Campaign Speeches
of American
Presidential Candidates
1948-1984

Campaign Speeches of American Presidential Candidates 1948-1984

—— ☆ ——

Edited and introduced by Gregory Bush

FREDERICK UNGAR PUBLISHING CO.
NEW YORK

Copyright © 1976, 1985 by FREDERICK UNGAR PUBLISHING Co., Inc.
Printed in the United States of America
Designed by Anita Duncan

Library of Congress Cataloging in Publication Data
Main entry under title:

Campaign speeches of American presidential
   candidates, 1948–1984.

   Original title: Campaign speeches of American
presidential candidates, 1928–1972.
   1. United States—Politics and government—
1945–   —Addresses, essays, lectures.
2. Campaign speeches—United States.   I. Bush, Gregory.
E743.C236   1985   973.92   85-3362
ISBN 0-8044-1137-9

The campaign speeches of the major candidates for the
elections of 1948 through 1972 are taken from the first edition
and were selected by Aaron Singer, editor of that edition.

CONTENTS

Introduction ix

1948

Campaign Background 1

HARRY S. TRUMAN, *Acceptance Speech, July 15* 4
HARRY S. TRUMAN, *Campaign Speech, October 29* 10
THOMAS E. DEWEY, *Acceptance Speech, June 24* 13
THOMAS E. DEWEY, *Campaign Speech, September 20* 16
HENRY A. WALLACE, *Campaign Speech, September 10* 22
J. STROM THURMOND, *Campaign Speech, October 26* 29

1952

Campaign Background 35

DWIGHT D. EISENHOWER, *Acceptance Speech, July 11* 38
DWIGHT D. EISENHOWER, *Campaign Speech, October 24* 41
ADLAI E. STEVENSON, *Acceptance Speech, July 26* 47
ADLAI E. STEVENSON, *Campaign Speech, October 31* 51

1956

Campaign Background 59

DWIGHT D. EISENHOWER, *Acceptance Speech, August 23* 62
DWIGHT D. EISENHOWER, *Campaign Speech, October 1* 72

CONTENTS

ADLAI E. STEVENSON, *Acceptance Speech, August 17*   79
ADLAI E. STEVENSON, *Campaign Speech, September 29*   85

1960
Campaign Background   92

JOHN F. KENNEDY, *Acceptance Speech, July 15*   95
JOHN F. KENNEDY, *Campaign Speech, September 12*   100
RICHARD M. NIXON, *Acceptance Speech, July 28*   104
RICHARD M. NIXON, *Campaign Speech, October 27*   116

1964
Campaign Background   123

LYNDON B. JOHNSON, *Acceptance Speech, August 27*   126
LYNDON B. JOHNSON, *Campaign Speech, October 7*   131
BARRY M. GOLDWATER, *Acceptance Speech, July 17*   134
BARRY M. GOLDWATER, *Campaign Speech, October 21*   142

1968
Campaign Background   149

RICHARD M. NIXON, *Acceptance Speech, August 8*   153
RICHARD M. NIXON, *Campaign Speech, September 19*   163
HUBERT H. HUMPHREY, *Acceptance Speech, August 29*   169
HUBERT H. HUMPHREY, *Campaign Speech, September 30*   177
GEORGE C. WALLACE, *Campaign Speech, October 24*   185

1972
Campaign Background   195

RICHARD M. NIXON, *Acceptance Speech, August 23*   199
RICHARD M. NIXON, *Campaign Speech, November 2*   209
GEORGE S. McGOVERN, *Acceptance Speech, July 14*   215
GEORGE S. McGOVERN, *Campaign Speech, August 5*   220

1976
Campaign Background   225

JIMMY CARTER, *Acceptance Speech, July 15*   230
JIMMY CARTER, *Campaign Speech, August 30*   237
GERALD R. FORD, *Acceptance Speech, August 19*   245
GERALD R. FORD, *Campaign Speech, September 17*   252

CONTENTS

1980

Campaign Background — 259

RONALD REAGAN, *Acceptance Speech, July 17* — 263
RONALD REAGAN, *Campaign Speech, September 9* — 274
JIMMY CARTER, *Acceptance Speech, August 14* — 281
JIMMY CARTER, *Campaign Speech, September 16* — 292
JOHN B. ANDERSON, *Campaign Speech,, April 24* — 299

1984

Campaign Background — 305

RONALD REAGAN, *Acceptance Speech, August 23* — 309
RONALD REAGAN, *Campaign Speech, September 24* — 321
WALTER F. MONDALE, *Acceptance Speech, July 19* — 332
WALTER F. MONDALE, *Campaign Speech, September 25* — 338

ACKNOWLEDGMENTS

I would like to acknowledge the assistance of Walter Kamphoefner and Carolina Amram for reading and commenting on the manuscript, Dean Richard Pfau and Don Carreau of the University of Miami's Otto Richter Library for helping to locate copies of campaign speeches, and Ruth Selden of Frederick Ungar for her editorial advice.

Copies of speeches by Strom Thurmond and John Anderson were provided by the Robert Muldrow Cooper Library at Clemson University and the National Unity Party in Washington.

G.B.

INTRODUCTION

On July 8, 1896, an obscure former Congressman from Nebraska named William Jennings Bryan made a speech on behalf of the free-silver issue to the Democratic Presidential convention in Chicago. It was an extraordinarily stirring speech, nostalgic for America's simpler days as an agricultural republic and angry at the "encroachments of organized wealth." Filling Chicago's great Coliseum with his melodic voice, Bryan concluded his dramatic oratory by asserting to those in favor of the gold standard that "you shall not press down upon the brow of labor this crown of thorns, you shall not crucify mankind on a cross of gold." Immediately after this, Bryan assumed the posture of a crucified man for a full five seconds, leaving his audience mesmerized by his performance.

Although this speech was only the climax of a successful strategy to win the Fresidential nomination, most Americans believed that the power of Bryan's single speech had been the sole reason the convention shifted in his favor. In the fall campaign, the candidate made over 600 speeches to an estimated five million listeners but lost his bid for the White House for reasons that are still the subject of much historical dispute.

The power of Bryan's oratory and the endurance he exhibited in promoting his message have probably never been duplicated in American presidential politics. More significantly, however, his face-to-face manner in presenting speeches has been superseded in the twentieth century by new media of mass persuasion through which a campaign's themes and the personalities of presidential candidates can reach far wider audiences. Some have understood and exploited these changes better than others. Bryan, for example, did not fully adapt to the advent of radio, losing his radio audience on several occasions while wandering around the speaker's platform while addressing another Democratic Presidential convention twenty-eight years later. By 1960, former Eisenhower aide Emmet John Hughes would write in the *New York Times* that the new medium of television "makes political life itself more fluid and more volatile. Men can surge or stumble with astonishing speed—either triumphing over obscurity or tripping over a hasty or graceless public word or gesture."

One of the chief victims of the advent of television and of professional media consultants is the presidential campaign speech itself. True, speeches are still given to numerous audiences by candidates seeking votes but they are seldom heard in their entirety through the broadcast media or reprinted in full in newspapers or magazines. Candidates seldom publish their speeches after elections, which they frequently used to do. It is a sad commentary that it is difficult to find the complete remarks of recent presidential candidates from published sources. We are a culture of fluid snippets. Television news provides brief clips of a candidate's remarks that are often taken out of context. Even campaign organizations primarily distribute capsule summaries of remarks and positions put forth by their candidates. Ours is an era when ostensibly sophisticated consultants place most of their client's campaign dollars into "spot" advertisements on television that may or may not even feature the candidate speaking to a significant issue in a few short phrases. As a result, it has become part of the common political wisdom that the attention span of the average American has been reduced to the commercialized demands of television itself. John Deardorff, a prominent consultant to many Republicans, asserted in 1980 that "I could tell voters all they might want to know about a candidate's position on any issue in 30 seconds or less if I choose to do that."

This book seeks to redress some of the neglect accorded Presidential campaign speeches in recent American history. Beginning with the first election following Franklin Roosevelt's death and ending with the campaign that reelected Ronald Reagan, fifty-two complete speeches are included, providing a small sample of the thousands given by Presidential contenders. Aside from updating the speeches through 1984 and revising all of the introductory notes, the present edition contains four speeches by minor party candidates. Exclusive reliance on the words of the major party candidates perpetuates the gross distortion that Americans are a people imbued with a clearly defined consensus of political ideals neatly contained within the two-party system.

A series of questions may recur as the reader goes through the book. How did the image of the federal government as benevolent assister or malevolent usurper of human welfare and civil liberties change through the thirty-six years covered in these pages? In which elections can a bipartisan consensus on foreign affairs be more clearly seen than in others and for what reasons? Which speeches exhibit a heightened concern with military defense issues and the threat of communism abroad or at home? How was communism used as a political weapon against opposition party candidates? Which past Presidents have been most frequently quoted and towards which ends? In what ways did both Democratic and Republican nominees identify with Franklin Roosevelt or assess the value of the New Deal? Which elections featured greater concern for moral issues involving family, religion, poverty, war, or nuclear weapons? Which candidates express greater compassion and sensitivity to the condition of the poor, farmers, urban dwellers, the "forgotten" middle class or those subject to racism? Do any of the candidates seek to alter significantly the economic and social structure of the country? If so, how specific are their prescriptions?

Another line of inquiry concerns the differing rhetorical styles. Whether a candidate is speaking to a political convention of the converted or a skeptical audience of business or labor leaders, whether he is pandering to particular interests or trying to elevate the ideals of his audience are all matters of importance in understanding these speeches. Does one candidate exhibit a lower conception of the mentality of his audience than another? Presidential candidates generally speak in optimistic tones about the future—especially if they are hoping to lead the country. Do any of these candidates use their platforms to issue significant warnings to the American people about crucial issues not widely addressed?

While in hindsight one can be highly critical of the vision and simplistic rhetoric presented by many of these speeches, it should be noted that they were written to gain political support. As Thurman Arnold noted in 1935, "the only realistic test of a political speech is its vote-getting effect." Each of these candidates projected their appeals to attract different matrixes of constituencies amidst the constantly changing demographic basis of the electorate.

Recent commentators have hinted that Presidential nominating conventions may become anachronistic as television and the political process make them more and more irrelevant and boring to viewers. Presidential campaign speeches may become relics of the twentieth century, but I doubt it. After all, Ronald Reagan gained the Presidency not simply because he was an actor but because he was a successful full-time speechmaker. Americans responded not simply to his conservative appeals but to his ability to put his personality across through the medium of televised speeches. Perhaps free air time should be provided not only for televised debates but for campaign speeches as well.

That American citizens seldom have the opportunity to read or experience Presidential campaign speeches in their entirety presents a serious cultural problem. A society promoting justice, equality of opportunity, and a dynamic spirit during these last years of the twentieth century surely needs an electorate that has access to print sources of such speeches and is able to "read" television with greater visual literacy. Let us hope that future campaigning will receive careful and serious attention from a voting public wishing to be fully informed.

Campaign Speeches
of American
Presidential Candidates
1948-1984

1948

☆

Franklin Roosevelt's death in April 1945 triggered an emotional outpouring of American grief that underscored the difficult position of anyone who sought to fill Roosevelt's long-time role as President. Harry Truman, a former Missouri judge, a U.S. Senator first elected in 1934, and Vice President since 1944, had been left poorly informed about policy and was little known to most Americans. Although World War II was rapidly drawing to a conclusion, important decisions had to be made. The difficult relations with America's allies, including the Soviet Union, the problems of conversion to a peacetime economy, and the growing attraction of voters to the Republican Party all confronted the new President with a myriad of complex decisions.

Within several months Truman had replaced much of the Roosevelt cabinet with his own choices but appeared to be continuing the outlines of the New Deal. He called for the expansion of unemployment insurance, a permanent Fair Employment Practices Commission, slum clearance, and low-rent housing, but he began to run into significant opposition from an increasingly conservative Congress. Strikes, inflation, and political conflict over the continuation of the wartime Office of Price Administration added to voters' increasing frustration with the Administration. Republicans were beginning to charge that the government was riddled with Communists, and in

November of 1946 the Democrats lost control of both houses of Congress for the first time since 1928.

While the completion of World War II had found the United States strongly supporting the creation of the United Nations, prospects for a peaceful postwar climate rapidly eroded as a cold war developed between the United States and the Soviet Union. By September, 1946, Truman fired Secretary of Commerce Henry Wallace for criticizing America's hostile policies toward the Soviet Union. A major rift was developing within the Democratic Party that would soon find progressive Democrats seeking to oust Truman in 1948. Truman was more concerned with Republican charges that Democrats were "soft on Communism." Partly to bolster his record as an anticommunist, Truman promoted aid to Greece and Turkey and a loyalty program aimed at government employees. In addition, Secretary of State George Marshall set forth a plan to help the recovery of the war-ravaged economies of Europe.

Republicans were increasingly confident they could win the Presidency from the Democrats. New York Governor Thomas Dewey, who had been defeated by only a slight margin when he had run against Roosevelt in 1944, was considered to be the frontrunner for the Republican nomination in 1948. He had achieved an impressive progressive record as Governor, including passage of the first state law prohibiting racial and religious discrimination in employment. Dewey was opposed by Senator Robert Taft of Ohio, Governor Earl Warren of California, and former Governor Harold Stassen of Minnesota. After a tumultuous primary campaign, Dewey triumphed at the Presidential convention in Philadelphia.

In his acceptance speech, Dewey called for national unity that was "more than material. . . . We have found the means to blow this world of ours apart, physically. We have not yet found the spiritual means to put together the world's broken pieces . . . to make . . . a community of men of good will that fits our dreams."

The Democratic Party throughout most of 1948 seemed to be a party waiting for its eviction notice from the White House. A young St. Louis lawyer named Clark Clifford is widely given credit for the political value of his 43-page memorandum outlining a strategy for Truman's eventual triumph at the polls that November. Clifford called for an aggressive attempt to shore up the New Deal coalition, including an aggressive advocacy of several civil rights measures.

Many at the Democratic Convention opening in Philadelphia on July 12th hoped that the party would be able to draft the war hero General Dwight Eisenhower to head their ticket, but Ike forcefully declined. Many liberals as well as states' rights advocates sought to deny Truman the nomination. The major controversy of the convention, which Truman had wanted to avoid, involved a battle over a civil rights plank in the party platform. A floor fight led by Minneapolis Mayor Hubert Humphrey successfully carried a vote that called upon Congress to "support our President in guaranteeing these basic and fundamental rights: (1) the right of full and equal political participation, (2) the right of equal opportunity of employment, (3) the right of security of person, and (4) the right of equal treatment in the service and defense of our nation."

This fight so antagonized southern states' rights advocates that many withdrew from the convention and met in Birmingham, Alabama, on July 17 to nominate South Carolina's governor, Strom Thurmond, to run on a states' rights and segregationist platform. Called Dixiecrats, these followers of Thurmond sought to gather enough electoral votes to throw the election into the House of Representatives. They did finally carry South Carolina, Alabama, Mississippi, and Louisiana. Thurmond's address in Fayetteville, Arkansas, near the end of the campaign provides a glimpse of his attempt to associate the major party nominees with Russian tyranny.

Henry Wallace was another wild card in the 1948 Presidential deck. After being fired from the Truman cabinet he allied himself with a number of left-wing forces and became the eventual nominee of a newly created Progressive Party, which the regular Democrats roundly chastised for being riddled with Communist sympathizers. Wallace never achieved any electoral votes in the final election, although both he and Thurmond racked up a little over a million votes apiece.

The fall campaign found Dewey speaking in rather broad generalities, giving addresses that sounded more like Fourth of July orations than campaign addresses. Truman, on the other hand, campaigned furiously as the underdog, covering over 20,000 miles and making some 250 addresses, most of which were "whistle stop" talks delivered from the platform of his train. Such speeches accommodated his informal style, which came across better in person than over the radio. Each speech was tied to a specific issue. His address in Harlem on October 24th provides evidence of his rhetorical strategy in dealing with the civil rights issue.

HARRY S. TRUMAN

Acceptance Speech

PHILADELPHIA, PENNSYLVANIA

July 15, 1948

I am sorry that the microphones are in your way, but they have to be where they are because I've got to be able to see what I'm doing, as I always am able to see what I am doing.

I can't tell you how very much I appreciate the honor which you've just conferred upon me. I shall continue to try to deserve it. I accept the nomination, and I want to thank this convention for its unanimous nomination of my good friend and colleague, Senator Barkley, of Kentucky.

He's a great man and a great public servant. Senator Barkley and I will win this election and make these Republicans like it, don't you forget that. We'll do that because they're wrong and we're right, and I'll prove it to you in just a few minutes.

This convention met to express the will and reaffirm the beliefs of the Democratic party. There have been differences of opinion. These differences have been settled by a majority vote, as they should be, and now it's time for us to get together and beat the common enemy and it's up to you.

We'll be working together for victory and a great cause. Victory has become a habit of our party. It's been elected four times in succession and I'm convinced it will be elected a fifth time next November.

The reason is that the people know the Democratic party is the people's party and the Republican party is the party of special interests and it always has been and always will be.

The record of the Democratic party is written in the accomplishments of the last sixteen years. I don't need to repeat them. They have been very ably placed before this convention by the keynote speaker, the candidate for Vice-President, and by the permanent chairman.

Confidence and security have been brought to the American people by the Democratic party. Farm income has increased from less than $2,500,000,000 in 1933 to more than $18,000,000,000 in 1947. Never in the world were the farmers of any republic or any kingdom or any other country, as prosperous as the farmers of the United States, and if they don't do their duty by the Democratic party they're the most ungrateful people in the world.

The wages and salaries in this country have increased from $29,000,000,000 in 1933 to more than $128,000,000,000 in 1947. That's labor, and labor never had but one friend in politics, and that was the Democratic party and Franklin D. Roosevelt.

And I'll say to labor just what I've said to the farmers. They are the most ungrateful people in the world if they pass the Democratic party by this year.

The total national income has increased from less than $40,000,000,000 in 1933 to $203,000,000,000 in 1947, the greatest in all the history of the world. These benefits have been spread to all the people because it's the business of the Democratic party to see that the people get a fair share of these things.

This last Eightieth Congress proved just the opposite for the Republicans. The record on foreign policy of the Democratic party is that the United States has been turned away permanently from isolationism, and we've converted the greatest and best of the Republicans to our viewpoint on that subject.

The United States has to accept its full responsibility for leadership in international affairs. We have been the backers and the people who organized and started the United Nations, first started under that great Democratic President Woodrow Wilson in the League of Nations. The League was sabotaged by the Republicans in 1920, and we must see that the United Nations continues a strong and going body, so we can have everlasting peace in the world.

We've removed the trade barriers in the world, which is the best asset we can have for peace. Those trade barriers must not be put back into operation again. We have started a foreign-aid program which means the recovery of Europe and China and the Far East. We instituted the program for Greece and Turkey, and I'll say to you that all these things were done in a co-operative bi-partisan manner.

The foreign-relations committees of the Senate and the House were taken into the full confidence of the President in every one of these moves.

As I've said time and time again, foreign policy should be the policy of the whole nation, and not a policy of one party or the other. Partisanship should stop at the water's edge, and I shall continue to preach that through this whole campaign.

I'd like to say a word or two now about what I think the Republican philosophy is, and I'll speak from actions and from history and from experience. The situation in 1932 was due to the policy of the Republican party control of the government of the United States.

The Republican party favors the privileged few and not the common, every-day man. Ever since its inception, that party has been under the control of special privilege, and they concretely proved it in the Eightieth Congress. They proved it by the things they did to the people and not for them. They proved it by the things they failed to do.

Now let's look at some of them, just a few. Time and time again I recommended the extension of price control before it expired on June 30, 1946. I asked for that extension in September, 1945. In November, 1945, in a message on the State of the Union in 1946. That price control legislation didn't come to my desk until June 30, 1946, on the day on which it was supposed to expire, and it was such a rotten bill that I couldn't sign it.

Then thirty days after that they sent me one that was just as bad and I had to sign it, because they quit and went home.

It was said when O. P. A. died that prices would adjust themselves, for the benefit of the country. They've adjusted themselves all right. They've gone all the way off the chart in adjusting themselves at the expense of the consumer and for the benefit of the people who hold the goods.

I called a special session of Congress in November, 1947—Nov. 17, 1947—and I set out a ten-point program for the welfare and benefit of this country; among other things, stand-by price controls. I got nothing. The Congress has still done nothing.

Way back, four and a half years ago while I was in the Senate we passed the housing bill in the Senate known as the Wagner-Ellender-Taft bill. It was a bill to clear the slums in the big cities, and to help erect low-rent housing. That bill, as I said, passed the Senate four years ago, but it died in the House. That bill was reintroduced in the Eightieth Congress as the Taft-Ellender-Wagner bill—the name was slightly changed.

But it was practically the same bill and it passed the Senate, but was allowed to die in the House of Representatives. The Banking and Currency Committee sat on that bill, and it was finally forced out of the committee when the Rules Committee took charge, and it's still in the Rules Committee.

But desperate pleas from Philadelphia, in that convention that met here three weeks ago, didn't get that housing bill passed. They passed a bill that's called a housing bill, which isn't worth the paper it's written on.

In the field of labor, we needed moderate legislation to promote labor-management relations. But Congress instead passed the so-called Taft-Hartley act, which has disrupted labor-management relations and will cause strife and bitterness for years to come if it's not repealed, and the Democratic platform says it's got to be repealed.

I tried to strengthen the Labor Deparment. The Republican platform in 1944 said if they were in power they'd build up a strong Labor Department. Do you know what they've done to the Labor Department? They've simply torn it up. There's only one bureau left that's functioning and they've cut the appropriation on that so it can hardly function.

I recommended an increase in the minimum wage. What did they do? Nothing, absolutely nothing. I suggested that the schools in this country are crowded, teachers underpaid, and that there is a shortage of teachers. One of the greatest national needs is more and better schools.

I urged the Congress to provide $300,000,000 to aid the states in meeting the present educational crisis. The Congress did nothing about it. Time and again I have recommended improvements in the social security law, including extending protection to those not now covered, to increase the amount of the benefits, reduce the eligibility age of women from sixty-five to sixty years. Congress studied the matter for two years but couldn't find time to extend increased benefits, but it did find time to take social security benefits away from 750,000 people.

And they passed that over my veto.

I repeatedly asked the Congress to pass a health program. The nation suffers from lack of medical care. That situation can be remedied any time the Congress wants to act upon it. Everybody knows that I recommended to the Congress a civil-rights program. I did so because I believe it to be my duty under the Constitution. Some of the members of my own party disagreed with me violently on this matter, but they stand up and do it openly. People can tell where they stand. But the Republicans all profess to be for these measures, but the Eightieth Congress didn't act and they had enough men there to do it, and they could have had cloture, and they didn't have to have a filibuster. There were enough people in that Congress to vote for cloture.

Now everybody likes to have a little surplus. But we must reduce the national debt in times of prosperity, and when tax relief can be given without regard to those who need it most, and not go to those who need it least, as this Republican rich-man's tax bill did when they passed it over my veto, on the third try.

The first one of these tax bills they sent me was so rotten that they couldn't even stomach it themselves. They finally did send one that was somewhat improved, but it still helps the rich and sticks the knife into the back of the poor.

Now the Republicans came here a few weeks ago and they wrote up a platform. I hope you've all read that platform. They adopted a platform, and that platform had a lot of promises and statements of what the Republican party is for and what they would do if they were in power.

They promised to do in that platform a lot of things I've been asking them to do, and that they've refused to do when they had the power. The Republican platform cries about cruelly high prices. I have been trying to get them to do something about high prices ever since they met the first time.

Now listen to this one. This one is equally as bad and as cynical. The Republican platform comes out for slum clearance and low rental housing. I've been trying to get them to pass that housing bill ever since they met the first time, and it's still resting in the Rules Committee today.

The Republican platform pledges equality of educational opportunity. I've been trying to get them to do something about that ever since they came there, and that bill is at rest in the House of Representatives.

The Republican platform urges extending and increasing social security benefits. Think of that—increasing social security benefits, and yet when they had the opportunity they took 750,000 people off the social security roles.

I wonder if they think they can fool the people of the United States with such poppycock as that?

There's a long list of these promises in that Republican platform and if it weren't so late I'd tell you about all of them.

I discussed a number of these failures of the Republican Eightieth Congress, and everyone of them is important. Two of them are of major concern to every American family; the failure to do anything about high prices, and the failure to do anything about housing.

My duty as President requires that I use every means within my power to get the laws the people need on matters of such importance and urgency. I am therefore calling this Congress back into session on the 26th of July.

On the twenty-sixth day of July, which out in Missouri they call Turnip Day, I'm going to call that Congress back and I'm going to ask them to pass laws halting rising prices and to meet the housing crisis which they say they're for in their platform. At the same time I shall ask them to act on other vitally needed measures such as aid to education, which they say they're for; a national health program, civil-rights legislation, which they say they're for; an increase in the minimum wage—which I doubt very much they're for; an extension of social security coverage and increased benefits, which they say they're for; funds for projects needed in our program to provide public power and cheap electricity.

By indirection, this Eightieth Congress has tried to sabotage the power policy which the United States has pursued for fourteen years. That power lobby is just as bad as the real estate lobby, which is sitting on the housing bill. I shall ask for adequate and decent law for displaced persons in place of the anti-Semitic, anti-Catholic law which this Eightieth Congress passed.

Now my friends, if there is any reality behind that Republican platform, we ought to get some action out of the short session of the Eightieth Congress. They could do this job in fifteen days if they wanted to do it. They'll still have time to go out and run for office. They're going to try and dodge their responsibility, they're going to drag all the red herrings they can across this campaign. But I'm here to say to you that Senator Barkley and I are not going to let them get away with it.

Now what that worst Eightieth Congress does in its special session will be the test. The American people will not decide by listening to mere words or by reading a mere platform. They will decide on the record. The record as it has been written. And in the record is the stark truth that the battle lines for 1948 are the same as they were back in 1932 when the nation lay prostrate and helpless as the result of Republican misrule and inaction.

In 1932 we were attacking the citadel of special privilege and greed; we were fighting to drive the money changers from the temple. Today in 1948 we are the defenders of the stronghold of democracy and of equal opportunity. The haven of the ordinary people of this land and not of the favored classes or of the powerful few.

The battle cry is just the same now as it was in 1932 and I paraphrase the words of Franklin D. Roosevelt as he issued the challenge in accepting his nomination at Chicago: This is more than a political call to arms. Give me your help. Not to win votes alone, but to win in this new crusade and keep America secure and safe for its own people.

Now my friends, with the help of God, and the wholehearted push which you can put behind this campaign, we can save this country from a continuation of the Eightieth Congress and from misrule from now on. I must have your help! You must get in and push and win this election. The country can't afford another Republican Congress.

☆

HARRY S. TRUMAN

Campaign Speech

HARLEM, NEW YORK

October 29, 1948

Dr. Johnson, and members of the Ministerial Alliance which has given me this award:

I am exceedingly grateful for it. I hope I shall always deserve it. This, in my mind, is a most solemn occasion. It's made a tremendous impression upon me.

Franklin Roosevelt was a great champion of human rights. When he led us out of the depression to the victory over the Axis, he enabled us to build a country in which prosperity and freedom must exist side by side. This is the only atmosphere in which human rights can thrive.

Eventually, we are going to have an America in which freedom and opportunity are the same for everyone. There is only one way to accomplish that great purpose, and that is to keep working for it and never take a backward step.

I am especially glad to receive the Franklin Roosevelt award on this day—October 29. This date means a great deal to me personally, and it is a significant date in the history of human freedom in this country.

One year ago today, on October 29, 1947, the President's Committee on Civil Rights submitted to me, and to the American people, its momentous report.

That report was drawn up by men and women who had the honesty to face the whole problem of civil rights squarely, and the courage to state their conclusions frankly.

I created the Civil Rights Committee because racial and religious intolerance began to appear after World War II. They threatened the very freedoms we had fought to save.

We Americans have a democratic way of acting when our freedoms are threatened.

We get the most thoughtful and representative men and women we can find, and we ask them to put down on paper the principles that represent freedom and a method of action that will preserve and extend that freedom. In that manner, we get a declaration of purpose and a guide for action that the whole country can consider.

That is the way in which the Declaration of Independence was drawn up.

That is the way in which the Constitution of the United States was written.

The report that the Civil Rights Committee prepared is in the tradition of these great documents.

It was the authors of the Declaration of Independence who stated the principle that all men are created equal in their rights, and that it is to secure these rights that governments are instituted among men.

It was the authors of the Constitution who made it clear that, under our form of government, all citizens are equal before the law, and that the Federal Government has a duty to guarantee to every citizen equal protection of the laws.

The Civil Rights Committee did more than repeat these great principles. It described a method to put these principles into action, and to make them a living reality for every American, regardless of his race, his religion, or his national origin.

When every American knows that his rights and his opportunities are fully protected and respected by the Federal, State, and local governments, then we will have the kind of unity that really means something.

It is easy to talk of unity. But it is the work that is done for unity that really counts.

The job that the Civil Rights Committee did was to tell the American people how to create the kind of freedom that we need in this country.

The Civil Rights Committee described the kind of freedom that comes when every man has an equal chance for a job—not just the hot and heavy job—but the best job he is qualified for.

The Committee described the kind of freedom that comes when every American boy and girl has an equal chance for an education.

The Committee described the kind of freedom that comes when every citizen has an equal opportunity to go to the ballot box and cast his vote and have it counted.

The Committee described the kind of freedom that comes when every man, woman, and child is free from the fear of mob violence and intimidation.

When we have that kind of freedom, we will face the evil forces that are abroad in the world—whatever or wherever they may be—with the strength that comes from complete confidence in one another and from complete faith in the working of our own democracy.

One of the great things that the Civil Rights Committee did for the country was to get every American to think seriously about the principles that make our country great.

More than 1 million copies of the full text of the civil rights report have been printed in books and newspapers.

More than 30 different pamphlets based on the report have been printed and distributed by private organizations.

Millions of Americans have heard the report discussed on the radio.

In making its recommendations, the Civil Rights Committee did not limit itself to action by the President or by the executive branch. The Committee's recommendations included action by every branch of the Federal Government, by State and local governments, and by private organizations, and by individuals.

That is why it is so important that the Civil Rights Committee's report be studied widely. For in the last analysis, freedom resides in the actions of each individual. That is the reason I like to hear that scriptural reading from the Gospel according to St. Luke. That's just exactly what it means. It means you and I must act out what we say in our Constitution and our Bill of Rights. It is in his mind and heart—and to his mind and heart—that we must eventually speak to the individual.

After the Civil Rights Committee submitted its report, I asked Congress to do ten of the things recommended by the Committee.

You know what they did about that.

So I went ahead and did what the President can do, unaided by the Congress.

I issued two Executive orders.

One of them established the President's Committee on Equality of Treatment and Opportunity in the Armed Services.

The other one covered regulations governing fair employment practices within the Federal establishment.

In addition to that, the Department of Justice went into the Supreme Court and aided in getting a decision outlawing restrictive covenants.

Several States and municipalities have taken action on the recommendations of the Civil Rights Committee, and I hope more will follow after them.

Today the democratic way of life is being challenged all over the world. Democracy's answer to the challenge of totalitarianism is its promise of equal rights and equal opportunity for all mankind.

The fulfillment of this promise is among the highest purposes of government.

Our determination to attain the goal of equal rights and equal opportunity must be resolute and unwavering.

For my part, I intend to keep moving toward this goal with every ounce of strength and determination that I have.

☆

THOMAS E. DEWEY

Acceptance Speech

PHILADELPHIA, PENNSYLVANIA

June 24, 1948

Speaker Martin and fellow Republicans:

You, the elected representatives of our Republican Party, have again given to me the highest honor you can bestow—your nomination for President of the United States.

I thank you with all my heart for your friendship and your confidence. I am profoundly sensible of the responsibility that goes with this nomination. I pray God that I may deserve this opportunity to serve our country. In all humility, I accept the nomination.

I am happy to be able to say to you that I come to you unfettered by a single obligation or promise to any living person. I come free to join with you in selecting to serve our nation the finest men and women in the country, free to unite our party and our country in meeting the grave challenge of our time.

United we can match this challenge with depth of understanding and largeness of spirit; with a unity which is above recrimination, above partisanship, and above self-interest. These are articles of faith from which the greatness of America has been fashioned. Our people are eager to know again the upsurging power of that faith. They are turning to us to put such a faith at the heart of our national life. That is what we are called upon to do, and that is what we will do.

In this historic Convention, you have had placed before you six other candidates, all high-minded men of character and ability and deeply devoted to their country—Senator Raymond E. Baldwin, General Douglas MacArthur, Governor Harold E. Stassen, Senator Robert A. Taft, Senator Arthur Vandenberg, and Governor Earl Warren. Never has any party produced so many fine, able, distinguished, and patriotic men.

I am deeply moved and grateful for the generous and gracious statements they have made in this hall tonight. I hope that I may be worthy of the trust. This has been a difficult choice in an honorable contest. It has been a stirring demonstration of the life and vitality and ideals of our Republican Party.

There has been honest contention, spirited disagreement, and I believe considerable hot argument. But do not let anybody be misled by that. You have given here in this hall a moving and dramatic proof of how Americans, who honestly differ, close ranks and move forward, for the Nation's well-being, shoulder to shoulder. Let me assure you that beginning next January 20, there will be teamwork in the Government of the United States of America.

The responsibility and the opportunity that have come to our party are the greatest in the history of free government. For tonight our future —our peace, our prosperity, the very fate of freedom—hangs in a precarious balance.

Mere victory in an election is not our purpose, it is not our task. Our task is to fill our victory with such meaning for mankind everywhere, yearning for freedom, that they will take heart and move forward out of this desperate darkness of today into the light of freedom's promise.

Our platform proclaims the guideposts that will mark our steadfast and certain endeavor in a fearful world. This magnificent statement of principles is concise and to the point.

You unanimously adopted it, and I am very proud to support it. That platform will be the heart of the message I will take to the country. After January 20th, it will be the cornerstone of our Republican Administration.

Fortunately, we are a united party. Our nation stands tragically in need of that same unity.

Our people are turning away from the meaner things that divide us, and they have a yearning to move to higher ground, to find a common purpose in the finer things which unite us. We, the Republican Party, must be the instrument of achieving that aspiration. We must be the means by which America's full powers are released and this uncertain future filled again with opportunity. That is our pledge. That will be, for the American people, the fruit of our victory.

If this unity is to be won and kept, it must have great dimensions. Its boundaries must be far above and beyond politics. Freedom can be saved —it can only be saved—if free men everywhere make this unity their common cause.

Unity in such a cause must be the chief cornerstone of peace. A peace won at the expense of liberty is a peace too dearly bought. Such a peace would not endure. Above all other purposes, we must labor by every peaceful means to build a world order founded upon justice and righteousness. That kind of world will have peace. That kind of peace will be worth having. That is the crowning responsibility that our people have laid upon us in this solemn hour. That is the crowning task to which we here dedicate ourselves.

The unity we seek is more than material. It is more than a matter of things and measures. It is most of all spiritual. Our problem is not outside ourselves. Our problem is within ourselves. We have found the means to blow this world of ours apart, physically. We have not yet found the spiritual means to put together the world's broken pieces, to bind up its wounds, to make a good society, a community of men of good will that fits our dreams. We have devised noble plans for a new world. Without a new spirit, our noblest plans will come to nought. We pray that, in the days ahead, a full measure of that spirit may be ours.

The next Presidential term will see the completion of the first half of the twentieth century. So far it has been a century of amazing progress and of terrible tragedy. We have seen the world transformed. We have seen mankind's age-long struggle against nature crowned by extraordinary success.

Yet our triumphs have been darkened by bitter defeats in the equally ancient struggle of men to live together in peace, security and understanding. For this age of progress, this twentieth century, has been dominated by two terrible world wars and, between the wars, the worst economic depression in the history of mankind.

We must learn to do better. The period that is drawing to a close has been one of scientific achievement. The era that is opening before us must be a period of human and spiritual achievement.

We propose, in this Convention, and as a party, and as a government, to continue to carry forward the great technological gains of our age. We shall harness the unimaginable possibilities of atomic energy, to bring men and women a larger, fuller life. But there is something more important than all this. With all the energy, intelligence and determination which mortal heart and mind can summon to the task, we must solve the problem of establishing a just and lasting peace in the world, and of securing to our own and other like-minded people the blessings of freedom and of individual opportunity.

To me, to be a Republican in this hour is to dedicate one's life to the freedom of men. As long as the world is half free and half slave, we must peacefully labor to help men everywhere to achieve liberty.

We have declared our goal to be a strong and free America in a free world of free men—free to speak their own minds, free to develop new ideas, free to publish whatever they believe, free to move from place to place, free to choose their occupations, free to enjoy and to save and to use the fruits of their labor, and free to worship God, each according to his own concept of His grace and His mercy.

When these rights are secure in this world of ours, the permanent ideals of the Republican Party shall have been realized.

The ideals of the American people are the ideals of the Republican Party. We have tonight, and in these days which preceded, here in Philadelphia lighted a beacon, in this cradle of our own independence. We have lighted a beacon to give eternal hope that men may live in liberty with human dignity and before God, and loving Him, stand erect and free.

☆

THOMAS E. DEWEY

Campaign Speech

DES MOINES, IOWA

September 20, 1948

Mr. Chairman, Senator Wilson, Senator Hickenlooper and fellow Americans:

I appreciate more deeply than I can tell you your wonderful welcome. Tonight we enter upon a campaign to unite all America.

On Jan. 20, we will enter on a new era. We propose to install in Washington an Administration which has faith in the American people, a warm understanding of their needs and the competence to meet those needs.

We will rediscover the essential unit of our people and the spiritual strength that makes our country great.

We'll begin to move forward again shoulder to shoulder toward an even greater America and a better life for every American, in a nation working effectively for the peace of the world.

This is my pledge to my fellow-citizens, the declaration of the principles and purposes of your next Administration.

I pledge to you that, as President, every act of mine will be determined by one principle above all others: Is this good for our country?

I pledge to you that my administration will be made up of men and women devoted to that same principle—of men and women whose love of their country comes ahead of every other consideration. They will know how to translate their devotion to our country into constructive action.

I pledge to you a foreign policy based upon the firm belief that we can have peace. That policy will be made effective by men and women who really understand the nature of the threat to peace and who have the vigor, the knowledge and the experience required to wage that peace.

I pledge to you a Government of team-work. The executive heads of your Government will be really qualified for their positions after Jan. 20 and they will be given full responsibility to do their job without loose talk, factional quarreling or appeals to group prejudice. They will know how to work together as a team and one of the most important members of that team will be the distinguished Governor of California, the next Vice President of the United States, Earl Warren.

I pledge to you an Administration which will know how to work with the elected representatives of the people in the Congress, an Administration that wants to work with them and will do so. The unity we need for the nation will be practiced in the nation's Capitol.

I pledge to you that on next Jan. 20 there will begin in Washington the biggest unraveling, unsnarling operation in our nation's history.

I pledge to you an Administration which knows in its mind and believes in its heart that every American is dependent on every other American; that no segment of our people can prosper without the prosperity of all; that in truth we must all go forward together.

This is what you may expect from your next, your Republican administration. It will be a government in which every member is enlisted to advance the well-being of all our people and is dedicated to the release of the enthusiasm, the energy and the enterprise of our people: a government that has faith in America and is resolved to prove its faith by its works.

This is the road on which I propose that we set out all together. As we advance we shall carry America's destiny with us. We shall also carry the hope of freedom and the living promise to a stricken world that men can be free and that free men can live in peace.

We're living in sorely troubled times. The unhappy difficulties of today are familiar to every one of us. Three years after the end of the war the world has still not found peace. As we wage the peace, we face problems as momentous as a any nation has ever confronted in history, either in peace or in war.

Our sons and daughters—the young people in all our grade schools, our high schools and our colleges have lived—it seems impossible but it's true—they have lived their whole lives in a troubled world. Their plans for education, for getting married—for getting ahead, are delayed and disrupted. Against the dangers of a sorely troubled world they are being called upon to keep America strong.

The wife and mother who's been out shopping today to buy meat for her family and clothes for her children has been up against the hard fact of high prices. Every married veteran living in a Quonset hut, or doubled up with his family, is up against the cruel fact that we do not have enough good homes for our people. Every family living in a crowded, unsanitary, cold-water tenement has the same urgent needs. Hard-working, frugal Americans find they don't make enough to lay anything by for a rainy day or for sickness, or unemployment, or old age.

Millions of Americans, too, face the intolerable fact that because of their race or their color or the way they choose to worship God, they are denied rights which are their birthrights and which, by American principle and law, are their just due.

These are some of the difficulties that confront us. It won't be easy to meet them, and I want no one to think that I believe it will be easy. These times require the cooperation of everyone of us and the highest order of devotion and intense labor by your Government. But it's part of my faith in America to believe that with restoration of faith in ourselves, of competence in our Government, of unity of purpose among our people there is nothing, as a people, we cannot do.

I deeply believe that with an administration which can unite our people will have taken the greatest single step toward solving these problems. This is our most urgent need.

Every four years, under our Constitution, it's our right as Americans to hear a full and thoughtful discussion of the issues before us. As this campaign progresses I shall place before you my views concerning every aspect of the grave problems at home and abroad and the steps, the concrete steps, by which I propose that we meet them.

I will not contend that all our difficulties today have been brought about by the present National Administration. They haven't. Some of these unhappy conditions are the result of circumstances beyond the control of any government. Any fair-minded person would agree that others are merely the result of the Administration's lack of judgment, or of faith in our people. Only part are deliberately caused for political purposes. But it's not too important how these conditions came about. The important thing is that, as Americans, we turn our faces forward and set about curing them with a stout purpose and a full heart. We can enlarge the opportunities of all our people and move toward peace with all the world.

And to all those in this country or abroad who hate freedom, as well as to all our friends everywhere who love freedom and look to us for aid and leadership, let me make this one thing very clear: So far as I am concerned—so far as the Republican party is concerned, this campaign will not create division among our people. Instead this campaign will unite us as we have never been united before. It will unite us so strongly that no force will again attack us and we will labor unceasingly and with unity to find common grounds of firm and peaceful agreement with all the nations of this earth.

As we chart our course for the years ahead, we must find the stars by which to sail. We must look to the fundamentals of our country. They're easy to find. Our America is not the lucky product of a rich continent discovered by seafaring adventurer looking for a pot of gold. The roots of our country are not material. They are moral and spiritual. Of course we are deeply concerned about things to live with. But we are also concerned about the values by which we live. You and I know that we can surmount our unhappy times by a restoration of our ideas and faith in our country.

We know that, we know it because we are Americans. It's no accident that our country stands like a beacon of hope to all the world today. Our magnificent America is the end result of the deep convictions of a great people devoted above everything else to faith in their God and the liberty and precious importance of every single human being.

We believe in freedom for our neighbors across the street or across the seas—the same freedom we expect for ourselves. We believe in honesty, loyalty, fair play, concern for our neighbors, the innate ability of men to achieve; these convictions, arched over by our faith in God, are the inner meaning of the American way of life. That is why the eyes of freedom-loving people everywhere in this troubled world are turning with hope to us. That is our America for which we cannot and will not fail.

But we are in a world and in a time when these convictions are doubted and sneered at and denied. The priceless rights of freedom of speech, of assembly, of religion, of the press, academic freedom, the fundamental freedom of choice of occupation, even of the right to own a car or a home or a farm—all these are denied to many millions of regimented people throughout the world. The ideals and the rights we hold to be good are held to be evil in those countries. No other fact about our world is of such ominous importance.

We live in a world in which tyranny is on the march. The evil idea is on the march that man is not destined to be free but to be enslaved. That idea is backed by a mobilization of enormous force. Millions of families who have known freedom are in fear of evil, unfamiliar footsteps and at every moment they expect the knock on the door. Millions who still enjoy freedom live in fear that today or tomorrow some crisis or excuse will be seized upon to blot out their freedom too.

Millions of human beings, it may be tens of millions—nobody knows—are being starved and worked to death in concentration camps and at slave labor. And yet, at this very moment in the history of the world the promise of America and the truth of what America believes are being vindicated. The oppressed peoples of these lands know there is a better life. They know there is a better way. The truth about America seeps through every obstacle of iron and steel. In millions of hearts the hope that is America is flaming. That's why we in America have such a solemn obligation to love and cherish all the freedoms we enjoy; that's why we have such a solemn obligation, every single one of us, not to divide our country but to unite it for all purposes and for all time.

We are the last, best hope of earth. Neither barbed wire nor bayonet have been able to suppress the will of men and women to cross from tyranny to freedom.

Let's call up some of them as witnesses. Let them testify to this thing we believe in. Call up Jan Masaryk of Czechoslovakia, the heroic son of a heroic father. We may never know whether he took his life or was murdered. But we do know this, that however it came, he preferred death to a life cut off from freedom. Jan Masaryk is our witness.

Call up Archbishop Stepinac who lies today in a Communist prison, a living martyr to the cause of freedom of religion. Call up Nicola Petkov, the executed leader of the free forces of Bulgaria. Call up General Bor Komorowski and Stanislaw Mikolajczyk, the great exiled leaders of Poland who gladly brushed elbows with death to escape from tyranny. All these are our witnesses.

Call up the athletes who came out from behind the iron curtain to compete in the Olympics only last month and refused to go home. Call up Oksana Kasenkina, the Russian school teacher. She was picked by the secret police to come to our country to teach the children of Soviet diplomats. She could not even understand the language of our country, but in her heart she came to understand America. And when she jumped to death or freedom from the window of her diplomatic prison, she gave her testimony. That was the day—the very same tragic day—that the American people were told that the exposure of communism in our own Government is a "red herring."

With mankind as our witness this is no time for doubting the rightness of free governments. This is a time—above all times—for a great American affirmation. Our faith reaffirmed holds our destiny and the hope of all the world.

As we look around us we can count our blessings and be humbly proud and grateful we are Americans.

Our fathers came from an old world in which few men knew the meaning of liberty. Yet they dared to found a nation and stake its future on their belief in what men could do if only they were free. The America of today is the living, towering symbol of the eternal rightness of that faith.

We've sometimes fallen short, we've sometimes failed, but in our hearts we believe and know that every man and woman and child has something of the Divine in him, that every single individual is of priceless importance and that free men against whatever odds have an unbeatable quality. That faith is my faith. It's the faith of our people. It's the faith in which we will go forward.

Never let anyone tell you that America's unfinished job is too big. Never let anyone tell you that we can meet our problems in this country only by surrendering to the devices borrowed from the police states. The free system is the only one where we can make a mistake and have a heaven-sent opportunity to cure it. It's the only one where opportunity always exists to improve. The free system is the only one where men can freely change their governments by peaceful means. This land of ours, almost alone in all the world, is still the place where youth—where every young man and every young woman—is free to plan for the future and to make their dreams come true.

As a nation we're troubled today by many problems and we must remove many fears. We're troubled by high prices and we must end the maladjustments which cause them. We need more homes for our people. We must widen the opportunities for our youth. We must increase the security for our older people. We must protect our enterprise system from monopoly, while encouraging free and fuller production for the benefit of all our citizens. We must, and we will, maintain support prices so our farmers can go ahead confidently with full production of the food our growing nation needs. We must, and we will, preserve the gains of labor so that its confidence and production will grow and flourish. We must work against intolerance and bigotry, against racial and religious discrimination. Above all we must confidently face the immense labor of making peace in this world and act wisely and with courage to achieve it.

As I make specific proposals dealing with these problems of ours in the course of this campaign, they will not be the product of any wishful thinking. I have no trick answers and no easy solutions. I will not offer one solution to one group and another solution to another group.

The American people have a right to expect honest answers and I propose to give them. The specific proposals I will make as this campaign goes along will not be born of fear—and I may add there will be no threats in any of them. They will come from my own deep faith in America. They will not set faction against faction or group against group. They will aim to join us together as a whole people in a more perfect union.

As we go on from here together, we shall know that our advance is carrying us into unexplored territory—on into the atomic age. Man has, at last, begun to tap the powers of the universe. We can do much, we Americans, to see that this new age is not one of catastrophe, but one of unimagined promise and achievements. That is our purpose. That is the measure of our opportunity. For such a future let us summon new wisdom, new courage and a new vision. Let us say, as one people: We welcome the challenge of tomorrow.

Let us go forward into this future as courageous, united Americans, bound together by an invincible faith that liberty and justice under God, is the most precious thing on earth.

☆

HENRY A. WALLACE
Campaign Speech
NEW YORK CITY
September 10, 1948

Delivered at a Progressive Party rally, Madison Square Garden

Just two years ago I spoke to many thousands of you who are here tonight. I said then as I say tonight that peace is the basic issue of the 1948 election campaign. I say now that the first job of national defense: the most important job in maintaining the peace is the job of conquering hate here at home, the job of protecting the civil rights of all Americans.

This is a great American meeting.

It is a meeting in the best American tradition—a meeting of men and women of all races, of all creeds.

Last week—in smaller gatherings—we proved that such meetings can be held in the much-maligned Southern states. We proved that such meetings—meetings of all the people—can be held wherever men respect the Constitution of the United States; and wherever they respect the Christian principles of brotherhood on which so much of our modern civilization has been built.

The news reported from the South last week was news of eggs and tomatoes. It was news of violence and threats of violence.

And there were eggs. And there were tomatoes. And there was violence and there were threats of violence.

Yes, and there were the ugly spewings of hate and prejudice; and the sad sight of men and women and children whose faces were contorted with hate.

But the significance of our trip south was not the dramatic proof that there are seeds of violence and fascism and deep prejudice in the Southern states. The significance was not in proving what is known.

No. The significance of our Southern trip lies in the two dozen completely unsegregated, peaceful meetings which we were able to hold.

The significance lies in those meetings in Virginia, North Carolina, Alabama, Mississippi, Arkansas and Tennessee which were held—even as this meeting tonight—in the best American tradition.

We held such meetings by insisting on our American rights to freely assemble and freely speak.

And if there is one message above all other messages which I bring you as a result of that Southern trip, it is this: Fear is a product of inactivity and the greatest remedy for fear is to stand up and fight for your rights.

In the course of private and public life I have traveled many places. I have experienced many fields. I have had a wide variety of emotional experiences. But I have never had such deeply moving experiences as those of the first week of September, 1948, when I traveled South to campaign for peace.

I had seen the victims of mass prejudice in a DP camp.

I had seen and felt—as any decent human being must feel—for the Jewish orphans interned in Italy.

I had visited foreign lands—Latin America, China and many parts of Europe, and had my heart go out to victims of oppression.

I have deplored and felt that I truly understood the plight of workers who have faced picket line violence.

I had been South before—many times—and I thought I understood the plight of our Negro citizens.

But I discovered last week that my understanding was only the limited understanding; the sympathetic feeling of a friend for a man who is afflicted.

To me fascism is no longer a second-hand experience—a motion picture, a photograph on the deeply moving words of a great writer.

It is no longer a mere definition of an economic and political system in which freedom is stifled by private power; in which prejudices are bred and nourished; in which man is set against man for the profit of powerful and greedy forces.

No, fascism has become an ugly reality—a reality which I have tasted.

I have tasted it neither so fully nor so bitterly as millions of others. But I have tasted it.

And in tasting it I have reinforced my solemn resolution to fight it wherever and whenever it appears so long as I live.

Last week—when I had a chance to live—to live very briefly and relatively mildly—the kind of life which millions of Americans live every waking hour, last week I learned what prejudice and hatred can mean. I learned to know the face of violence, although I was spared the full force of violence. I saw the ugly reality of how hate and prejudice can warp good men and women; turn Christian gentlemen into raving beasts; turn good mothers and wives into jezebels.

I didn't like that part of what I saw. I didn't like to see men and women fall victims to the catchwords of prejudice and the slogans of hate, even as the poor people of Germany were victimized by the catchwords and slogans of Hitler and Streicher.

I saw how a few hate mongers carefully placed in a crowd of decent folks can set off a dangerous spark.

I saw a young college student—a Progressive party worker—who was severely cut across his chest and arms by the agents of hate.

I was a passenger in the car of a prominent businessman in a Southern city as he raced down dark streets and alleys to elude all who might be following us, so that he could take me, unknown to anyone else, to his home for dinner.

He was a courageous man. The precautions he took were necessary. His business in that Southern town would have been ruined, if it were known that a candidate for the Presidency, a former Vice President, was having dinner at his home.

I saw an irate landlord rouse a quiet neighborhood where I had gone quietly to rest and work on a radio speech at the apartment of a young couple.

I saw how fear is bred and perpetuated and capitalized—and I didn't like it.

But I also saw the kind of courage; the kind of real, deep human fighting spirit which promises a new day for the South and for the world.

I saw men and women, white and Negro, who have been leading the fight against hate and prejudice and intolerance in the South.

I saw them standing up and fighting for the very foundations of our American way of life—standing up to all kinds of intimidation. And from them radiates a contagious spirit; the same kind of spirit of resistance which stopped the armies of Adolf Hitler in half a dozen European countries.

I heard Clark Foreman say so truthfully that "Down here, to believe in the Constitution means you are automatically called a Communist"; and I heard a young college student, a veteran, add: "It's like General Carlson said, 'To be called a Red here is a badge of honor.'"

I am confident that their spirit—the spirit of the progressive Southerners—will triumph in the South. I am hopeful that our trip helped to build their forces; helped rally new strength; helped along the movement which will free the South. Rich in resources—proud and courageous, the South must be—and will be—freed from the shackles in which it has been held by huge corporations with headquarters only four miles south of here—not in Virginia, not in Tennessee, but in Wall Street.

The free South and the feudal South live side by side in the State of Alabama. In one day we received courteous receptions and held free meetings in the best American tradition in Decatur and Huntsville and Gunthersville in the great TVA area; and on the same day we could not hold meetings in Gadsden and Birmingham and Bessemer, cities which are dominated by Northern-owned steel corporations. We did not hold meetings because the police insisted on dividing Americans by the color of their skins. We did not hold meetings because the constitutional right to freely assemble and speak was denied by the police authorities of those company towns.

Here—in Alabama—in a single day, we saw the economic basis of hate and segregation.

In the steel towns it is profitable to keep labor divided.

North against South, race against race, farmer against worker— the profits of the men who own the South are multiplied by keeping the people divided.

But their days are numbered.

The good people of the South have learned their scriptures. They know the fundamental Christian doctrine of the Fatherhood of God and the Brotherhood of Man. They know that "God hath made of one blood all the nations to dwell upon the face of the earth." They know that we are all members, one of another. Just as surely as men everywhere, they want the Kingdom of Heaven here on earth; and they are not going to be stopped any longer by those who spew hate.

It is the owners of the mines and mills, the great plantations, and newspapers who incite violence.

They don't personally engage in lynching either free speech or human beings, just as they don't personally engage in fighting the wars from which they profit.

But they inflame the passions of others. They have had others do their dirty work. But the ranks of new recruits for their dirty work are narrowing as more and more men and women of the South see how they have been victimized by prejudice—as they see how it has profited the few, and brought misery for themselves and their neighbors.

And the workers and farmers and independent businessmen of the South are turning from the false leadership of those who have been styled "Southern liberals"—they are turning from those who have preached the tolerance of intolerance, tolerance of segregation; tolerance of murderous Jim Crow. They are learning that such men are only slightly to the left of Hitler and Rankin.

They are learning that no man can believe in both segregation and democracy.

In a radio interview the editor of an Arkansas paper asked me about FEPC. He wanted to know if I would interfere with the right of men to choose their own associates. And I replied that I considered that a most important right. I replied that it was precisely my devotion to that right that leads me to fight segregation—segregation which deprives both white and Negro from freely choosing their own associates.

I told this same man; this same champion of segregation that while I knew we couldn't legislate love, we most certainly could and will legislate against the acts of hate.

Throughout the South we spoke for the full protection of all citizens under the Constitution of the United States. Tonight, I want to call upon the candidates of the Republican and Democratic parties to pledge with me that whosoever shall be elected, he will enforce the second section of the Fourteenth Amendment no less than the other provisions of the Constitution. That section of our Constitution calls for the reduction of the number of Congressmen for each state where the right to vote is abridged.

In 1946 the votes cast to elect fourteen Congressmen from Louisiana and Mississippi were less than the votes cast in the Twenty-fifth Congressional District here in New York.

John Rankin and thirteen others, all together, received less votes than are cast here in the Twenty-fifth District.

That is not only unfair to the people of New York's Twenty-fifth District; it is grossly unfair to the people of the Southern states whose freedom has been limited by the failure of the Congress to enforce the Fourteenth Amendment.

If every Congressional candidate, if each of the Presidential candidates will take a pledge to secure constitutional reapportionment on the basis of the next census, I predict that we shall see an end to the many hindrances to free suffrage in the South.

We pledge ourselves to enforce this constitutional right.

In pledging to live by the Constitution, we have earned enemies. And we are proud of our enemies.

The men who stand for Jim Crow.

The men who stand for Taft-Hartley.

The men who support fascists in Greece and China.

The men who prefer an atmosphere of war, because they profit by it.

The men who hated Franklin Roosevelt and the New Deal and who now find their unity in hatred for the Progressive party.

These men, Republicans and Democrats bound together by hate, are using every mechanism which bipartisan fear can suggest to defeat congressional candidates who stand for peace.

The Democrats, the Republicans, and the self-styled Liberals have joined hands to support single candidates against the candidates of the Progressive party; against candidates of the American Labor party.

They have joined hands in their bipartisan wrath against two men with the best liberal and labor voting records in the Congress of the United States.

They have honored—these corrupt and dangerous men—they have honored two real servants of the people. Vito Marcantonio and Leo Isacson. They have honored Leo Isacson with a single opponent. They have honored Vito Marcantonio with a joint campaign of vituperation and hate.

They are afraid of our strength. They saw what the people could do last February when they sent Leo Isacson to the Congress.

They have seen, time and again, the devotion of Vito Marcantonio's constituents to that dynamic champion of progressive principles. They have reason for their fear—and though they have combined their resources and efforts, we shall lick them on election day and return Vito Marcantonio and Leo Isacson to the Congress.

It is with great sadness that I note that the bipartisans have some new allies; fearful men who call themselves liberals and leaders of labor; men who cry out against Wall Street running the country and then ask workers to give dollar bills to keep President Truman and his Wall Street gang in Washington.

I say such action, such double talk, such duplicity is shameful, immoral, and corrupt.

These illiberal liberals; these labor leaders who fight monopoly with words, but whose actions support the candidates of monopoly, these men make possible the Truman double talk. They make it possible for Truman to condemn Taft-Hartley while using it to destroy unions and the Wagner Act; to call for civil rights, while maintaining segregation in the Armed Forces and conducting loyalty purges; to call for price controls after killing them; to call for peace, while preparing for war.

The surest proof that we of the Progressive party are not impractical in our politics is in the alliances of hate which have been formed against us.

Some of the liberals, some of the Pied Pipers of labor will tell us that they have compromised because Roosevelt compromised; but they slander a great man when they draw that comparison.

Roosevelt, by the deftest political maneuvering in all history, made many a political deal, but always advancing the cause of the common man.

The men who are bargaining with corruption today hope for no gains, no advancements. They are bargaining to minimize losses. They are fearful men. They are men who might well heed the lesson that the only cure for fear is to stand up and fight for right.

The bipartisans have learned that the Progressives are not for sale. They have found out—through their leading agent in New York City, Mayor O'Dwyer, that the party in which Fiorello LaGuardia was proud to enroll himself is not for sale.

Bill O'Dwyer found it out when he tried with his fanciest offers to get John Rogge to quit the race for the surrogate's bench. Bill O'Dwyer heard Vito Marcantonio say "no." He heard John Rogge say "no." And he knows that John Rogge will conduct the kind of dynamic, fighting campaign against corruption which he himself should have fought against Tammany.

O'Dwyer, who has Trumanized his local administration by serving the same interests as the Republicans, by pitting police against strikers, by fighting inflation with increased subway fares, by invoking local loyalty orders; Bill O'Dwyer has found that Progressives know double-talk when they hear it.

As President Truman has demonstrated that he could not fill the shoes of Roosevelt; so Mayor O'Dwyer has shown that he cannot fill the shoes of LaGuardia.

Yes, our "no sale" sign has earned us many names. But it does not matter if they call us red or black, if they lie about us or egg us or stone us. We will not join the Republican-Democratic poker match which governs out of the backroom—from the bottom of the deck.

The shop-worn, the discredited, the cheap political tricksters have joined with those who all their lives have practiced black reaction. They have set up one camp, though there are many banners.

And what are they joined against? What are we that they should forget old feuds to fight against us?

We are those who stand against the course which leads to war.

We are those who would take from the hands of monopoly the power to say who shall starve and who shall feast. We are those who protest a policy toward minority groups that is administered by a policeman's nightstick. We are those who feel attacked whenever the color of man's skin or the color of his political beliefs is the official excuse for brutality, whether in Mississippi or in Harlem, whether at home or abroad.

We must go now into every building of this city, into every suburban home, onto every street corner. We must tell the people who we are. We will stand up and take the jeers of hirelings.

We must work—we will work, so that on Nov. 2, Americans can clearly choose.

☆

J. STROM THURMOND
Campaign Speech
FAYETTEVILLE, ARKANSAS

October 26, 1948

My fellow Americans:

At the close of a most enjoyable and inspiring visit with the good people of Arkansas, I am happy to be privileged to be with you here in the great educational center of Fayetteville.

As a candidate for President who is just old-fashioned enough to believe in government by the Constitution of the United States, I am struck by the meaning of the state motto of Arkansas—"The People Rule." A short motto, but within those words may be found the full meaning of the American system of government and the American way of life.

We are ruled by the people—not by any one man or group of men who may have seized power.

It is time that we as Americans look more closely at the manner in which we have perpetuated government by the people. It is time that we examine the way in which our system differs from that of Soviet Russia, for instance.

We hold that our government is safeguarded by the terms of a constitution, written by the people. Soviet Russia, however, also have a constitution which Soviet leaders claim was written by the people.

We hold that we in America have a democracy. Soviet Russia, however, also claims to have a democracy.

Yet everyone knows that a few selfish men in the Kremlin maintain an iron control over the lives of Russian people which apparently the people cannot throw off. While in the United States any group which sought to monopolize power has always been quickly crushed.

Where is the difference?

It is not hard to find. In the United States we have maintained a system of checks and balances, with power divided between the state governments and the federal government. By reserving most of the power of government to the states, men like Thomas Jefferson made it certain that power could never be taken away from the people.

The new American system of government was different from the patterns of centralized control in Europe, because it enabled the people of the various states to govern themselves according to their own needs.

If that system had not been laid down in crystal clear language in the Constitution, there would have been nothing to prevent the United States from falling into the hands of a tyrant.

Today, the balance of power between the states and the Federal Government is no less a protection against tyranny than it was in the early days. It is the only guarantee we have that a kind of Kremlin will not be established in Washington. It is our only protection against the desire of Stalin to spread his doctrine of one-party, centralized control into our own land.

And yet we Americans have witnessed a wholesale assault upon the principle of local self-government in this political year of 1948. We have seen three Presidential candidates—Truman, Dewey, and Wallace—endorse and support platforms which would destroy the American system of balanced power.

We have seen them adopt a program which would be the entering wedge for the breaking down of our state lines, just as Hitler broke down the German states when he came to power.

Out of their desire to bid against each other for the votes of a minority bloc in the big-city states, Truman, Dewey, and Wallace have all three advocated the breaking down of states' rights.

But those of us who place love for country above the desire for political power were unwilling to let these three candidates go unchallenged. We were unwilling to sit idly at home while the American people were denied the right to express their opposition to a program that is openly in violation of the Constitution.

The States Rights Democrats are resisting this betrayal of American ideals. We oppose this attempt to change our form of government and to change the very way in which we live in this country!

When these candidates first made their cheap appeal to the minority groups, a great many people believed that the effects of the program would be felt only in the South. Today, millions of Americans are realizing that once the principle of state sovereignty is destroyed, the freedoms of all Americans everywhere will be in mortal danger. They are recognizing that the fight which has been thrust upon us is a governmental one, and not a racial fight—all of the high-powered propaganda of our opponents to the contrary notwithstanding.

Americans are beginning to realize, too, that the vicious program endorsed by the National Democrats and the Republicans would not only have a drastic effect upon the South, but that it would change the way of life and affect the liberties of every citizen in every state.

The proponents of this program are trying to sell it to the nation on the basis that it guarantees—or creates—human rights. These claims are false. It is ridiculous to suppose that human rights may be created by destroying the framework of the Constitution. It is by means of the United States Constitution and its guarantees of local self-government that human rights are protected.

The so-called "Civil Rights" program of Truman, Dewey, and Wallace is full of the same kind of deception that prostrated Europe, and that is spreading out of Russia today into every corner of the earth. It is time we in America girded ourselves against that evil doctrine by renewing our faith in our own kind of democracy. It is most certainly not logical that we should begin now to undermine the Constitution and to change the American system.

Those who advocate that we depart from the Constitution, do so at the risk of treason of their country. We must make this plain to them, whether they be Republican or Democrat or Progressive. And we can make it plain to them only in the traditional American way—by the use of our privilege of voting.

A vote cast for the States Rights Democrats is therefore a vote of loyalty to the American way of life.

Those who engaged in the un-American performance of the Philadelphia conventions committed a deep offense against the Southern states. Their action jeopardizes the forward strides recently achieved in liberal and progressive thought and viewpoint in the South. Catering in high places to the favor of professional agitators and mercenary missionaries of ill-will has set the stage for new racial antagonisms which had been almost entirely stamped out over the years by the increasingly enlightened public opinion of our people.

Those of us in the South who have worked hard in the cause of liberalism and constructive endeavor in the field of human and economic progress, have been forced to turn aside to meet an attack upon the Constitution, and upon our right to direct and guide ourselves. The task of the liberal in the South today is to save the hard-won ground which we have gained from destruction by ill-advised and irresponsible meddling from without.

When that inter-meddling takes the form of Federal usurpation of the rights of states, no responsible Southerner can be silent. No loyal Southerner can afford to endorse it with his vote. And no loyal Democrat can follow the lead of the machine minority bosses and the parlor pinks in the prostration of that great Party to an un-American and unconstitutional program.

All over the South and in many other states, millions of good Democrats are determined that our Party shall be restored to the principles for which it was organized. We shall reclaim and rebuild the Democratic Party, beginning with this election, and make it once again a great voice for the sovereignty of states and for the personal freedom of the individual man.

Those who join with us in this effort may feel that they have had a great share in the restoration of the Democratic Party to its historic devotion to the Constitution!

Those of you who have studied the so-called Civil Rights proposals, know that I do not speak lightly when I say they would change our way of life.

We Americans enjoy a Constitutional right to regulate elections within our states, and to fix voting qualifications. That right is under attack in the Anti-Poll Tax Bill.

We enjoy the right to control our state courts, to pass laws for the control of crimes within our states, and to regulate and control our own police. All these rights are under attack in the Anti-Lynching Bill.

We enjoy the right to pass laws concerning the separation of the races, in states where it is considered needful. Such laws enable us to maintain peace and harmony between the races, according to the needs of our individual states. Our right to do so is attacked by the Anti-Segregation proposals.

We Americans also enjoy the right of private enterprise, which means the right to employ in our businesses and our industrial plants those persons most suitable to the progress and prosperity of our businesses. But the so-called Fair Employment Practices Act would take away that right.

Finally, we enjoy the right to control the policing of our states and the regulation of crime. That right is under attack in the enforcement proposals of the Civil Rights legislation, which provide for a national police not very different from the Gestapo of Hitler.

All these proposals were endorsed by Truman, Dewey, and Wallace at the demands of a minority bloc which has as its first aim the breaking down of separation of the races in our homes, our schools, our theatres, and in all public places. To gain that end, they are willing to break down the Constitution at the same time that they are breaking down segregation.

This is another attempt to drive the South into doing the impractical and the impossible in our racial relations. Racial harmony in the South, and the progress of all races in the South depends upon state laws which fit our own situations. Violations of those laws can mean only new obstacles to progress. But, because the selfish minority groups demand it, Truman, Dewey, and Wallace have promised to force the South to get into line.

They make these promises in spite of the fact that the Negro race has made greater progress under the Southern bi-racial civilization than any other race ever did in a similar period. They have adopted this program in spite of the fact that, under its own customs and laws, the South is now entering upon an era of economic gains which promises to be the greatest in our history, for all races.

These things are promised under the guise of human rights. As a matter of fact, the FEPC, which is the worst phase of the program sponsored by these three candidates, is a direct violation of human rights. Heretofore, we have always recognized the right of the individual to choose his own associates, at work or during recreation. Yet the FEPC would fine or imprison a working man who refused to stay on the job beside someone he does not like. We have always recognized the right of a business man to employ those persons who he believes are best suited to his business, and who will get along well together. But the FEPC would force such a man to employ persons he does not wish to employ.

Under this law, a working man could not even quit his job in protest, without facing severe punishment. He could not even decide who shall be members of his labor unions, and use his union hall.

No thinking American would deny that the right to employ persons of your choice, and the right to associate with persons of your choice, are civil rights guaranteed by the Constitution.

The endorsement of the FEPC by the Republicans should make

you want to take a closer look at their candidate, Governor Dewey. As a leading sponsor of the national FEPC, Dewey claims credit for enforcing this vicious law in New York State, which is of course his privilege under our system of government.

But let us look at the New York FEPC regulations so as to determine what Dewey's national law might be. In New York it is unlawful to ask an applicant for a job what his former name was if he had changed it. You can't ask him for a birth certificate, or whether he is native-born, or to show his naturalization papers. You can't ask him whether he is an atheist. You can't ask him what his complexion is, or to send a photograph if he is applying by mail. You can't even ask him what his military service has been, or where he was during World War I.

My friends, we all admit Governor Dewey's right to sponsor such a law in New York State. But we cannot permit him, or Truman, or Wallace, to impose it upon the whole country!

There is no middle ground in this election. A vote for either of these three candidates is an indication that you want an FEPC and all the other vicious laws that go with it. A vote for the States Rights Democrats is your only means of preserving your right to participate in your own government.

As good Americans, we must join together to repudiate the un-American influence which pervaded our national conventions at Philadelphia this year.

Let us repudiate forever the influences which would break down our state control, and reach down to change our everyday lives.

We Americans, unlike may hundreds of millions of oppressed people on this earth, have within our grasp the means by which mankind may destroy political oppression for all time. We can, by the example we set, lead the peoples of the world into a new life of self-fulfillment and happiness. That is our challenge today.

Let us meet that challenge by our opposition to tyranny in government, and our faith in the democratic ideal.

☆

1952

☆

Harry Truman's term as President, which began March 4, 1949, was a frustrating one. He had regarded his surprise victory at the polls in 1948 as a mandate for liberalism, for what he called a "Fair Deal" for the American people. But Congress rejected his proposals for national health insurance, federal aid to education, and an agricultural plan to uphold farm incomes instead of farm prices.

The conflict with Communism also grew in intensity. What Republicans labeled the "loss" of China by the Truman Administration seemed, to some, part of a conspiracy to sell out American interests to the Communists. The entertainment industry was rocked by a blacklisting campaign that deeply affected the lives of many performers who, in most cases, were accused of vague leftist tendencies. The Rosenberg spy case, the Alger Hiss case, and the Korean War all reverberated through the press as palpable proof that America was in a relentless war with Communism. Powerful interest groups such as the American Medical Association had even associated the Truman Administration proposal for national medical insurance with Communism.

On September 4, 1951, Senator Henry Cabot Lodge of Massachusetts arrived in Europe to attempt to convince Dwight Eisenhower, then Supreme Commander of NATO, to run for President in 1952 as a Republican. Three years before, significant elements in both major political parties had unsuccessfully approached the General to run for President on their respective tickets. Eisenhower had just led the largest army in world history to a smashing victory over the Nazis; his popularity and unknown political allegiance were major assets. In 1951, however, Lodge tried a new tack, arguing that there had been a dangerous accumulation of power in Washington that needed to be opposed. From 1932 to 1948, the Democratic Party had dominated the political landscape and, as Eisenhower relates in his memoirs, "unless this one-sided partisan dominance could be promptly reversed, the record presaged the virtual elimination of the two-party system, which, we agreed, was vital to the ultimate preservation of our national institutions."

Although Eisenhower did not immediately allow his name to be used in primary ballots for the nomination, he relented after winning several important primaries on write-in ballots. The eastern internationalist wing of the Republican Party, led by Governor Dewey of New York, promoted Eisenhower against Senator Robert Taft of Ohio. Taft was known as "Mr. Republican" for his domestic conservatism, although he had supported federal aid to education and public housing. In foreign policy he was perceived as a "unilateralist," opposing America's entanglement in foreign alliances such as NATO.

The Republican Convention was held in Chicago in early July, and Eisenhower was able to best Senator Robert Taft, who led at the end of the first ballot. Perhaps a little defensively, Eisenhower later wrote that his "acceptance speech did not attempt to reach for eloquence or to become a vehicle for displaying any fancied oratorical ability."

The Democratic convention was also held in Chicago—to facilitate television coverage. Harry Truman had publicly declined to run for renomination on March 29th. A number of favorite-son candidates such as W. Averill Harriman and Senator Robert Kerr competed with Senators Estes Kefauver and Alben Barkley for the nomination. But a late-blooming draft movement, combined with the last-minute endorsement of President Truman, gave the nomination to the Governor of Illinois, Adlai Stevenson. Significantly, this was the last Presidential nomination in our history that took more than one ballot to decide on a nominee. The Governor, a former assistant to the Secretary of the Navy and U.S. delegate to the U.N. General Assembly, was not widely known outside his native state. Stevenson's acceptance speech is a model of modesty, brevity, and eloquence that has found few peers in the ensuing years.

The fall campaign was fought over the Korean War, the containment of Communism within and beyond America's borders, and corruption within the Democratic Administration. Both Presidential candidates traveled over 32,000 miles in their campaigns and made hundreds of speeches.

This was the first campaign in which television became a significant factor in political advertising and in projecting campaign speeches. After the General's initial reluctance to perform in a "spot" television advertising campaign, he finally acquiesced and was seen widely by the public in numerous rather trivial ads promoting his candidacy. In mid-September television also became crucial to his campaign when Vice Presidential candidate Richard Nixon used the medium to defend himself against allegations of having a secret campaign fund. In his address, labeled afterward the "Checkers Speech," Nixon blunted criticism of his political behavior by diverting attention to his family, his dog, and his emotional life.

On October 24th in a speech in Detroit, Michigan, Eisenhower made a dramatic announcement that he would go to Korea in order to try and secure peace in that war-torn country. The diplomatic front seemed to be bogged down in stalemate. Eisenhower was attempting to demonstrate that he could provide new leadership in solving this problem. He was highly critical of the Truman Administration's withdrawal of troops from the region in 1949, which had led to the North Korean attack in June 1950.

A week after Eisenhower's speech, Adlai Stevenson criticized Eisenhower's position on Korea before a Brooklyn audience by asserting that "a stalemate is better than surrender—and it is better than atomic war." He called for an honorable conclusion to the war in order to avoid death for the 50,000 prisoners held by the Communists and to be in a position to lead the "coalition of the free world." Ironically, sixteen years later in the midst of another land war that America was fighting in Asia, a similar issue would rebound to the electoral favor of the Republicans under the leadership of Richard Nixon.

DWIGHT D. EISENHOWER

Acceptance Speech

CHICAGO, ILLINOIS

July 11, 1952

Mr. Chairman, my Fellow Republicans:

May I first thank you on behalf of Mrs. Eisenhower and myself for the warmth of your welcome. For us both this is our first entry into a political convention and it is a heartwarming one. Thank you very much.

And before I proceed with the thoughts that I should like to address briefly to you, may I have the temerity to congratulate this convention on the selection of their nominee for Vice-President. A man who has shown statesmanlike qualities in many ways, but as a special talent an ability to ferret out any kind of subversive influence wherever it may be found and the strength and persistence to get rid of it.

Ladies and Gentlemen, you have summoned me on behalf of millions of your fellow Americans to lead a great crusade—for Freedom in America and Freedom in the world. I know something of the solemn responsibility of leading a crusade. I have led one. I take up this task, therefore, in a spirit of deep obligation. Mindful of its burdens and of its decisive importance. I accept your summons. I will lead this crusade.

Our aims—the aims of this Republican crusade—are clear: to sweep from office an administration which has fastened on every one of us the wastefulness, the arrogance and corruption in high places, the heavy burdens and anxieties which are the bitter fruit of a party too long in power.

Much more than this, it is our aim to give to our country a program of progressive policies drawn from our finest Republican traditions; to unite us wherever we have been divided; to strengthen freedom wherever among any group is has been weakened; to build a sure foundation for sound prosperity for all here at home and for a just and sure peace throughout our world.

To achieve these aims we must have total victory; we must have more Republicans in our state and local offices; more Republican governments in our states; a Republican majority in the United States House of Representatives and in the United States Senate; and, of course, a Republican in the White House.

Today is the first day of this great battle. The road that leads to Nov. 4 is a fighting road. In that fight I will keep nothing in reserve.

Before this I stood on the eve of battle. Before every attack it has always been my practice to seek out our men in their camps and on the roads and talk with them face to face about their concerns and discuss with them the great mission to which we were all committed.

In this battle to which all of us are now committed it will be my practice to meet and talk with Americans face to face in every section, every corner, every nook and cranny of this land.

I know that such a momentous campaign cannot be won by a few or by divided or by uncertain forces. So to all those from the precinct level up who have worked long hours at difficult tasks in support of our party—and for our party's candidates—I extend an earnest call to join up; join up for longer hours and harder work and even greater devotion to this cause. I call on you to bring into this effort your neighbors next door and across the street. This is not a job for any one of us or for just a few of us.

Since this morning I have had helpful and heartwarming talks with Senator Taft, Governor Warren and Governor Stassen. I wanted them to know, as I want you to know, that in the hard fight ahead we will work intimately together to promote the principles and aims of our party. I was strengthened and heartened by their instant agreement to support this cause to the utmost. Their cooperation means that the Republican party will unitedly move forward in a sweeping victory.

We are now at a moment in history when, under God, this nation of ours has become the mightiest temporal power and the mightiest spiritual force on earth. The destiny of mankind—the making of a world that will be fit for our children to live in—hangs in the balance on what we say and what we accomplish in these months ahead.

We must use our power wisely for the good of all our people. If we do this, we will open a road into the future on which today's Americans, young and old, and the generations that come after them, can go forward—go forward to a life in which there will be far greater abundance of material, cultural, and spiritual rewards than our forefathers or we ever dreamed of.

We will so undergird our freedom that today's aggressors and those who tomorrow may rise up to threaten us, will not merely be deterred but stopped in their tracks. Then we will at last be on the road to real peace.

The American people look to us to direct our nation's might to these purposes.

As we launch this crusade we call to go forward with us the youth of America. This cause needs their enthusiasm, their devotion, and the lift their vision of the future will provide. We call to go forward with us the women of America; our workers, farmers, businessmen. As we go to the country, Americans in every walk of life can have confidence that our single-minded purpose is to serve their interest, guard and extend their rights and strengthen the America that we so love.

The noble service to which we Republicans summon all Americans is not only for one campaign or for one election. Our summons is to a lifetime enrollment. And our party shall always remain committed to a more secure, a brighter and an even better future for all our people.

We go out from here with unbounded trust in the American people. We go out from here to merit their unbounded trust in us.

Wherever I am, I will end each day of this coming campaign thinking of millions of American homes, large and small; of fathers and mothers working and sacrificing to make sure that their children are well cared for, free from fear; full of good hope for the future, proud citizens of a country that will stand among the nations as the leader of a peaceful and prosperous world.

Ladies and gentlemen, my dear friends that have heaped upon me such honors, it is more than a nomination I accept today. It is a dedication —a dedication to the shining promise of tomorrow. As together we face that tomorrow, I beseech the prayers of all our people and the blessing and guidance of Almighty God.

☆

DWIGHT D. EISENHOWER

Campaign Speech

DETROIT, MICHIGAN

October 24, 1952

In this anxious autumn for America, one fact looms above all others in our people's mind. One tragedy challenges all men dedicated to the work of peace. One word shouts denial to those who foolishly pretend that ours is not a nation at war.

This fact, this tragedy, this word is: Korea.

A small country, Korea has been, for more than two years, the battleground for the costliest foreign war our nation has fought, excepting the two world wars. It has been the burial ground for 20,000 American dead. It has been another historic field of honor for the valor and skill and tenacity of American soldiers.

All these things it has been—and yet one thing more. It has been a symbol—a telling symbol—of the foreign policy of our nation.

It has been a sign—a warning sign—of the way the Administration has conducted our world affairs.

It has been a measure—a damning measure—of the quality of leadership we have been given.

Tonight I am going to talk about our foreign policy and of its supreme symbol—the Korean war. I am not going to give you elaborate generalizations—but hard, tough facts. I am going to state the unvarnished truth.

What, then, are the plain facts?

The biggest fact about the Korean war is this: It was never inevitable, it was never inescapable, no fantastic fiat of history decreed that little South Korea—in the summer of 1950—would fatally tempt Communist aggressors as their easiest victim. No demonic destiny decreed that America had to be bled this way in order to keep South Korea free and to keep freedom itself self-respecting.

We are not mute prisoners of history. That is a doctrine for totalitarians, it is no creed for free men.

There is a Korean war—and we are fighting it—for the simplest of reasons: Because free leadership failed to check and to turn back Communist ambition before it savagely attacked us. The Korean war—more perhaps than any other war in history—simply and swiftly followed the collapse of our political defenses. There is no other reason than this: We failed to read and to outwit the totalitarian mind.

I know something of this totalitarian mind. Through the years of World War II, I carried a heavy burden of decision in the free world's crusade against the tyranny then threatening us all. Month after month, year after year, I had to search out and to weigh the strengths and weaknesses of an enemy driven by the lust to rule the great globe itself.

World War II should have taught us all one lesson. The lesson is this: To vacillate, to hesitate—to appease even by merely betraying unsteady purpose—is to feed a dictator's appetite for conquest and to invite war itself.

That lesson—which should have firmly guided every great decision of our leadership through these later years—was ignored in the development of the Administration's policies for Asia since the end of World War II. Because it was ignored, the record of these policies is a record of appalling failure.

The record of failure dates back—with red-letter folly—at least to September of 1947. It was then that Gen. Albert Wedemeyer—returned from a Presidential mission to the Far East—submitted to the President this warning: "The withdrawal of American military forces from Korea would result in the occupation of South Korea by either Soviet troops or, as seems more likely, by the Korean military units trained under Soviet auspices in North Korea."

That warning and his entire report were disregarded and suppressed by the Administration.

The terrible record of these years reaches its dramatic climax in a series of unforgettable scenes on Capitol Hill in June of 1949. By then the decision to complete withdrawal of American forces from Korea—despite menacing signs from the North—had been drawn up by the Department of State. The decision included the intention to ask Congress for aid to Korea to compensate for the withdrawal of American forces.

This brought questions from Congress. The Administration parade of civilian and military witnesses before the House Foreign Affairs Committee was headed by the Secretary of State. He and his aides faced a group of Republican Congressmen both skeptical and fearful.

What followed was historic and decisive.

I beg you to listen carefully to the words that followed, for they shaped this nation's course from that date to this.

Listen, then:

First: Republican Congressman John Lodge of Connecticut asked "(do) you feel that the Korean Government is able to fill the vacuum caused by the withdrawal of the occupation forces?"

The Administration answered: "Definitely."

Second: A very different estimate of the risk involved came from Republican Congressman Walter Judd of Minnesota. He warned: "I think the thing necessary to give security to Korea at this stage of the game is the presence of a small American force and the knowledge (on the Soviet side) that attack upon it would bring trouble with us."

"I am convinced," Representative Judd continued, "that if we keep even a battalion there, they are not going to move. And if the battalion is not there"—listen now to his warning—"the chances are they will move within a year."

What a tragedy that the Administration shrugged off that accurate warning!

Third: The Secretary of State was asked if he agreed that the South Koreans alone—and I quote—"will be able to defend themselves against any attack from the northern half of the country." To this the Secretary answered briskly: "We share the same view. Yes, sir."

Rarely in Congressional testimony has so much misinformation been compressed so efficiently into so few words.

Fourth: Republican Congressman Lodge had an incisive comment on all this. "That," he said, "is wishful thinking. . . . I am afraid it confesses a kind of fundamental isolationism that exists in certain branches of the Government, which I think is a very dangerous pattern. I think the presence of our troops there is a tremendous deterrent to the Russians."

Finally: This remarkable scene of the summer of 1949 ends with a memorable document. The minority report of five Republican members of the House Foreign Affairs Committee on July 26, 1949, submitted this solemn warning.

Listen to it:

"It is reliably reported that Soviet troops, attached to the North Korean puppet armies, are in position of command as well as acting as advisors. . . . This development may well presage the launching of a full-scale military drive across the Thirty-eighth Parallel.

"Our forces . . . have been withdrawn from South Korea at the very instant when logic and common sense both demanded no retreat from the realities of the situation."

The report continues: "Already along the Thirty-eighth Parallel aggression is speaking with the too-familiar voices of howitzers and cannons. Our position is untenable and indefensible.

"The House should be aware of these facts."

These words of eloquent, reasoned warning were spoken eleven months before the Korean war broke.

Behind these words was a fervent, desperate appeal. That appeal was addressed to the Administration. It begged at least some firm statement of American intention that might deter the foreseen attack.

What was the Administration answer to that appeal?

The first answer was silence—stubborn, sullen silence for six months.

Then, suddenly, came speech—a high Government official at long last speaking out on Asia. It was now January of 1950. What did he say? He said, "The United States Government will not provide military aid or advice to Chinese forces on Formosa."

Then, one week later, the Secretary of State announced his famous "defense perimeter"—publicly advising our enemies that, so far as nations outside this perimeter were concerned, "no person can guarantee these areas against military attack." Under these circumstances, it was cold comfort to the nations outside this perimeter to be reminded that they could appeal to the United Nations.

These nations, of course, included Korea. The armies of communism, thus informed, began their big build-up. Six months later they were ready to strike across the Thirty-eighth Parallel. They struck on June 25, 1950.

On that day, the record of political and diplomatic failure of this Administration was completed and sealed.

The responsibility for this record cannot be dodged or evaded. Even if not a single Republican leader had warned so clearly against the coming disaster, the responsibility for the fateful political decisions would still rest wholly with the men charged with making those decisions—in the Department of State and in the White House. They cannot escape that responsibility now or ever.

When the enemy struck, on that June day of 1950, what did America do? It did what it always has done in all its times of peril. It appealed to the heroism of its youth.

This appeal was utterly right and utterly inescapable. It was inescapable not only because this was the only way to defend the idea of collective freedom against savage aggression. That appeal was inescapable because there was now in the plight into which we had stumbled no other way to save honor and self-respect.

The answer to that appeal has been what any American knew it would be. It has been sheer valor—valor on all the Korean mountainsides that, each day, bear fresh scars of new graves.

Now—in this anxious autumn—from these heroic men there comes back an answering appeal. It is no whine, no whimpering plea. It is a question that addresses itself to simple reason. It asks: Where do we go from here? When comes the end? Is there an end?

These questions touch all of us. They demand truthful answers. Neither glib promises nor glib excuses will serve. They would be no better than the glib prophecies that brought us to this pass.

To these questions there are two false answers—both equally false. The first would be any answer that dishonestly pledged an end to war in

Korea by any imminent, exact date. Such a pledge would brand its speaker as a deceiver.

The second and equally false answer declares that nothing can be done to speed a secure peace. It dares to tell us that we, the strongest nation in the history of freedom, can only wait—and wait—and wait. Such a statement brands its speaker as a defeatist.

My answer—candid and complete—is this:

The first task of a new Administration will be to review and re-examine every course of action open to us with one goal in view: To bring the Korean war to an early and honorable end. This is my pledge to the American people.

For this task a wholly new Administration is necessary. The reason for this is simple. The old Administration cannot be expected to repair what it failed to prevent.

Where will a new Administration begin?

It will begin with its President taking a simple, firm resolution. That resolution will be: To forego the diversions of politics and to concentrate on the job of ending the Korean war—until that job is honorably done.

That job requires a personal trip to Korea.

I shall make that trip. Only in that way could I learn how best to serve the American people in the cause of peace.

I shall go to Korea.

That is my second pledge to the American people.

Carefully, then, this new Administration, unfettered by past decisions and inherited mistakes, can review every factor—military, political and psychological—to be mobilized in speeding a just peace.

Progress along at least two lines can instantly begin. We can—first—step up the program of training and arming the South Korean forces. Manifestly, under the circumstances of today, United Nations forces cannot abandon that unhappy land. But just as troops of the Republic of Korea covet and deserve the honor of defending their frontiers, so should we give them maximum assistance to insure their ability to do so.

Then, United Nations forces in reserve positions and supporting roles would be assurance that disaster would not again strike.

We can—secondly—shape our psychological warfare program into a weapon capable of cracking the Communist front.

Beyond all this we must carefully weigh all interrelated courses of action. We will, of course, constantly confer with associated free nations of Asia and with the cooperating members of the United Nations. Thus we could bring into being a practical plan for world peace.

That is my third pledge to you.

As the next Administration goes to work for peace, we must be guided at every instant by that lesson I spoke of earlier. The vital lesson is this:

To vacillate, to appease, to placate is only to invite war—vaster war—bloodier war. In the words of the late Senator [Arthur H.] Vandenberg, appeasement is not the road to peace; it is only surrender on the installment plan.

I will always reject appeasement.

And that is my fourth pledge to you.

A nation's foreign policy is a much graver matter than rustling papers and bustling conferences. It is much more than diplomatic decisions and trade treaties and military arrangements.

A foreign policy is the face and voice of a whole people. It is all that the world sees and hears and understands about a single nation. It expresses the character and the faith and the will of that nation. In this, a nation is like any individual of our personal acquaintance; the simplest gesture can betray hesitation or weakness, the merest inflection of voice can reveal doubt or fear.

It is in this deep sense that our foreign policy has faltered and failed.

For a democracy, a great election, such as this, signifies a most solemn trial. It is the time when—to the bewilderment of all tyrants—the people sit in judgment upon the leaders. It is the time when these leaders are summoned before the bar of public decision. There they must give evidence both to justify their actions and explain their intentions.

In the great trial of this election, the judges—the people—must not be deceived into believing that the choice is between isolationism and internationalism. That is a debate of the dead past. The vast majority of Americans of both parties know that to keep their own nation free, they bear a majestic responsibility for freedom through all the world. As practical people, Americans also know the critical necessity of unimpaired access to raw materials on other continents for our own economic and military strength.

Today the choice—the real choice—lies between policies that assume that responsibility awkwardly and fearfully—and policies that accept that responsibility with sure purpose and firm will. The choice is between foresight and blindness, between doing and apologizing, between planning and improvising.

In rendering their verdict, the people must judge with courage and with wisdom. For—at this date—any faltering in America's leadership is a capital offense against freedom.

In this trial, my testimony, of a personal kind, is quite simple. A soldier all my life, I have enlisted in the greatest cause of my life—the cause of peace.

I do not believe it a presumption for me to call the effort of all who have enlisted with me—a crusade.

I use that word only to signify two facts. First: We are united and devoted to a just cause of the purest meaning to all humankind. Second: We know that—for all the might of our effort—victory can come only with the gift of God's help.

In this spirit—humble servants of a proud ideal—we do soberly say: This is a crusade.

☆

ADLAI E. STEVENSON

Acceptance Speech

CHICAGO, ILLINOIS

July 26, 1952

I accept your nomination—and your program.

I should have preferred to hear those words uttered by a stronger, a wiser, a better man than myself. But, after listening to the President's speech, I feel better about myself!

None of you, my friends, can wholly appreciate what is in my heart. I can only hope that you may understand my words. They will be few.

I have not sought the honor you have done me. I *could* not seek it because I aspired to another office, which was the full measure of my ambition. One does not treat the highest office within the gift of the people of Illinois as an alternative or as a consolation prize.

I *would* not seek your nomination for the Presidency because the burdens of that office stagger the imagination. Its potential for good or evil now and in the years of our lives smothers exultation and converts vanity to prayer.

I have asked the Merciful Father—the Father of us all—to let this cup pass from me. But from such dread responsibility one does not shrink in fear, in self-interest, or in false humility.

So, "If this cup may not pass from me, except I drink it, Thy will be done."

That my heart has been troubled, that I have not sought this nomination, that I could not seek it in good conscience, that I would not seek it in honest self-appraisal, is not to say that I value it the less. Rather it is that I revere the office of the Presidency of the United States.

And now, my friends, that you have made your decision, I will fight to win that office with all my heart and soul. And, with your help, I have no doubt that we will win.

You have summoned me to the highest mission within the gift of any people. I could not be more proud. Better men than I were at hand for this mighty task, and I owe to you and to them every resource of mind and of strength that I possess to make your deed today a good one for our country and for our party. I am confident too, that your selection of a candidate for Vice President will strengthen me and our party immeasurably in the hard, the implacable work that lies ahead for all of us.

I know you join me in gratitude and respect for the great Democrats and the leaders of our generation whose names you have considered here in this Convention, whose vigor, whose character, whose devotion to the Republic we love so well have won the respect of countless Americans and have enriched our party. I shall need them, we shall need them, because I have not changed in any respect since yesterday. Your nomination, awesome as I find it, has not enlarged my capacities. So I am profoundly grateful and emboldened by their comradeship and their fealty, and I have been deeply moved by their expressions of good will and support. And I cannot, my friends, resist the urge to take the one opportunity that has been afforded me to pay my humble respects to a very great and good American, whom I am proud to call my kinsman, Alben Barkley of Kentucky.

Let me say, too, that I have been heartened by the conduct of this Convention. You have argued and disagreed, because as Democrats you care and you care deeply. But you have disagreed and argued without calling each other liars and thieves, without despoiling our best traditions in any naked struggles for power.

And you have written a platform that neither equivocates, contradicts nor evades. You have restated our party's record, its principles and its purposes, in language that none can mistake, and with a firm confidence in justice, freedom and peace on earth that will raise the hearts and the hopes of mankind for that distant day when no one rattles a saber and no one drags a chain.

For all these things I am grateful to you. But I feel no exultation, no sense of triumph. Our troubles are all ahead of us. Some will call us appeasers; other will say we are the war party. Some will say we are reactionary. Others will say that we stand for socialism. There will be the inevitable cries of "throw the rascals out"; "it's time for a change"; and so on and so on.

We'll hear all those things and many more besides. But we will hear nothing that we have not heard before. I am not too much concerned with partisan denunciation, with epithets and abuse, because the workingman, the farmer, the thoughtful businessmen, all know that they are better off than ever before and they all know that the greatest danger to free enterprise in this country died with the great depression under the hammer blows of the Democratic Party.

Nor am I afraid that the precious two-party system is in danger. Certainly the Republican Party looked brutally alive a couple of weeks ago, and I mean both Republican parties! Nor am I afraid that the Democratic Party is old and fat and indolent. After 150 years it has been old for a long time; and it will never be indolent as long as it looks forward and not back, as long as it commands the allegiance of the young and the hopeful who dream the dreams and see the visions of a better America and a better world.

You will hear many sincere and thoughtful people express concern about the continuation of one party in power for twenty years. I don't belittle this attitude. But change for the sake of change has no absolute merit in itself. If our greatest hazard is preservation of the values of Western civilization, in our self-interest alone, if you please, is it the part of wisdom to change for the sake of change to a party with a split personality; to a leader, whom we all respect, but who has been called upon to minister to a hopeless case of political schizophrenia?

If the fear is corruption in official position, do you believe with Charles Evans Hughes that guilt is personal and knows no party? Do you doubt the power of any political leader, if he has the will to do so, to set his own house in order without his neighbors having to burn it down?

What does concern me, in common with thinking partisans of both parties, is not just winning the election, but how it is won, how well we can take advantage of this great quadrennial opportunity to debate issues sensibly and soberly. I hope and pray that we Democrats, win or lose, can campaign not as a crusade to exterminate the opposing party, as our opponents seem to prefer, but as a great opportunity to educate and elevate a people whose destiny is leadership, not alone of a rich and prosperous, contented country as in the past, but of a world in ferment.

And, my friends, more important than winning the election is governing the nation. That is the test of a political party—the acid, final test. When the tumult and the shouting die, when the bands are gone and the lights are dimmed, there is the stark reality of responsibility in an hour of history haunted with those gaunt, grim specters of strife, dissension and materialism at home, and ruthless, inscrutable and hostile power abroad.

The ordeal of the twentieth century—the bloodiest, most turbulent era of the Christian age—is far from over. Sacrifice, patience, understanding and implacable purpose may be our lot for years to come. Let's face it. Let's talk sense to the American people. Let's tell them the truth, that there are no gains without pains, that we are now on the eve of great decisions, not easy decisions, like resistance when you're attacked, but a long, patient, costly struggle which alone can assure triumph over the great enemies of man—war, poverty and tyranny—and the assaults upon human dignity which are the most grievous consequences of each.

Let's tell them that the victory to be won in the twentieth century, this portal to the Golden Age, mocks the pretensions of individual acumen and ingenuity. For it is a citadel guarded by thick walls of ignorance and of mistrust which do not fall before the trumpets' blast or the politicians' imprecations or even a general's baton. They are, my friends, walls that must be directly stormed by the hosts of courage, of morality and of vision, standing shoulder to shoulder, unafraid of ugly truth, contemptuous of lies, half truths, circuses and demagoguery.

The people are wise—wiser than the Republicans think. And the Democratic Party is the people's party, not the labor party, not the farmers' party, not the employers' party—it is the party of no one because it is the party of everyone.

That I think, is our ancient mission. Where we have deserted it we have failed. With your help there will be no desertion now. Better we lose the election than mislead the people; and better we lose than misgovern the people. Help me to do the job in this autumn of conflict and of campaign; help me to do the job in these years of darkness, doubt and of crisis which stretch beyond the horizon of tonight's happy vision, and we will justify our glorious past and the loyalty of silent millions who look to us for compassion, for understanding and for honest purpose. Thus we will serve our great tradition greatly.

I ask of you all you have; I will give to you all I have, even as he who came here tonight and honored me, as he has honored you—the Democratic Party—by a lifetime of service and bravery that will find him an imperishable page in the history of the Republic and of the Democratic Party—President Harry S. Truman.

And finally, my friends, in the staggering task you have assigned me, I shall always try "to do justly and to love mercy and to walk humbly with my God."

☆

ADLAI E. STEVENSON

Campaign Speech

ACADEMY OF MUSIC, BROOKLYN, NEW YORK

October 31, 1952

Brooklyn has meant good fortune for Franklin Roosevelt and good fortune for Harry Truman. In fact, it seems to have meant good fortune for practically everybody, except the Dodgers.

I will never forget the time during the war when I was driving through Brooklyn from the Navy Yard with the Secretary of the Navy behind a motorcycle escort; we slowed down at a crowded corner, and I overhead somebody in the curious crowd say, "It must be dem bums." I was never more flattered in my life.

Now, as usual, my friends, the pre-election thunder comes from the Republicans. They have most of the nation's newspapers and magazines. They have the slickest slogans and the shiniest posters. They win most of the pre-election polls, and sometimes they win them in a "Gallup." It is not a very good pun but it is the best I could do.

Then—then the people will vote on Tuesday. I understand that on Wednesday the newspapers plan to publish a 5-Star Final.

Many thousands of our votes will come from rank-and-file Republicans who will vote with us. No doubt some Democrats will vote for the Republican candidates. We have already, for example, traded a couple of Southern Governors for the Senator from Oregon and the Vice Chairman of the National Young Republicans. And I regard this as a profitable exchange for us. I would be happy to throw in a second baseman—but not Jackie Robinson.

But, let's not speak of the approaching Republican sorrow without compassion. You in Brooklyn, of all places, know how melancholy is the sound of the words, "wait till next year."

The choice next Tuesday is a fateful one. It is a choice of parties, between the party whose affirmative leadership for many years is written in the strength and the prosperity of our nation and in the widening opportunity and security of our lives, and the party whose only consistent record is one of opposition, obstruction and stubborn negation. It is also a choice of leadership. My opponent has been making a great effort—here in the East anyway, and especially in New York—to persuade the people to forget the last three months. His friends are suggesting that what he said in

Champaign, Illinois, doesn't count, that those words in Milwaukee really weren't uttered, that none of his Midwestern tour expressed the real Eisenhower. But those words were spoken, those speeches were made; the visits with Senator Jenner and Senator McCarthy were all too real. The General may forget, but those Senators won't, and if they should be returned to the Senate and the General sent to the White House, they won't forget and won't let the General forget either.

A man who has the confidence of the public has a public trust not to abuse that confidence for any ends, let alone his own.

In the field of foreign policy the obligation is even stronger. The issues are the relations of our country with our allies and our enemies, the issues of peace or war.

Deception cannot be condoned as campaign oratory. I thought for a time that the issues of foreign policy and of our future could be freely and honestly debated between us on a level worthy of the American people. But the Republicans have concentrated not on discussing, but on systematically disparaging the policies which, with all their defects, have brought the United States to a peak of world prestige and power and responsibility never before dreamed of. Confronted with the great achievements and potentialities of the Marshall Plan, the Truman Doctrine, the North Atlantic Pact, Point Four, the Trade Agreements Program, the Good Neighbor Policy, they have fallen back upon the parrot-like repetition of a monotonous charge. The Democratic foreign policy, they say, does not promise quick solutions; the answers are not all to be found in the back of the book.

As a result, they have now got their own candidates into a trap. For they feel, unless he can come up with the big answer, unless he can promise a quick and easy road to peace and world leadership, the American people will begin to find out how good our foreign policy really has been. The General's advisers seem to have assured him that the American people will buy any merchandise so long as you package it gaudily enough. But the public has rejected the General's merchandise, piece by piece as second-hand and deceptive.

Now, let us, if you will, review this dreary history because it is important in these last hours of this fateful campaign.

The General's experience in Europe and in working with Europeans should have made him unusually sensitive to the importance of guarding and strengthening our European alliances. Yet in his first major policy speech last August, what did he do? He said, speak "with cold finality," to the Soviet Union and prepare to roll back Soviet power and liberate the satellite states. How we were to accomplish this, he did not say; but these words, spoken on the General's eminent authority, raised momentary hopes among those Americans whose friends or relatives were trapped behind the Iron Curtain.

As the idea sank in, however, the effect was greatly different. It became apparent that the General's proposal would lead, not to the liberation of the captive peoples, but to their obliteration—not to release, but to war.

Caught out in this manner, the General explained that he didn't mean what he had said. Yet the damage in Europe had already been done— damage not only to the General himself—which you and I have all regretted—but, far more important, to that funded capital of confidence in American stability and judgment which we have so carefully built up in the postwar years.

And this was only the beginning.

I was surprised that the General should have recklessly gambled with the confidence of our European allies in view of his experience as the head of the North Atlantic Treaty Organization. I was even more surprised when he showed a willingness to undermine that organization itself. In May of 1952, the General had told the Congress that a cut of more than one billion dollars in the foreign-aid program would endanger the proposed military buildup which he said he considered essential in the interests of United States security.

As soon as he took off his uniform, however, he changed his tune.

What this country needed, he said, was a forty-billion-dollar budget cut and a major tax reduction. Pressed by his own astonished colleagues, he qualified this claim. He did not propose, he said, to cut the budget immediately by forty billion, but to work toward a reduction of that amount over a period of five years.

It was at this point that Senator Taft took the General firmly by the hand. The forty-billion figure, he apparently dismissed as a typographical error. In his Morningside Heights Manifesto he pledged the General to a mere ten-billion-dollar cut next year, and a twenty-five-billion cut the following year.

Again false hopes were raised—hopes that we could quickly reduce our taxes and still not reduce our safety. And once again the hopes were doomed to disappointment.

Before the Chicago Convention the General appeared willing to keep Korea out of the campaign. Last June, at Abilene, he denied that there was, and I quote him, "any clear-cut answer" to the Korean problem. He said he did not think it would be possible for our forces to carry through a decisive attack; he ruled out the alternative of retreat; and he ended with this candid conclusion: "We have got to stand firm and take every possible step we can to reduce our losses and stand right there and try to get a decent armistice."

But a few weeks as a political candidate began to alter his opinion. Where once he had sought to unite public sentiment behind our stand in Korea, he now sought out the possibilities of division and of mistrust, echoing the views of his Republican advisers who had even called this first, great, historic case of collective security under arms a "useless war" and "Truman's war."

He first began to speak of what he called the truly terrible blunders that led up to the Korean War, including the very decision to withdraw our troops from Korea, in which he had participated as Chief of Staff of the Army.

Then he reversed his position on the all-important question of bombing the Manchurian bases across the Yalu and expanding the war—a question which the nation had pondered through the weeks of the MacArthur hearings and had decided in the negative. On June 5th, at Abilene, the General declared that he was against bombing bases in Chinese territory on the other side of the Yalu. Yet in September, he could say that he had always stood behind MacArthur on bombing those bases.

And now, as this political campaign has grown in intensity, and as each day sees the increase in Democratic strength, the General is indulging in something far more insidious than self-contradiction. He is seeking one easy solution after another for the Korean War.

Early this month in Illinois, the General propounded the startling theory that the American forces could soon be withdrawn and replaced by South Korean troops. "If there must be a war there," he said, "let it be Asians against Asians."

Now, there are several things wrong with this proposal. In the first place, the General put it forward as though it were a brand-new idea, although he knew that it has been our policy since the start of the Korean conflict to arm and train South Korean forces as fast as possible. In the second place, he suggested that it would be relatively easy to replace our American boys with Koreans; yet our Commander on the spot immediately stated that no matter how much training and equipment we supplied, it would be impossible for the South Koreans to take over the entire front.

Apart from these military questions, however, the General's statement displayed an alarming disdain for the sensibilities of our allies both in Europe and in Asia. The General talked as if we had entered Korea to fight Asians; yet he must know that we entered Korea to resist communist aggression, and that in such a fight there can be no color line. And, as the former head of NATO, how could the General be unaware that such talk would undermine the confidence of all our allies in the sincerity of our world leadership?

"Let Asians fight Asians" is the authentic voice of a resurgent isolationist. In 1939 the Republican Old Guard, faced with the menace of the Nazi world, was content to say, "Let Europeans fight Europeans," ignoring completely the fact that the menace of Nazism was a menace to Americans as much as to Frenchmen and Englishmen. What a curious remark for a man who led the crusade against a Nazi tyranny!

Again the General raised false hopes of a quick solution, and again the false hopes were doomed to disappointment. Confronted with scathing comment for this proposal, even from members of his own party, such as Senator Smith of Maine, the General has now put forth a new proposal—a proposal suggested not by an experienced diplomat, or even by an experienced soldier, but rather by one of the General's new ghost writers, recruited from the staff of a slick magazine.

This new proposal is simplicity itself. "Elect me President," the General says, "and you can forget about Korea; I will go there personally." I don't think for a moment that the American people are taken in by a promise without a program. It is not enough to say, "I will fix it for you." The principle of blind leadership is alien to our tradition. And, unfortunately, the ghost writer who provided the proposal failed to give it content. The General was to go to Korea, but nobody indicated what he should do when he got there. The American people were quick to realize also that the conduct of a military campaign is the task of a field commander, whereas the making of peace requires negotiation with the central adversary—and in this case the central adversary is in Moscow, not in Korea.

And so, once again having raised the hopes of American families, he has been forced to beat a retreat from his first proposals. In a series of statements in the last two days he has abandoned his promise of making peace. At Kew Gardens he said that he was going out only to—and I quote him—"improve our plans." At Mineola he referred to his duty to go to Korea to see what our problems were and—I quote him—"how we can bring that situation under better control."

In the Bronx, on Wednesday, he referred to his Korean trip as an opportunity, "to see how we stand in organizing the forces of the Republic of Korea in order to prepare the Koreans to defend their own line."

And in New York City on the same day he again talked in terms of increasing the contribution of the Republic of Korea.

Now, these are admirable objectives, and such a trip would be informative. But, the label on the bottle was different, and the contents are misbranded.

If we are to bring about an honorable peace in Korea—which is what the General talked about in his Detroit speech—we must face the facts. There are only four possible courses open to us: Get out, or enlarge the war, or purchase a truce through the abandonment of our moral position, or continue the negotiations with all of the resource and self-discipline at our command.

Last summer the General excluded the alternatives of extending the war or retreating from it. I don't know what his position is now. Retreat can only mean the loss of the whole Far East to communism. And extending the war to China would tie up the bulk of our armed strength in Asia while the Red Army was left free for new adventures in the industrial heart of Europe.

But if he would neither enlarge the war nor abandon it, what would he do? Would he make new concessions in the truce negotiations, or has he forgotten the nature of the problem which has caused the deadlock?

Negotiations with communists are never easy, always exasperating, but not necessarily hopeless.

At the time we instituted the Berlin Airlift many impatient Americans said that we were undertaking a hopeless task; but we regained access to Berlin and our prestige in Europe was greater than ever.

The Korean truce negotiations have dragged on through many months, but they have not been without result. Most of the problems which first confronted us in reaching an agreement have now, one by one, been eliminated. Only one major issue remains, and this is not a military but a moral issue.

It is whether we and the other United Nations fighting in Korea should force thousands of Chinese and North Korean prisoners to return to communist territory and almost certain death.

We sent our troops into Korea two and one-half years ago because we knew that mobsters who get away with one crime are only encouraged to start on another. Korea was a crucial test in the struggle between the free world and communism.

The question of the forcible return of prisoners of war is an essential part of that test. Fifty thousand prisoners have stated that they would rather kill themselves than return to their homeland. Many of those prisoners surrendered in response to our own appeals. They surrendered to escape the communist world. They surrendered because in their eyes the United States stood for freedom from slavery. So far the United States *has* stood for freedom—and this is our greatest asset in our struggle against communism. How many of you suppose that we could retain that asset if we sent these men back to their death at the point of a bayonet?

This is the sole question remaining unresolved in the truce negotiations. Is this the question General Eisenhower intends to settle by going to Korea? I do not ask this idly. Quite recently at Richmond, Senator Capehart, one of the Republican Old Guard whom General Eisenhower has embraced, accused President Truman of prolonging the war by refusing to force these prisoners to return. The Senator's position with respect to these prisoners is identical with that of the communists. It is a position which no government in the world has taken except the Soviet Union and its satellites.

And I think it is worth noting that this was the same Senator Capehart who said on October 12th, "In another two weeks, General Eisenhower will be thinking and talking on foreign policy just like Senator Taft."

Now I think the General should answer one question. In embracing the Republican Old Guard has he embraced their contention that we should give up our moral position? And in asking the General this question, let me state my own views.

I have the profoundest sympathy for every mother and father in the United States who is affected by this tragic war. No one is more determined than I to see that it is brought to a conclusion. But that conclusion must be honorable, for if we do not maintain our moral position we have lost everything—our young men will have died in vain. If we give up on this point, if we send these 50,000 prisoners to their death, we will no longer lead the coalition of the free world. Today we stand in that position of leadership not merely because we are physically strong but because our cause is just. Once we commit a gross injustice, our allies will fall away like the leaves in autumn.

With patience and restraint and with the building up of our strength the communists will be compelled to yield, even as they yielded on the Berlin Airlift.

As of the moment we have a stalemate, and stalemates are abhorrent to Americans. But let us not deceive ourselves. A stalemate is better than surrender—and it is better than atomic war. And let us not forget that a stalemate exists for the enemy as well as for ourselves.

There is no greater cruelty, in my judgment, than the raising of false hopes—no greater arrogance than playing politics with peace and war. Rather than exploit human hopes and fears, rather than provide glib solutions and false assurances, I would gladly lose this Presidential election.

There is strength in freedom—strength far greater than we know. I have no fear that our present ordeal is without end. Working together, united in respect for human beings, and united in respect for ourselves, the free peoples can stop the communist conquest, save the peace, and move together to build a new and spacious and friendly world.

If we have the courage and the fortitude to walk through the valley of the shadow boldly and mercifully and justly, we shall yet emerge in the blazing dawn of a glorious new day.

☆

1956

☆

Eisenhower's first term as President was marked by negotiations ending the Korean War, the demise of Joseph McCarthy's power of intimidation in the United States Senate, and the Brown desegregation decision issued by the Supreme Court under Eisenhower's new Chief Justice, Earl Warren. Eisenhower's personal popularity notwithstanding, Republicans lost control of Congress in the elections of 1954 and were forced to work closely with the southern Democratic Party leadership in formulating policy. Instead of rolling back many of the social welfare programs initiated during the New Deal, Eisenhower continued to request modest additions in such areas as federal aid to housing and extending minimum wage benefits.

In foreign policy, Eisenhower and his Secretary of State, John Foster Dulles, completed negotiations ending the Korean War and created a web of anti-Communist alliances around the world. In addition, through the CIA, the governments of Guatemala and Iran were overthrown. After American aid had failed to stem the Viet Minh Communists' defeat of the French in Indochina, Dulles and Eisenhower refused to abide by the Final Declaration of the Geneva Convention in 1954. Eventually, Eisenhower backed the repressive Diem regime in South Vietnam, which became the target of renewed Communist guerilla warfare by the late 1950s.

The President suffered a heart attack in September 1955 but in

February 1956 announced that he would run for a second term. He was renominated by the Republican Convention in August by acclamation. There had been a flurry of opposition by Republican liberals against retaining Vice President Nixon, but the Californian was duly renominated in San Francisco in late August.

Eisenhower's acceptance speech attempted to prove that the Republicans were the party of the future whereas the Democratic Party's obsession with the Depression of the 1930s "still blinds [them] to the insistent demands of today." One significant comment of Eisenhower's was that it "is madness to suppose that there could be an island of tranquility and prosperity in a sea of wretchedness and frustration." Living in an era of thermonuclear bombs necessitated attempts to "bridge the great chasm that separates us from the people under Communist rule."

The Democrats met in Chicago in mid-August and renominated Adlai Stevenson for the Presidency. He had forced the withdrawal of rival Tennessee Senator Estes Kefauver after winning several significant primary contests and defeated a late entrant, New York Governor W. Averill Harriman, on the first ballot for the nomination. The party platform attacked the Eisenhower administration for its "favoritism" to big business and accepted the Supreme Court decisions on desegregation, although it opposed "all proposals for the use of force to interfere with the orderly determination of these matters by the courts."

In his acceptance speech Stevenson chose to walk a tightrope between those favoring increased civil rights for black Americans and southerners who were gearing up for campaigns of "massive resistance" against desegregation rulings. He also condemned the Republican attempts to manipulate the minds of Americans by "the arts of advertising" and issued a warning that Americans should not let their "aspirations so diminish that our worship becomes rather of bigness—bigness of material achievement."

The political historian Theordore White in his book *America in Search of Itself: The Making of the President 1956–1980* believes that this convention was the last of an older system:

> where states, sovereignties, interests, pressure groups, machine blocs, unions, ethnics, all regarded the national convention as the ultimate bargaining place where wheeler-dealers, cause people, and vested interests traded claims. . . . After 1956, conventions would no longer choose the nominee; he would emerge as the survivor of the primary trail. And the excitement of the convention would be largely synthetic, packaged for projection outward in the contest between the two parties to grab, dominate, or control public attention.

The fall campaign saw Stevenson change the style of his speeches from those he had given in 1952, aiming them more directly at the mass of voters instead of at the highly educated and the policy makers. His major addresses were televised. By late September, in speeches such as the one he made in Minneapolis, Stevenson began to question the efficacy of the draft by observing that "we must not let the Selective Service become our Maginot Line." Further, he suggested a moratorium "on the testing of more super H-bombs."

Eisenhower's campaign started off at a leisurely pace, but a Democratic gubernatorial victory in Maine in mid-September forced the Republicans to campaign more vigorously. One issue that caused concern was the low agricultural prices in the farm belt. Eisenhower later wrote in his memoirs that "we were unwilling to return to a program of increased governmental bribes designed to create a false and fleeting prosperity—and to purchase votes." His speech in Cleveland on October 1st addressed both the farm problem and his belief that the Democrats were primarily in favor of a "continuous extension of political control over our economy."

The last few days of the campaign were fought amidst the drama of the Hungarian Revolt against the Russians and the crisis over control of the Suez Canal that pitted France, Great Britain and Israel against Egypt. In a televised speech on October 31st Eisenhower condemned violence in both areas of the world, intoning that "there can be no peace without law. And there can be no law if we were to invoke one code of international conduct for those who oppose us and another for our friends." Stevenson could do little to match Eisenhower at this point and was again soundly defeated at the polls several days later.

DWIGHT D. EISENHOWER

Acceptance Speech

SAN FRANCISCO, CALIFORNIA

August 23, 1956

Chairman Martin, delegates and alternates to this great convention, distinguished guests and my fellow Americans wherever they may be in this broad land.

I should first tell you that I have no words in which to express the gratitude that Mrs. Eisenhower and I feel for the warmth of your welcome, the cordiality you extended to us and to the members of our family —our son and daughter, my brothers and their wives—touches our hearts deeply. Thank you very much, indeed.

I thank you additionally and personally for the high honor you have accorded me in entrusting me once more with your nomination for the Presidency. And I should like to say that it is a great satisfaction to me that the team of individuals you selected in 1952 you've selected to keep intact for this campaign.

I am not here going to attempt a eulogy of Mr. Nixon. You have heard his qualifications described in the past several days. I merely want to say this: that whatever dedication to country, loyalty and patriotism and great ability can do for America, he will do—and that I know.

Ladies and gentlemen, when Abraham Lincoln was nominated in 1860, and a committee brought the news to him at his home in Springfield, Ill., his reply was two sentences long. Then, while his friends and neighbors waited in the street, and while bonfires lit up the May evening, he said simply, "And now I will not longer defer the pleasure of taking you, and each of you, by the hand."

I wish I could do the same—speak two sentences, and then take each of you by the hand, all of you who are in sound of my voice. If I could do so, I would first thank you individually for your confidence and your trust. Then, as I am sure Lincoln did as he moved among his friends in the light of the bonfires, we could pause and talk a while about the questions that are uppermost in your minds.

I am sure that one topic would dominate all the rest. That topic is: the future.

This is a good time to think about the future, for this convention is celebrating its one hundredth anniversary. And a centennial is an occasion not just for recalling the inspiring past, but even more for looking ahead to the demanding future.

Just as on New Year's Day we instinctively think, "I wonder where I will be a year from now," so it is quite natural for the Republican party to ask today, "What will happen, not just in the coming election, but even 100 years from now?"

My answer is this: If we and our successors are as courageous and forward-looking and as militantly determined, here under the Klieg lights of the twentieth century, as Abraham Lincoln and his associates were in the bonfire light of the nineteenth, the Republican party will continue to grow in the confidence and affection of the American people, not only to November next, but indeed to and beyond, its second centennial.

Now, of course, in this convention setting you and I are momentarily more interested in November, 1956, than in 2056. But the point is this: Our policies are right today only as they are designed to stand the test of tomorrow.

The great Norwegian, Henrik Ibsen, once wrote:

"I hold that man is in the right who is most clearly in league with the future."

Today I want to demonstrate the truth of a single proposition:

The Republican party is the party of the future.

I hold that the Republican party and platform are right in 1956, because they are "most closely in league with the future." And for this reason the Republican party and program are and will be decisively approved by the American people in 1956.

My friends, I have just made a very flat statement for victory for the Republican party in November. And I believe it from the bottom of my heart, but what I say is based upon certain assumptions and those assumptions must become true if the prediction I make is to be valid.

And that is this: that every American who believes as we do—the Republicans, the independents, the straight-thinking Democrats must carry the message of the record and the pledges that we have made and here make to all the people in the land.

We must see as we do our civic duty that not only do we vote but that everybody is qualified to vote—that everybody registers, then everybody goes to the polls in November.

Here is the task—not only for the Republican National Committee, for the women's organizations, for the citizen's organizations, for the so-called Youth For Eisenhower—everybody that bears this message in his heart must carry it to the country. In that way we will win.

And which reminds me, my friends, there are only a few days left for registering in a number of our states. That is one thing you cannot defer. The records show that our registration as compared to former years at this time is way down across the land—registration across the board.

Let's help the American Heritage, let's help the Boy Scouts, let's help everybody to get people out and registered to vote.

Now of special relevance, and to me particularly gratifying, is the fact that the country's young people show a consistent preference for this Administration. After all, let us not forget these young people are America's future. Parenthetically, may I say I shall never cease to hope that the several states will give them the voting privilege at a somewhat earlier age than is now generally the case.

Now, the first reason of the five I shall give you why the Republican party is the party of the future is this:

Because it is the party of long-range principle, not short-term expediency.

One of my predecessors is said to have observed that in making his decisions he had to operate like a football quarterback—he could not very well call the next play until he saw how the last play turned out. Well, that may be a good way to run a football team, but in these times it is no way to run a government.

Now why is it so important that great government programs be based upon principle rather than upon shifting political opportunism?

It is because what government does affects profoundly the daily lives and plans of every person in the country. If governmental action is without the solid guidelines of enduring principle, national policies flounder in confusion. And more than this, the millions of individuals, families and enterprises, whose risk-taking and planning for the future are our country's very life force, are paralyzed by uncertainty, diffidence and indecision.

Change based on principle is progress. Constant change without principle becomes chaos.

I shall give you several examples of rejecting expediency in favor of principle.

First, the farm issue.

Expediency said: "Let's do something in a hurry—anything—even multiply our price-depressing surpluses at the risk of making the problem twice as bad next year—just so we get through this year."

People who talk like that do not care about principle, and do not know farmers. The farmer deals every day in basic principles of growth and life. His product must be planned, and cultivated, and harvested over a long period. He has to figure not just a year at a time but over cycles and spans of years, as to his soil, his water, his equipment, the strains of his stock—and the strains on his income.

And so, for this man of principle, we have designed our program of principle. In it, we recognize that we have received from our forebears a rich legacy: our continent's basic resource of soil. We are determined that, through such measures as the soil bank and the great plains program, this legacy shall be handed on to our children even richer than we received it.

We are equally determined that farm prices and income, which were needlessly pushed down under surpluses—surpluses induced first by war and then by unwise political action that was stubbornly and recklessly prolonged, shall in the coming months and years get back on a genuinely healthy basis.

This improvement must continue until a rightful share of our prosperity is permanently enjoyed by agriculture—on which our very life depends.

A second example: labor relations.

Expediency said: "When a major labor dispute looms, the Government must do something—anything—to settle the dispute even before the parties have finished negotiating. Get an injunction. Seize the steel mills. Appoint a board. Knock their heads together."

Principle says: "Free collective bargaining without Government interference is the cornerstone of American philosophy of labor-management relations."

If the Government charges impatiently into every major dispute, the negotiations between parties will become a pointless preliminary farce, while everyone waits around to see what the Government will do. This Administration has faith in the rightness of the collective bargaining principle. It believes in the maturity of both labor and business leaders, and in their determination to do what is best not only for their own side but for the country as a whole.

The results: for the first time in our history a complete steel contract was negotiated and signed without direct Government intervention, and the last three and a half years have witnessed one of the most remarkable periods of labor peace on record.

Another example: concentration of power in Washington.

Expediency said: "We cannot allow our fine new ideas to be at the mercy of fifty-one separate state and territorial Legislatures. It is so much easier to plan, finance and direct all major projects from Washington."

Principle says: "Geographical balance of power is essential to our form of free society. If you take the centralization short-cut every time something is to be done, you will perhaps sometimes get quick action. But there is no perhaps about the price you will pay for your impatience: the growth of a swollen, bureaucratic, monster government in Washington, in whose shadow our state and local governments will ultimately wither and die."

And so we stemmed the heedless stampede to Washington. We made a special point to build up state activities, state finances, and state prestige.

Our founding fathers showed us how the Federal Government could exercise its undoubted responsibility for leadership, while still stopping short of the kind of interference that deadens local vigor, variety, initiative and imagination.

So today we say to our young people: the party of their future will pass along to you undamaged the unique system of division of authority which has proved so successful in reconciling our oldest ideas of personal freedom with the twentieth-century need for decisiveness in action.

My second reason for saying that the Republican party is the party of the future is this: it is the party which concentrates on the facts and issues of today and tomorrow, not the facts and issues of yesterday.

More than twenty years ago, our opponents found in the problems of the depression a battleground on which they scored many political victories. Now economic cycles have not been eliminated. Still, the world has moved on from the Nineteen Thirties: good times have supplanted depression; new techniques for checking serious recession have been learned and tested and a whole new array of problems has sprung up. But their obsession with the depression still blinds many of our opponents to the insistent demands of today.

The present and future are bringing new kinds of challenge to Federal and local governments: water supply, highways, health, housing, power development, and peaceful uses of atomic energy. With two-thirds of us living in big cities, questions of urban organization and redevelopment must be given high priority. Highest of all, perhaps, will be the priority of first-class education to meet the demands of our swiftly growing school-age population.

The party of the young and all ages says: Let us quit fighting the battles of the past and let us all turn our attention to these problems of the present and future, on which the long-term well-being of our people so urgently depends.

Third: The Republican party is the party of the future because it is the party that draws people together, not drives them apart.

Our party despises the technique of pitting group against group for cheap political advantage. Republicans view as a central principle of conduct—not just as a phrase on nickels and dimes—that old motto of ours: "E Pluribus Unum"—"Out of Many—One."

Our party as far back as 1856 began establishing a record of bringing together, as its largest element, the working people and small farmers, as well as the small business men. It attracted minority groups, scholars and writers, not to mention reformers of all kinds, free-soilers, independent Democrats, conscience Whigs, barn-burners, "soft hunkers," teetotallers, vegetarians and transcendentalists!

Now, 100 years later, the Republican party is again the rallying point for Americans of all callings, ages, races and incomes. They see in its broad, forward-moving, straight-down-the-road, fighting program the best promise for their own steady progress toward a bright future. Some opponents have tried to call this a "one-interest party." Indeed it is a one-interest party; and that one interest is the interest of every man, woman and child in America! And most surely as long as the Republican party continues to be this kind of a one-interest party—a one-universal-interest party—it will continue to be the party of the future.

And now the fourth reason: The Republican party is the party of the future because it is the party through which the many things that still need doing will soonest be done—and will be done by enlisting the fullest energies of free, creative, individual people.

Republicans have proved that it is possible for a government to have a warm, sensitive concern for the everyday needs of people, while steering clear of the paternalistic "big-brother-is-watching-you" kind of interference. The individual—and especially the idealistic young person—has no faith in a tight Federal monopoly on problem-solving. He seeks and deserves opportunity for himself and every other person who is burning to participate in putting right the wrongs of the world.

In our time of prosperity and progress, one thing we must always be on guard against is smugness. True, things are going well; but there are thousands of things still to be done. There are still enough needless sufferings to be cured, enough injustices to be erased to provide careers for all the young crusaders we can produce or find.

We want them all! Republicans, independents, discerning Democrats, come on in and help.

One hundred years ago the Republican party was created in a devout belief in equal justice and equal opportunity for all in a nation of free men and women.

What is more, the Republican party's record on social justice rests, not on words and promises, but on accomplishment. The record shows that a wide range of quietly effective actions, conceived in understanding and good will for all, has brought about more genuine—and often voluntary—progress toward equal justice and opportunity in the last three years than was accomplished in all the previous twenty put together.

Elimination of various kinds of discrimination in the armed services, the District of Columbia, and among the employes of government contractors provides specific examples of this progress. In this work, incidentally, no one has been more effective and more energetic than our Vice President, who is head of one of the great committees in this direction.

Now, in all existing kinds of discrimination there is much to do. We must insure a fair chance to such people as mature workers who have trouble getting jobs, older citizens with problems of health, housing, security and recreation, migratory farm laborers and physically-handicapped workers. We have with us, also, problems involving American Indians, low-income farmers and laborers, women who sometimes do not get equal pay for equal work, small businessmen, and employers and workers in areas which need special assistance for redevelopment.

Specific new programs of action are being pushed for all of these, the most recent being a new fourteen-point program for small businessmen which was announced early in August. And the everyday well-being of people is being advanced on many other fronts. This is being done, not by paternalistic regimentation. It is done by clear cut, aggressive Federal leadership and by releasing the illimitable resources and drives of our millions of self-reliant individuals and our thousands of private organizations of every conceivable kind and size—each of these is consecrated to the task of meeting some human need, curing some human evil, or enriching some human experience.

Finally, a party of the future must be completely dedicated to peace, as indeed must all Americans. For without peace there is no future.

It was in the light of this truth that the United States proposed its atoms-for-peace plan in 1953, and since then has done so much to make this new science universally available to friendly nations in order to promote human welfare. We have agreements with more than thirty nations for research reactors, and with seven for power reactors, while many others are under consideration. Twenty thousand kilograms of nuclear fuel have been set aside for the foreign programs.

In the same way, we have worked unceasingly for the promotion of effective steps in disarmament so that the labor of men could with confidence be devoted to their own improvement rather than wasted in the building of engines of destruction.

No one is more aware than I that it is the young who fight the wars, and it is the young who give up years of their lives to military training and service. It is not enough that their elders promise "peace in our time": it must be peace in their time too, and in their children's time; indeed, my friends, there is only one real peace now, and that is peace for all time.

Now there are three imperatives of peace—three requirements that the prudent man must face with unblinking realism.

The first imperative is the elementary necessity of maintaining our own national strength—moral, economic and military.

It is still my conviction, as I wrote in 1947:

"The compelling necessities of the moment leave us no alternative to the maintenance of real and respectable strength—not only in our moral rectitude and our economic power, but in terms of adequate military preparedness."

During the past three and one-half years, our military strength has been constantly augmented, soberly and intelligently. Our country has never before in peacetime been so well prepared militarily. So long as the world situation requires, our security must be vigorously sustained.

Our economic power, as everyone knows, is displaying a capacity for growth which is both rapid and sound, even while supporting record military budgets. We must keep it growing.

But moral strength is also essential. Today we are competing for men's hearts, and minds, and trust all over the world. In such a competition, what we are at home and what we do at home is even more important than what we say abroad. Here again, my friends, we find constructive work for each of us. What each of us does, how each of us acts has an influence on this question.

Now the second imperative of peace is collective security.

We live in a shrunken world, a world in which oceans are crossed in hours, a world in which a single-minded despotism menaces the scattered freedoms of scores of struggling independent nations. To insure the combined strength of friendly nations is for all of us an elementary matter of self-preservation—as elementary as having a stout militia in the days of the flintlock.

Again the strength I speak of is not military strength alone. The heart of the collective security principle is the idea of helping other nations to realize their own potentialities—political, economic and military. The strength of the free world lies not in cementing the free worlds into a second monolithic mass to compete with that of the Communists. It lies rather in the unity that comes of the voluntary association of nations which, however diverse, are developing their own capacities and asserting their own national destinies in a world of freedom and of mutual respect.

There can be no enduring peace for any nation while other nations suffer privation, oppression, and a sense of injustice and despair. In our modern world, it is madness to suppose that there could be an island of tranquillity and prosperity in a sea of wretchedness and frustration. For America's sake, as well as the world's, we must measure up to the challenge of the second imperative: the urgent need for mutual economic and military cooperation among the free nations, sufficient to deter or repel aggression wherever it may threaten.

But even this is no longer enough.

We are in the era of the thermonuclear bomb that can obliterate cities and can be delivered across continents. With such weapons, war has become, not just tragic, but preposterous. With such weapons, there can be no victory for anyone. Plainly the objective now must be to see that such a war does not occur at all.

And so the third imperative of peace is this: without for a moment relaxing our internal and collective defenses, we must actively try to bridge the great chasm that separates us from the people under Communist rule. In those regions are millions of individual human beings who have been our friends, and who themselves have sincerely wanted peace and freedom, throughout so much of our mutual history.

Now for years the Iron Curtain was impenetrable. Our people were unable to talk to these individuals behind the curtain, or travel among them, or share their arts or sports, or invite them to see what life is like in a free democracy, or even get acquainted in any way. What future was there in such a course, except greater misunderstanding and an ever deepening division in the world?

Of course, good will from our side can do little to reach these peoples unless there is some new spirit of conciliation on the part of the Governments controlling them. Now, at last, there appear to be signs that some small degree of friendly intercourse among peoples may be permitted. We are beginning to be able—cautiously and with our eyes open—to encourage some interchange of ideas, of books, magazines, students, tourists, artists, radio programs, technical experts, religious leaders and governmental officials. The hope is, little by little, mistrust based on falsehoods will give way to international understanding based on truth.

Now as this development gradually comes about, it will not seem futile for young people to dream of a brave and new and shining world, or for older people to feel that they can in fact bequeath to their children a better inheritance than that which was their own. Science and technology, labor-saving methods, management, labor organization, education, medicine—and not least, politics and government—all these have brought within our grasp a world in which backbreaking toil and longer hours will not be necessary.

Travel all over the world, to learn to know our brothers abroad, will be fast and cheap. The fear and pain of crippling disease will be greatly reduced. The material things that make life interesting and pleasant will be available to everyone. Leisure, together with educational and recreational facilities, will be abundant, so that all can develop the life of the spirit, of reflection, of religion, of the arts, of the full realization of the good things of the world. And political wisdom will ensure justice and harmony.

This picture of the future brings to mind a little story.

A Government worker, when he first arrived in Washington in 1953, was passing the National Archives Building in a taxi, where he saw this motto carved on one of its pedestals: "What is past is prologue." He had heard that Washington cab drivers were noted for knowing all the Washington answers, so he asked the driver about the motto. "Oh, that," said the driver. "That's just bureaucrat talk. What it really means is—you ain't seen nothing yet."

My fellow Americans, the kind of era I have described is possible. But it will not be attained by revolution. It will not be attained by the sordid politics of pitting group against group. It will be brought about by the ambitions and judgments and inspirations and darings of 168,000,000 free Americans working together and with friends abroad toward a common ideal in a peaceful world.

Lincoln, speaking to a Republican state convention in 1858, began with the biblical quotation: "A house divided against itself cannot stand."

Today the world is a house divided.

But—as is sometimes forgotten—Lincoln followed this quotation with a note of hope for his troubled country:

"I do not expect the house to fall," he said, "but I do expect it will cease to be divided."

A century later, we too must have the vision, the fighting spirit, and the deep religious faith in our Creator's destiny for us, to sound a similar note of promise for our divided world; that out of our time there can, with incessant work and with God's help, emerge a new era of good life, good will and good hope for all men.

One American put it this way: "Every tomorrow has two handles. We can take hold of it with the handle of anxiety or the handle of faith."

My friends, in firm faith, and in the conviction that the Republican purposes and principles are "in league" with this kind of future, the nomination that you have tendered me for the Presidency of the United States I now—humbly but confidently—accept.

☆

DWIGHT D. EISENHOWER

Campaign Speech

CLEVELAND, OHIO

October 1, 1956

Mr. Chairman, Secretary Humphrey, Senator Bricker, Senator Bender, members of the Ohio Republican contingent in the Congress, Republican candidates for State Office—let me pause here long enough to say I wish for each of them overwhelming success where they are standing for election this fall—and My fellow citizens in this great throng and over the Nation:

Almost two years have passed since I last visited Cleveland, but I find that even a few hours in this city provide a tremendous tonic for me, as an American. From my heart, I thank you for the warmth of your welcome.

This time I am here in the midst of a political campaign—a political campaign to determine what kind of government this country is going to have for the next four years.

Now let there be no mistake. There are deep and essential differences in the beliefs and convictions of the two major parties as established by the words of their candidates and by their records in office.

Speaking simply and directly to the problem: one of the most vital of these differences is that a dominant element in the other party believes primarily in big government and paternalistic direction by Washington bureaucrats of important activities of the entire nation. Those people have in the past sponsored the Brannan plan and price controls in time of peace. They have flirted with socialized medicine. In general, they preach continuous extension of political control over our economy.

On the other hand, we of this Administration and this Party believe that the great American potential can be realized only through the unfettered and free initiative, talents and energies of our entire people.

We believe that the government has the function of insuring the national security and domestic tranquillity, and beyond this, has to perform, in Lincoln's phrase—all those things which individuals cannot well do for themselves.

We believe that government must be alert—and this Administration has been alert—to every need of our people, especially in those things affecting their health and education and their human rights. A sound nation is built of individuals sound in body and mind and spirit. Government dares not ignore the individual citizen.

But we emphatically reject every unnecessary invasion into the daily lives of our people and into their occupations, both industrial and on the farm.

Let no one tell you that this difference is either merely doctrinal or fanciful. It is practical. It is real. It affects your lives, the life of the nation today and the life of the nation tomorrow.

Now naturally, the busy orators of the opposition deplore—and even attempt to deny—this faith of ours, in you, the people.

Daily I read about politicians—some of them candidates for high office—who go about the country expressing at length their worries about America and the American people. They profess to be alarmed, scared, and convinced that in all ways we are slipping badly. They cry that the country is going to pot and only they—prescribing for our ills from the seat of government in Washington—can save it.

Now I have a simple prescription for their worries and fears. It is this:

Let them forget themselves for awhile, and their partisan speeches. When they visit a city like Cleveland, let them look around at the hustle and bustle; talk to, and especially listen to, the people here. Let these politicians absorb some of the spirit that animates Clevelanders, all of them—whether they work in banks, in factories, in orchards and fields or in kitchens. Their worries and fears of the future of America should begin to sound foolish—even to them.

Now, my friends, despite this good advice, I am sure these men of fretting fear and worried doubt will reject my prescription instantly. They want too much to have you believe in the story of gloom they spread. For, you see, they assert that these fancied ills can be cured only if the government in Washington—with they themselves occupying its important posts—runs the entire country, including Cleveland.

Now, for a few years in the past, they, and men like them, almost succeeded in selling us this philosophy. But, now the shoe is on the other foot and they are extremely unhappy about it.

For Cleveland, and the rural areas in Ohio, and the citizens of all the other 47 States, are not only running their own jobs efficiently, but are doing their part to run Washington. The result is a better America, an America of increasing peace, security and progress.

Together, we Americans have moved along way forward in the last four years.

For, you see, Cleveland is not an island of prosperity in an ocean of stagnation. All America has advanced in the past four years.

Now that advance didn't happen just by accident. Your Government in Washington has adopted policies that have created a tremendous confidence in America's future.

And with that confidence, you people of Cleveland, your neighbors in Detroit and Toledo—yes, all the people of the United States—you have done the rest.

You here in this Square, the tens of millions like you all over the country, are the source of this tremendous advance—not a group of bureaucrats in Washington or a group of politicians bewailing the fix the country is in. And how did you do this? You accomplished this by hard work; by investing your money; by sticking to your job and doing a good job. You did it because you had faith in yourselves, in your community, and your country. You did it by using your Government as a servant, not turning to it as a kindly master who could parcel out to you—in its great wisdom—the measure of prosperity it believes you merit.

Now the results have been wonderful.

The cost of living has been remarkably stabilized—only about 2½ percent increase in 3½ years. During the final six years of the previous Administration the cost of living increase was twenty times as great as that.

Today, we have a stable dollar. One man who has powerfully helped restore its honesty and dependability is your own fellow citizen, your great Secretary of the Treasury, George Humphrey.

You have a right—a definite right—to be proud of him. With the late Senator Taft, he has added stature to the Republican Party in this generation.

Now, my friends, we have balanced the Federal Budget, and have even made some payment on our huge national debt.

We have record high employment—66.8 million jobs in August—and without war.

Just before I left Washington, one of the technicians gave me the latest figures on unemployment in the month of September, and it looks like it's down below three percent—almost a record in our entire history.

Working people have higher wages than ever—for the average factory worker, 12 percent more than when the prior Administration left office—and this worker has greatly increased his purchasing power.

Production of goods and services is at a rate exceeding 400 billion dollars a year.

In the first three years of this Administration there were more single-family homes built in America than in any prior three-year period.

A nation-wide highway construction program is now under way.

Those are the facts—that is where America is today. Now while Americans were accomplishing this—were making these tremendous advances—what has your Government been doing?

In virtually every area of human concern, it is moving forward.

Government has had a heart as well as a head.

Now, my friends, in telling you about some of the things this Administration has been doing, I hope you will not take it that I am boasting. There will never be room for boasting in this regard until there is not a single needy person left in the United States, when distress and disease have been eliminated. I am talking about progress—how far we have gone ahead.

Now here are some things the opposition would like you to forget:

Social Security has been extended to an additional 10 million Americans—unemployment compensation to an additional 4 million Americans.

Our health program has been greatly improved—research into the causes of crippling and killing diseases has been markedly stepped up.

The minimum wage has been increased, even though my recommendation for its wider coverage was not acted on in the Congress.

We have had a 7.4 billion dollar tax cut—the largest in our Nation's history. And despite opposition charges, two thirds of that cut was given to individuals.

Sympathetic understanding has been fostered and intelligent progress has been made in civil rights. Segregation has been ended in restaurants, theatres, hotels, and schools in the District of Columbia—ended in Government departments, the Armed Forces, veterans' hospitals.

And we have been vigilant and successful in preserving the nation's security—and peace.

Now let me say, this peace is not all that we could wish, and not all that—with God's help—it will one day be. Centuries of mutual hatreds and prejudices and quarrels cannot disappear in a few short years.

But why this anguished cry of some politicians that we have no peace?

Do they think they can make America's parents and wives believe that their sons and husbands are being shot at?

Do they think they can bring Americans to believe that our nation's powerful voice is not daily urging conciliation, mutual understanding and justice?

That is exactly what we are doing in the Suez problem.

Do they believe that Americans do not know how strong have been our efforts to dedicate the atom to constructive instead of destructive purposes?

Are they so deluded as to believe they can conceal from all our people the steady policies directed toward removing the causes of war?

Let them think of these names: Korea, Trieste, Austria, Guatemala, West Germany. If they so think of them, they will realize that they would be very wise to stop this effort of fooling all the people all the time.

Not only is this Administration dedicated to peace, but we have established a record in behalf of peace that all the world respects.

Now these are just some of the things this Administration has been doing.

Let us look for a moment at a simple question: Which Party, in these recent years, has done more to help all citizens meet the problems of their daily lives? Which Party has helped more—not with words, with deeds?

As an early demonstration of its concern for the human problems of health, education and welfare, the Administration raised that agency to Cabinet level. Now national health, the proper education of our children, and the human welfare of all Americans are discussed at the same table—and with the same exhaustive care—as such great subjects as foreign affairs and national security.

The men of the opposition know perfectly well that one of the main reasons they were thrown out of office four years ago was their tolerance of the thievery of inflation. Just in the final seven years of their tenure of office this economic fever had cut the value of the dollar by almost one-third, damaging the livelihood of the aged—the pensioned—all salaried workers. The opposition did nothing effectively to stop this economic thievery. And they know it.

Take the St. Lawrence Seaway. For twenty years the opposition talked about the Seaway. Yet it was repeatedly shelved, by-passed, and blocked. This Administration acted and got the Seaway going. As a result, two years from now, great ocean ships will dock here in Cleveland.

All the money the Federal government could spend for this purpose won't hold a candle to the increased prosperity the Seaway will bring to the Great Lakes—to the Middle West. This Administration made it a reality. And they—the opposition—know it.

Take agriculture. They—the opposition—had 20 long years to do something for the most needy families on our farms. At the end of those 20 years, they had done nothing—except to by-pass the small farmer as they made corporation and big area farming more profitable than ever before. And the Administration's new rural development program is the first—I repeat the first—full-scale and integrated Federal effort to help these lowest-income families. Another Administration program enables the small farmer—often a young veteran—to get full and comprehensive credit in financing his farm and buildings and equipment and seed. And he can refinance his existing debts in the same way as any other business or industry. That's another "first" for this administration. And the opposition knows it.

Now, let's take small business. Just 18 years ago small business people from all over America gathered in Washington at the request of the Administration then in power. They made 23 recommendations—appeals

—for action. Yet for the next 14 years—for all the years when the opposition held power—virtually nothing was done. This Administration is the first Administration that has made a major attack upon the problems of small business. And they—the opposition—know it.

Take labor. The opposition say that they alone truly care for the working men and women of America and that the Republican Party is really a vague kind of political conspiracy by big business to destroy organized labor and to bring hunger and torment to every worker in America.

This is more than political bunk. It is willful nonsense. It is wicked nonsense.

Let's see what the record shows about this:

The record shows: Organized labor is larger in numbers and greater in strength today—after these years of Republican Administration—than ever in our Nation's history.

The record shows: Not under the opposition's leadership, but under the leadership of this Administration, the workers of America have received the greatest rise in real wages—the kind of wages that buys groceries and cars and homes—the greatest rise in 30 years.

The record shows: We—not they—have made the most successful fight to stop inflation's robbery of every paycheck.

The record shows that this check upon inflation is most vital—not for the few who are rich—but for the millions who depend upon salaries or pensions, those who are old, those who are sick, those who are needy.

The record shows: We—not they—have brought a reduction in the cost of Federal Government and a reduction in taxes—a reduction benefiting, not a favored few, but every taxpayer in the land. In fact, 11 out 12 increases that have been made in the individual income tax since it started were made under our opponents, while 5 out of 7 reductions were made under Republican Administrations.

And now I want to add this simple fact. We have given to our Nation the kind of government that is a living witness to the basic virtues in a democracy—public morality, public service, and public trust. In this Administration you cannot find those ugly marks of the past: Special favoritism, cronyism, and laxity in administration.

You have here in Ohio a vigorous exponent of the Administration's program—George Bender.

Two years ago I came here to add my voice to his campaign for the United States Senate. He ran on one basic platform pledge—to support the President and his Administration in Washington. In this he has a splendid record.

He has done an effective job for this State and for all the States of the Union. He has served with vigor and forthrightness. He has shown us a great dedication.

And this Administration is dedicated to the welfare—the peace and the prosperity—of 168 million American citizens. This dedication is equal for all. It is equal for all regardless of race or color or creed—regardless of region or section or of occupation—and regardless of social or economic fortune.

This is the kind of government that we have been developing for the past four years.

Now the Republican Party does not base its appeal on sectionalism, on playing worker against manager, housewife against storekeeper, farmer against manufacturer.

The Republican Party believes that none of us can truly prosper unless all of us prosper. It believes we cannot be secure unless we are strong—that no nation can enjoy true peace unless all nations are free from war.

If the Republican Party were not this sort of Party, I would not belong to it. I would not belong to it and I would not be running as its candidate. What benefits America benefits farmers and industrial workers, the school children and the aged, the West and North and South—all of us. We are one people, one Nation.

And finally, let me say this to you. One of my chief objectives and my greatest hope prior to taking office was to restore the respect of the American people for the Government of the United States. I think you agree with me that honor and integrity have been the landmarks of all that we have done during the last four years. But much remains to be done in the cause of good government for the future of America.

I sincerely and devotedly want to continue the job. To be successful two things are necessary: time; and your help.

With your help between now and November, we can gain the time for the next four years in which we can permanently establish an understanding of these truths—in Washington and throughout the country. There will be restored the faith and belief of the American people in our national processes.

The confidence of the American people in our institutions and our leaders must be strong and secure, if we are to lead the peoples and the nations toward the lasting and just peace, which we all so devoutly seek.

Friends, again I thank you for your welcome and for your courtesy in listening to me so attentively. Thank you very much.

☆

ADLAI E. STEVENSON

Acceptance Speech

CHICAGO, ILLINOIS

August 17, 1956

I accept your nomination and your program. And I pledge to you every resource of mind and strength that I possess to make your deed today a good one for our country and for our party.

Four years ago I stood in this same place and uttered those same words to you. But four years ago we lost. This time we will win!

My heart is full tonight, as the scenes and faces and events of these busy years in between crowd my mind.

To you here tonight and across the country who have sustained me in this great undertaking for months and even years, I am deeply, humbly grateful; and to none more than the noble lady who is also the treasurer of a legacy of greatness—Mrs. Eleanor Roosevelt, who has reminded us so movingly that this is 1956 and not 1932, nor even 1952; that our problems alter as well as their solutions; that change is the law of life, and that political parties, no less than individuals, ignore it at their peril.

I salute also the distinguished American who has been more than equal to the hard test of disagreement and has now reaffirmed our common cause so graciously—President Harry Truman. I am glad to have you on my side again, sir!

I am sure that the country is as grateful to this convention as I am for its action of this afternoon. It has renewed and reaffirmed our faith in free democratic processes.

The office of the Vice-Presidency has been dignified by the manner of your selection as well as by the distinction of your choice. Senator Kefauver is a great Democrat and a great campaigner—as I have reason to know better than anybody!

If we are elected and it is God's will that I do not serve my full four years, the people will have a new President whom they can trust. He has dignity; he has convictions, and he will command the respect of the American people and the world.

Perhaps these are simple virtues, but there are times when simple virtues deserve comment. This is such a time. I am grateful to you for my running mate—an honorable and able American—Senator Estes Kefauver and may I add that I got as excited as any of you about that photo-finish between Senator Kefauver and that great young American Senator John Kennedy.

When I stood here before you that hot night four years ago we were at the end of an era—a great era of restless forward movement, an era of unparalleled social reform and of glorious triumph over depression and tyranny. It was a Democratic era.

Tonight, after an interval of marking time and aimless drifting, we are on the threshold of another great, decisive era. History's headlong course has brought us, I devoutly believe, to the threshold of a new America—to the America of the great ideals and noble visions which are the stuff our future must be made of.

I mean a new America where poverty is abolished and our abundance is used to enrich the lives of every family.

I mean a new America where freedom is made real for all without regard to race or belief or economic condition.

I mean a new America which everlastingly attacks the ancient idea that men can solve their differences by killing each other.

These are the things I believe in and will work for with every resource I possess. These are the things I know you believe in and will work for with everything you have. These are the terms on which I accept your nomination.

Our objectives are not for the timid. They are not for those who look backward, who are satisfied with things as they are, who think that this great nation can ever sleep or ever stand still.

The program you have written is, I think, more than a consensus of the strongly held convictions of strong men; it is a signpost toward that new America. It speaks of the issues of our time with passion for justice, with reverence for our history and character, with a long view of the American future, and with a sober, fervent dedication to the goal of peace on earth.

Nor has it evaded the current problems in the relations between the races who comprise America, problems which have so often tormented our national life. Of course there is disagreement in the Democratic party on desegregation. It could not be otherwise in the only party that must speak responsibly and responsively in both the North and the South. If all of us are not wholly satisfied with what we have said on this explosive subject it is because we have spoken the only way a truly national party can—by the understanding accommodation of conflicting views.

But in so doing, in substituting realism and persuasion for the extremes of force or nullification, our party has preserved its effectiveness, it has avoided a sectional crisis, and it has contributed to our national unity as only a national party could.

As President it would be my purpose to press on in accordance with our platform toward the fuller freedom for all our citizens which is at once our party's pledge and the old American promise.

I do not propose to make political capital out of the President's illness. His ability to personally fulfill the demands of his exacting office is a matter between him and the American people. So far as I am concerned that is where the matter rests. As we all do, I wish deeply for the President's health and well-being.

But if the condition of President Eisenhower is not an issue as far as I am concerned, the condition and the conduct of the President's office and of the Administration is very much an issue.

The men who run the Eisenhower Administration evidently believe that the minds of Americans can be manipulated by shows, slogans and and the arts of advertising. And that conviction will, I dare say, be backed up by the greatest torrent of money ever poured out to influence an American election—poured out by men who fear nothing so much as change and who want everything to stay as it is—only more so.

This idea that you can merchandise candidates for high office like breakfast cereal—that you can gather votes like box tops—is, I think, the ultimate indignity to the democratic process. And we Democrats must also face the fact that no administration has ever before enjoyed such an uncritical and unenthusiastic support from so much of the press as this one.

But let us ask the people of our country to what great purpose for the republic has the President's popularity and this unrivaled opportunity for leadership been put? Has the Eisenhower Administration used this opportunity to elevate us? To enlighten us? To inspire us? Did it, in a time of headlong, world-wide revolutionary change, prepare us for stern decisions and great risks? Did it, in short, give men and women a glimpse of the nobility and vision without which peoples and nations perish?

Or did it just reassure us that all is well, everything is all right, that everyone is prosperous and safe, that no great decisions are required of us, and that even the Presidency of the United States has somehow become an easy job?

I will have to confess that the Republican Administration has performed a minor miracle—after twenty years of incessant damnation of the New Deal they not only haven't repealed it but they have swallowed it, or most of it, and it looks as though they could keep it down at least until after the election.

I suppose we should be thankful that they have caught up with the New Deal at last, but what have they done to take advantage of the great opportunities of these times—a generation after the New Deal?

Well, I say they have smothered us in smiles and complacency while our social and economic advancement has ground to a halt and which our leadership and security in the world have been imperiled.

In spite of these unparalleled opportunities to lead at home and abroad, they have, I say, been wasting our opportunities and losing our world.

I say that what this country needs is not propaganda and a personality cult. What this country needs is leadership and truth. And that's what we mean to give it.

What is the truth?

The truth is that the Republican party is a house divided. The truth is that President Eisenhower, cynically coveted as a candidate but ignored as a leader, is largely indebted to Democrats in Congress for what accomplishments he can claim.

The truth is that everyone is not prosperous. The truth is that the farmer, especially the family farmer who matters most, has not had his fair share of the national income and the Republicans have done nothing to help him—until an election year.

The truth is that 30,000,000 Americans live today in families trying to make ends meet on less than $2,000 a year. The truth is that the small farmer, the small business man, the teacher, the white collar worker, and the retired citizen trying to pay today's prices on yesterday's pension—all these are in serious trouble.

The truth is that in this Government of big men—big financially—no one speaks for the little man.

The truth is that in this government policy abroad has the Communists on the run. The truth, unhappily, is not—in the Republican President's words—that our "prestige since the last world war has never been as high as it is this day." The truth is that it has probably never been lower.

The truth is that we are losing the military advantage, the economic initiative and the moral leadership.

The truth is not that we are winning the cold war. The truth is that we are losing the cold war.

Don't misunderstand me. I, for one, am ready to acknowledge the sincerity of the Republican President's desire for peace and happiness for all. But good intentions are not good enough and the country is stalled on dead center—stalled in the middle of the road—while the world goes whirling by. America, which has lifted man to his highest economic state, which has saved freedom in war and peace, which saved collective security, no longer sparks and flames and gives off new ideas and initiatives. Our lights are dimmed. We chat complacently of this and that while, in Carlyle's phrase, "death and eternity sit glaring." And I could add that opportunity, neglected opportunity, sits glaring too!

But you cannot surround the future with arms, you cannot dominate the racing world by standing still. And I say it is time to get up and get moving again. It is time for America to be herself again.

And that's what this election is all about!

Here at home we can make good the lost opportunities; we can recover the wasted years; we can cross the threshold to the new America.

What we need is a rebirth of leadership—leadership which will give us a glimpse of the nobility and vision without which peoples and nations perish. Woodrow Wilson said that "when America loses its ardor for mankind it is time to elect a Democratic President." There doesn't appear to be much ardor in America just now for anything, and it's time to elect a Democratic Administration and a Democratic Congress, yes, and a Democratic Government in every state and local office across the land.

In our hearts we know that the horizons of the new America are as endless, its promise as staggering in its richness as the unfolding miracle of human knowledge. America renews itself with every forward thrust of the human mind.

We live at a time when automation is ushering in a second industrial revolution, and the powers of the atom are about to be harnessed for ever greater production. We live at a time when even the ancient spectre of hunger is vanishing. This is the age of abundance. Never in history has there been such an opportunity to show what we can do to improve the equality of living now that the terrible, grinding anxieties of daily bread, of clothing and shelter, are disappearing.

With leadership, Democratic leadership, we can do justice to our children, we can repair the ravages of time and neglect in our schools. We can and we will!

With leadership, Democratic leadership, we can restore the vitality of the American family farm. We can preserve the position of small business without injury to the large. We can strengthen labor unions and collective bargaining as vital institutions in a free economy. We can and our party history proves that we will!

With leadership, Democratic leadership, we can conserve our resources of land and forest and water and develop them for the benefit of all. We can and the record shows that we will!

With leadership, Democratic leadership, we can rekindle the spirit of liberty emblazoned in the bill of rights; we can build this new America where the doors of opportunity are open equally to all, yes, the doors of our factories and the doors of our school rooms. We can make this a land where opportunity is founded only on responsibility and freedom on faith, and where nothing can smother the lonely defiant spirit of the free intelligence. We can, and by our traditions as a party we will!

All these things we can do and we will. But in the international field the timing is only partially our own. Here the "unrepentant minute" once missed, may be missed forever. Other forces, growing yearly in potency, dispute with us the direction of our times. Here more than anywhere guidance and illumination are needed in the terrifying century of the hydrogen bomb. Here more than anywhere we must move, and rapidly, to repair the ravages of the past four years to America's repute and influence abroad.

We must move with speed and confidence to reverse the spread of communism. We must strengthen the political and economic fabric of our alliances. We must launch new programs to meet the challenge of the vast social revolution that is sweeping the world and turn the violent forces of change to the side of freedom.

We must protect the new nations in the exercise of their full independence; and we must help other peoples out of Communist or colonial servitude along the hard road to freedom.

And we must place our nation where it belongs in the eyes of the world—at the head of the struggle for peace. For in this nuclear age peace is no longer a visionary ideal. It has become an absolute, imperative, practical necessity. Humanity's long struggle against war has to be won and won now. Yes, and I say it can be won.

It is time to listen again to our hearts, to speak again our ideals, to be again our own great selves.

There is a spiritual hunger in the world today and it cannot be satisfied by material things alone. Our forebears came here to worship God. We must not let our aspirations so diminish that our worship becomes rather of bigness—bigness of material achievement.

For a century and a half the Democratic party has been the party of respect for people, of reverence for life, of hope for each child's future, of belief that "the highest revelation is that God is in every man."

Once we were not ashamed in this country to be idealists. Once we were proud to confess that an American is a man who wants peace and believes in a better future and loves his fellow man. We must reclaim these great Christian and humane ideas. We must dare to say again that the American cause is the cause of all mankind.

If we are to make honest citizens of our hearts we must unite them again to the ideals in which they have always believed and give those ideals the courage of our tongues.

Standing as we do here tonight at this great fork of history, may we never be silenced, may we never lose our faith in freedom and the better destiny of man.

☆

ADLAI E. STEVENSON
Campaign Speech
MINNEAPOLIS, MINNESOTA

September 29, 1956

Minnesota is the great overarching bridge between the old Midwest and the new Northwest, where people breathe freer and look higher and, somehow, the blood is quickened in the clean North air, where men are not afraid to speak their minds or vote their deep convictions. Up here in Minnesota men are never satisfied that things can't be better than they are.

Minnesota has always led the great traditions of protest in the upper Midwest—the protest against things that could be better.

In recent years across your Eastern border the heirs of the Wisconsin Progressives have found a home in the Democratic party; today to the west in North Dakota the Nonpartisan League is moving in with us, too.

Here in Minnesota the heirs of that same great tradition have fused their strength in the Democratic-Farmer-Labor party.

And two men who have helped to write the Democratic-Farmer-Labor story are its great leaders today—Hubert Humphrey and Orville Freeman.

These men—and the national leaders of the Democratic party down the years—had several things in common. They were not afraid of new ideas. They were not content to leave well enough alone. They had a passion for human life—they cared and, they cared deeply about people. And they tackled the people's problems with an enthusiasm that was boundless and unbeatable.

I want to talk to you tonight about the need for enthusiasm and new ideas in our national life.

Of course today the Republicans would have us feel all the problems are solved, that what we need is not enthusiasm and new ideas but caution, complacency and a passion not for the people but for things as they are.

Well, here is how things are for some of our people unfortunately.

Farmers and their wives and children are being forced to pack up and leave the farm—a good farm—and uproot their whole lives.

Men are being forced to sell the store on Main Street that for years has provided for their family and served their community well.

Too many of our older citizens are spending what ought to be the golden years in want and neglect.

Too many children are going to school in crowded ramshackle buildings with teachers that are only half-trained.

Millions of sick people can't afford to call a doctor.

Hundreds of thousands of our mental patients are consigned to disgraceful medieval institutions.

One family out of five must get by on less than $2,000 in times like these.

Millions of American citizens are still barred from schools and jobs and an equal chance merely because of their color.

In the city slums children are roaming the alleys behind the tenement buildings, and in some parts of our country poverty is converting farmland into a rural slum.

I say this is not right. And I say that only the Democratic party has the passion for human justice, the enthusiasm and determination and the new ideas, to drive want and suffering from all American homes, not just some of them.

But beyond this lies another goal—the goal of peace, and I want to say something about that tonight.

Like most Americans, I've read some of what that wise New England philosopher, Ralph Waldo Emerson, wrote. I fear I've forgotten a lot of what he said, but I've remembered this:

"Nothing great," Emerson said, "was ever achieved without enthusiasm." How true that is. As we look back over the centuries, we can see that nearly all the glorious achievements of mankind, nearly all the best things that characterize our society, sprang from the uncrushable enthusiasm of those who believed in the genius of man, and who believed in the possibility of doing the seemingly impossible. To these enthusiasts, whose optimism often exposed them to scorn and ridicule, we chiefly owe all the good things of our civilization.

This thought of Emerson's—this tribute to the power of man's ability to master his destiny—came to me again only recently when I heard the President's recent expression of views on war and peace—the area above all others where we need fresh and positive thinking.

I was distressed to see that the President not only had nothing new to suggest for the future but he seemed resentful over the efforts of others —including myself—to find some new and more hopeful answers to the problems of life and death that now confront us.

To be more specific, I have said before and I'll say it again that I, for one, am not content to accept the idea that there can be no end to compulsory military service. While I, like most others who have had intimate experience with our armed forces in war and peace, have felt that it was and is necessary, at the same time I have felt, and many others likewise, that the draft is a wasteful, inefficient, and often unfair way of maintaining our armed forces, and now it is fast becoming an obsolete way.

Let me make it perfectly clear that as long as danger confronts us, I believe we should have stronger, not weaker, defenses than we have now. Ever since Mr. Eisenhower became President we Democrats have fought hard to prevent the Administration from putting dollars ahead of defense. The Democrats in Congress forced the Administration to reverse itself and restore deep cuts in the strategic Air Force even during this last session of Congress.

But my point is that the draft does not necessarily mean a strong defense. Conditions change, and no conditions have changed more in our time than the conditions of warfare. Nothing is more hazardous in military policy than rigid adherence to obsolete ideas. France learned this in 1939; she crouched behind the Maginot Line, which was designed for an earlier war, and German panzers overran France. The Maginot Line gave France a false—and fatal sense of security. We must not let Selective Service become our Maginot Line.

What I am suggesting is that we ought to take a fresh and open-minded look at the weapons revolution and the whole problem of recruiting and training military manpower. We may very well find that in the not far distant future we can abolish the draft and at the same time have a stronger defense and at lower cost.

Defense is now so complex, its demand for highly skilled and specialized manpower so great, that the old fashioned conscript army, in which many men serve short terms of duty, is becoming less and less suited to the needs of modern arms. And it is becoming more and more expensive.

Let me say right here in all frankness that I have no special pride, no conceit, in the suggestions that I have tried to advance. No one will be happier than I if others find better solutions.

Once we start exploring this possibility seriously many new ideas will be forthcoming; that is always the case when men turn their creative energies full time upon a problem. Right now I had hoped to do no more than get this kind of creative thinking started.

I am distressed that President Eisenhower should dismiss this objective out of hand. If anyone had proposed the abolition of the draft right now, today, the President's attitude would be understandable; indeed, I would share it. But I don't see how we can ever get anywhere against the rigid, negative position that we cannot even discuss the matter, or even look forward to a time when we can do away with compulsory military service. I say it's time we stopped frowning and started thinking about them.

I am even more distressed that this attitude on the part of Mr. Eisenhower carries over into the all-important problem of controlling the hydrogen bomb, for here we are talking about the actual survival of the human race itself.

The testing alone of these super bombs is considered by scientists to be dangerous to man; they speak of the danger of poisoning the atmosphere; they tell us that radioactive fall-out may do genetic damage with effects on unborn children which they are unable to estimate.

I think almost everyone will agree that some measure of universal disarmament—some means of taming the nuclear weapons—is the first order of business in the world today.

It is not enough to say, well, we have tried and failed to reach agreement with the Russians. It is not enough to throw up our hands and say it's no use to try this or that new approach. This is one time we cannot take no for an answer, for life itself depends on our ultimately finding the right yes.

Again, I have no foolish pride in my own ideas on this subject. But there must be a beginning, a starting point, a way to get off the dead center of disagreement. I have proposed a moratorium on the testing of more super H-bombs. If the Russians don't go along, well then at least the world will know we tried. And we will know if they don't because we can detect H-bomb explosions without inspection.

It may be that others will come forward with other ideas; indeed, I hope they do. But I say to you that in this field, as in many others, fresh and openminded thinking is needed as never before—and in this field we may not have unlimited time to get the answers. We'd better start thinking now.

Furthermore, I do not see how we can ever hope to get the answers if fresh ideas, new proposals, new solutions, are not encouraged.

I was shocked when Mr. Eisenhower the other night brushed off my suggestion as a theatrical gesture. I don't believe that was worthy of the President of the United States. I have never questioned his sincerity on a matter that I am sure means more to both of us than anything else in the world—the matter of permanent peace—and I do not think he should have questioned mine.

All decent men and women everywhere hate war. We don't want our boys to be drafted and we don't want to live forever in the shadow of a radioactive mushroom cloud. And when I say "we," I mean Democrats and Republicans alike—I mean mankind everywhere.

Peace is not a partisan issue. Every American, Democrat and Republican alike, wants peace. There is no war party in this country; there is no peace party.

And the way to get started on the difficult road to disarmament and peace is not, I repeat, to scorn new ideas.

Just because this Administration has not been able to make any progress toward safe disarmament or even toward controlling H-bomb development, does not mean that such agreements are forever impossible. No matter which party wins in November, another supreme effort must be undertaken, and, if that fails, then another and another, for leaders must lead, and the conquest of this scourge is a more imperative goal of mankind than the conquest of the black plague in the Middle Ages.

I shall continue to concentrate my own attention on this problem, and I shall also do everything I can to encourage others to do likewise, for, as I have said, I know in my heart that Emerson was right when he said that "nothing great was ever achieved without enthusiasm."

And we saw it proved in our own time. For many years, you will recall, the world had dreamed of splitting the atom and releasing its boundless energy.

But most men despaired of ever making this dream come true. Had it not been for Franklin D. Roosevelt and his determination, the so-called impossible might still seem impossible. Then, as now, there were the skeptic, the defeatists, the non-enthusiasts who thought Roosevelt was off on a wild goose chase, who dubbed Oakridge his billion dollar folly. But he was not deterred.

He would not take no for an answer. Nuclear energy was finally placed at the disposal of man, and if we, who survived Franklin Roosevelt, show the will to control this energy that he showed in creating it, then it still may prove to be one of the greatest blessings of all time.

Franklin Roosevelt was not a physicist. He knew nothing about the hidden secrets of uranium. But he had to a supreme degree the first attributes of political leadership—that is, he had the enthusiastic will to act, and the genius for organizing great undertakings.

I, too, know little or nothing about the mechanics of the H-bomb. But I do know this: if man is capable of creating it, he also is capable of taming it. And nothing—including Presidential frowns—can make me believe otherwise.

My friends, this is not the first time the Republicans have dismissed or scorned Democratic efforts to make this a better world.

When Woodrow Wilson had his immortal dream of a League of Nations, the Republicans called it worse names than a "theatrical gesture"—yet American participation might have prevented a second World War.

Franklin Roosevelt proposed the United Nations. Yet even today many Republican leaders, even Senator Knowland, are still suspicious of it or positively hostile. The U.N. isn't perfect. Like most human institutions it probably never will be, and certainly not without the wholehearted support of America's leaders.

This negative, defeatist attitude among Republican leaders comes in an unbroken line down to the present. President Hoover's Fortress America concept is familiar. Senator Taft's negative, isolationist views are still shared by many of his followers.

And the fact is that the Republican party has been so divided since the first war and the League of Nations fight that even to this day it cannot conduct a coherent, consistent foreign policy, and the purpose of foreign policy for the United States is peace. Time and again in the past four years we have seen allied unity abroad sacrificed to Republican unity at home.

This is not to suggest for a second that the Republican party is, therefore, the war party, or that the Democratic party is the party of peace. I have no patience with such blanket charges.

Both parties are dedicated to peace, but historically they differ on how to realize this great objective. I think it is fair to say that, generally speaking, the Republican way has been the narrow, nationalistic one of the low, limited horizon, while the Democratic way has been that of the wide horizon, dotted with the ships and sails of beckoning hope.

One way, of course, is just as patriotic as the other. But in my opinion the Democratic way has usually been more attuned to the changes, the challenge and surprise, of this everchanging world. And I think this is just as true today as it has ever been.

And I think our Democratic enthusiasm for new ideas can better solve our problems here at home, too. For on the record it is the Democratic party that has always made new gains for the good of all the people.

Ours is the party that stopped child labor and started the nation on an eight-hour day, invented Social Security and built the T.V.A. It was the Democratic party that rescued the farmer with the Triple-A in the great depression, curbed the excesses of the stock promoters, built housing for the people, and wrote the G.I. Bill of Rights, I could go on and on.

I spoke a few minutes ago of the Democratic-Farmer-Labor story written here in Minnesota. We're going to tell a larger story, too, this year. Woodrow Wilson restrained the excesses of a new industrialism and met the challenge of the Kaiser; Franklin Roosevelt lifted the people from the slough of depression and beat down totalitarianism; Harry Truman made the great decision that lifted prostrate Europe and gave our nation leadership of the free in the world—and that is our story, written in the Twentieth Century here in blessed America.

I say there is yet much to be done. Great work lies ahead. I believe with all my heart and soul that this nation is about to enter a richer age than man has ever known. The question is: Shall we use our riches for all the people, or just for some of them? And, can we master the new machines, or must we serve them? And, can we put the atom to our peaceful use, or will it destroy us?

These are great questions, they require great answers, and those answers can come only from the strength and wisdom of you, the American people. And they will not be drawn forth by leadership that fails to lead, that frowns on new ideas. They will be drawn forth only by leadership that dares to try the new, that meets the crises of our time with unbeatable enthusiasm.

"Nothing great," I repeat, "was ever achieved without enthusiasm." Let us go forward in the spirit of you of Minnesota, never satisfied with things as they are, daring always to try the new, daring nobly and doing greatly, and so building a New America.

It is in this spirit that I come to you tonight. It is in this spirit that we will win in November.

☆

1960

— ☆ —

By 1960 a new generation of postwar politicians emerged into the Presidential arena, all subtly trying to exude more dynamic leadership than that practiced by Eisenhower. Although the personal popularity of Dwight Eisenhower remained at a high level, he was prevented by his age (he was seventy years old) and by constitutional amendment from serving another term. His second term had not been an unqualified success. Corruption involving Eisenhower's assistant Sherman Adams reverberated through the press. The recession of 1957–58 took place as the Soviet Union launched the Sputnik satellite into space. Further accentuating this growing American insecurity, Cuban Premier Fidel Castro's attraction to Communism and the collapse of a May 1960 U.S.-Soviet summit meeting in Paris raised serious questions about America's "will" and imagination in providing an attractive worldwide alternative to Communism.

Democratic Presidential contenders included Minnesota's liberal Senator Hubert Humphrey, Senate Majority Leader Lyndon Johnson from Texas, and the young, wealthy, and Catholic John Kennedy from Massachusetts. The second son of Franklin Roosevelt's one-time Ambassador to England, Kennedy had been a PT-boat skipper during World War II before winning election to the House of Representatives after the war. In 1952 he beat Henry Cabot Lodge in the first of two successful campaigns for the Senate. Aside from Kennedy's access to his father's vast fortune, he had the advantage of a superb political organization headed by his brother Robert.

Lyndon Johnson chose to seek support among states choosing delegates by caucuses and avoid primary contests. But by 1960 it was becoming mandatory for Presidential candidates to demonstrate their popular appeal in primary battles. Within twenty years the primary system would grow to include thirty-six states. In 1960 Kennedy beat Humphrey first in New Hampshire, then in Wisconsin and West Virginia. As the Los Angeles Democratic convention drew near, liberals, who were wary of Kennedy's rather undistinguished legislative record, sought to draft Adlai Stevenson. Their efforts failed to stop Kennedy from gaining his first ballot victory.

In his acceptance speech Kennedy made an explicit appeal for "a new generation of leadership." After references to Woodrow Wilson's New Freedom and Franklin Roosevelt's New Deal, Kennedy envisioned a "New Frontier" of challenges in "uncharted areas of science and space, unsolved problems of peace and war, unconquered pockets of ignorance and prejudice, unanswered questions of poverty and surplus."

The Democratic candidate also hit the controversial issue of his religion head on. No Catholic had ever been elected President. First in his acceptance speech and then in an address in Houston, the candidate poured scorn on those who repeated the old admonition that the Pope in Rome would be the power behind any Catholic in the White House. Historian Richard Polenberg has written in his book *One Nation Divisible* that Kennedy handled the religious issue "so skillfully as to remove it from pubic discourse for the remainder of the campaign." Another issue that Kennedy raised during the campaign was the existence of what he called a "missle gap" between the United States and the Soviet Union. Historians have since discounted the existence of this gap.

Similar to Kennedy, Republican Richard Nixon had first been elected to the U.S. Congress in 1946 after serving in the armed forces in World War II. He achieved notoriety for his prosecution of Alger Hiss in the House trials in the late 1940s and was elected to the Senate in 1950 by using red-baiting tactics against Helen Gahagan Douglas. His selection as Republican Vice Presidential candidate in 1952 by Eisenhower's political managers was aimed at attracting western and younger voters to the ticket.

Nixon's role as Vice President is recounted in his 1962 book *Six Crises*. While Eisenhower was generally indifferent to Republican party matters, Nixon traveled extensively around the country meeting local Republicans and presenting himself effectively as spokesman for the Administration. Although New York's newly elected Governor Nelson Rockefeller showed some initial interest in challenging Nixon for the nomination in 1959, he ultimately declined to run, and Nixon was able to secure a first-ballot nomination in Chicago by making several minor platform concessions to liberals. The Republicans nominated former Massachusetts Senator and United Nations Ambassador Henry Cabot Lodge to run as Nixon's Vice Presidential candidate.

Nixon foolishly pledged to campaign in all fifty states in his acceptance speech. By the end of the campaign, when his presence could have been used to solidify support in some of the big states, he found himself in arduous journeys to states with few electoral votes.

Since 1948 questions involving the advance of worldwide Communism had been important rhetorical elements to American Presidential candidates. Yet in reading the speeches of major party contenders up to 1960, it may be noted that anti-Communism was but one line of thought presented in each of the candidates' appeal. In Richard Nixon's Chicago acceptance speech, however, the overriding centrality of his anti-Communism becomes apparent. Little is heard about housing, education, or racism unless it is tied to the triumph of freedom defined only in contrast to Communism. The candidate called for a "total commitment" from wage earners, students, and scientists to excell in their fields so that Communism could be defeated. He also exhibited a rather naive belief that "because of the dramatic breakthroughs in science for the first time in human history we have the resources—the resources to wage a winning war against poverty, misery and disease wherever it exists in the world."

Nixon's boundless faith in atomic technology was also demonstrated in his Toledo, Ohio, address of late October in which he lauded Project Plowshare as the kind of effort that "has been a discernible part of the American character and the American purpose from the beginning of our century."

The 1960 campaign is, of course, especially notable because it marked the first set of televised debates between the major party contenders for the Presidency. Four debates were held in the fall, and it is generally believed that Kennedy's telegenic presence in the first debate had a strong impact on the outcome of the election. Issues debated included American policy toward Cuba and the small islands off the coast of Asia threatened by the People's Republic of China.

JOHN F. KENNEDY
Acceptance Speech
LOS ANGELES, CALIFORNIA

July 15, 1960

With a deep sense of duty and high resolve, I accept your nomination. I accept it with a full and grateful heart—without reservation—and with only one obligation—the obligation to devote every effort of body, mind and spirit to lead our party back to victory and our nation back to greatness.

I am grateful, too, that you have provided me with such an eloquent statement of our party's platform. Pledges which are made so eloquently are made to be kept. "The rights of man"—the civil and economic rights essential to the human dignity of all men—are indeed our goal and our first principles. This is a platform on which I can run with enthusiasm and conviction.

And I am grateful, finally, that I can rely in the coming months on so many others—on a distinguished running-mate who brings unity to our ticket and strength to our platform, Lyndon Johnson—on one of the most articulate statesmen of our time, Adlai Stevenson—on a great spokesman for our needs as a nation and a people, Stuart Symington—and on that fighting campaigner whose support I welcome, President Harry S. Truman.

I feel a lot safer now that they are on my side again. And I am proud of the contrast with our Republican competitors. For their ranks are apparently so thin that not one challenger has come forth with both the competence and the courage to make theirs an open convention.

I am fully aware of the fact that the Democratic party, by nominating someone of my faith, has taken on what many regard as a new and hazardous risk—new, at least, since 1928. But I look at it this way:

The Democratic Party has once again placed its confidence in the American people, and in their ability to render a free, fair judgment.

And you have, at the same time, placed your confidence in me, and in my ability to render a free, fair judgment—to uphold the Constitution and my oath of office—and to reject any kind of religious pressure or obligation that might directly or indirectly interfere with my conduct of the Presidency in the national interest.

My record of fourteen years supporting public education—supporting complete separation of church and state—and resisting pressures from any source on any issue should be clear by now to everyone.

I hope that no American, considering the really critical issues facing this country, will waste his franchise by voting either for me or against me solely on account of my religious affiliation. It is not relevant, I want to stress, what some other political or religious leader may have said on this subject. It is not relevant what abuses may have existed in other countries or in other times. It is not relevant what pressures, if any, might conceivably be brought to bear on me.

I am telling you now what you are entitled to know:

That my decisions on every public policy will be my own—as an American, a Democrat and a free man.

Under any circumstances, however, the victory we seek in November will not be easy. We all know that in our hearts. We recognize the power of the forces that will be aligned against us. We know they will invoke the name of Abraham Lincoln on behalf of their candidate—despite the fact that his political career has often seemed to show charity toward none and malice for all.

We know that it will not be easy to campaign against a man who has spoken or voted on every known side of every known issue. Mr. Nixon may feel it is his turn now, after the New Deal and the Fair Deal—but before he deals, someone had better cut the cards.

That "someone" may be the millions of Americans who voted for President Eisenhower but balk at his would-be, self-appointed successor. For just as historians tell us that Richard I was not fit to fill the shoes of bold Henry II—and that Richard Cromwell was not fit to wear the mantle of his uncle—they might add in future years that Richard Nixon did not measure to the footsteps of Dwight D. Eisenhower.

Perhaps he could carry on the party policies—the policies of Nixon, Benson, Dirksen and Goldwater. But this nation cannot afford such a luxury. Perhaps we could afford a Coolidge following Harding. And perhaps we could afford a Pierce following Fillmore.

But after Buchanan this nation needed a Lincoln—after Taft, we needed a Wilson—after Hoover we needed Franklin Roosevelt—and after eight years of drugged and fitful sleep, this nation needs strong, creative Democratic leadership in the White House.

But we are not merely running against Mr. Nixon. Our task is not merely one of itemizing Republican failures. Nor is that wholly necessary. For the families forced from the farm will know how to vote without our telling them. The unemployed miners and textile workers will know how to vote. The old people without medical care—the families without a decent home—the parents of children without adequate food or schools—they all know that it's time for a change.

But I think the American people expect more from us than cries of indignation and attack. The times are too grave, the challenge too urgent, and the stakes too high—to permit the customary passions of political debate. We are not here to curse the darkness, but to light the candle that can guide us through that darkness to a safe and sane future. As Winston Churchill said on taking office some twenty years ago:

"If we open a quarrel between the present and the past, we shall be in danger of losing the future."

Today our concern must be with that future. For the world is changing. The old era is ending. The old ways will not do.

Abroad, the balance of power is shifting. There are new and more terrible weapons—new and uncertain nations—new pressures of population and deprivation. One-third of the world, it has been said, may be free—but one-third is the victim of cruel repression—and the other one-third is rocked by the pangs of poverty, hunger and envy. More energy is released by the awakening of these new nations than by the fission of the atom itself.

Meanwhile, Communist influence has penetrated further into Asia, stood astride the Middle East and now festers some ninety miles off the coast of Florida. Friends have slipped into neutrality—and neutrals into hostility. As our keynoter reminded us, the President who began his career by going to Korea ends it by staying away from Japan.

The world has been close to war before—but now man, who has survived all previous threats to his existence, has taken into his mortal hands the power to exterminate the entire species some seven times over.

Here at home, the changing face of the future is equally revolutionary. The New Deal and the Fair Deal were bold measures for their generations—but this is a new generation.

A technological revolution on the farm has led to an output explosion—but we have not yet learned to harness that explosion usefully, while protecting our farmers' right to full parity income.

An urban population revolution has overcrowded our schools, cluttered up our suburbs, and increased the squalor of our slums.

A peaceful revolution for human rights—demanding an end to racial discrimination in all parts of our community life—has strained at the leashes imposed by timid Executive leadership.

A medical revolution has extended the life of our elder citizens without providing the dignity and security those later years deserve. And a revolution of automation finds machines replacing men in the mines and mills of America, without replacing their income or their training or their need to pay the family doctor, grocer and landlord.

There has also been a change—a slippage—in our intellectual and moral strength. Seven lean years of drouth and famine have withered the field of ideas. Blight has descended on our regulatory agencies—and a dry rot, beginning in Washington, is seeping into every corner of America—in the payola mentality, the expense account way of life, the confusion between what is legal and what is right. Too many Americans have lost their way, their will and their sense of historic purpose.

It is time, in short, for a new generation of leadership—new men to cope with new problems and new opportunities.

All over the world, particularly in the newer nations, young men are coming to power—men who are not bound by the traditions of the past—men who are not blinded by the old fears and hates and rivalries—young men who can cast off the old slogans and delusions and suspicions.

The Republican nominee-to-be, of course is also a young man. But his approach is as old as McKinley. His party is the party of the past. His speeches are generalities from Poor Richard's Almanac. Their platform, made up of left-over Democratic planks, has the courage of our old convictions. Their pledge is a pledge to the status quo—and today there can be no status quo.

For I stand tonight facing west on what was once the last frontier. From the lands that stretch 3,000 miles behind me, the pioneers of old gave up their safety, their comfort and sometimes their lives to build a new world here in the West.

They were not the captives of their own doubts, the prisoners of their own price tags. Their motto was not "every man for himself"—but "all for the common cause." They were determined to make that new world strong and free, to overcome its hazards and its hardships, to conquer the enemies that threatened from without and within.

Today some would say that those struggles are all over—that all the horizons have been explored—that all the battles have been won—that there is no longer an American frontier.

But I trust that no one in this vast assemblage will agree with those sentiments. For the problems are not all solved and the battles are not all won—and we stand today on the edge of a new frontier—the frontier of the 1960's—a frontier of unknown opportunities and perils—a frontier of unfulfilled hopes and threats.

Woodrow Wilson's New Freedom promised our nation a new political and economic framework. Franklin Roosevelt's New Deal promised security and succor to those in need. But the New Frontier of which I speak is not a set of promises—it is a set of challenges. It sums up not what I intend to offer the American people, but what I intend to ask of them. It appeals to their pride, not their pocketbook—it holds out the promise of more sacrifice instead of more security.

But I tell you the New Frontier is here, whether we seek it or not. Beyond that frontier are uncharted areas of science and space, unsolved problems of peace and war, unconquered pockets of ignorance and prejudice, unanswered questions of poverty and surplus.

It would be easier to shrink back from that frontier, to look to the safe mediocrity of the past, to be lulled by good intentions and high rhetoric —and those who prefer that course should not cast their votes for me, regardless of party.

But I believe the times demand invention, innovation, imagination, decision. I am asking each of you to be new pioneers on that New Frontier. My call is to the young in heart, regardless of age—to the stout in spirit, regardless of party—to all who respond to the scriptural call:

"Be strong and of good courage; be not afraid, neither be thou dismayed."

For courage—not complacency—is our need today—leadership—not salesmanship. And the only valid test of leadership is the ability to lead, and lead vigorously. A tired nation, said David Lloyd George, is a tory nation—and the United States today cannot afford to be either tired or tory.

There may be those who wish to hear more—more promises to this group or that—more harsh rhetoric about the men in the Kremlin—more assurances of a golden future, where taxes are always low and subsidies ever high. But my promises are in the platform you have adopted. Our ends will not be won by rhetoric and we can have faith in the future only if we have faith in ourselves.

For the harsh facts of the matter are that we stand on this frontier at a turning-point in history. We must prove all over again whether this nation—or any nation so conceived—can long endure—whether our society—with its freedom of choice, its breadth of opportunity, its range of alternatives—can compete with the single-minded advance of the Communist system.

Can a nation organized and governed such as ours endure? That is the real question. Have we the nerve and the will? Can we carry through in an age where we will witness not only new breakthroughs in weapons of destruction—but also a race for mastery of the sky and the rain, the ocean and the tides, the far side of space and the inside of men's minds?

Are we up to the task? Are we equal to the challenge? Are we willing to match the Russian sacrifice of the present for the future? Or must we sacrifice our future in order to enjoy the present?

That is the question of the New Frontier. That is the choice our nation must make—a choice that lies not merely between two men or two parties, but between the public interest and private comfort—between national greatness and national decline—between the fresh air of progress and the stale, dank atmosphere of "normalcy"—between determined dedication and creeping mediocrity.

All mankind waits upon our decision. A whole world looks to see what we will do. We cannot fail their trust; we cannot fail to try.

It has been a long road from that first snowy day in New Hampshire to this crowded convention city. Now begins another long journey, taking me into your cities and homes all over America. Give me your help, your hand, your voice, your vote. Recall with me the words of Isaiah:

"They that wait upon the Lord shall renew their strength; they shall mount up with wings as eagles; they shall run, and not be weary."

As we face the coming challenge, we too, shall wait upon the Lord and ask that He renew our strength. Then shall we be equal to the test. Then we shall not be weary. And then we shall prevail.

☆

JOHN F. KENNEDY

Campaign Speech

HOUSTON, TEXAS

September 12, 1960

I am grateful for your generous invitation to state my views.

While the so-called religious issue is necessarily and properly the chief topic here tonight, I want to emphasize from the outset that I believe that we have far more critical issues in the 1960 election: the spread of Communist influence, until it now festers only ninety miles off the coast of Florida—the humiliating treatment of our President and Vice-President by those who no longer respect our power—the hungry children I saw in West Virginia, the old people who cannot pay their doctor's bills, the families forced to give up their farms—an America with too many slums, with too few schools, and too late to the moon and outer space.

These are the real issues which should decide this campaign. And they are not religious issues—for war and hunger and ignorance and despair know no religious barrier.

But because I am a Catholic, and no Catholic has ever been elected President, the real issues in this campaign have been obscured—perhaps deliberately, in some quarters less responsible than this. So it is apparently necessary for me to state once again—not what kind of church I believe in, for that should be important only to me, but what kind of America I believe in.

I believe in an America where the separation of church and state is absolute—where no Catholic prelate would tell the President (should he be a Catholic) how to act and no Protestant minister would tell his parishioners for whom to vote—where no church or church school is granted any public funds or political preference—and where no man is denied public office merely because his religion differs from the President who might appoint him or the people who might elect him.

I believe in an America that is officially neither Catholic, Protestant nor Jewish—where no public official either requests or accepts instructions on public policy from the Pope, the National Council of Churches or any other ecclesiastical source—where no religious body seeks to impose its will directly or indirectly upon the general populace or the public acts of its officials—and where religious liberty is so indivisible that an act against one church is treated as an act against all.

For while this year it may be a Catholic against whom the finger of suspicion is pointed, in other years it has been, and may someday be again, a Jew—or a Quaker—or a Unitarian—or a Baptist. It was Virginia's harassment of Baptist preachers, for example, that led to Jefferson's statute of religious freedom. Today, I may be the victim—but tomorrow it may be you—until the whole fabric of our harmonious society is ripped apart at a time of great national peril.

Finally, I believe in an America where religious intolerance will someday end—where all men and all churches are treated as equal—where every man has the same right to attend or not to attend the church of his choice—where there is no Catholic vote, no antiCatholic vote, no bloc voting of any kind—and where Catholics, Protestants and Jews, both the lay and the pastoral level, will refrain from those attitudes of disdain and division which have so often marred their works in the past, and promote instead the American ideal of brotherhood.

That is the kind of America in which I believe. And it represents the kind of Presidency in which I believe—a great office that must be neither humbled by making it the instrument of any religious group, nor tarnished by arbitrarily withholding it, its occupancy, from the members of any religious group. I believe in a President whose views on religion are his own private affair, neither imposed upon him by the nation or imposed by the nation upon him as a condition to holding that office.

I would not look with favor upon a President working to subvert the First Amendment's guarantees of religious liberty (nor would our system of checks and balances permit him to do so). And neither do I look with favor upon those who would work to subvert Article VI of the Constitution by requiring a religious test—even by indirection—for if they disagree with that safeguard, they should be openly working to repeal it.

I want a Chief Executive whose public acts are responsible to all and obligated to none—who can attend any ceremony, service or dinner his office may appropriately require him to fulfill and whose fulfillment of his Presidential office is not limited or conditioned by any religious oath, ritual or obligation.

This is the kind of America I believe in—and this is the kind of America I fought for in the South Pacific and the kind my brother died for in Europe. No one suggested than that we might have a "divided loyalty," that we did "not believe in liberty" or that we belonged to a disloyal group that threatened "the freedoms from which our forefathers died."

And in fact this is the kind of America for which our forefathers did die when they fled here to escape religious test oaths, that denied office to members of less favored churches, when they fought for the Constitution, the Bill of Rights, the Virginia Statute of Religious Freedom—and when they fought at the shrine I visited today—the Alamo. For side by side with Bowie and Crocket died Fuentes and McCafferty and Bailey and Bedillio and Carey—but no one knows whether they were Catholics or not. For there was no religious test there.

I ask you tonight to follow in that tradition, to judge me on the basis of fourteen years in the congress—on my declared stands against an ambassador to the Vatican, against unconstitutional aid to parochial schools, and against any boycott of the public schools (which I attended myself)—instead of judging me on the basis of these pamphlets and publications we have all seen that carefully select quotations out of context from the statements of Catholic Church leaders, usually in other countries, frequently in other centuries, and rarely relevant to any situation here—and always omitting, of course, that statement of the American bishops in 1948 which strongly endorsed church-state separation.

JOHN F. KENNEDY

I do not consider these other quotations binding upon my public acts—why should you? But let me say, with respect to other countries, that I am wholly opposed to the state being used by any religious group, Catholic or Protestant, to compel, prohibit or persecute the free exercise of any other religion. And that goes for any persecution at any time, by anyone, in any country.

And I hope that you and I condemn with equal fervor those nations which deny their Presidency to Protestants and those which deny it to Catholics. And rather than cite the misdeeds of those who differ, I would also cite the record of the Catholic Church in such nations as France and Ireland—and the independence of such statesmen as de Gaulle and Adenauer.

But let me stress again that these are my views—for, contrary to common newspaper usage, I am not the Catholic candidate for President. I am the Democratic Party's candidate for President, who happens also to be a Catholic.

I do not speak for my church on public matters—and the church does not speak for me.

Whatever issues may come before me as President, if I should be elected—on birth control, divorce, censorship, gambling, or any other subject—I will make my decision in accordance with these views, in accordance with what my conscience tells me to be in the national interest, and without regard to outside religious pressure or dictate. And no power or threat of punishment could cause me to decide otherwise.

But if the time should ever come—and I do not concede any conflict to be remotely possible—when my office would require me to either violate my conscience, or violate the national interest, then I would resign the office, and I hope any other conscientious public servant would do likewise.

But I do not intend to apologize for these views to my critics of either Catholic or Protestant faith, nor do I intend to disavow either my views or my church in order to win this election. If I should lose on the real issues, I shall return to my seat in the Senate, satisfied that I tried my best and was fairly judged.

But if this election is decided on the basis that 40,000,000 Americans lost their chance of being President on the day they were baptized, then it is the whole nation that will be the loser in the eyes of Catholics and non-Catholics around the world, in the eyes of history, and in the eyes of our own people.

But if, on the other hand, I should win this election, I shall devote every effort of mind and spirit to fulfilling the oath of the Presidency—practically identical, I might add, with the oath I have taken for fourteen years in the Congress. For, without reservation, I can, and I quote, "solemnly swear that I will faithfully execute the office of President of the United States and will to the best of my ability preserve, protect and defend the Constitution, so help me God."

☆

RICHARD M. NIXON

Acceptance Speech

CHICAGO, ILLINOIS

July 28, 1960

Mr. Chairman, delegates to this convention, my fellow Americans:
I have made many speeches in my life and never have I found it more difficult to find the words adequate to express what I feel as I find them tonight.

To stand here before this great convention, to hear your expression of affection for me, for Pat, for our daughters, for my mother, for all of us who are representing our party is, of course, the greatest moment of my life.

And I just want you to know that my only prayer as I stand here is that in the months ahead I may be in some way worthy of the affection and the trust which you have presented to me on this occasion in everything that I say, everything that I do, everything that I think in this campaign and afterwards.

May I say also that I have been wanting to come to this convention, but because of the protocol that makes it necessary for a candidate not to attend the convention until the nominations are over, I've had to look in on it on television. But I want all of you to know that I have never been so proud of my party as I have been in these last three days, and as I have compared this convention, the conduct of our delegates and our speakers with what went on in my native state of California just two weeks ago.

And I congratulate Chairman Halleck and Chairman Morton and all of those who have helped to make this convention one that will stand in the annals of our party forever as one of the finest we have ever held.

Have you ever stopped to think of the memories you will take away from this convention?

The things that run through my mind are these: that first day with the magnificent speech by Mr. Hoover with his great lesson for the American people, Walter Judd with one of the most outstanding keynote addresses in either party in the history and last night our beloved fighting President making the greatest speech that I have ever heard him make before this convention.

Your platform and its magnificent presentation by Chuck Percy, the chairman. For these and for so many other things, I want to congratulate you tonight and to thank you from the bottom of my heart and on behalf of Americans—not just Republicans—Americans everywhere for making us proud of our country and of our two-party system for what you have done.

And tonight, too, I particularly want to thank this convention for nominating as my running mate, a world statesman of the first rank, my friend and colleague, Henry Cabot Lodge of Massachusetts.

In refreshing contrast to what happened in Los Angeles you nominated a man who shares my views on the great issues and who will work with me and not against me in carrying out our magnificent platform.

And may I say that during this week we Republicans who feel our convictions strongly about our party and about our country have had our differences but as the speech by Senator Goldwater indicated yesterday and the eloquent and gracious remarks of my friend Nelson Rockefeller indicated tonight, we Republicans know that the differences that divide us are infinitesimal compared to the gulf beween us and what the Democrats would put upon us from what they did at Los Angeles at their convention two weeks ago.

It was only eight years ago that I stood in this very place after you had nominated as our candidate for the President one of the great men of our century, and I say to you tonight that for generations to come Americans, regardless of party, will gratefully remember Dwight Eisenhower as the man who brought peace to America, as the man under whose leadership Americans enjoyed the greatest progress and prosperity in history, but above all they will remember him as the man who restored honesty, integrity and dignity to the conduct of government in the highest office of this land.

My fellow Americans, I know now that you will understand what I next say because the next President of the United States will have his great example to follow; because the next President will have new and challenging problems in the world of utmost gravity this truly is the time for greatness in America's leadership.

I am sure you will understand why I do not say tonight that I alone am the man who can furnish that leadership. That question is not for me but for you to decide. And I only ask that the thousands in this hall and the millions listening to me on television, I only ask that you make that decision in the most thoughtful way that you possibly can because what you decide this November will not only affect your lives, and your future, it will affect the future of millions throughout the world.

And I urge you study the records of the candidates, listen to my speeches and that of my opponent and that of Mr. Lodge and that of his opponent and then after you have studied our records and listened to our speeches decide—decide on the basis of what we say and what we believe which is best qualified to lead America and the free world in this critical period.

And to help you make this decision I would like to discuss tonight some of the great problems which will confront the next President of the United States and the policies I believe that should be adopted to meet them.

One hundred years ago in this city Abraham Lincoln was nominated for President of the United States. The problems which will confront our next President will be even greater than those that confronted him.

The question then was freedom for the slaves and survival of the nation. The question now is freedom for all mankind and the survival of civilization and the choice you make—each of you listening to me makes this November—can affect the answer to that question.

What should your choice be and what is it?

Well, let's first examine what our opponents offered in Los Angeles two weeks ago.

They claim theirs was a new program but you know what it was? It was simply the same old proposition that a political party should be all things to all men and nothing more than that.

And they promised—everything to everybody with one exception. They didn't promise to pay the bill. And I say tonight that with their convention, their platform and their ticket they composed a symphony of political cynicism which is out of harmony with our times today.

Now we come to the key question: what should our answer be? And some might say, why, do as they do. Out-promise them, because that's the only way to win.

And I want to tell you my answer. I happen to believe that their program would be disastrous for America. It would wreck our economy; it would dash our people's high hopes for a better life.

And I serve notice here and now that whatever the political consequences, we are not going to try to out-promise our opponents in this campaign.

We are not going to make promises we cannot and should not keep and we are not going to try to buy the people's votes with their own money.

And to those who say that this position will mean political defeat, my answer is this: We have more faith than that in the good sense of the American people, provided the people know the facts, and that's where we come in.

And I pledge to you tonight that we will bring the facts home to the American people, and we will do it with a campaign such as this country has never seen before.

I have been asked by the newsmen sitting on my right and my left all week long, when is this campaign going to begin, Mr. Vice President, on the day after Labor Day or one of the other traditional starting dates? And this is my answer: This campaign begins tonight, here and now, and it goes on.

And this campaign will continue from now until Nov. 8 without any let up.

And I've also been asked by my friends in the press on either side here. They say, "Mr. Vice President, where are you going to concentrate. What states are you going to visit?" And this is my answer: In this campaign, we are going to take no states for granted and we aren't going to concede any states to the opposition!

And I announce to you tonight and I pledge to you that I, personally, will carry this campaign into every one of the fifty states of this nation between now and Nov. 8.

And in this campaign I make a prediction. I say that just as in 1952 and 1956, millions of Democrats will join us not because they are deserting their party but because their party deserted them at Los Angeles two weeks ago.

Now I have suggested to you what our friends of the opposition offered to the American people. What do we offer?

First, we are proud to offer the best eight-year record of any Administration in the history of this country.

But, my fellow Americans, that isn't all, and that isn't enough, because we happen to believe that a record is not something to stand on but something to build on, and building on the great record of this Administration we shall build a better America. We shall build an America in which we shall see the realization of the dreams, the dreams of millions of people not only in America but throughout the world for a fuller, freer, richer life than men have ever known in the history of mankind.

Let me tell you something of the goal of this better America towards which we will strive.

In this America, our older citizens shall not only have adequate protection against the hazards of ill-health but a greater opportunity to lead a useful and productive life by participating to the extent they are able in the nation's exciting work rather than sitting on the sidelines.

And in this better America, young Americans shall not only have the best basic education in America but every boy and girl of ability regardless of his financial circumstances shall have the opportunity to develop his intellectual capabilities to the full.

Our wage-earners shall enjoy increasingly higher wages in honest dollars with better protection against the hazards of unemployment and old age and for those millions of Americans who are still denied equality of rights and opportunity, I say there shall be the greatest progress in human rights since the days of Lincoln, 100 years ago.

And America's farmers—America's farmers—to whose hard work and almost incredible efficiency we owe the fact that we are the best fed, best clothed people in the world, I say American farmers must and will receive what they do not have today and what they deserve—a fair share of America's ever-increasing prosperity.

And to accomplish these things, we will develop to the full the untapped natural resources our water, our minerals, our power with which we are so fortunate to be blessed in this rich land of ours.

And we shall provide for our scientists, the support they need for the research that will open exciting new highways into the future—new highways in which we shall have progress which we cannot even dream of today. And above all, in this decade of the Sixties, this decade of decision and progress, we will witness the continued revitalization of America's moral and spiritual strength with the renewed faith in the eternal ideals of freedom and justice under God which are our priceless heritage as a people.

And now I am sure that many of you in this hall and many of you on television might well ask, "but Mr. Nixon, don't our opponents favor just such goals as these?" And my answer is yes, of course. All Americans regardless of party want a better life for our people. What's the difference then? And I'll tell you what it is. The difference is in the way we propose to reach these goals, and the record shows that our way works and theirs doesn't. And we're going to prove it in this campaign.

We produce on the promises that they make. We succeed where they fail. Do you know why? Because we put, as Governor Rockefeller said in his remarks, we put our primary reliance not upon government but upon people for progress in America. That is why we will succeed.

And we must never forget that the strength of America is not in its government but in its people. And we say tonight that there is no limit to the goals America can reach provided we stay true to the great American tradition.

A government has a role and a very important one but the role of government is not to take responsibility from people but to put responsibility on them. It is not to dictate to people but to encourage and stimulate the creative productivity of 180,000,000 free Americans. That's the way to progress in America.

In other words, we have faith in the people and because our programs for progress are based on that faith, we shall succeed where our opponents will fail in building the better America that I've described.

But if these goals are to be reached, the next President of the United States must have the wisdom to choose between the things government should and should not do. He must have the courage to stand against the pressures of the few for the good of the many, and he must have the vision to press forward on all fronts for the better life our people want.

I have spoken to you of the responsibilities of our next President at home. Those which he will face abroad will be infinitely greater. But before I look to the future, let me say a word about the past.

At Los Angeles two weeks ago, we heard the United States—our Government—blamed for Mr. Khrushchev's sabotage of the Paris conference. We heard the United States blamed for the actions of communist-led mobs in Caracas and Tokyo. We heard that American education and American scientists are inferior. We heard that America militarily and economically is a second-rate country. We heard that America's prestige is at an all-time low.

This is my answer: I say that at a time the Communists are running us down abroad it's time to speak up. And my friends, let us recognize America has its weaknesses, and constructive criticism of those weaknesses is essential, essential so that we can correct our weaknesses in the best traditions of our democratic process.

But let us also recognize that while it is dangerous to see nothing wrong in America, it is just as wrong to refuse to recognize what is right about America.

And tonight I say to you: no criticism—no criticism—should be allowed to obscure the truth either at home or abroad that today America is the strongest nation militarily, economically and ideologically in the world and we have the will and the stamina, the resources to maintain that strength in the years ahead.

And now, if we may turn to the future. We must recognize that the foreign policy problems of the Sixties will be different and they will be vastly more difficult than those of the Fifties through which we have just passed.

We are in a race tonight, my fellow Americans, in a race for survival in which our lives, our fortunes, our liberties are at stake. We are ahead now. But the only way to stay ahead in a race is to move ahead and the next President will make decisions which will determine whether we win or whether we lose this race.

What must we do?

These things, I believe:

He must resolve first and above all that the United States must never settle for second-best in anything.

Let's look at the specifics:

Militarily the security of the United States must be put before all other consideration. Why? Not only because this is necessary to deter aggression but because we must make sure that we are never in a position at the conference table so Mr. Khrushchev or his successor is able to coerce an American President because of his strength and our weakness.

Diplomatically, let's look at what this problem is. Diplomatically, our next President must be firm, firm on principle. But he must never be belligerent. He must never engage in a war of words which might heat up the international climate to the igniting point of nuclear catastrophe. But, while he must never answer insults in kind, he must leave no doubt at any time that whether it is in Berlin or in Cuba or anywhere else in the world, America will not tolerate being pushed around by anybody, any place.

Because we have already paid a terrible price in lives and resources to learn that appeasement leads not to peace but to war.

It will indeed take great leadership to steer us through these years, and avoiding the extremes of belligerency on the one hand and appeasement on the other.

Now, Mr. Kennedy has suggested that what the world needs is young leadership, and understandably this has great appeal. Because it is true, true, that youth does bring boldness and imagination, and drive to leadership, and we need all these things.

But I think most people will agree with me tonight when I say that President de Gaulle, Prime Minister Macmillan, Chancellor Adenauer, are not young men.

But we are indeed fortunate that we have their wisdom and their experience, and their courage on our side in the struggle for freedom today in the world.

And I might suggest that as we consider the relative merits of youth and age, it's only fair to point out that it was not Mr. de Gaulle, or Mr. Macmillan, or Mr. Adenauer, but Mr. Kennedy who made the rash and impulsive suggestion that President Eisenhower should have apologized and sent regrets to Mr. Khrushchev for the U-2 flight which the President had ordered to save our country from surprise attack.

But formidable as will be the diplomatic and military problems confronting the next President, far more difficult and critical will be the decisions he must make to meet and defeat the enemies of freedom in an entirely different kind of struggle.

And now, I want to speak to you of another kind of aggression—

aggression without war, for the aggressor comes not as a conqueror but as a champion of peace, of freedom, offering progress and plenty and hope to the unfortunates of the earth.

And I say tonight that the major problem—the biggest problem—confronting the next President of the United States will be to inform the people of the character of this kind of aggression, to arouse the people to the mortal danger it presents and to inspire the people to meet that danger.

And he must develop a brand new strategy which will win the battle for freedom for all men and women without a war. That is the great task of the next President of the United States.

And this will be a difficult task. Difficult because at times our next President must tell the people not what they want to hear but what they need to hear. Why, for example, it may be just as essential to the national interest to build a dam in India as in California. It will be difficult, too, because we Americans have always been able to see and understand the danger presented by missiles and airplanes and bombs, but we found it hard to recognize the even more deadly danger of the propaganda that warps the mind, the economic offensive that softens the nation, the subversion that destroys the will of a people to resist tyranny.

And yet may I say tonight that the fact that this threat is as I believe it to be the greatest danger we have ever confronted this is no reason for lack of confidence in the outcome.

You know why?

Because there is one great theme that runs through our history as a nation. Americans are always at their best when the challenge is greatest.

And I say tonight that we Americans shall rise to our greatest heights in this Decade of the Sixties as we mount the offensive to meet those forces which threaten peace and the rights of free men everywhere.

But there are some things we can do and things we must do, and I would like to list them for you tonight.

First, we must take the necessary steps which will assure that the American economy grows at a maximum rate so that we can maintain our present massive lead over the Communist bloc.

How do we do this? There isn't any magic formula by which government in a free nation can bring this about. The way to insure maximum growth in America is not by expanding the functions of government but by increasing the opportunities for investment and creative enterprise for millions of individual Americans.

And at a time when the Communists have found it necessary to turn to decentralization of their economy and to turn to the use of individual incentive to increase productivity, at a time, in other words when they are turning our way, I say we must and we will not make the mistake of turning their way.

There is another step that we must take—a second one. Our government activity must be reorganized—reorganized to take the initiative from the Communists and to develop and carry out a world-wide strategy, an offensive for peace and freedom.

The complex of agencies which has grown up through the years for exchange of persons, for technical assistance, for information, for loans and for grants, all these must be welded together into one powerful economic and ideological striking force under the direct supervision and leadership of the President of the United States.

Because what we must do you see is to wage the battles for peace and freedom with the same unified direction and dedication with which we wage battles in wars.

And if these activities are to succeed, we must develop a better training program for the men and women who will represent our country at home and abroad.

And what we need are men with broad knowledge of the intricacies and techniques of the strategy of communism, with a keen knowledge of the great principles for which free people stand and above all men who with zeal and dedication which the Communists cannot match will outthink and outwork and outlast the enemies of freedom wherever they meet them anyplace in the world.

This is the kind of men we must train.

And we must recognize something else. Government can't do this job alone. The most effective proponents of freedom are not governments but free people.

And this means that every American, every one of you listening tonight who works or travels abroad must represent his country at its best in everything that he does.

And the United States, the United States, big as it is, strong as it is, we can't do this job alone.

The best brains, the fullest resources of other free nations which have as great a stake in freedom as we have must be mobilized to participate with us in this task to the extent they are able.

But do you know what is most important of all—above all—we must recognize that the greatest economic strength that we can imagine, the finest of government organizations—all this will fail if we are not united and inspired by a great idea—an idea which will be a battle cry for a grand offensive to win the minds and the hearts and the souls of men.

Do we have such an idea?

The Communists proclaim over and over again that their aim is the victory of communism throughout the world. It is not enough for us to reply that our aim is to contain communism, to defend the free world against communism, to hold the line against communism. The only answer to a strategy of victory for the communist world is a strategy of victory for the free world.

But let the victory we seek be not victory over any other nation or any other people. Let it be the victory of freedom over tyranny, of plenty over hunger, of health over disease in every country of the world.

When Mr. Khrushchev says our grandchildren will live under communism, let us say his grandchildren will live in freedom.

When Mr. Khrushchev says the Monroe Doctrine is dead in the Americas, we say the doctrine of freedom applies everywhere in the world.

And I say tonight let us welcome Mr. Khrushchev's challenge to peaceful competition of our system. But let us reply, let us compete in the Communist world as well as in the free world, because the Communist dictators must not be allowed the privileged sanctuary from which to launch their guerrilla attacks on the citadels of freedom.

And we say further, extend this competition—extend it to include not only food and factories as he has suggested but extend it to include the great spiritual and moral values which characterize our civilization.

And further, let us welcome, my friends, let us welcome the challenge, not be disconcerted by it, not fail to meet it. The challenge, presented by the revolution of peaceful peoples' aspirations in South America, in Asia, in Africa. We can't fail in this mission. We can't fail to assist them in finding a way to progress with freedom, so that they will be faced with the terrible alternative of turning to communism with its promise of progress at the cost of freedom.

Let us make it clear to them that our aim in helping them is not merely to stop communism but that in the great American tradition of concern for those less fortunate than we are, that we welcome the opportunity to work with people everywhere in helping them to achieve their aspirations for a life of human dignity.

And this means that our primary aim must be not to help government but to help people—to help people attain the life they deserve.

In essence, what I am saying tonight is that our answer to the threat of Communist revolution is renewed devotion to the great ideals of the American Revolution—ideals that caught the imagination of the world 180 years ago and it still lives in the minds and hearts of people everywhere.

I could tell you tonight that all you need to do to bring all these things about that I have described is to elect the right man as President of this country and leave these tasks to him. But my fellow Americans, America demands more than that of me and of you.

When I visited the Soviet Union, in every factory there was a huge sign which read: "Work for the victory of communism."

And what America needs today is not just a President, not just a few leaders, but millions of Americans working for the victory of freedom.

Each American must make a personal and total commitment to the cause of freedom and all it stands for. It means wage earners and employers making an extra effort to increase the productivity of our factories. It means our students in schools striving for excellence rather than adjusting to mediocrity.

It means supporting, encouraging our scientists to explore the unknown, not for just what we can get but for what we can learn. And it means on the part of each American assuming personal responsibility to make this country which we love a proud example of freedom for all the world. Each of us for example doing our part in ending the prejudice which 100 years after Lincoln, to our shame, still embarrasses us abroad and saps our strength at home. Each of us participating in this or other political campaigns, not just by going to the polls and voting but working with the candidate of your choice.

And it means, my fellow Americans, it means sacrifice. But not the grim sacrifice of desperation but the rewarding sacrifice of choice which lifts us out of the humdrum life in which we live and gives us the supreme satisfaction which comes from working together in a cause greater than ourselves, greater than our nation, as great as the whole world itself.

What I proposed tonight is not new. It is as old as America and as young as America because America will never grow old.

You will remember. Listen, Thomas Jefferson said "We act not for ourselves alone but for the whole human race." Lincoln said, "In giving freedom to the slaves we assure freedom to the free. We shall nobly save or meanly lose the last best hope of earth." And Teddy Roosevelt said, "Our first duty as citizens of the nation is owed to the United States but if we are true to our principles we must also think of serving the interests of mankind at large."

And Woodrow Wilson said, "A patriotic American is never so proud of the flag under which he lives as when it comes to mean to others as well as to himself a symbol of hope and liberty."

And we say—we say today—that a young America shall fulfill her destiny by helping to build a new world in which men can live together in peace and justice and freedom with each other.

But there is a difference today, an exciting difference. And the difference is because of the dramatic breakthroughs in science for the first time in human history we have the resources—the resources to wage a winning war against poverty, misery and disease wherever it exists in the world, and upon the next President of the United States will rest the responsibility to inspire and to lead the forces of freedom toward this goal.

I am sure now that you understand why I said at the beginning that it would be difficult for any man to say that he was qualified to provide this kind of leadership.

I can only say tonight to you that I believe in the American dream because I have seen it come true to my own life.

I know something of the threat which confronts us, and I know something of the effort which will be needed to meet it.

I have seen hate for America, not only in the Kremlin, but in the eyes of Communists in our own country, and on the ugly face of a mob in Caracas.

I have heard doubts about America, expressed not just by Communists but by sincere students and labor leaders in other countries, searching for the way to a better life and wondering if we had lost the way.

And I have seen love for America in countries throughout the world, in a crowd in Jakarta, in Bogota; in the heart of Siberia, in Warsaw— 250,000 people on the streets on a Sunday afternoon singing, crying with tears running down their cheeks and shouting: "Nacheea! Nacheea!" "Long live the United States."

And I know, my fellow Americans, I know tonight that we must resist the hate. We must remove the doubts, but above all we must be worthy of the love and the trust of millions on this earth for whom America is the hope of the world.

A hundred years ago Abraham Lincoln was asked during the dark days of the tragic war between the states whether he thought God was on his side. His answer was "my concern is not whether God is on our side, but whether we are on God's side."

My fellow Americans, may that ever be our prayer for our country, and in that spirit with faith in America, with faith in her ideals and in her people I accept your nomination for President of the United States.

☆

RICHARD M. NIXON

Campaign Speech

TOLEDO, OHIO

October 27, 1960

Tonite I want to talk about a question of major significance, both to our survival as a nation and our progress as a society—our atomic policy both as it affects peaceful uses and weapons.

We are not a warlike people. We yearn as deeply as any nation to convert our wealth, energy, and science into the pursuit of peaceful progress.

Unfortunately for all men, there are others in the world who boldly assert, by word and deed, that force and violence are justified to accomplish their political ambitions. War and threats of war are to them just as worthy tactics of basic policy as words of peace. They have repeatedly used the sword to deprive people of their freedom and compel them to serve the purposes of a tyrannical state.

Because of this continuing menace, America must stay powerfully armed and vigilant. But we have hoped, and we continue to hope, that the Communists would fully comprehend that a thermonuclear war can only destroy attacker and defender alike. Thus, two years ago we sat down with the Soviets in Geneva to negotiate on control of nuclear weapons testing.

Both sides agreed that control was desirable but the obstacle was Soviet refusal to accept adequate inspection. The Soviets have remained intent upon keeping their society walled off from the rest of mankind. They have insisted that we simply take their word that they would adhere to any agreed controls. This has been unacceptable to ourselves and our allies as we earnestly seek the way to world peace. Years of the big and little lie, ignored pledges, broken promises, and violated agreements, make obvious the necessity of a foolproof inspection system. Until now, the Soviet atomic negotiators have stalled in implementing Chairman Khrushchev's letters of April 23, 1959, to President Eisenhower and Prime Minister Macmillan, when he stated that "we are quite able to find a solution to the problem of discontinuing tests . . . and to establish such controls as would guarantee strict observance of the treaty."

In an open society like ours, a ban on atom testing is self-policing, in that any activities of this nature are widely reported immediately. The

Soviets, by contrast, simply do not permit people, even their own people, to move freely about the country and speak or write what they see. The limited inspection system which they are willing to accept would permit them to cheat and allow the cheating to go undetected.

During these two years of negotiations, we have not detonated any nuclear devices and the Soviets know that we have not. However, during the same period, the Soviets have fired at least one large underground explosion and several smaller ones. They state that these have not been nuclear shots, simply high explosives. We have no way of knowing whether this is the fact. Nor will the Soviets permit us, or the United Nations, or neutral nations, to make an inspection.

Only a few days ago, the new seismic station at Fort Sill, Oklahoma, recorded a disturbance in the Soviet Union. It might have been an earthquake. Or it might have been a large underground nuclear explosion. We have no way of knowing.

The seriousness of this great uncertainty becomes clear when we consider where we are in point of time as it concerns weapons development. Originally, the moratorium on testing was fixed for one year; then, in a carefully calculated risk, the President decided to extend the moratorium, a risk which he accepted for the purpose of going the second mile, and beyond, to reach agreement with the Soviets.

Now consider the situation. For two years we have not tested our nuclear technology. And the history of weapons development is such that it requires only between three and four years to complete a new breakthrough. Two years of this time has run, as the United States has worked earnestly for this positive step toward eliminating the war threat to all humanity.

Where has this left us? We have no agreement, There is reason to believe that the Soviets may have used the time to attempt to overtake us. We cannot prolong the risk much longer without seriously jeopardizing the very objective toward which we hoped the Geneva negotiations would point—peace and human survival.

Recently my opponent made a campaign statement on the question of atomic testing, in the form of a reply to an open letter to us both from former Atomic Energy Commissioner Thomas E. Murray. He stated that "this subject like all other public issues is properly a matter for critical discussion and debate." Then he outlined his course of action.

I will deal briefly with Senator Kennedy's proposals because of the fact that one or the other of us is going to have the responsibility for resolving this question bearing on our very survival. I will deal with them because his approach is different from the one which I believe this nation must follow if we are to keep our vital military and technological superiority over the Soviets in the crucial years ahead.

My opponent said that he did not believe that underground nuclear weapons tests " should be resumed at this time." He would want, he said, even at this late date, to continue or reopen negotiations with the Soviets with new negotiators and new instructions. Noting specifically that the present negotiators "are not representatives chosen by me," he added that he would "direct vigorous negotiation, in accordance with my personal instructions on policy."

He is saying, in effect, that the negotiations of the past two years by the United States representatives have not been sufficiently vigorous and that their instructions have not been adequate to the task. He is proposing a course of action which would delay any possible resolution of this vital matter for much too long—far beyond any margin of safety—since he is proposing to handle the matter with new men and new instructions. And he is suggesting nothing more concrete toward resolving the issue than to imply that his "personal instructions" must be more effective than President Eisenhower's have been during the past two years.

The delay, and Senator Kennedy's reasons for it, are both unacceptable. I say to him that it is impossible to imply in truth that these negotiations could have been pursued with greator vigor or sincerity on the part of Ambassador [James J.] Wadsworth and our career negotiators and our top scientists. I say to him no instruction would have produced agreement to date, except and unless we had been willing to sacrifice the principles of adequate inspection.

The only major obstacle to an atomic test agreement has been, and is now, the Soviet refusal to accept adequate inspection. Clearly, then, the only "new policy instructions" through which the United States could remove this obstacle would entail surrender on this point. The security of the United States, and of the entire free world, simply will not permit either such a surrender or the indefinite continuation of the present moratorium, entirely without inspection.

And I say that we cannot and should not blame ourselves, our policies, our negotiators, their scientific advisers, or their instructions for the unyielding refusal of the Soviets to make an agreement at Geneva. The time and patience which we have already expended to explore this way out of the disarmament dilemma have been fulsome proof of our own intentions and of the Soviets'. The blame rests squarely on them. We cannot permit further delay.

This is exactly what Mr. Khrushchev and his intransigent negotiators are seeking to accomplish. They are trying to buy critical time, critical time designed to arrest our atomic development, both military and peaceful, while they are free to proceed with their own. Another delay, of the length indicated in Senator Kennedy's proposals, could be decisive in the struggle for peace and freedom.

We must resolve the issue now. We must never allow the Soviets, by deceit, to make America second in nuclear technology. This outcome could defeat us without even the direct horror of atomic war.

As President Eisenhower already has for the present Administration, I will make the settlement of the atomic-test negotiations a question of the highest priority of American policy.

We must act now to break this Soviet filibuster against peace and the security of the free nations.

To allow this Soviet filibuster against a test agreement to continue would dangerously increase the risk of war, the risk of war in the most frightful form in human history, an annihilating atomic war.

It has become one of the grim facts of our times that whatever increases Soviet strength relative to our own thereby increases the risk of war. Hearing Mr. Khrushchev bluster and threaten to launch his rockets from his present position of significant military inferiority leaves us small room for doubt about what he would be tempted to do if he ever gained the overall advantage.

The peace of the world, the very survival of the human race, demands that we break this fateful filibuster. We must and will take the necessary steps to maintain the peace. If I am elected, I will on November 9 ask the President to designate Ambassador Lodge to go to Geneva personally to participate in the present negotiations with a view to resolving this question by February 1. There is no conceivable, no honest reason why this cannot be accomplished if the Soviets have any intention of ever coming to an agreement. After two years they are still haggling over matters that can only be construed as naked attempts to further obstruct and delay.

I would have Mr. Khrushchev know that if Amabassador Lodge and the Soviet negotiator are able to bring an agreement in sight in this eighty-day period, I would be prepared to meet with Prime Minister Macmillan and—so important do I hold this question to be—with Mr. Khrushchev to make the final agreement at the summit.

But I would have him understand that, if at the end of the eighty-day period—by February 1—there is no progress, the United States will be prepared to detonate atomic devices necessary to advance our peaceful technology. Such devices already are prepared for underground use in such a way as to guarantee no contamination.

Further, I would have him understand that the United States is willing to continue negotiations for a nuclear weapons test ban as long as the Soviet representatives will sit, but not under an uninspected moratorium of indefinite duration. I would have Mr. Khrushchev understand that if an agreement is not signed within a reasonable period after February 1, the United States will have no alternative but resume underground testing of atomic weapons.

I say underground testing because there is no question of resuming tests in the atmosphere, where some still undetermined danger of contamination exists. The United States has abandoned such testing, certainly until more knowledge is available as to the exact consequences.

We must not, and will not, continue the present moratorium on weapons testing without adequate safeguards of inspection for an extended period of time such as implicit in Senator Kennedy's position.

On the other hand, if before then an agreement can be negotiated, the United States will proceed, in concert with all nations, to realize the enormous potential which nuclear energy holds for the human race. It must, of course, be an integral part of such an atomic agreement that the nations will continue—with proper safeguards—to experiment for peaceful purposes.

As things now stand, we face a fateful alternative. We can and must go forward with our atomic technology in one of these two ways:

1. With an agreement guaranteeing that nuclear energy will not further be developed into still greater weapons of annihilation, but for the benefit of humanity, or—

2. With no agreement, each nation insuring its own survival and maintaining its technological progress, military and peaceful, as it sees fit.

We are on the threshold of developing major peaceful uses of the atom. Large power reactors are coming into being, next year we will witness the sea trials of the Savannah—the world's first atomic merchant ship. By 1965 we will have from Project Rover a nuclear-fueled space engine that will be capable of propelling space probes.

However, without exploding atomic devices we cannot achieve many peaceful benefits of our nuclear technology. This is particularly true of a new and imaginative peaceful use of the atom which has tremendous potential—the use of explosive power for great engineering projects which would otherwise not be practical or economical. Our plan to develop peaceful constructive uses of nuclear explosives has been given the name of Project Plowshare because it literally is an attempt to convert the most destructive weapon in history into a tool for human betterment. Through Project Plowshare, we now have a great opportunity to turn our atomic armory into a tool for peace.

From the study on the very few subsurface shots that were conducted prior to the Geneva talks, we have gained tantalizing glimpses of great new vistas of future achievement. In Project Plowshare, scientists and engineers already know of some things they expect to find and some hints as to what else they may find. Exciting as these factors may be, the other still unknown findings may outshine all the rest.

In numerous private and official discussions with our scientists and our leaders in this exciting new field, I have full reports on both the progress and the promise of this development. I will discuss them briefly tonite.

First a word about safety from atomic radiation. I am assured by all scientists familiar with Project Plowshare that the underground projects can go forward without fear of the consequences of radiation. Eventually, with further development and more knowledge, ways can be found to explore all of the promising areas which the Plowshare researchers now suggest. It would be my firm policy that projects of this character would only be undertaken after the most thorough consideration and with the utmost regard for public health and safety.

In small underground explosions, the scientists advise, the fireball is small—only a few feet in diameter—and it transmits its heat through the ground for a radius of sixty to 150 feet. Everything immediately around the fireball is vaporized. A few feet beyond everything is melted. As the intense heat of the fireball diminishes, all this molten material cools and forms a glasslike shell. A major portion of the radioactivity produced by the explosion is permanently trapped inside the shell.

And in this underground shell and the broken rock formations around it—between 100,000 and 100,000,000 tons of broken and crushed rock—is enormous potential to be extracted for man's benefit. First the scientists believe the heat which is trapped may be trapped for a long enough time to produce steam for the economical generation of electric power.

Think of the implications for a moment—the energy unit of an atomic power plant to be available wherever engineers want to place it. Think of the vast mineral riches in remote areas of Alaska, Canada, South America, Africa, Asia, which lie untapped because there presently is no way to bring in electricity or any other conventional form of energy to mine and extract the ores. Any of these areas would be vastly benefited and enriched if they sought to avail themselves of such scientific development.

Moreover, we have in this country, in our Rocky Mountain states, oil deposits that equal the reserves of the entire Middle East, oil deposits that are denied to us because they are tightly locked in shale rock. At present we know of no economical way to get oil out of the shale. Plowshare offers a solution.

There is another great potential of enormous significance to millions of Americans, particularly in the presently depressed coal-mining regions. For some time the coal industry has searched for cheap and reasonable methods to accomplish coal "gasification," to convert this resource, not presently in great enough demand, into one that is. The Plowshare scientists have been led to believe from results of previous underground tests that an answer may lie in their researches.

The versatility of Project Plowshare goes on and on. Of immediate and far-reaching importance to the peoples of all the world is the use of atomic energy in this form for massive engineering projects, the costs of which heretofore have been prohibitive. Plowshare scientists anticipate that, with further research and testing, nuclear explosions will make it possible to build harbors where none now exist, thus accelerating by many times the economic development of such areas as Alaska and many other areas of the world. They are already drawing plans and designing devices to adapt the "nuclear dynamite" of Plowshare to cut sea-level canals between the oceans and other navigable bodies, dredge rivers, literally to lift the face of the earth to the benefit of all mankind.

Our determination to proceed with these works of great general benefit to humanity is fully in accord with the great American tradition. I repeat that, with or without a trustworthy agreement with the Soviets in the next few months, we must get on with our work.

Significantly, this kind of effort has been a discernible part of the American character and the American purpose from the beginnings of our century. Early in the nineteenth century the French observer de Tocqueville noted this difference between the American character and the Russian:

"The American struggles against the obstacles that nature opposes to him.

"The adversaries of the Russian are men. The conquests of the American are therefore gained by the plowshare; those of the Russian by the sword."

We will continue to gain our conquests by the plowshare, in the modern context of the atomic plowshares. At the same time we will maintain our military superiority so that the Soviets can never again gain new conquests by the sword.

And ultimately we will realize the vision of the prophet Isaiah for the community of man: ". . . and they shall beat their swords into plowshares, and their spears into pruning hooks; nation shall not lift up sword against nation. Neither shall they learn war any more."

☆

1964

― ☆ ―

Traumatized by the assasination of its young President in November 1963, the United States entered a decade during which violence and disorder would slowly turn its citizens to new political patterns. After assuming the Presidency, Lyndon Johnson pushed for a series of measures increasing the scope of federal responsiblity for social welfare and civil rights. He tried to coalesce a liberal consensus to attack the problems of poverty and racism, poor housing, and inadequate employment opportunities. Johnson retained many of Kennedy's cabinet officers and assistants, including Attorney General Robert Kennedy, but inevitable strains appeared. Even though the new President was largely successful in passing much of the liberal legislation initiated by the Kennedy administration, many loyalists hoped that Johnson would choose Robert Kennedy as his Vice Presidential running mate in 1964. Instead, Johnson chose Senator Hubert Humphrey; Kennedy ran and won a Senate seat from New York that fall.

Beginning with the Montgomery bus boycott in November 1955, the civil rights movement picked up momentum so that by May 1963 it was becoming a regular feature on television news and in print journalism. In the summer of 1964, Lyndon Johnson signed the most significant piece of civil rights legislation since the Reconstruction period. Among other far-reaching results, the Civil Rights Act of 1964 outlawed discrimination in public facilities and accommodations. Racial violence in the South as well as in northern cities was becoming a growing reality, however, as the federal government sought to extend its protection of the rights of black Americans.

Johnson's main opponent in the winter and spring Democratic primaries was Alabama Governor George Wallace, who had vowed to continue segregation "forever" when confronted by federal power several years before. It was thus both startling and ominous to liberals that Wallace gained 43 percent of the Democratic vote in the border state of Maryland as well as 30 percent in Indiana and 34 percent in Wisconsin. Wallace demonstrated that there was a pervasive anger toward blacks in white working-class neighborhoods.

The Democratic Convention took place in Atlantic City in August. Conflict had grown up over the seating of a largely black Mississippi Freedom Democratic Party in place of the all-white regular delegation. A compromise was eventually worked out that satisified no one but provided a preview of future conflict over delegate selection procedures. The final night of the convention featured a moving film and a eulogy to John Kennedy. In his acceptance speech, Johnson warned the nation about "reckless acts of violence," that were beginning to gain greater attention. He called for broad social programs to be initiated by government. Johnson was seldom a stirring orator, and this performance was, in comparison to the rousing speech of Vice Presidential candidate Hubert Humphrey, a tepid finale to the convention.

Johnson was opposed in the national election by Arizona Senator Barry Goldwater, the most conservative Republican candidate since Calvin Coolidge. After Kennedy's assassination, Goldwater was reluctant to run but eventually was convinced to enter the race. He was the eventual victor over the recently divorced and remarried New York Governor Nelson Rockefeller in the critical California primary. The Republican Convention in San Francisco's Cow Palace was an acrimonious affair stimulated by the conservatives' ire against the Rockefeller wing of the party and the "liberal" media. This convention signaled the end of political control of the Republican Party by the older eastern establishment leaders who had championed Willkie, Dewey, and Eisenhower and had reluctantly swallowed the candidacy of Nixon in 1960.

Goldwater's acceptance speech lamented the Democratic Party failures in allowing the erection of the Berlin Wall, in presiding over the Bay of Pigs fiasco, as well as the "slow death of freedom in Laos" and Vietnam. He spoke about raising the Atlantic civilization to new heights of leadership and condemned the increasing bureaucratization of American life in unprecedentedly stark terms. "we are plodding along at a pace set by centralized planning," he said, "red tape, rules without responsiblity and regimentation without recourse." He did frankly acknowledge that "we are at war in Vietnam" and chastised Johnson for not being candid about the nature of America's mission in that part of the world. In fact, in August Johnson would use the ostensible attack by North Vietnamese gunboats on several American ships off Vietnam to secure sufficient executive authority to wage war through Congressional passage of the Gulf of Tonkin Resolution. Stigmatized by the press as an extremist within the Republican Party, however, Goldwater lashed out with the famous lines that "extremism in the defense of liberty is no vice! And let me remind you also that moderation in the pursuit of justice is no virtue!"

The fall campaign was marked by both a number of Republicans who refrained from actively supporting Goldwater's candidacy and the emergence of Ronald Reagan as an effective advocate for Barry Goldwater's candidacy. Reagan's televised speech, in fact, helped launch his political career. Wealthy businessmen promoted the former actor for the Governorship of California in 1966. Goldwater's campaign was hobbled by disorganization and a rather ineffective "spot" TV campaign. His Washington speech of October 21st warned of an impending Sino-Soviet rapprochement, and exhibited his contempt for the idea of "peaceful coexistence" with Communists. Democrats were dangerously misled to believe that there were "good" and "bad" Communists.

The President did not begin to campaign actively until October. In an October 7th address Johnson struck the basic themes of his campaign: that the prosperity of the country was the result of Democratic policies, that his election offered the people a "basic choice," and that Goldwater's program represented a "radical departure." His unprecedented electoral mandate came from his appeals for a bipartisan liberal consensus, the effective advertising strategy of the Doyle, Dane, Bernbach advertising firm, the Kennedy legacy, and the prosperity the country was experiencing that year. Unfortunately for the incumbent President, that liberal consensus would very rapidly come under fire from pressures in the black ghettoes and college campuses of the nation as well as from the mountains and rice paddies of Southeast Asia.

LYNDON B. JOHNSON

Acceptance Speech

ATLANTIC CITY, NEW JERSEY

August 27, 1964

Chairman McCormack. My fellow Americans:

I accept your nomination.

I accept the duty of leading this party to victory this year.

And I thank you, I thank you from the bottom of my heart for placing at my side the man that last night you so wisely selected to be the next Vice President of the United States.

I know I speak for each of you and all of you when I say we—he proved himself tonight in that great acceptance speech.

And I speak for both of us when I tell you that from Monday on he's going to be available for such speeches in all 50 states.

We will try to lead you as we were led by that great champion of freedom, the man from Independence, Harry S. Truman.

But the, but the gladness of his high occasion cannot mask the sorrow which shares our hearts. So let us here tonight, each of us, all of us, rededicate ourselves to keeping burning the golden torch of promise which John Fitzgerald Kennedy set aflame.

And let none of us stop to rest until we have written into the law of the land all the suggestions that made up the John Fitzgerald Kennedy program and then let us continue to supplement that program with the kind of laws that he would have us write.

Tonight we offer ourselves on our records and by our platform as a party for all Americans, an all-American party for all Americans!

This prosperous people, this land of reasonable men, has no place for petty partisanship or peevish prejudice.

The needs of all can never be met by parties of the few.

The needs of all cannot be met by a business party, or a labor party, not a war party or a peace party; not by a Southern party or a Northern party.

Our deeds will meet our needs only if we are served by a party which serves all our people.

We are members together of such a party—the Democratic party of 1964.

We have written a proud record of accomplishments for all Americans. If any ask what we have done, just let them look at what we promised to do.

For those promises have become our deeds; and the promises of tonight, I can assure you, will become the deeds of tomorrow.

We are in the midst of the largest and the longest period of peacetime prosperity in our history.

And almost every American listening to us tonight has seen the results in his own life. But prosperity for most has not brought prosperity to all.

And those who have received the bounty of this land, who sit tonight secure in affluence and safe in power, must not now turn from the needs of their neighbors.

Our party and our nation will continue to extend the hand of compassion and extend the hand of affection and love, to the old and the sick and the hungry.

For who among us dares betray the command: Thou shalt open thy hand unto thy Brother, to thy poor and to thy needy in the Land?

The needs that we seek to fill, the hopes that we seek to realize, are not our needs, our hopes alone. They are the needs and hopes of most of the people.

Most Americans want medical care for older citizens, and so do I.

Most Americans want fair and stable prices and decent income for our farmers, and so do I.

Most Americans want a decent home in a decent neighborhood for all, and so do I.

Most Americans want an education for every child to the limit of his ability, and so do I.

Most Americans want a job for every man who wants to work, and so do I.

Most Americans want victory in our war against poverty, and so do I.

Most Americans want continually expanding and growing prosperity, and so do I.

These are your goals; these are our goals; these are the goals and will be the achievements of the Democratic party.

These are the goals of this great, rich nation; these are the goals toward which I will lead if the American people choose to follow.

For 30 years, year by year, step by step, vote by vote, men of both parties have built a solid foundation for our present prosperity.

Too many have worked too long and too hard to see this threatened now by policies which promise to undo all that we have done together over these years.

I believe most of the men and women in this hall tonight and I believe most Americans understand that to reach our goals in our own land we must work for peace among all lands.

America's cause is still the cause of all mankind. Over the last four years, the world has begun to respond to a simple American belief—the belief that strength and courage and responsibility are the keys to peace.

Since 1961, under the leadership of that great President, John F. Kennedy, we have carried out the greatest peacetime build-up of national strength of any nation, at any time in the history of the world.

And I report tonight that we have spent $30 billions more on preparing this nation in the four years of the Kennedy Administration than would have been spent if we had followed the appropriations of the last of the previous Administration.

I report tonight as President of the United States and as Commander in Chief of the Armed Forces on the strength of your country and I tell you that it is greater than any adversary's.

I assure you that it is greater than the combined might of all the nations in all the wars in all the history of this planet.

And I report our superiority is growing.

Weapons do not make peace; men make peace. And peace comes not through strength alone, but through wisdom and patience and restraint.

And these qualities under the leadership of President Kennedy brought a treaty banning nuclear tests in the atmosphere and a hundred other nations in the world joined us.

Other agreements were reached and other steps were taken. And their single guide was to lessen the danger to men without increasing the danger of freedom.

Their single purpose was peace in the world. And as a result of these policies, the world tonight knows where we stand and our allies know where we stand, too.

And our adversaries have learned again that we will never waver in the defense of freedom.

The true courage of this nuclear age lies in the quest for peace. There is no place in today's world for recklessness.

We cannot act rashly with the nuclear weapons that could destroy us all. The only course is to press with all our minds and all our will to make sure, doubly sure, that these weapons are never really used at all.

This is a dangerous and a difficult world in which we live tonight. I promise no easy answers. But I do promise this: I pledge the firmness to defend freedom; the strength to support that firmness, and a constant, patient effort to move the world toward peace instead of war.

And here, at home, one of our greatest responsibilities is to assure fair play for all of our people.

Every American has the right to be treated as a person. He should be able to find a job. He should be able to educate his children. He should be able to vote in elections.

And he should be judged on his merits as a person.

Well, this is the fixed policy and the fixed determination of the Democratic party and the United States of America.

So long as I am your President, I intend to carry out what the Constitution demands and justice requires. Equal justice under law for all Americans.

We cannot and we will not allow this great purpose to be endangered by reckless acts of violence.

Those who break the law, those who create disorder, whether in the North or the South, must be caught and must be brought to justice.

And I believe that every man and woman in this room tonight joins me in saying that in every part of this country the law must be respected and violence must be stopped.

And wherever local officers seek help or Federal law is broken, I have pledged and I will use the full resources of the Federal Government.

Let no one tell you that he can hold back progress and at the same time keep the peace. This is a false and empty promise. So to stand in the way of orderly progress is to encourage violence.

And I say tonight to those who wish us well and to those who wish us ill the growing forces in this country are the forces of common human decency and not the forces of bigotry and fear and smears.

Our problems are many and are great. But our opportunities are even greater. And let me make this clear. I ask the American people for a mandate, not to preside over a finished program, not just to keep things going. I ask the American people for a mandate to begin.

This nation, this generation, in this hour has man's first chance to build a great society, a place where the meaning of man's life matches the marvels of man's labor.

We seek a nation where every man can find reward in work and satisfaction in the use of his talents. We seek a nation where every man can seek knowledge and touch beauty and rejoice in the closeness of family and community.

We seek a nation where every man can work—follow the pursuit of happiness—not just security, but achievement and excellence and fulfillment of the spirit. So let us join together in this great task. Will you join me tonight in starting, in rebuilding our cities to make them a decent place for our children to live in?

Will you join me tonight in starting a program that will protect the beauty of our land and the air that we breathe?

Won't you join me tonight in starting a program that will give every child education of the highest quality that he can take?

So let us, let us join together in giving every American the fullest life which he can hope for, for the ultimate test of our civilization, the ultimate test of our faithfulness to our past has not been our goods and has not been our guns. It is in the quality—the quality of our people's lives and in the men and women that we produce.

This goal can be ours. We have the resources; we have the knowledge. But tonight we must seek the courage.

Because tonight the contest is the same that we have faced at every turning point in history. It is not between liberals and conservatives, it is not between party and party or platform and platform. It is between courage and timidity.

It is between those who have visions and those who see what can be and those who want only to maintain the status quo.

It is between those who welcome the future and those who turn away from its promise. This is the true cause of freedom. The man who is hungry, who cannot find work or educate his children, who is bowed by want—that man is not fully free. For more than 30 years, from Social Security to the war against poverty, we have diligently worked to enlarge the freedom of man, and as a result Americans tonight are freer to live as they want to live, to pursue their ambitions to meet their desires, to raise their families than in any time in all of our glorious history.

And every American knows in his heart that this is right!

I am determined in all the time that is mine to use all the talents that I have for bringing this great lovable land, this great nation, for ours together, together in greater unity in pursuit of this common purpose.

I truly believe that some day we will see an America that knows no North or South, no East nor West, an America, an America that is undivided by creed or color and untorn by suspicion or class.

The Founding Fathers dreamed America before it was. The pioneers dreamed of great cities on the wilderness that they had crossed. Our tomorrow is on its way. It can be a shape of darkness or it can be a thing of beauty. The choice is ours—is yours. For it will be the dream that we dare to dream.

I know what kind of a dream Franklin Delano Roosevelt and Harry S. Truman and John F. Kennedy would dream if they were here tonight.

And I think that I know what kind of a dream you want to dream.

Tonight we of the Democratic party confidently go before the people offering answers, not retreats; offering unity, not division; offering hope, not fear or smear.

We do offer the people a choice. A choice of continuing on the courageous and the compassionate course that has made this nation the strongest and the freest and the most prosperous and the most peaceful nation in history of mankind.

To those who have sought to divide us, they have only helped to unite us.

To those who would provoke us, we have turned the other cheek.

So as we conclude our labors, let us tomorrow turn to our new task. Let us be on our way.

☆

LYNDON B. JOHNSON

Campaign Speech

WASHINGTON, D. C.

October 7, 1964

My fellow Americans:

I have been in this office for almost a year—ever since that black and unforgetttable day when America lost one of its greatest leaders—cut down in the fullness of his manhood and promise.

I have drawn much of my strength in this task from loyal and dedicated public servants. Most of all I have drawn strength from the warm support and understanding of the American people.

I will always be grateful to you for that.

I am now on a tour that will take me to every section of the country—to discuss with you the important issues of this campaign.

Few presidential elections in our entire history have presented—as this one does—a basic choice that involves the fundamental principles of American life.

We must decide whether we will move ahead by building on the solid structure created by forward-looking men of both parties over the past 30 years. Or whether we will begin to tear down this structure and move in a radically different, and—I believe—a deeply dangerous direction.

Most of you listening to me have felt the steady progress of American prosperity in your own life and the life of your family. Most of you, more than ever before, can look forward, with confidence, to a steadily improving life for your children.

Our prosperity is not just good luck. It rests on basic beliefs which a generation of leaders has carefully woven into the fabric of American life.

Our prosperity rests on the basic belief that the work of free individuals makes a nation—and it is the job of Government to help them do the best they can.

Our prosperity rests on the basic belief that our greatest resource is the health and skills and knowledge of our people. We have backed up this belief with public and private investment in education and training, and many other programs.

Our prosperity rests on the basic belief that older Americans—those who have fought our wars and built our Nation—are entitled to live out ther lives in dignity. We have backed up this belief, for over 30 years, with the social security system—supported by every President of both parties.

Our prosperity rests on the basic belief that individual farmers and individual workers have a right to some protection against those forces which might deprive them of a decent income from the fruits of their labor. We have backed up this belief with a system of fair collective bargaining. We have backed it with agricultural programs which have kept the farmer from suffering the neglect and despair of only a few decades ago.

Today our whole approach to these problems is under attack.

We are now told that we the people acting through Government should withdraw from education, from public power, from agriculture, from urban renewal, and from a host of other vital programs.

We are now told that we should end social security as we know it, sell TVA, strip labor unions of many of their gains, and terminate all farm subsidies.

We are told that the object of leadership is not to pass laws but to repeal them.

And these views have been supported by a consistent record of opposition in the Congress to every progressive proposal of both parties—Democratic and Republican.

This is a radical departure from the historic and basic current of American thought and action. It would shatter the foundation on which our hopes for the future rest.

Too many have worked too hard and too long to let this happen now.

I propose to build on the basic beliefs of the past, to innovate where necessary, to work to bring us closer to a growing abundance in which all Americans can seek to share.

The choice is yours.

For 20 years our country has been the guardian at the gate of freedom. Our cause has been the cause of all mankind.

The strength of that leadership has come from the fact that every President, and the leaders of both parties, have followed the same basic principles of foreign policy. They have built our strength—so that today America is the greatest military power on earth.

They have moved with courage and firmness to the defense of freedom. President Truman met Communist aggression in Greece and Turkey. President Eisenhower met Communist aggression in the Formosa Strait. President Kennedy met Communist aggression in Cuba.

And, when our destroyers were attacked, we met Communist aggression in the waters around Viet-Nam.

But each of these Presidents has known that guns and rockets alone do not bring peace. Only men can bring peace.

They have used great power with restraint—never once taking a reckless risk which might plunge us into large-scale war.

They have patiently tried to build bridges of understanding between people and nations. They have used all their efforts to settle disputes peacefully—working with the United Nations. They have never been afraid to sit down at the council table to work out agreements which might lessen the danger of war without increasing the danger to freedom.

But today these established policies are under the severest attack.

We are told we should consider using atomic weapons in Viet-Nam, even in Eastern Europe should there be an uprising.

We are told we should break off relations with Russia—and with it any hope of lasting agreement. We are urged to withdraw from the United Nations and stop our help to other countries.

We have heard the test ban treaty denounced. This is the treaty that has halted the radioactive poisoning of the air we breathe.

We are urged to threaten others with force if they don't do as we say.

We are told, in effect, to withdraw into an armed camp—with a few carefully selected friends—and try to intimidate our adversaries into submission.

This kind of attack contradicts the entire course of America in the postwar period.

If we should follow this course—if we should discard the tested policies of the last 20 years—the peace of the world will be in grave danger.

I will not discard them. I will continue them. I will match firmness to strength. And I will continue, with all the skill at my command, the patient search for lasting peace.

Here, again, the choice is yours.

I will discuss these issues in the next few weeks. They are among the most important questions ever presented to the American people.

It is you who will decide these questions. And you will decide them on November 3 in polling booths across the Nation. No person can afford to sit comfortably at home, confident that others will take care of the job. You must work, and register, and vote.

For this is a turning point in the history of our Nation. At stake is all that we have so carefully built, and all the hopes that rest upon it.

I will do all I can.

I need your help.

Then we can turn to our work. Together we will build the Great Society—a place where every one of us has the chance to seek happiness and fulfillment to the limit of his abilities.

And we will work together to make the world a place where free men can live in peace.

☆

BARRY M. GOLDWATER

Acceptance Speech

SAN FRANCISCO, CALIFORNIA

July 17, 1964

My good friend and great Republican, Dick Nixon and your charming wife, Pat; my running mate—that wonderful Republican who has served us so well for so long—Bill Miller and his wife, Stephanie; to Thurston Morton, who's done such a commendable job in chairmaning this convention; to Mr. Herbert Hoover who I hope is watching, and to that great American and his wife, General and Mrs. Eisenhower. To my own wife, fellow Republicans here assembled, and Americans across this great nation:

From this moment, united and determined, we will go forward together dedicated to the ultimate and undeniable greatness of the whole man.

Together we will win.

I accept your nomination with a deep sense of humility. I accept, too, the responsibility that goes with it, and I seek your continued help and your continued guidance. My fellow Republicans, our cause is too great for any man to feel worthy of it. Our task would be too great for any man did he not have with him the heart and the hands of this great Republican party.

And I promise you tonight that every fibre of my being is consecrated to our cause, that nothing shall be lacking from the struggle that can be brought to it by enthusiasm, by devotion and plain hard work.

In this world no person, no party can guarantee anything, but what we can do and what we shall do is to deserve victory and victory will be ours. The Good Lord raised this mighty Republican—Republic to be a home for the Brave and to flourish as the land of the free—not to stagnate in the swampland of collectivism, not to cringe before the bully of Communism.

Now my fellow Americans, the tide has been running against freedom. Our people have followed false prophets. We must, and we shall, return to proven ways—not because they are old, but because they are true.

We must, and we shall, set the tide running again in the cause of freedom. And this party, with its every action, every word, every breath and every heart beat, has but a single resolve, and that is freedom.

Freedom made orderly for this nation by our constitutional government. Freedom under a government limited by laws of nature and of nature's God. Freedom balanced so that order lacking liberty will not become the slavery of the prison cell; balanced so that liberty lacking order will not become the license of the mob and of the jungle.

Now, we Americans understand freedom, we have earned it; we have lived for it, and we have died for it. This nation and its people are freedom's models in a searching world. We can be freedom's missionaries in a doubting world.

But, ladies and gentlemen, first we must renew freedom's mission in our own hearts and in our own homes.

During four futile years the Administration which we shall replace has distorted and lost that faith. It has talked and talked and talked and talked the words of freedom but it has failed and failed and failed in the works of freedom.

Now failure cements the wall of shame in Berlin; failures blot the sands of shame at the Bay of Pigs; failures marked the slow death of freedom in Laos; failures infest the jungles of Vietnam, and failures haunt the houses of our once great alliances and undermine the greatest bulwark ever erected by free nations, the NATO community.

Failures proclaim lost leadership, obscure purpose, weakening wills and the risk of inciting our sworn enemies to new aggressions and to new excesses.

And because of this Administration we are tonight a world divided. We are a nation becalmed. We have lost the brisk pace of diversity and the genius of individual creativity. We are plodding along at a pace set by centralized planning, red tape, rules without responsibility and regimentation without recourse.

Rather than useful jobs in our country, people have been offered bureaucratic makework; rather than moral leadership, they have been given bread and circuses; they have been given spectacles, and, yes, they've even been given scandals.

Tonight there is violence in our streets, corruption in our highest offices, aimlessness among our youth, anxiety among our elderly, and there's a virtual despair among the many who look beyond material success toward the inner meaning of their lives. And where examples of morality should be set, the opposite is seen. Small men seeking great wealth or power have too often and too long turned even the highest levels of public service into mere personal opportunity.

Now, certainly simple honesty is not too much to demand of men in government. We find it in most. Republicans demand it from everyone.

They demand it from everyone no matter how exalted or protected his position might be.

The growing menace in our country tonight, to personal safety, to life, to limb and property, in homes, in churches, on the playgrounds and places of business, particularly in our great cities, is the mounting concern or should be of every thoughtful citizen in the United States. Security from domestic violence, no less than from foreign aggression, is the most elementary and fundamental purpose of any government, and a government that cannot fulfill this purpose is one that cannot long command the loyalty of its citizens.

History shows us, demonstrates that nothing, nothing prepares the way for tyranny more than the failure of public officials to keep the streets safe from bullies and marauders.

Now we Republicans see all this as more—much more—than the result of mere political differences, or mere political mistakes. We see this as the result of a fundamentally and absolutely wrong view of man, his nature and his destiny.

Those who seek to live your lives for you, to take your liberty in return for relieving you of yours; those who elevate the state and downgrade the citizen, must see ultimately a world in which earthly power can be substituted for Divine Will. And this nation was founded upon the rejection of that notion and upon the acceptance of God as the author of freedom.

Now those who seek absolute power, even though they seek it to do what they regard as good, are simply demanding the right to enforce their own version of heaven on earth, and let me remind you they are the very ones who always create the most hellish tyranny.

Absolute power does corrupt, and those who seek it must be suspect and must be opposed. Their mistaken course stems from false notions, ladies and gentlemen, of equality. Equality, rightly understood as our founding fathers understood it, leads to liberty and to the emancipation of creative differences; wrongly understood, as it has been so tragically in our time, it leads first to conformity and then to despotism.

Fellow Republicans, it is the cause of Republicanism to resist concentrations of power, private or public, which enforce such conformity and inflict such despotism.

It is the cause of Republicanism to insure that power remains in the hands of the people—and, so help us God, that is exactly what a Republican President will do with the help of a Republican Congress.

It is further the cause of Republicanism to restore a clear understanding of the tyranny of man over man in the world at large. It is our cause to dispel the foggy thinking which avoids hard decisions in the delusion that a world of conflict will somehow resolve itself into a world of harmony, if we just don't rock the boat or irritate the forces of aggression—and this is hogwash.

It is, further, the cause of Republicanism to remind ourselves, and the world, that only the strong can remain free; that only the strong can keep the peace.

Now, I needn't remind you, or my fellow Americans regardless of party, that Republicans have shouldered this hard responsibility and marched in this cause before. It was Republican leadership under Dwight Eisenhower that kept the peace, and passed along to this Administration the mightiest arsenal for defense the world has ever known.

And I needn't remind you that it was the strength and the believable will of the Eisenhower years that kept the peace by using our strength, by using it in the Formosa Strait, and in Lebanon, and by showing it courageously at all times.

It was during those Republican years that the thrust of Communist imperialism was blunted. It was during those years of Republican leadership that this world moved closer not to war but closer to peace than at any other time in the last three decades.

And I needn't remind you, but I will, that it's been during Democratic years that our strength to deter war has been stilled and even gone into a planned decline. It has been during Democratic years that we have weakly stumbled into conflicts, timidly refusing to draw our own lines against aggression, deceitfully refusing to tell even our own people of our full participation and tragically letting our finest men die on battlefields unmarked by purpose, unmarked by pride or the prospect of victory.

Yesterday it was Korea: tonight it is Vietnam. Make no bones of this. Don't try to sweep this under the rug. We are at war in Vietnam. And yet the President, who is the Commander in Chief of our forces, refuses to say, refuses to say mind you, whether or not the objective over there is victory, and his Secretary of Defense continues to mislead and misinform the American people, and enough of it has gone by.

And I needn't remind you, but I will, it has been during Democratic years that a billion persons were cast into Communist captivity and their fate cynically sealed.

Today—today in our beloved country we have an Administration which seems eager to deal with Communism in every coin known—from gold to wheat; from consulates to confidence, and even human freedom itself.

Now the Republican cause demands that we brand communism as the principal disturber of peace in the world today. Indeed, we should brand it as the only significant disturber of the peace. And we must make clear that until its goals of conquest are absolutely renounced, and its relations with all nations tempered, Communism and the governments it now controls are enemies, of every man on earth who is or wants to be free.

Now, we here in America can keep the peace only if we remain vigilant, and only if we remain strong. Only if we keep our eyes open and keep our guard up can we prevent war.

And I want to make this abundantly clear—I don't intend to let peace or freedom be torn from our grasp because of lack of strength, or lack of will—and that I promise you Americans.

I believe that we must look beyond the defense of freedom today to its extension tomorrow. I believe that the Communism which boasts it will bury us will instead give way to the forces of freedom. And I can see in the distant and yet recognizable future the outlines of a world worthy of our dedication, our every risk, our every effort, our every sacrifice along the way. Yes, a world that will redeem the suffering of those who will be liberated from tyranny.

I can see, and I suggest that all thoughtful men must contemplate, the flowering of an Atlantic civilization, the whole world of Europe reunified and free, trading openly across its borders, communicating openly across the world.

This is a goal far, far more meaningful than a moon shot.

It's a truly inspiring goal for all free men to set for themselves during the latter half of the twentieth century. I can see and all free men must thrill to the events of this Atlantic civilization joined by a straight ocean highway to the United States. What a destiny! What a destiny can be ours to stand as a great central pillar linking Europe, the Americas and the venerable and vital peoples and cultures of the Pacific.

I can see a day when all the Americas—North and South—will be linked in a mighty system—a system in which the errors and misunderstandings of the past will be submerged one by one in a rising tide of prosperity and interdependence.

We know that the misunderstandings of centuries are not to be wiped away in a day or wiped in an hour. But we pledge, we pledge, that human sympathy—what our neighbors to the South call an attitude of sympatico—no less than enlightened self-interest will be our guide.

And I can see this Atlantic civilization galvanizing and guiding emergent nations everywhere. Now I know this freedom is not the fruit of every soil. I know that our own freedom was achieved through centuries of unremitting efforts by brave and wise men. And I know that the road to freedom is a long and a challenging road, and I know that some men may walk away from it, that some men resist challenge, accepting the false security of governmental paternalism.

And I pledge that the America I envision in the years ahead will extend its hand in help in teaching and in cultivation so that all new nations will be at least encouraged to go our way; so that they will not wander down the dark alleys of tyranny or to the dead-end streets of collectivism.

My fellow Republicans, we do no man a service by hiding freedom's light under a bushel of mistaken humility.

I seek an America proud of its past, proud of its ways, proud of its dreams and determined actively to proclaim them. But our examples to the world must, like charity, begin at home.

In our vision of a good and decent future, free and peaceful, there must be room, room for the liberation of the energy and the talent of the individual, otherwise our vision is blind at the outset.

We must assure a society here which while never abandoning the needy, or forsaking the helpless, nurtures incentives and opportunity for the creative and the productive.

We must know the whole good is the product of many single contributions. And I cherish the day when our children once again will restore as heroes the sort of men and women who, unafraid and undaunted, pursue the truth, strive to cure disease, subdue and make fruitful our natural environment, and produce the inventive engines of production, science and technology.

This nation, whose creative people have enhanced this entire span of history, should again thrive upon the greatness of all those things which we—we as individual citizens—can and should do.

During Republican years, this again will be a nation of men and women, of families proud of their role, jealous of their responsibilities, unlimited in their aspirations—a nation where all who can will be self-reliant.

We Republicans see in our constitutional form of government the great framework which assures the orderly but dynamic fulfillment of the whole man, and we see the whole man as the great reason for instituting orderly government in the first place.

We see in private property and in economy based upon and fostering private property the one way to make government a durable ally of the whole man rather than his determined enemy.

We see in the sanctity of private property the only durable foundation for constitutional government in a free society.

And beyond that we see and cherish diversity of ways, diversity of thoughts, of motives, and accomplishments. We don't seek to live anyone's life for him. We only seek to secure his rights, guarantee him opportunity, guarantee him opportunity to strive with government performing only those needed and constitutionally sanctioned tasks which cannot otherwise be performed.

We, Republicans, seek a government that attends to its inherent responsibilities of maintaining a stable monetary and fiscal climate, encouraging a free and competitive economy and enforcing law and order.

Thus do we seek inventiveness, diversity and creative difference within a stable order, for we Republicans define government's role where needed at many, many levels, preferably through the one closest to the people involved: our towns and our cities, then our counties, then our states then our regional contacts and only then the national government.

That, let me remind you, is the land of liberty built by decentralized power. On it also we must have balance between the branches of government at every level.

Balance, diversity, creative difference—these are the elements of Republican equation. Republicans agree, Republicans agree heartily, to disagree on many, many of their applications. But we have never disagreed on the basic fundamental issues of why you and I are Republicans.

This is a party—this Republican party is a party for free men. Not for blind followers and not for conformists.

Back in 1858 Abraham Lincoln said this of the Republican party, and

I quote him because he probably could have said it during the last week or so: It was composed of strained, discordant, and even hostile elements. End of the quote, in 1958 [sic].

Yet all of these elements agreed on one paramount objective: to arrest the progress of slavery, and place it in the course of ultimate extinction.

Today, as then, but more urgently and more broadly than then, the task of preserving and enlarging freedom at home and of safeguarding it from the forces of tyranny abroad is great enough to challenge all our resources and to require all our strength.

Anyone who joins us in all sincerity we welcome. Those, those who do not care for our cause, we don't expect to enter our ranks in any case. And let our Republicanism so focused and so dedicated not be made fuzzy and futile by unthinking and stupid labels.

I would remind you that extremism in the defense of liberty is no vice!

And let me remind you also that moderation in the pursuit of justice is no virtue!

By the—the beauty of the very system we Republicans are pledged to restore and revitalize, the beauty of this Federal system of ours is in its reconciliation of diversity with unity. We must not see malace in honest differences of opinion, and no matter how great, so long as they are not inconsistent with the pledges we have given to each other in and through our Constitution.

Our Republican cause is not to level out the world or make its people conform in computer-regimented sameness. Our Republican cause is to free our people and light the way for liberty throughout the world. Ours is a very human cause for very humane goals. This party, its good people, and its unquestionable devotion to freedom will not fulfill the purposes of this campaign which we launch here now until our cause has won the day, inspired the world, and shown the way to a tomorrow worthy of all our yesteryears.

I repeat, I accept your nomination with humbleness, with pride and you and I are going to fight for the goodness of our land. Thank you.

☆

BARRY M. GOLDWATER

Campaign Speech

WASHINGTON, D. C.

October 21, 1964

Good evening, my fellow Americans. Before doing anything else I want to call your attention to two headlines in this week's news.

"Kremlin shift hints harder line."

"Brezhnev hints at improved links with Peking."

These tell a story which seems to contradict the story you heard from President Johnson last Sunday evening. That is why I am here tonight.

I come before you this evening to discuss two events of great importance to the security of this nation and the free world.

As you all know, Khrushchev has been thrown out of the Government of the Soviet Union and the dictatorship of that country has been put into the hands of new leaders.

As you also know, a nuclear explosion took place in Red China within hours of this change of government.

These are momentous events. They present both a challenge and an opportunity to this country. You deserve a straight and honest explanation from each candidate for the Presidency on how he proposes to meet this challenge and exploit this opportunity.

I have said many times, and I repeat it again tonight, that every President owes it to the American people to take them into his full confidence when critical decisions confront the nation. This is particularly true when national security is at stake. We cannot afford—and let me stress that—we simply cannot afford any security risks.

Now what is the significance of these events in the Communist world?

First, the Communist threat to our security has become grave. The dissension in Communist ranks brought on by a clash of personalities is being repaired. Red China and the Soviet Union seem to be patching up their differences, and we must look forward to being faced by a more unified Communist movement.

Second, the foreign policy of the present Administration—based on a belief that there are "good" and "bad" Communists—has been an utter failure. It has failed to halt the march of Communism and the testing of nuclear weapons and the spread of nuclear power through the Communist world. This policy, if I may call it that, has instead helped the

Communist world through a time of troubles and allowed it to emerge as a greater threat than ever to the freedom of the West.

Third, these events have laid bare—for all to see—the real meaning of "peaceful coexistence." By this slogan the Communists simply mean, "We won't hurt you if you peacefully surrender to us."

Now let's see why these conclusions are so clear. Over the last several years we have all read about the troubles besetting the Communist world. There were grave economic difficulties everywhere—in the Soviet Union, in its European satellites, in Red China and its satellites, in Cuba—everywhere. Beyond that, Mao Tse-tung, the dictator of Red China, was quarreling with Khrushchev, the dictator of the Soviet Union. They were quarreling over who would be the big boss of the entire Communist movement and what would be the best way to bury us.

Meanwhile, the Communist countries of Eastern Europe were becoming restless and were demanding more independence.

Khrushchev decided that the best way to get out of trouble and to stay on top was to get the West to bail him out. And so he dusted off the old slogan of "peaceful coexistence" and worked it on the leaders of the present Administration with a soft sell. And they fell for it.

Khrushchev, we were being told, was a "good" Communist—one who was concerned, as we were, with finding a peaceful resolution of the conflict between Communist aggression and Western resistance. Only last Sunday Lyndon Johnson paid tribute to him as a man of "good sense and sober judgment."

We were also being told that standing against Khrushchev were the "bad" Communists—namely, his personal enemies in Red China. Why were they "bad"? Because they openly admitted that Communism could not conquer the world without fighting wars against the free nations.

Never mind that Khrushchev vowed to bury us. Never mind that the only difference between "good" and "bad" Communists is a disagreement on how to bury us. Khrushchev thought we would simply surrender without putting up a fight, while the Chinese and some other Communists thought some fighting would be necessary.

But never mind those things. This Administration embarked on the dangerous policy of being nice to the "good" Communists. If their economy fails, sell them wheat at bargain prices. If they are short of cash, give them credit. If they promise not to blow up any more nuclear bombs, sign a treaty giving our solemn and faithful word not to do the same. If they object to our armaments program, cut it back unilaterally. If our pursuit of national interest in Cuba makes them nervous, promise never to rock the boat as long as Communism reigns.

In these and other ways we actively helped Khrushchev over his difficult times. We helped this man who did not hesitate to remind us that he intended to bury us. Listen, for example, to what he said last July:

"Of course, when I say that we are against war, I mean aggressive, predatory wars. But there are other wars, wars of national liberation; such wars are just and sacred. We support the peoples who take up arms and uphold their independence and freedom, and we support them not only in words but by concrete deeds."

In other words, it's all right to kill our boys in Vietnam, or Cuba, or the Congo, or anywhere people are being "liberated" by Communism. Do you think for a moment that the United States is not also marked for Communist "liberation"?

And let's just see what the Communists really mean by "peaceful coexistence." Here's what an official journal of the international Communist movement says:

"Peaceful coexistence being a form of the class struggle between capitalism and Socialism, provides, as the events of recent years have shown, a favorable climate for the revolutionary struggle of all peoples. It is in the conditions of peaceful coexistence that the colonial system of imperialism has disintegrated, that the Socialist revolution has triumphed in Cuba, and that the working class and democratic movements have grown in the capitalist countries. Peaceful coexistence, then, does not signify 'accommodation' with imperialism, 'reconciliation' between the oppressed and the oppressors, or 'coexistence of ideologies' but the future development of the class struggle economic, political and ideological."

Mark these words well. This is what the Communists really mean by "peaceful coexistence." They do not mean "peace." "Peaceful coexistence" is simply the Communist strategy for world conquest. Communists may sometimes disagree about the best tactics for carrying out this strategy, but they all agree on the strategy.

Now the only thing any reasonable man can conclude is that the present Administration has made the mistake of thinking that "peaceful coexistence" is the same as "peace." And it has made the mistake of trying to distinguish different kinds of Communism and of supporting some and not others. It has ignored the fact that all Communists agree on the same goal—a Communist-dominated world. And so this Administration chose Khrushchev as the "good" Communist who should be supported. But some months ago it began to be clear that Khrushchev was not doing so well, even with help from the United States.

Khrushchev pushed his tactical differences with the Chinese leaders too far last summer. His call for a conference of all Communist parties gave those parties an opportunity to disapprove of him and his tactics. Such objections came out in the open in the testament supposedly left by

Togliatti, the leader of the Italian Communist party, who died during a visit to the Soviet Union last July. Finally—just a little over a week ago —the French Communist party flatly refused to attend the conference and declared its support for the greater independence of parties.

While this opposition was growing outside the Soviet Union, interesting changes in party and government were taking place inside as well. Khrushchev's self-appointed successor, Frol Kozlov, disappeared. They said only that he had suffered a stroke. A man named Brezhnev gradually took his place in the party organization, moving from his ceremonial post as head of state. Some old Communists, such as Suslov, who prosecuted the case against Khrushchev, remained in power. Men little known in the West, such as Panomorov, seemed to have increasing influence. Mikoyan, the hardy perennial of the Soviet scene, and Kosygin, a relative newcomer who was to take Khrushchev's place in the Government, shifted about in their positions. New men rose up in the party and Government structure —men like Ustinov, who has been connected with the armament industry. There were other organizational changes and counter-changes.

Soviet and Chinese party emissaries met in a conference in East Germany. Rumors flew of an imminent nuclear explosion in Red China, and these were given credence by our own Secretary of State.

In short, there were many signs that something was afoot.

Yet this Administration was caught completely by surprise when Khrushchev was deposed. Last Sunday on television, the Secretary of State confirmed the fact that the Administration was caught flat-footed by Khrushchev's fall.

The Administration was undoubtedly caught even more by surprise when the leaders of Red China immediately congratulated the new rulers of the Soviet Union and forecast a new era of friendly relations between the two countries. Here is what their message said:

"On learning that Comrade Brezhnev has been elected first secretary of the Central Committee of the Communist party of the Soviet Union and that Comrade Kosygin has been appointed chairman of the Council of Ministers, we extend you our warm greetings.

"It is our sincere wish that the fraternal Soviet people will achieve new successes in their constructive work in all fields and in the struggle for the defense of world peace.

"The Chinese Communist party, the Chinese Government, and the Chinese people rejoice at every progress made by the great Soviet Union, the Communist party of the Soviet Union, and the Soviet people on their road of advance.

"The recent successful launching and landing of the Soviet spaceship represented another great achievement of the working people of the

Soviet Union. We wish to avail ourselves of this opportunity to convey our sincere congratulations to you, and through you to the great Soviet people.

"The Chinese and Soviet parties and the two countries unite on the basis of Marxism-Leninism and proletarian internationalism.

"May the fraternal, unbreakable friendship between the Chinese and Soviet peoples continuously develop.

"May the Chinese and Soviet peoples win one victory after another in their common struggle against imperialism headed by the United States and for the defense of world peace."

Can you imagine a stronger message of friendship and declaration of unity? And remember this was sent by the four top leaders of Red China —the chairman of the party, the President, the head of the armed forces, and the Prime Minister. And here is the response given this week by Brezhnev, the new Communist leader.

"Our party will strive for the strengthening of the unity of the great community of the fraternal Socialist countries on a fully equal footing and on the basis of correct combination of the common interests of the Socialist community with the interests of the people of each country, the development of an all-sided cooperation between the Socialist states, in our common struggle for peace and socialism."

Where is the Chinese-Soviet rift today? Can we even be sure that the Soviet Union did not take a hand in the nuclear explosion? What does the test ban treaty mean now—if it ever meant anything? You may recall that I warned of the possibility, when the test-ban treaty was before the Senate, that the Soviets might easily evade the treaty by conducting their tests in Red China. Surely nothing prevents them from doing so.

So where do we stand?

Every sign before us now says that our policy toward the Communists has been a failure. It was bad enough to make a fatal mistake about Nikita Khrushchev. It was bad enough to have a foreign policy—if we may call it that—based on a choice between "good" and "bad" Communists. It was bad enough to count on personal diplomacy to solve the problems of a clash of systems.

But worst of all was the insane policy of strengthening an enemy who has sworn to bury us.

We are now brought face to face with reality. We must now confront an enemy reunified and strengthened by our policy of aid.

This Administration once faced an enemy plagued with disunity and trouble, and it followed a policy that brought back unity and greater strength.

This Administration once had friends in the free world who were unified in purpose and strength, and it followed a policy that tore them asunder. This Administration has lived in the world of empty wishes and slogans.

It is now time for this nation to move forward into the world of reality and good sense. And I pledge to you that I will lead you back to sanity in our foreign relations.

Here are the three things we must do immediately in establishing a sensible policy toward Communism.

First, we must rebuild our once grand alliance. And we must start with the North Atlantic Treaty Organization. Here in these 15 countries rests more than two-thirds of the world's productive capacity. Here live 470 million intelligent and able people. The economic power of our North Atlantic allies, taken together, equals our own.

Here are the elements of power in the free world. Here are all the elements we need, already in being—just waiting to be put to use in ending the Communist threat.

Only one thing is missing, but it means everything. That one thing is unity—unity in cause, unity in purpose and unity in action. In its place we have disunity and disarray, brought to the free world by four years of drift, deception, defeat.

How can we create unity out of chaos? It will not be easy, but it can be done by a bold and joint attack on the roots of the problem.

I have already pledged that one of my first acts as President will be to initiate a call for a North Atlantic conclave. That conclave will have a single purpose—to create a North Atlantic community unified in spirit, purpose and action.

As the first move, I will name a blue ribbon delegation of American citizens to meet with the delegates from other NATO nations to plan the conclave. Those great statesmen of this nation who helped build NATO should join in leading the American delegation.

Only through such a bold venture can we create a climate of true friendship and partnersship. We must reclaim our friends and reassure them of our own friendship through concrete deeds. We must treat them as genuine partners in the pursuit of freedom.

The second thing we must do is to recognize that Communism is our enemy—the whole of Communism, not just some faction of the movement. After all, we spend $50 billion a year to defend ourselves against the "good" Communists—so-called by this Administration. We must understand the nature, aim, and strategy of the international Communist movement. We must never let the zigs and zags in tactics take our eyes off the ultimate strategy, which is plainly and simply a blueprint for world revolution and world conquest.

The third thing to do is to confront Communism with a firm policy of resistance. We must move as quickly as possible to rebuild a policy of strength and resolution with the overriding goal of promoting our national interests. This is the only policy Communist leaders understand and respect. We will keep the peace if—and only if—we take a firm stand against Communist aggression: if—and only if—we insist on concrete concessions and safeguards every step of the way toward a lasting peace.

Of course we must act prudently and cautiously. Of course we must make responsible use of our great power.

But let us never again fall into the trap of thinking that weakness means prudence, or that inaction means caution. These are the truly irresponsible policies. These are the policies that have led this Administration down the road to failure and our nation to the brink of disaster.

We face a challenge and an opportunity. Before us lies a new team in control of the Soviet Union. There will be days and months and perhaps even years of jockeying for power. We cannot see the final outcome.

But what we do now—in the immediate future—will play a major role in shaping the future of freedom throughout the world. If we have the will and wisdom to show the Communist leaders that we firmly intend to protect and promote our interests, we will blunt the thrust of Communist aggression. We will deny success to their ambitions for expansion. We will cause the Communist leaders to look inward to their own internal problems and to work out solutions—solutions that can be found only through relaxing the totalitarian despotism that now reigns in the Communist world. Then we can have a real hope for lasting peace.

My fellow Americans, you have a clear choice to make. You may continue the bankrupt policy of this Administration—a policy of drift and deception. This can only lead to defeat, to an ultimate choice between total war or total surrender.

Or you can strike out once again on the path of peace through strength and resolution. This is the only responsible course, the only course to peace and freedom.

I have faith in the choice you will make. And with your help and with God's blessing, I will take up the task of leadership.

☆

1968

☆

Lyndon Johnson used his great electoral mandate in 1964 to expand the welfare state and enlarge the powers of the federal bureaucracy. Federal aid to housing and education, the creation of the Corporation for Public Broadcasting, Medicare, the Voting Rights Act of 1965 were but the tip of the legislative iceberg.

Yet the liberal consensus that Johnson seemed to embody in 1964 soon began to unravel. Domestic tensions and foreign involvements, especially in Vietnam, revealed a rising level of violence that had become deeply entangled in American life. Beginning with the assassination of John Kennedy, continuing with both white and black militants participating in the civil rights movement and campus disorders, and culminating with the American involvement in the Vietnam War, the nation was becoming increasingly divided. White backlash focused on counterculture youths and the New Left, who were contemptuous of the draft and the tyranny of "respectability" and American wealth. Race riots erupted in dozens of American cities in the summer of 1967; that fall a nonviolent march on the Pentagon attracted 75,000 demonstrators. Generation gaps and crediblity gaps became heated topics in the news. Finally, a growing number of liberal Democratic members of Congress began to perceive that America was exhibiting what Senator J. William Fulbright called an "arrogance of power."

One Democratic member of the Senate who came forth by late fall 1967 to oppose America's Vietnam policy and President Johnson's renomination was Wisonsin Senator Eugene McCarthy. His campaign in New Hampshire attracted a vast cast of student volunteers and press attention to the antiwar cause. After McCarthy's strong showing, New York Senator Robert Kennedy also entered the race. Two weeks later, on March 31st, under premonitions of defeat in the upcoming Wisconsin primary, Lyndon Johnson withdrew from consideration as a presidential contender while simultaneously announcing a bombing halt in Vietnam. Nearly half a million soldiers were then in that Asian country, with the death toll of Americans mounting in the evening news body counts. The news media's coverage of the Tet offensive by the Viet Cong and North Vietnamese that winter undoubtedly was one factor in undermining America's earlier more naïve determination to "win" in Vietnam.

The stage was set for one of the most traumatic periods in all of American political history. That spring saw Hubert Humphrey enter the Democratic Presidential race as the candidate of the "regular" Democrats, who were mostly those supporting Johnson's Vietnam policies. Spring added further violence to the American scene as both the Nobel Prize-winning civil rights leader Martin Luther King and Robert Kennedy were cut down by assassins' bullets. King's death instigated a new round of race riots in early April.

Kennedy's death left the antiwar elements of the Democratic Party in disarray. McCarthy was unacceptable to many liberals because of his preoccupation with Vietnam. Senator George McGovern of South Dakota eventually entered the race to rally the Kennedy delegates. The Democratic Convention in Chicago that August elicited widely televised violence involving demonstrators and the Chicago police. Inevitably, this image of disorder associated with the Democratic Party was transmitted to millions of Americans. The party of Jackson and Roosevelt was in the process of wrecking itself in its attempt to fulfill an overextended dream in domestic and foreign affairs.

Hubert Humphrey's speech at the convention and in a September 30th television address from Salt Lake City were attempts to square his candidacy with the policies of his dominating boss, Lyndon Johnson. The vehemence of those who opposed Johnson's war policies left him politically vulnerable. In his Salt Lake City speech Humphrey attempted, too late in the campaign, to put distance between himself and Johnson's bombing policies by calling for a halt in the bombing of the North as "an acceptable risk for peace."

Running for the Presidency after an eight-year absence, Richard

Nixon seemed more temperate to many observers, but he also ran his campaign with more control over his televised image than ever before. Having lost a race for the Governorship of California in 1962 and gone to New York City to practice law and reap large financial rewards, Nixon surfaced in 1964 and 1966 as a tireless speaker on behalf of Republican political candidates around the country. By 1968, he told audiences that he did not want to criticize Johnson's handling of the war but asserted that he had a secret plan to end the conflict. He also attempted to address the rising fear of crime and violence in the country by calling for a new Attorney General who would inculcate a no-nonsense brand of law and order in the criminal justice system.

Nixon's initial Republican opponent for the Presidential nomination in 1968 was Michigan Governor George Romney. But due to an unfortunate statement in which he had admitted to having been "brainwash[ed]" by American military and diplomatic personnel in Vietnam, his candidacy lost steam. Nixon coasted to the nomination, even after the late entrance into the race by Nelson Rockefeller and Ronald Reagan.

Nixon's acceptance speech in Miami Beach reflected the sense of frustration Americans were feeling at their impotence as a great nation. Unable to win in Vietnam or to stem the tide of domestic violence, America had Nixon's promise that "the dark long night for America is about to end." Prophetically, Nixon extended an olive branch of "peaceful competition" to the Russian and Chinese people. In contrast to his 1960 acceptance speech, Nixon also showed more sensitivity to the problems of black Americans and sought to identify his rather ill-defined concept of the American dream with a wide variety of ethnic groups.

Nixon's radio address on leadership broadcast on September 19th should be read in conjunction with history books that describe the reality of his Presidency. His assertion that as President he would "bring dissenters into policy discussions" did not square with the reality of the "siege mentality" he developed over the next five years, tragically revealed in the transcripts of the Watergate tapes.

As if Presidential politics were not confused enough in 1968, Governor George Wallace of Alabama also entered the race at the head of what generally went by the name of the American Independence Party. Having run up impressive totals in several Democratic primaries in 1964, Wallace in 1968 eventually gained a place on the ballots of all fifty states, a difficult feat in a nation that has structured its election laws against third-party challengers. His appeal had originated in a blatantly racist appeal for whites reacting against federal promotion of civil rights for blacks. By 1968, however, Wallace's appeal was more subtle, condemning federal interference in local schools, ridiculing the Supreme Court, while courting those offended by Vietnam demonstrators and the counterculture. In a speech at Madison Square Garden in late October, Wallace proclaimed that "anarchy prevails today in the streets of the large cities of our country. . . . The liberals and the left-wingers in both national parties have brought us to the domestic mess we are in now," he said. Frequently heckled while addressing the crowd, Wallace's response to them shows his awareness of the power of television's coverage of the event.

The popularity of Wallace's appeal for "law and order" was not lost on Richard Nixon, who attempted to make sure that most of the 13 percent of the electorate who voted for Wallace in the close election in 1968 would be attracted to Nixon four years later.

RICHARD M. NIXON

Acceptance Speech

MIAMI BEACH, FLORIDA

August 8, 1968

Mr. Chairman, delegates to this convention, my fellow Americans.

Sixteen years ago I stood before this convention to accept your nomination as the running mate of one of the greatest Americans of our time or of any time—Dwight D. Eisenhower.

Eight years ago I had the highest honor of accepting your nomination for President of the United States.

Tonight I again proudly accept that nomination for President of the United States.

But I have news for you. This time there's a difference—this time we're going to win.

We're going to win for a number of reasons. First a personal one.

General Eisenhower, as you know, lies critically ill in the Walter Reed Hospital tonight. I have talked, however, with Mrs. Eisenhower on the telephone.

She tells me that his heart is with us. She says that there is nothing that he lives more for, and there is nothing that would lift him more than for us to win in November.

And I say let's win this one for Ike.

We're going to win because this great convention has demonstrated to the nation that Republican party has the leadership, the platform and the purpose that America needs.

We're going to win because you have nominated as my running mate a statesman of the first rank who will be a great campaigner, and one who is fully qualified to undertake the new responsibilities that I shall give to the next Vice President of the United States.

And he is a man who fully shares my conviction and yours that after a period of 40 years when power has gone from the cities and the states to the Government in Washington, D. C., it's time to have power go back from Washington to the states and to the cities of this country all over America.

We're going to win because at a time that America cries out for the unity that this Administration has destroyed, the Republican party, after a spirited contest for its nomination for President and Vice President, stands united before the nation tonight.

And I congratulate Governor Reagan, I congratulate Governor Rockefeller, I congratulate Governor Romney, I congratulate all those who have made the hard fight that they have for this nomination, and I know that you will all fight even harder for the great victory our party is going to win in November because we're going to be together in that election campaign.

And a party that can unite itself will unite America.

My fellow Americans, most important we're going to win because our cause is right. We make history tonight, not for ourselves but for the ages. The choice we make in 1968 will determine not only the future of America but the future of peace and freedom in the world for the last third of the 20th century, and the question that we answer tonight: can America meet this great challenge?

Let us listen to America to find the answer to that question.

As we look at America, we see cities enveloped in smoke and flame. We hear sirens in the night. We see Americans dying on distant battlefields abroad. We see Americans hating each other; fighting each other; killing each other at home.

And as we see and hear these things, millions of Americans cry out in anguish: Did we come all this way for this? Did American boys die in Normandy and Korea and in Valley Forge for this?

Listen to the answers to these questions.

It is another voice, it is a quiet voice in the tumult of the shouting. It is the voice of the great majority of Americans, the forgotten Americans, the non-shouters, the non-demonstrators. They're not racists or sick; they're not guilty of the crime that plagues the land; they are black, they are white; they're native born and foreign born; they're young and they're old.

They work in American factories, they run American businesses. They serve in government; they provide most of the soldiers who die to keep it free. They give drive to the spirit of America. They give lift to the American dream. They give steel to the backbone of America.

They're good people. They're decent people; they work and they save and they pay their taxes and they care.

Like Theodore Roosevelt, they know that this country will not be a good place for any of us to live in unless it's a good place for all of us to live in.

And this I say, this I say to you tonight, is the real voice of America. In this year 1968, this is the message it will broadcast to America and to the world.

Let's never forget that despite her faults, America is a great nation. And America is great because her people are great.

With Winston Churchill we say, we have not journeyed all this way, across the centuries, across the oceans, across the mountains, across the prairies because we are made of sugar candy.

America's in trouble today not because her people have failed, but because her leaders have failed. And what America needs are leaders to match the greatness of her people.

And this great group of Americans—the forgotten Americans and others—know that the great question Americans must answer by their votes in November is this: Whether we shall continue for four more years the policies of the last five years.

And this is their answer, and this is my answer to that question: When the strongest nation in the world can be tied down for four years in a war in Vietnam with no end in sight, when the richest nation in the world can't manage its own economy, when the nation with the greatest tradition of the rule of law is plagued by unprecedented lawlessness, when a nation has been known for a century for equality of opportunity is torn by unprecedented racial violence, and when the President of the United States cannot travel abroad or to any major city at home without fear of a hostile demonstration—then it's time for new leadership for the United States of America.

Thank you. My fellow Americans, tonight I accept the challenge and the commitment to provide that new leadership for America and I ask you to accept it with me.

And let us accept this challenge not as a grim duty but as an exciting adventure in which we are privileged to help a great nation realize its destiny and let us begin by committing ourselves to the truth, to see it like it is and tell it like it is, to find the truth, to speak the truth and to live the truth. That's what we will do.

We've had enough of big promises and little action. The time has come for an honest government in the United States of America.

And so tonight I do not promise the millenium in the morning. I don't promise that we can eradicate poverty and end discrimination and eliminate all dangers of wars in the space of four, or even eight years. But I do promise action. A new policy for peace abroad, a new policy for peace and progress and justice at home.

Look at our problems abroad. Do you realize that we face the stark truth that we are worse off in every area of the world tonight than we were when President Eisenhower left office eight years ago? That's the record.

And there is only one answer to such a record of failure, and that is the complete house cleaning of those responsible for the failures and that record.

The answer is the complete reappraisal of America's policies in every section of the world. We shall begin with Vietnam.

We all hope in this room that there's a chance that current negotiations may bring an honorable end to that war. And we will say nothing during this campaign that might destroy that chance.

But if the war is not ended when the people choose in November, the choice will be clear. Here it is: For four years this Administration has had at its disposal the greatest military and economic advantage that one nation has ever had over another in a war in history. For four years America's fighting men have set a record for courage and sacrifice unsurpassed in our history. For four years this Administration has had the support of the loyal opposition for the objective of seeking an honorable end to the struggle.

Never has so much military and economic and diplomatic power been used so ineffectively. And if after all of this time, and all of this sacrifice, and all of this support, there is still no end in sight, then I say the time has come for the American people to turn to new leadership not tied to the mistakes and policies of the past. That is what we offer to America.

And I pledge to you tonight that the first priority foreign policy objective of our next Administration will be to bring an honorable end to the war in Vietnam.

We shall not stop there. We need a policy to prevent more Vietnams. All of America's peace-keeping institutions and all of America's foreign commitments must be reappraised.

Over the past 25 years, America has provided more than $150-billion in foreign aid to nations abroad. In Korea, and now again in Vietnam, the United States furnished most of the money, most of the arms, most of the men to help the people of those countries defend themselves against aggression. Now we're a rich country, we're a strong nation, we're a populous nation but there are 200 million Americans and there are two billion people that live in the free world, and I say the time has come for other nations in the free world to bear their fair share of the burden of defending peace and freedom around this world.

What I call for is not a new isolationism. It is a new internationalism in which America enlists its allies and its friends around the world in those struggles in which their interest is as great as ours.

And now to the leaders of the Communist world we say, after an era of confrontations, the time has come for an era of negotiations.

Where the world superpowers are concerned there is no acceptable alternative to peaceful negotiation. Because this will be a period of negotiations we shall restore the strength of America so that we shall always negotiate from strength and never from weakness.

And as we seek through negotiations let our goals be made clear. We do not seek domination over any other country. We believe deeply in our ideas but we believe they should travel on their own power and not on the power of our arms. We shall never be belligerent. But we shall be as firm in defending our system as they are in expanding theirs.

We believe this should be an era of peaceful competition not only in the productivity of our factories but in the quality of our ideas. We extend the hand of friendship to all people. To the Russian people. To the Chinese people. To all people in the world. And we shall work toward the goal of an open world, open sky, open cities, open heart, open minds. The next eight years my friends. . . .

This period in which we're entering—I think we will have the greatest opportunity for world peace, but also face the greatest danger of world war of anytime in our history.

I believe we must have peace. I believe that we can have peace. But I do not underestimate the difficulty of this task.

Because, you see, the art of preserving peace is greater than that of waging war, and much more demanding.

But I am proud to have served in an Administration which ended one war and kept the nation out of other wars for eight years afterward.

And it is that kind of experience, and it is that kind of leadership, that America needs today and that we will give to America, with your help.

And as we commit the new policies for America tonight, let me make one further pledge—For five years hardly a day has gone by when we haven't read or heard a report of the American flag being spit on, and our embassy being stoned, a library being burned, or an ambassador being insulted some place in the world, and each incident reduced respect for the United States until the ultimate insult inevitably occurred.

And I say to you tonight that when respect for the United States of

America falls so low that a fourth-rate military power like Korea will seize an American naval vessel in the high seas, it's time for new leadership to restore respect for the United States of America.

Thank you very much. My friends, America is a great nation. It is time we started to act like a great nation around the world.

It's ironic to note, when we were a small nation, weak militarily and poor economically, America was respected. And the reason was that America stood for something more powerful than military strength or economic wealth.

The American Revolution was a shining example of freedom in action which caught the imagination of the world, and today, too often, America is an example to be avoided and not followed.

A nation that can't keep the peace at home won't be trusted to keep the peace abroad. A president who isn't treated with respect at home will not be treated with respect abroad. A nation which can't manage its own economy can't tell others how to manage theirs.

If we are to restore prestige and respect for America abroad, the place to begin is at home—in the United States of America.

My friends, we live in an age of revolution in America and in the world. And to find the answers to our problems, let us turn to a revolution—a revolution that will never grow old, the world's greatest continuing revolution, the American Revolution.

The American Revolution was and is dedicated to progress. But our founders recognized that the first requisite of progress is order.

Now there is no quarrel between progress and order because neither can exist without the other.

So let us have order in America, not the order that suppresses dissent and discourages change but the order which guarantees the right to dissent and provides the basis for peaceful change.

And tonight it's time for some honest talk about the problem of order in the United States. Let us always respect, as I do, our courts and those who serve on them, but let us also recognize that some of our courts in their decisions have gone too far in weakening the peace forces as against the criminal forces in this country.

Let those who have the responsibility to enforce our laws, and our judges who have the responsibility to interpret them, be dedicated to the great principles of civil rights. But let them also recognize that the first civil right of every American is to be free from domestic violence. And that right must be guaranteed in this country.

And if we are to restore order and respect for law in this country, there's one place we're going to begin: We're going to have a new Attorney General of the United States of America.

I pledge to you that our new Attorney General will be directed by the President of the United States to launch a war against organized crime in this country.

I pledge to you that the new Attorney General of the United States will be an active belligerent against the loan sharks and the numbers racketeers that rob the urban poor in our cities.

I pledge to you that the new Attorney General will open a new front against the pill peddlers and the narcotics peddlers who are corrupting the lives of the children of this country.

Because, my friends, let this message come through clear from what I say tonight. Time is running out for the merchants of crime and corruption in American society. The wave of crime is not going to be the wave of the future in the United States of America.

We shall re-establish freedom from fear in America so that America can take the lead of re-establishing freedom from fear in the world.

And to those who say that law and order is the code word for racism, here is a reply: Our goal is justice—justice for every American. If we are to have respect for law in America, we must have laws that deserve respect. Just as we cannot have progress without order, we cannot have order without progress.

And so as we commit to order tonight, let us commit to progress.

And this brings me to the clearest choice among the great issues of this campaign.

For the past five years we have been deluged by Government programs for the unemployed, programs for the cities, programs for the poor, and we have reaped from these programs an ugly harvest of frustrations, violence and failure across the land. And now our opponents will be offering more of the same—more billions for Government jobs, Government housing, Government welfare. I say it's time to quit pouring billions of dollars into programs that have failed in the United States of America.

To put it bluntly, we're on the wrong road and it's time to take a new road to progress.

Again we turn to the American Revolution for our answers. The war on poverty didn't begin five years ago in this country; it began when this country began. It's been the most successful war on poverty in the history of nations. There's more wealth in America today, more broadly shared than in any nation in the world.

We are a great nation. And we must never forget how we became great. America is a great nation today, not because of what government did for people, but because of what people did for themselves over 190 years in this country.

And so it is time to apply the lessons of the American Revolution to our present problems.

Let us increase the wealth of America so we can provide more generously for the aged and for the needy and for all those who cannot help themselves.

But for those who are able to help themselves, what we need are not more millions on welfare rolls but more millions on payrolls in the United States of America.

Instead of Government jobs and Government housing let Government use its tax and credit policies to enlist in this battle the greatest engine of progress ever developed in the history of man—American private enterprise.

Let us enlist in this great cause the millions of Americans in volunteer organizations who will bring a dedication to this task that no amount of money can ever buy.

And let us build bridges, my friends, build bridges to human dignity across the gulf that separates black America from white America.

Black Americans—no more than white Americans—do not want more Government programs which perpetuate dependency. They don't want to be a colony in a nation. They want the pride and the self-respect and the dignity that can only come if they have an equal chance to own their own homes, to own their own businesses, to be managers and executives as well as workers, to have a piece of the action in the exciting ventures of private enterprise.

I pledge to you tonight that we shall have new programs which will provide that equal chance. We make great history tonight. We do not fire a shot heard round the world, but we shall light the lamp of hope in millions of homes across this land in which there is no hope today.

And that great light shining out from America will again become a beacon of hope for all those in the world who seek freedom and opportunity.

My fellow Americans, I believe that historians will recall that 1968 marked the beginning of the American generation in world history. Just to be alive in America, just to be alive at this time is an experience unparalleled in history. Here's where the action is.

Think: Thirty-two years from now most of Americans living today will celebrate a New Year that comes once in a thousand years.

Eight years from now, in the second term of the next President, we will celebrate the 200th anniversary of the American Revolution.

And by our decision in this we—all of us here, all of you listening on television and radio—we will determine what kind of nation America will be on its 200th birthday. We will determine what kind of a world America will live in in the year 2000.

This is the kind of a day I see for America on that glorious Fourth eight years from now: I see a day when Americans are once again proud of their flag; when once again at home and abroad it is honored as the world's greatest symbol of liberty and justice.

I see a day when the President of the United States is respected and his office is honored because it is worthy of respect and worthy of honor. I see a day when every child in this land, regardless of his background, has a chance for the best education that our wisdom and schools can provide, and an equal chance to go just as high as his talents will take him.

I see a day when life in rural America attracts people to the country rather than driving them away.

I see a day when we can look back on massive breakthroughs in solving the problems of slums and pollution and traffic which are choking our cities to death.

I see a day when our senior citizens and millions of others can plan for the future with the assurance that their government is not going to rob them of their savings by destroying the value of their dollar.

I see a day when we will again have freedom from fear in America and freedom from fear in the world. I see a day when our nation is at peace and the world is at peace and everyone on earth—those who hope, those who aspire, those who crave liberty will look to America as the shining example of hopes realized and dreams achieved.

My fellow Americans, this is the cause I ask you to vote for. This is the cause I ask you to work for. This is the cause I ask you to commit to not just for victory in November but beyond that to a new Administration because the time when one man or a few leaders could save America, is gone. We need tonight nothing less than the total commitment and the total mobilization of the American people if we are to succeed.

Government can pass laws but respect for law can come only from people who take the law into their hearts and their minds and not into their hands.

Government can provide opportunity, but opportunity means nothing unless people are prepared to seize it.

A president can ask for reconciliation in the racial conflict that divides Americans, but reconciliation comes only from the hearts of people.

And tonight, therefore, as we make this commitment, let us look into our hearts, and let us look down into the faces of our children.

Is there anything in the world that should stand in their way? None of the old hatreds mean anything when you look down into the faces of our children. In their faces is our hope, our love and our courage.

Tonight, I see the face of a child. He lives in a great city, he's black or he's white, he's Mexican, Italian, Polish, none of that matters. What matters he's an American child.

That child in that great city is more important than any politician's promise. He is America, he is a poet, he is a scientist, he's a great teacher, he's a proud craftsman, he's everything we've ever hoped to be in everything we dare to dream about.

He sleeps the sleep of a child, and he dreams the dreams of a child. And yet when he awakens, he awakens to a living nightmare of poverty, neglect and despair.

He fails in school, he ends up on welfare. For him the American system is one that feeds his stomach and starves his soul. It breaks his heart. And in the end it may take his life on some distant battlefield.

To millions of children in this rich land this is their prospect, but this is only part of what I see in America.

I see another child tonight. He hears a train go by. At night he dreams of faraway places where he'd like to go. It seems like an impossible dream. But he is helped on his journey through life. A father who had to go to work before he finished the sixth grade sacrificed everything he had so that his sons could go to college.

A gentle Quaker mother with a passionate concern for peace, quietly wept when he went to war but she understood why he had to go.

A great teacher, a remarkable football coach, an inspirational minister encouraged him on his way. A courageous wife and loyal children stood by him in victory and also in defeat.

And in his chosen profession of politics, first there was scores, then hundreds, then thousands, and finally millions who worked for his success.

And tonight he stands before you, nominated for President of the United States of America.

You can see why I believe so deeply in the American dream.

For most of us the American revolution has been won, the American dream has come true. What I ask of you tonight is to help me make that dream come true for millions to whom it's an impossible dream today.

One hundred and eight years ago the newly elected President of the United States, Abraham Lincoln, left Springfield, Ill., never to return again.

He spoke to his friends gathered at the railroad station. Listen to his words:

"Today I leave you. I go to assume a greater task than devolved on General Washington. The Great God which helped him must help me. Without that great assistance I will surely fail. With it, I cannot fail."

Abraham Lincoln lost his life but he did not fail.

The next President of the United States will face challenges which in some ways will be greater than those of Washington or Lincoln, because for the first time in our nation's history an American President will face not only the problem of restoring peace abroad, but of restoring peace at home.

Without God's help, and your help, we will surely fail.

But with God's help and your help, we shall surely succeed.

My fellow Americans, the dark long night for America is about to end.

The time has come for us to leave the valley of despair and climb the mountain so that we may see the glory of the dawn, a new day for America, a new dawn for peace and freedom to the world.

☆

RICHARD M. NIXON

Campaign Speech

RADIO BROADCAST

September 19, 1968

During the course of this campaign, I have discussed many issues with the American people. Tonight, I would like to talk with you about a subject often debated by scholars and the public, but seldom dealt with directly in the Presidential campaign: The nature of the Presidency itself.

What *kind* of leadership should a President give? Is the office too strong, or not strong enough? How can it be made more responsive? Should a President lead public opinion, or follow it? What are the priorities for Presidential attention, and the range of Presidential responsibilities?

Perhaps the best way to begin my own answer is with another question, one I am often asked as I travel around the country: "Why do you seek the office? With all the troubles that we have, why would *anyone* want to be President today?"

The answer is not one of glory, or fame; today the burdens of the office outweigh its privileges. It's not because the Presidency offers a chance to *be* somebody, but because it offers a chance to *do* something.

Today, it offers a greater opportunity to help shape the future than ever before in the nation's history—and if America is to meet its challenges, the next President must seize that opportunity.

We stand at a great turning point—when the nation is groping for a new direction, unsure of its role and its purposes, caught in a tumult of change. And for the first time, we face serious, simultaneous threats to the peace both at home and abroad.

In the watershed year of 1968, therefore, America needs Presidential leadership that can establish a firm focus, and offer a way out of a time of towering uncertainties. Only the President can hold out a vision of the future and really the people behind it.

The next President must unite America. He must calm its angers, ease its terrible frictions, and bring its people together once again in peace and mutual respect. He has to take *hold* of America before he can move it forward.

This requires leadership that believes in law, and has the courage to enforce it; leadership that believes in justice, and is determined to promote it; leadership that believes in progress, and knows how to inspire it.

The days of a passive Presidency belong to a simpler past. Let me be very clear about this: The next President must take an activist view of his office. He must articulate the nation's values, define its goals and marshal its will. Under a Nixon Administration, the presidency will be deeply involved in the entire sweep of America's public concerns.

The first responsibility of leadership is to gain mastery over events, and to shape the future in the image of our hopes.

The President today cannot stand aside from crisis; he cannot ignore division; he cannot simply paper over disunity. He must lead.

But he must bear in mind the distinction between forceful leadership and stubborn willfulness. And he should not delude himself into thinking that he can do everything himself. America today cannot afford vest-pocket government, no matter who wears the vest.

In considering the kind of leadership the next President should give, let us first consider the special relationship—the special trust—that has developed between President and people.

The President is trusted, not to follow the fluctuations of the public-opinion polls, but to bring his own best judgment to bear on the best *ideas* his administration can muster.

There are occasions on which a President must take unpopular measures.

But his responsibility does not stop there. The President has a duty to decide, but the people have a right to know why. The President has a responsibility to tell them—to lay out all the facts, and to explain not only why he chose as he did but also what it means for the future. Only through an open, candid dialogue with the people can a President maintain his trust and his leadership.

It's time we once again had an open administration—open to ideas *from* the people, and open in its communication *with* the people—an administration of open doors, open eyes and open minds.

When we debate American commitments abroad, for example, if we expect a decent hearing from those who now take to the streets in protest, we must recognize that neither the Department of State nor of Defense has a monopoly on all wisdom. We should bring dissenters into policy discussions, not freeze them out; we should invite constructive criticism, not only because the critics have a right to be heard, but also because they often have something worth hearing.

And this brings me to another, related point: The President cannot isolate himself from the great intellectual ferments of his time. On the contrary, he must consciously and deliberately place himself at their center. The lamps of enlightenment are lit by the spark of controversy; their flame can be snuffed out by the blanket of consensus.

This is one reason why I don't want a government of yesmen. It's why I do want a government drawn from the broadest possible base—an administration made up of Republicans, Democrats and independents, and drawn from politics, from career government service, from universities, from business, from the professions—one including not only executives and administrators, but scholars and thinkers.

While the President is a leader of thought, he is also a user of thought, and he must be a catalyst of thought. The thinking that he draws upon must be the best in America—and not only in government. What's happening today in America and the world is happening not only in politics and diplomacy, but in science, education, the arts—and in all areas a President needs a constant exposure to ideas that stretch the mind.

Only if we have an Administration broadly enough based philosophically to ensure a true ferment of ideas, and to invite in interplay of the best minds in America, can we be sure of getting the best and most penetrating ideas.

We cannot content ourselves with complacency, with an attitude that because something worked once before, it must be good enough for us now. The world is changing, America is changing, and so must our ideas and our policies change—and our pursuit of the new must be an unremitting pursuit of excellence.

When we think of leadership, we commonly think of persuasion. But the coin of leadership has another side.

In order to lead, a President today must listen. And in this time of searching and uncertainty, government must learn to listen in new ways.

A President has to hear not only the clamorous voices of the organized, but also the quiet voices, the *inner voices*—the voices that speak through the silences, and that speak from the heart and the conscience.

These are the voices that carry the real meaning and the real message of America.

He's got to articulate these voices so that they can be heard, rather than being lost in the wail and bellow of what too often passes today for public discourse. He must be, in the words of Woodrow Wilson, "the spokesman for the real sentiment and purpose of the country."

The President is the one official who represents every American—rich and poor, privileged and underprivileged. He represents those whose misfortunes stand in dramatic focus, and also the great, quiet forgotten majority—the non-shouters and the non-demonstrators, the millions who ask principally to go their own way in decency and dignity, and to have their own rights accorded the same respect they accord the rights of others. Only if he listens to the quiet voices can he be true to this trust.

This I pledge, that in a Nixon Administration, America's citizens will not have to break the law to be heard, they will not have to shout or resort to violence. We can restore peace only if we make government attentive to the quiet as well as the strident, and this I intend to do.

But what of the burdens of the Presidency? Have they, as some maintain, grown beyond the capacity of any one man?

The Presidency has been called an impossible office.

If I thought it were, I would not be seeking it. But its functions have become cluttered, the President's time drained away in trivia, the channels of authority confused.

When questions of human survival may turn on the judgments of one man, he must have time to concentrate on those great decisions that only he can make.

One means of achieving this is by expanding the role of the Vice President—which I will do.

I also plan a re-organized and strengthened Cabinet, and a stronger White House staff than any yet put together.

The people are served not only by a President, but by an Administration, and not only by an Administration, but by a government.

The President's chief function is to lead, not to administer; it is not to oversee every detail, but to put the right people in charge, to provide them with basic guidance and direction, and to let them do the job. As Theodore Roosevelt once put it, "the best executive is the one who has enough sense to pick good men to do what he wants done, and self-restraint enough to keep from meddling with them while they do it."

This requires surrounding the President with men of stature, including young men, and giving them responsibilities commensurate with that stature. It requires a Cabinet made up of the ablest men in America, leaders in their own right and not merely by virtue of appointment—men who will command the public's respect and the President's attention by the power of their intellect and the force of their ideas.

Such men are not attracted to an Administration in which all credit is gathered to the White House and blame parceled out to scapegoats, or in which high officials are asked to dance like puppets on a Presidential string. I believe in a system in which the appropriate Cabinet officer gets credit for what goes right, and the President takes the blame for what goes wrong.

Officials of a new Administration will not have to check their consciences at the door, or leave their powers of independent judgment at home.

Another change I believe necessary stems directly from my basic concept of government. For years now, the trend has been to sweep more and more authority toward Washington. Too many of the decisions that would better have been made in Seattle or St. Louis have wound up on the President's desk.

I plan a streamlined Federal system, with a return to the states, cities and communities of decision-making powers rightfully theirs.

The purpose of this is not only to make government more effective and more responsive, but also to concentrate Federal attention on those functions that can only be handled on the Federal level.

The Presidency is a place where priorities are set, and goals determined.

We need a new attention to priorities, and a new realism about goals.

We are living today in a time of great promise—but also of too much wishful imagining that all the ills of man could be set right overnight, merely by making a national "commitment."

A President must tell the people what cannot be done immediately, as well as what can. Hope is fragile, and too easily shattered by the disappointment that follows inevitably on promises unkept and unkeepable. America needs charts of the possible, not excursions into the impossible.

Our cause today is not a nation, but a planet—for never have the fates of all the peoples of the earth been so bound up together.

The tasks confronting the next President abroad are among the most complex and difficult ever faced. And, as Professor Clinton Rossiter has observed, "Leadership in foreign affairs flows today from the President— or it does not flow at all."

The whole structure of power in the world has been undergoing far-reaching changes. While these pose what may be our period of greatest danger, they open what also may be our greatest opportunity. This is a time when miscalculation could prove fatal; a time when the destructive power amassed by the world's great nations threatens the planet. But it is also a time when leaders both East and West are developing a new, sobering awareness of the terrible potential of that power and the need to restrain it.

The judgments of history can bestow no honor greater than the title of peacemaker. It is this honor—this destiny—that beckons America, the chance to lead the world at last out of turmoil and onto that plateau of peace man has dreamed of since the dawn of time. This is our summons to greatness. If we answer the call, generations yet unborn will say of this generation of Americans that we truly mastered our moment, that we at last made the world safe for mankind.

The President cannot stand alone. Today, more than ever in modern times, he must reach out and draw upon the strength of the people.

Theodore Roosevelt called the Presidency "a bully pulpit;" Franklin Roosevelt called it pre-eminently "a place of moral leadership." And surely one of a President's greatest resources is the moral authority of his office. It's time we restored that authority—and time we used it once again, to its fullest potential—to rally the people, to define those moral imperatives which are the cement of a civilized society, to point the ways in which the *energies* of the people can be enlisted to serve the *ideals* of the people.

What has to be done, has to be done by President and people together, or it won't be done at all.

In asking you to join this great effort, I am asking not that you give something *to* your country, but that you do something *with* your country; I am asking not for your gifts, but for your hands. Together, we can hardly fail, for there is no force on earth to match the will and the spirit of the people of America, if that will and that spirit are mobilized in the service of a common aim.

Let me add a personal note. I made a point of conducting my campaign for the nomination in a way that would make it possible to unite the party after the convention. That was successful. I intend now to conduct my election campaign in a way that will make it possible to unite the nation after November. It is not my intention to preside over the disintegration of America or the dissolution of America's force for good in the world. Rather, I want the Presidency to be a force for pulling our people back together once again, and for making our nation whole by making our people one. We have had enough of discord and division, and what we need now is a time of healing of renewal, and of realistic hope.

No one who has been close to the Presidency would approach its powers lightly, or indifferently, or without a profound sense of the awesome responsibility these powers carry.

Nor should the American people approach this time of challenge without a sense of the majesty of the moment.

Greatness comes from stepping up to events, not from sitting on the sidelines while history is made by others.

History will be made in these years just ahead—history that can change the world for generations to come. So let us seize the moment, and accept the challenge—not as a burden, and not in fear—but in the full confidence that no people have ever had such resources to meet its challenge. Ours is the chance to see the American dream fulfilled at last in the destiny of man. This is the role that history offers; this is the hope that summons us; this is our generation's call to greatness as a nation. This, today, is America's opportunity.

☆

HUBERT H. HUMPHREY

Acceptance Speech

CHICAGO, ILLINOIS

August 29, 1968

Mr. Chairman, my fellow Americans, my fellow Democrats—

I proudly accept the nomination of our party. This moment—this moment is one of personal pride and gratification. Yet one cannot help but reflect the deep sadness that we feel over the troubles and the violence which have erupted, regrettably and tragically, in the streets of this great city, and for the personal injuries which have occurred.

Surely we have now learned the lesson that violence breeds counter-violence and it cannot be condoned, whatever the source.

I know that every delegate to this convention shares tonight my sorrow and my distress over these incidents. And for just one moment, in sober reflection and serious purpose, may we just quietly and silently, each in our own way, pray for our country. And may we just share for a moment a few of those immortal words of the prayer of St. Francis of Assisi, words which I think may help heal the wounds, ease the pain and lift our hearts.

Listen to this immortal saint: "Where there is hatred, let me know love. Where there is injury, pardon. Where there is doubt, faith. Where there is despair, hope. Where there is darkness, light."

Those are the words of a saint. And may those of us of less purity listen to them well and may America tonight resolve that never, never again shall we see what we have seen.

Yes, I accept your nomination in this spirit and I have spoken knowing that the months and the years ahead will severely test our America. And might I say that as this America is tested, that once again we give our testament to America. And I do not think it is sentimental nor it is cheap, but I think it is true that each and everyone of us in our own way should once again reaffirm to ourselves and our posterity that we love this nation, we love America!

But take heart my fellow Americans. This is not the first time that our nation has faced a challenge to its life and its purpose. And each time that we've had to face these challenges we have emerged with new greatness and with new strength.

We must make this moment of crisis—we must make it a moment of creation.

As it has been said, in the worst of times a great people must do the best of things—and let us do it.

We stand at such a moment now in the affairs of this Nation, because, my fellow Americans, something new, something different has happened. There is an end of an era, and there is the beginning of a new day.

And it is the special genius of the Democratic party that it welcomes change—not as an enemy but as an ally—not as a force to be suppressed but as an instrument of progress to be encouraged.

This week our party has debated the great issues before America in this very hall, and had we not raised these issues—troublesome as they were—we would have ignored the reality of change.

Had we just papered over the differences of frank, hard debate, we would deserve the contempt of our fellow citizens and the condemnation of history.

Yes, we dare to speak out and we have heard hard and sometimes bitter debate. But I submit that this is the debate, and this is the work of a free people, the work of an open convention and the work of a political party responsive to the needs of this nation.

Democracy affords debate, discussion and dissent. But, my fellow Americans, it also requires decision. And we have decided here, not by edict, but by vote; not by force, but by ballot.

Majority rule has prevailed but minority rights are preserved.

There is always the temptation, always the temptation to leave the scene of battle in anger and despair, but those who know the true meaning of democracy accept the decision of today but never relinquishing their right to change it tomorrow.

In the space of but a week this convention has literally made the foundations of a new Democratic party structure in America. From precinct level to the floor of this convention, we have revolutionized our rules and procedures.

And that revolution is in the proud tradition of our party. It is in the tradition of Franklin Roosevelt, who knew that America had nothing to fear but fear itself!

And it is in the tradition of that one and only Harry Truman, who let 'em have it and told it like it was.

And that's the way we're going to do it from here on out.

And it is in the tradition of that beloved man, Adlai Stevenson, who talked sense to the American people—and oh, tonight, how we miss this great, good and gentle man of peace in America—

And my fellow Americans, all that we do and all that we ever hope to do, must be in the tradition of John F. Kennedy, who said to us: Ask not what your country can do for you, but what can you do for your country.

And, my fellow Democrats and fellow Americans, in that spirit of that great man let us ask what together we can do for the freedom of man.

And what we are doing is in the tradition of Lyndon B. Johnson, who rallied a grief-stricken nation when our leader was stricken by the assassin's bullet and said to you and said to me, and said to all the world—let us continue.

And in the space, and in the space of five years since that tragic moment, President Johnson has accomplished more of the unfinished business of America than any of his modern predecessors.

And I truly believe that history will surely record the greatness of his contribution to the people of this land.

And tonight to you, Mr. President, I say thank you. Thank you, Mr. President.

Yes, my fellow Democrats, we have recognized and indeed we must recognize the end of an era and the beginning of a new day—and that new day, and that new day belongs to the people—to all the people, everywhere in this land of the people, to every man, woman and child that is a citizen of this Republic.

And within that new day lies nothing less than the promise seen a generation ago by that poet Thomas Wolfe—to every man his chance, to every man regardless of his birth his shining golden opportunity, to every man the right to live and to work and be himself, and to become whatever thing his manhood and his vision can combine to make him—this is the promise of America.

Yes, the new day is here across America. Throughout the entire world forces of emancipation are at work. We hear freedom's rising course—"Let me live my own life, let me live in peace, let me be free," say the people.

And that cry is heard today in our slums, on our farms and in our cities. It is heard from the old as well as from the young. It is heard in Eastern Europe and it is heard in Vietnam. And it will be answered by us, in how we face the three realities that confront this nation.

The first reality is the necessity for peace in Vietnam and in the world.

The second reality, the second reality is the necessity for peace and justice in our cities and in our nation.

And the third reality is the paramount necessity for unity—unity in our country.

Let me speak first, then, about Vietnam.

There are differences of course, serious differences within our party on this vexing and painful issue of Vietnam, and these differences are found even within the ranks of all of the Democratic Presidential candidates.

But I might say to my fellow Americans that once you have examined the differences I hope you will also recognize the much larger areas of agreement.

Let those who believe that our cause in Vietnam has been right, or those who believe that it has been wrong, agree here and now, agree here and now, that neither vindication nor repudiation will bring peace or be worthy of this country!

The question is not the yesterdays but the question is what do we do now? No one knows what the situation in Vietnam will be when the next President of the United States takes that oath of office on Jan. 20, 1969.

But every heart in America prays that by then we shall have reached a cease-fire in all Vietnam and be in serious negotiation toward a durable peace.

Meanwhile, as a citizen, a candidate and Vice President, I pledge to you and to my fellow Americans that I will do everything within my power, within the limits of my capacity and ability to aid the negotiations and to bring a prompt end to this war!

May I remind you of the words of a truly great citizen of the world, Winston Churchill. It was he who said—and we should heed his words well—"those who use today and the present to stand in judgment of the past may well lose the future."

And if there is any one lesson that we should have learned, it is that the policies of tomorrow need not be limited by the policies of yesterday.

My fellow Americans, if it comes my high honor to serve as President of these states and people, I shall apply that lesson to the search for peace in Vietnam as to all other areas of national policy.

Now let me ask you, do you remember these words at another time, in a different place: Peace and freedom do not come cheap. And we are destined—all of us here today—to live out most if not all of our lives in uncertainty and challenge and peril. The words of a prophet—yes, the words of a President—yes, the words of the challenge of today—yes. And the words of John Kennedy to you, and to me, and to posterity!

Last week we witnessed once again in Czechoslovakia the desperate attempt of tyranny to crush out the forces of liberalism by force and brutal power, to hold back change.

But in Eastern Europe as elsewhere the old era will surely end, and there, as here, a new day will dawn.

And to speed this day we must go far beyond where we've been—beyond containment to communication; beyond the emphasis of differences to dialogue; beyond fear to hope.

We must cross those remaining barriers of suspicion and despair. We must halt the arms race before it halts humanity.

And is this, is this a vain hope, is it but a dream? I say the record says no.

Within the last few years we have made progress, we have negotiated a nuclear test ban treaty, we have laid the groundwork for a nuclear non-proliferation treaty.

We have reached agreement on banning weapons in outer space. We have been building patiently—stone by stone, each in our own way—the cathedral of peace.

And now we must take new initiative, new initiative with prudence and caution but with perseverance. We must find the way and the means to control and reduce offensive and defensive nuclear missile systems. The world cannot indefinitely hope to avoid nuclear war which one last act, one erring judgment, one failure in communication could unleash upon all humanity and destroy all of mankind.

But the search for peace is not for the timid or the weak, it must come from a nation of high purpose—firm without being belligerent, resolute without being bellicose, strong without being arrogant. And that's the kind of America that will help build the peace of this world.

But the task of slowing down the arms race, of halting the nuclear escalation—there is no more urgent task than ending this threat to the very survival of our planet, and if I am elected as your President, I commit myself body, mind and soul to this task.

Now our second reality is the necessity for peace at home. There is, my friends, let's see it as it is—there is trouble in America. But it does not come from a lack of faith. But it comes from the kindling of hope.

When the homeless can find a home, they do not give up the search for a better home. When the hopeless find hope, they seek higher hopes. And in 1960 and again in 1964, you, the American people, gave us a mandate to awaken America. You asked us to get America moving again, and we have—and America is on the move.

And we have, we have awakened expectations. We have aroused new voices and new voices that must and will be heard.

We have inspired new hope in millions of men and women, and they are impatient—and rightfully so, impatient now to see their hopes and their aspirations fulfilled.

We have raised a new standard of life in our America, not just for the poor but for every American—wage earner, businessman, farmer, school child and housewife. A standard by which the future progress must be judged.

Our most urgent challenge is in urban America, where most of our people live. Some 70 percent of our people live on 2 percent of our land, and within 25 years 100 million more will join our national family.

I ask you tonight—where shall they live? How shall they live? What shall be their future? We're going to decide in the next four years those questions. The next President of the United States will establish policies not only for this generation but for children yet unborn. Our task is tremendous and I need your help.

The simple solution of the frustrated and the frightened to our complex urban problems is to lash out against society. But we know—and they must know—that this is no answer.

Violence breeds more violence: disorder destroys, and only in order can we build. Riot makes for ruin; reason makes for solution.

So from the White House to the court house to the city hall, every official has the solemn responsibility of guaranteeing to every American—black and white, rich and poor—the right to personal security—life.

Every American, black or white, rich or poor, has the right in this land of ours to a safe and a decent neighborhood, and on this there can be no compromise.

I put it very bluntly—rioting, burning, sniping, mugging, traffic in narcotics, and disregard for law are the advance guard of anarchy, and they must and they will be stopped.

But may I say most respectfully, particularly to some who have spoken before, the answer lies in reasoned, effective action by state, local and Federal authority. The answer does not lie in an attack on our courts, our laws or our Attorney General.

We do not want a police state. But we need a state of law and order.

We do not want a police state but we need a state of law and order, and neither mob violence nor police brutality have any place in America.

And I pledge to use every resource that is available to the Presidency, every resource available to the President, to end once and for all the fear that is in our cities.

Now let me speak of other rights. Nor can there be any compromise with the right of every American who is able and who is willing to work to have a job—that's an American right, too.

Who is willing to be a good neighbor, to be able to live in a decent home in the neighborhood of his own choice.

Nor can there be any compromise with the right of every American who is anxious and willing to learn, to have a good education.

And it is to these rights—the rights of law and order, the rights of life, the rights of liberty, the right of a job, the right of a home in a decent neighborhood, and the right of an education—it is to these rights that I pledge my life and whatever capacity and ability I have.

And now the third reality, essential if the other two are to be achieved, is the necessity, my fellow Americans, for unity in our country, for tolerance and forbearance for holding together as a family, and we must make a great decision. Are we to be one nation, or are we to be a nation divided, divided between black and white, between rich and poor, between north and south, between young and old? I take my stand—we are and we must be one nation, united by liberty and justice for all, one nation under God, indivisible with liberty and justice for all. This is our America.

Just as I said to you there can be no compromise on the right of personal security, there can be no compromise on securing of human rights.

If America is to make a crucial judgment of leadership in this coming election, then let that selection be made without either candidate hedging or equivocating.

Winning the Presidency, for me, is not worth the price of silence or evasion on the issue of human rights.

And winning the Presidency—and listen well—winning the Presidency is not worth a compact with extremism.

I choose not simply to run for President. I seek to lead a great nation.

And either we achieve through justice in our land or we shall doom ourselves to a terrible exhaustion of body and spirit.

I base my entire candidacy on the belief which comes from the very depths of my soul—which comes from basic religious conviction that the American people will stand up, that they will stand up for justice and fair play, and that they will respond to the call of one citizenship—one citizenship open to all for all Americans!

So this is the message that I shall take to the people, and I ask you to stand with me.

To all of my fellow Democrats now who have labored hard and openly this week, at the difficult and sometimes frustrating work of democracy, I pledge myself to that task of leading the Democratic Party to victory in November.

And may I say to those who have differed with their neighbor, or those who have differed with fellow Democrats, may I say to you that all of your goals, that all of your high hopes, that all of your dreams, all of them will come to naught if we lose this election and many of them can be realized with the victory that can come to us.

And now a word to two good friends. To my friends—and they are my friends—and they're your friends—and they're fellow Democrats.

To my friends Gene McCarthy and George McGovern—to my friends Gene McCarthy and George McGovern, who have given new hope to a new generation of Americans that there can be greater meaning in their lives, that America can respond to men of moral concern, to these two good Americans: I ask your help for our America, and I ask you to help me in this difficult campaign that lies ahead.

And now I appeal, I appeal to those thousands—yea millions—of young Americans to join us, not simply as campaigners but to continue as vocal, creative and even critical participants in the politics of our time. Never were you needed so much, and never could you do so much if you want to help now.

Martin Luther King, Jr. had a dream. Robert F. Kennedy as you saw tonight had a great vision. If Americans will respond to that dream and that vision, if Americans will respond to that dream and that vision, their deaths will not mark the moment when America lost its way. But it will mark the time when America found its conscience.

These men, these men have given us inspiration and direction, and I pledge from this platform tonight we shall not abandon their purpose— we shall honor their dreams by our deeds now in the days to come.

I am keenly aware of the fears and the frustrations of the world in which we live. It is all too easy, isn't it, to play on these emotions. But I do not intend to do so. I do not intend to appeal to fear, but rather to hope. I do not intend to appeal to frustration, but rather to your faith.

I shall appeal to reason and to your good judgment.

The American Presidency, the American Presidency is a great and powerful office, but it is not all-powerful. It depends most of all upon the will and the faith and the dedication and the wisdom of the American people.

So I call you forth—I call forth that basic goodness that is there—I call you to risk the hard path of greatness.

And I say to America. Put aside recrimination and dissension. Turn away from violence and hatred. Believe—believe in what America can do, and believe in what America can be, and with the vast—with the help of that vast, unfrightened, dedicated, faithful majority of Americans, I say to this great convention tonight, and to this great nation of ours, I am ready to lead our country!

☆

HUBERT H. HUMPHREY
Campaign Speech
SALT LAKE CITY, UTAH

September 30, 1968

Tonight I want to share with you my thoughts as a citizen and a candidate for President of the United States. I want to tell you what I think about great issues which I believe face this nation.

I want to talk with you about Vietnam, and about another great issue in the search for peace in the world—the issue of stopping the threat of nuclear war.

After I have told you what I think, I want you to think.

And if you agree with me, I want you to help me.

For the past several weeks, I have tried to tell you what was in my heart and on my mind.

But sometimes that message has been drowned out by the voices of protesters and demonstrators.

I shall not let the violence and disorder of a noisy few deny me the right to speak or to destroy the orderly democratic process.

I have paid for this television time this evening to tell you my story uninterrupted by noise . . . by protest . . . or by second-hand interpretation.

When I accepted the Democratic party's nomination and platform, I said that the first reality that confronted this nation was the need for peace in Vietnam.

I have pledged that my first priority as President shall be to end the war and obtain an honorable peace.

For the past four years I have spoken my mind about Vietnam, frankly and without reservation, in the Cabinet and in the National Security Council—and directly to the President.

When the President has made his decisions, I have supported them.

He has been the Commander in Chief. It has been his job to decide. And the choices have not been simple or easy.

President Johnson will continue—until Jan. 20, 1969—to make the decisions in Vietnam. The voice at the negotiating table must be his. I shall not compete with that voice. I shall cooperate and help.

We all pray that his efforts to find peace will succeed.

But, 112 days from now, there will be a President . . . a new Administration . . . and new advisers.

If there is no peace by then, it must be their responsibility to make a complete reassessment of the situation in Vietnam—to see where we stand and to judge what we must do.

As I said in my acceptance speech: The policies of tomorrow need not be limited by the policies of yesterday.

We must look to the future. For neither vindication nor repudiation of our role in Vietnam will bring peace or be worthy of our country.

The American people have a right to know what I would do—if I am President—after Jan. 20, 1969, to keep my pledge to honorably end the war in Vietnam.

What are the chances for peace?

The end of the war is not yet in sight. But our chances for peace are far better today than they were a year or even a month ago.

On March 31, the war took on an entirely new dimension.

On that date President Johnson by one courageous act removed the threat of bombing from 90 percent of the people, and 78 percent of the land area, of North Vietnam.

On that date President Johnson sacrificed his own political career in order to bring negotiations that could lead to peace.

Until that time, the struggle was only on the battlefield.

Now our negotiators are face to face across the table with negotiators from North Vietnam.

A process has been set in course. And lest that process be set back, our perseverance at the conference table must be great as our courage has been in the war.

There have been other changes during these past few months.

The original Vietnam decision—made by President Eisenhower—was made for one basic reason.

President Eisenhower believed it was in our national interest that Communist subversion and aggression should not succeed in Vietnam.

It was his judgment—and the judgment of President Kennedy and President Johnson since then—that if aggression did succeed in Vietnam, there was a danger that we would become involved on a more dangerous scale in a wider area of Southeast Asia.

While we have stood with our allies in Vietnam, several things have happened.

Other nations of Southeast Asia—given the time we have bought for them—have strengthened themselves . . . have begun to work together . . . and are far more able to protect themselves against any future subversion or aggression.

In South Vietnam itself, a constitution has been written . . . elections have been stepped up . . . and the South Vietnamese Army has increased its size and capacity, and improved its equipment, training and performance—just as the Korean Army did during the latter stages of the Korean War.

So—in sharp contrast to a few months ago—we see peace negotiations going on.

We see a stronger Southeast Asia.

We see a stronger South Vietnam.

Those are the new circumstances which a new President will face in January.

In light of those circumstances—and assuming no marked change in the present situation—how would I proceed as President?

Let me first make clear what I would not do.

I would not undertake a unilateral withdrawal.

To withdraw would not only jeopardize the independence of South Vietnam and the safety of other Southeast Asian nations. It would make meaningless the sacrifices we have already made.

It would be an open invitation to more violence . . . more aggression . . . more instability.

It would, at this time of tension in Europe, cast doubt on the integrity of our word under treaty and alliance.

Peace would not be served by weakness or withdrawal.

Nor would I escalate the level of violence in either North or South Vietnam. We must seek to de-escalate.

The platform of my party says that the President should take reasonable risks to find peace in Vietnam. I shall do so.

North Vietnam, according to its own statements and those of others, has said it will proceed to prompt and good faith negotiations, if we stop the present limited bombing of the North.

We must always think of the protection of our troops.

As President, I would stop the bombing of the North as an acceptable risk for peace because I believe it could lead to success in the negotiations and thereby shorten the war. This would be the best protection for our troops. . . . In weighing that risk—and before taking action—I would place key importance on evidence—direct or indirect—by deed or word—of Communist willingness to restore the demilitarized zone between North and South Vietnam.

Now if the Government of North Vietnam were to show bad faith, I would reserve the right to resume the bombing.

Now secondly, I would take the risk that South Vietnamese would meet the responsibilities they say they are now ready to assume in their own self-defense.

I would move, in other words, toward de-Americanization of the war.

I would sit down with the leaders of South Vietnam to set a specific timetable by which American forces could be systematically reduced while South Vietnamese forces took over more and more of the burden.

The schedule must be a realistic one—one that would not weaken the over-all Allied defense posture. I am convinced such action would be as much in South Vietnam's interest as in ours.

What I am proposing is that it should be basic to our policy in Vietnam that the South Vietnamese take over more and more of the defense of their own country.

That would be an immediate objective of the Humphrey-Muskie Administration as I sought to end the war.

If the South Vietnamese Army maintains its present rate of improvement, I believe this will be possible next year—without endangering either our remaining troops or the safety of South Vietnam.

I do not say this lightly. I have studied this matter carefully.

Third, I would propose once more an immediate cease-fire—with United Nations or other international supervision and supervised withdrawal of all foreign forces from South Vietnam.

American troops are fighting in numbers in South Vietnam today only because North Vietnamese forces were sent to impose Hanoi's will on the South Vietnamese people by aggression.

We can agree to bring home our forces from South Vietnam, if the North Vietnamese agree to bring theirs home at the same time.

External forces assisting both sides could and should leave at the same time, and should not be replaced.

The ultimate key to an honorable solution must be free elections in South Vietnam—with all people, including members of the National Liberation Front and other dissident groups, able to participate in those elections if they were willing to abide by peaceful processes.

That, too, would mean some risk.

But I have never feared the risk of one man, one vote. I say: let the people speak. And accept their judgment, whatever it is.

The Government of South Vietnam should not be imposed by force from Hanoi or by pressure from Washington. It should be freely chosen by all the South Vietnamese people.

A stopping of the bombing of the North—taking account of Hanoi's actions and assurances of prompt good faith negotiations and keeping the option of resuming that bombing if the Communists show bad faith.

Careful, systematic reduction of American troops in South Vietnam— a de-Americanization of the war—turning over to the South Vietnamese Army a greater share of the defense of its own country.

An internationally supervised cease-fire—and supervised withdrawal of all foreign forces from South Vietnam.

Free elections, including all people in South Vietnam willing to follow the peaceful process.

Those are risks I would take for peace.

I do not believe any of these risks would jeopardize our security or be contrary to our national interest.

There is, of course, no guarantee that all these things could be successfully done.

Certainly, none of them could be done if North Vietnam were to show bad faith.

But I believe there is a good chance these steps could be undertaken with safety for our men in Vietnam.

As President, I would be dedicated to carrying them out—as I would be dedicated to urging the Government of South Vietnam to expedite all political, economic and social reforms essential to broadening popular participation including high priority to land reform . . . more attention to the suffering of refugees . . . and constant Government pressure against inflation and corruption.

I believe all of these steps could lead to an honorable and lasting settlement, serving both our own national interest and the interests of the independent nations of Southeast Asia.

We have learned a lesson from Vietnam.

The lesson is not that we should turn our backs on Southeast Asia, or on other nations or people in less familiar parts of the world neighborhood.

The lesson is, rather, that we should carefully define our goals and priorities. And within those goals and priorities, that we should formulate policies which will fit new American guidelines.

Applying the lesson of Vietnam, I would insist as President that we review other commitments made in other times, that we carefully decide what is and is not in our national interest.

I do not condemn any past commitment.

I do not judge the decisions of past Presidents when, in good conscience, they made those decisions in what they thought were the interests of the American people.

But I do say, if I am President, I owe it to this nation to bring our men and resources in Vietnam back to America where we need them so badly, and to be sure we put first things first in the future.

Let me be clear: I do not counsel withdrawal from the world.

I do not swerve from international responsibility.

I only say that, as President, I would undertake a new strategy for peace in this world, based not on American omnipotence, but on American leadership, not only military and economic but moral.

That new strategy for peace would emphasize working through the United Nations . . . strengthening and maintaining our key alliances for mutual security, particularly including NATO . . . supporting international peacekeeping machinery . . . and working with other nations to build new institutions and instruments for cooperation.

In a troubled and dangerous world we should seek not to march alone, but to lead in such a way that others will wish to join us.

Even as we seek peace in Vietnam, we must for our own security and well-being seek to halt and turn back the costly and even more dangerous arms race.

Five nations now have nuclear bombs.

The United States and the Soviet Union already possess enough weapons to burn and destroy every human being on this earth.

Unless we stop the arms race . . . unless we stop 15 to 20 more nations from getting nuclear bombs and nuclear bomb technology within the next few years, this generation may be the last.

For 20 years we have lived under the constant threat that some irresponsible action or even some great miscalculation could blow us all up in the wink of an eye.

There is danger that we have become so used to the idea that we no longer think it abnormal—forgetting that our whole world structure depends for its stability on the precarious architecture of what Winston Churchill called the "balance of terror." This is no longer an adequate safeguard for peace.

There is a treaty now before the Senate which would stop the spread of nuclear weapons. That treaty must be ratified now.

If this nation cannot muster the courage to ratify this treaty—a treaty which in no way endangers our national security, but adds to it by keeping these weapons out of the hands of a Nassar, a Castro . . . and many others —then there can be little hope for our future in this world. We must ratify this treaty.

I also believe that we must have the courage—while keeping our guard up and fulfilling our commitments to NATO—to talk with the Soviet Union as soon as possible about a freeze and a reduction of offensive and defensive nuclear missiles systems.

To escalate the nuclear missile arms race is to raise the level of danger and total destruction. It is costly, menacing, fearsome and offers no genuine defense.

Beyond that, if I am President, I shall take the initiative to find the way—under carefully safeguarded, mutually acceptable international inspection—to reduce arms budgets and military expenditures systematically among all countries of the world.

Our country's military budget this year is $80-billion.

It is an investment we have to make under existing circumstances. It protects our freedom.

But if we can work with other nations so that we can all reduce our military expenditures together, with proper safeguards and inspection, then it will be a great day for humanity.

All of us will have moved further away from self-destruction. And all of us will have billions of dollars with which to help people live better lives.

The American people must choose the one man they believe can best face these great issues.

I would hope that Mr. Nixon, Mr. Wallace and I could express our views on Vietnam not only individually, but on the same public platform.

I call for this because—on the basis of our past records and past careers—there are great differences between our policies and programs.

Those views of Governor Wallace which I have seen reported indicate that he would sharply escalate the war.

Mr. Nixon's past record reveals his probable future policies.

In 1954—at the time of the French defeat at Dienbienphu—he advocated American armed intervention in Vietnam in aid of French colonialism. It was necessary for President Eisenhower to repudiate his proposal.

Since then, he has taken a line on Vietnam policy which I believe could lead to greater escalation of the war.

In January of this year, Mr. Nixon described as "bunk" the idea that free elections in South Vietnam were of importance.

In February of this year, when questioned about the use of nuclear weapons in Vietnam, Mr. Nixon said that a general "has to take the position that he cannot rule out the use of nuclear-weapons in extreme situations that might develop."

Since then, he has indicated he has a plan to end the war in Vietnam but will not disclose it until he becomes President.

If he has such a plan, he has an obligation to so inform President Johnson and the American people.

A few days ago the Republican Vice-Presidential nominee said there is not now and never has been a Nixon-Agnew plan for peace in Vietnam. It was, he said, a ploy "to maintain suspense."

And then he said: "Isn't that the way campaigns are run?"

I think we need some answers about this from Mr. Nixon.

Mr. Nixon's public record shows, also, consistent opposition to measures for nuclear arms controls.

He attacked Adlai Stevenson and myself for advocating a nuclear test ban treaty—a treaty to stop radioactive fallout from poisoning and crippling people the world over. He called our plan "a cruel hoax." We can be thankful that President Kennedy and the Congress did not follow his advice.

Today, he is asking for delay of ratification of a treaty carefully negotiated over several years and signed by 80 nations—the nuclear nonproliferation treaty designed to stop the spread of nuclear weapons.

I speak plainly: I do not believe the American Presidency can afford a return to leadership which would increase tension in the world; which would, on the basis of past statements, escalate the Vietnam war; and which would turn the clock back on progress that has been made at a great sacrifice to bring the great powers of the world into a saner relationship in this nuclear age.

On the great issues of Vietnam, of the arms race and of human rights in America, I have clear differences with Mr. Nixon and Mr. Wallace.

I call on both of these men to join me in open debate before the American people.

Let us put our ideas before the people. Let us offer ourselves for their judgment—as men and as leaders.

Let us appear together—in front of the same audiences or on the same television screens, and at the same time—to give the people a choice.

We must not let a President be elected by the size of his advertising budget.

We cannot let a President be elected without having met the issues before the people.

I am willing to put myself, my programs, my capacity for leadership, before the American people for their judgment.

I ask the Republican nominee and the third-party candidate to do the same.

I ask, before Election Day, that we be heard together as you have heard me alone tonight.

I appeal to the people—as citizens of a nation whose compassion and sense of decency and fair play have made it what Lincoln called "the last best hope on earth."

I appeal to you as a person who wants his children to grow up in that kind of country.

I appeal to you to express and vote your hopes and not your hates.

I intend, in these five weeks, to wage a vigorous, tireless and forthright campaign for the Presidency. I shall not spare myself, or those who will stand with me.

I have prepared myself. I know the problems facing this nation. I do not shrink from these problems. I challenge them. They were made by men. I believe they can be solved by men.

If you will give me your confidence and support, together we shall build a better America.

☆

GEORGE C. WALLACE
Campaign Speech
NEW YORK CITY
October 24, 1968

Well, thank you very much ladies and gentlemen. Thank you very much for your gracious and kind reception here in Madison Square Garden. I'm sure that the *New York Times* took note of the reception that we've received here in the great city of New York. I'm very grateful to the people of this city and this state for the opportunity to be on the ballot on November 5, and as you know we're on the ballot in all 50 states in this union. This is not a sectional movement. It's a national movement, and I am sure that those who are in attendance here tonight, especially of the press, know that our movement is a national movement and that we have an excellent chance to carry the great Empire State of New York.

I have a few friends from Alabama with me and we have a number of others who were with us last week, but we have with us Willie Kirk, past president of Local 52, United Association of Plumbers and Pipefitters.

Well, I want to tell you something. After November 5, you anarchists are through in this country. I can tell you that. Yes, you'd better have your say now, because you are going to be through after November 5, I can assure you that.

I have also with me W. C. Williamson, business manager of Local 52, UAPP, Montgomery, Alabama, and R. H. Low, president of the Mobile Building and Construction Trades Council and business manager of Local 653 Operating Engineers.

And, you came for trouble, you sure got it.

And we have R. H. Bob Low, president of the MBC—We—why don't you come down after I get through and I'll autograph your sandals for you, you know?

And Charlie Ryan, recording secretary of the Steam Fitters Local 818, New York City. We have been endorsed in Alabama by nearly every local in our state: textiles workers, paper workers, steel workers, rubber workers, you name it. We've been endorsed by the working people of our state.

Regardless of what they might say, your national leaders, my wife carried every labor box in 1966, when she ran for governor of Alabama in the primary and the general election. And I also was endorsed by labor when I was elected governor in 1962.

Now, if you fellows will—I can drown—listen—if you'll sit down, ladies and gentlemen, I can drown that crowd out. If you'll just sit down, I'll drown 'em out—that—all he needs is a good haircut. If he'll go to the barbershop, I think they can cure him. So all you newsmen look up this way now. Here's the main event. I've been wanting to fight the main event a long time in Madison Square Garden, so here we are. Listen, that's just a preliminary match up there. This is the main bout right here. So let me say again as I said a moment ago, that we have had the support of the working people of our state. Alabama's a large industrial state, and you could not be elected governor without the support of people in organized labor.

Let me also say this about race, since I'm here in the state of New York, and I'm always asked the question. I am very grateful for the fact that in 1966 my wife received more black votes in Alabama than did either one of her opponents. We are proud to say that they support us now in this race for the presidency, and we would like to have the support of people of all races, colors, creeds, religions, and national origins in the state of New York.

Our system is under attack: the property system, the free enterprise system, and local government. Anarchy prevails today in the streets of the large cities of our country, making it unsafe for you to even go to a political rally here in Madison Square Garden, and that is a sad commentary. Both national parties in the last number of years have kowtowed to every anarchist that has roamed the streets. I want to say before I start on this any longer, that I'm not talking about race. The overwhelming majority of all races in this country are against this breakdown of law and order as much as those who are assembled here tonight. It's a few anarchists, a few activists, a few militants, a few revolutionaries, and a few Communists. But your day, of course, is going to be over soon. The American people are not going to stand by and see the security of our nation imperiled, and they're not going to stand by and see this nation destroyed, I can assure you that.

The liberals and the left-wingers in both national parties have brought us to the domestic mess we are in now. And also this foreign mess we are in.

You need to read the book "How to Behave in a Crowd." You really don't know how to behave in a crowd, do you?

Yes, the liberals and left-wingers in both parties have brought us to the domestic mess we are in also to the foreign policy mess we find our nation involved in at the present time, personified by the no-win war in Southeast Asia.

Now what are some of the things we are going to do when we become president? We are going to turn back to you, the people of the states, the right to control our domestic institutions. Today you cannot even go to the school systems of the large cities of our country without fear. This is a sad day when in the greatest city in the world, there is fear not only in Madison Square Garden, but in every school building in the state of New York, and especially in the City of New York. Why has the leadership of both national parties kowtowed to this group of anarchists that makes it unsafe for your child and for your family? I don't understand it. But I can assure you of this—that there's not ten cents worth of difference with what the national parties say other than our party. Recently they say most of the same things we say. I remember six years ago when this anarchy movement started, Mr. Nixon said: "It's a great movement," and Mr. Humphrey said: "It's a great movement." Now when they try to speak and are heckled down, they stand up and say: "We've got to have some law and order in this country." "We've got to have some law and order in this country." They ought to give you law and order back for nothing, because they have helped to take it away from you, along with the Supreme Court of our country that's made up of Republicans and Democrats.

It's costing the taxpayers of New York and the other states in the union almost a half billion dollars to supervise the schools, hospitals, seniority and apprenticeship lists of labor unions, and businesses. Every year on the federal level we have passed a law that would jail you without a trial by jury about the sale of your own property. Mr. Nixon and Mr. Humphrey, both three or four weeks ago, called for the passage of a bill on the federal level that would require you to sell or lease your own property to whomsoever they thought you ought to lease it to. I say that when Mr. Nixon and Mr. Humphrey succumb to the blackmail of a few anarchists in the streets who said we're going to destroy this country if you do not destroy that adage that a man's home is his castle, they are not fit to lead the American people during the next four years in our country. When I become your president, I am going to ask that Congress repeal this so-called open occupancy law and we're going to, within the law, turn back to the people of every state their public school system. Not one dime of your federal money is going to be used to bus anybody any place that you don't want them to be bussed in New York or any other state.

Yes, the theoreticians and the pseudo-intellectuals have just about destroyed not only local government but the school systems of our country. That's all right. Let the police handle it. So let us talk about law and order. We don't have to talk about it much up here. You understand what I'm talking about in, of course, the City of New York, but let's talk about it.

Yes, the pseudo-intellectuals and the theoreticians and some professors and some newspaper editors and some judges and some preachers have looked down their nose long enough at the average man on the street: the pipe-fitter, the communications worker, the fireman, the policeman, the barber, the white collar worker, and said we must write you a guideline about when you go to bed at night and when you get up in the morning. But there are more of us than there are of them because the average citizen of New York and of Alabama and of the other states of our union are tired of guidelines being written, telling them when to go to bed at night and when to get up in the morning.

I'm talking about law and order. The Supreme Court of our country has hand-cuffed the police, and tonight if you walk out of this building and are knocked in the head, the person who knocks you in the head is out of jail before you get in the hospital, and on Monday morning, they'll try a policeman about it. I can say I'm going to give the total support of the presidency to the policemen and the firemen in this country, and I'm going to say, you enforce the law and you make it safe on the streets, and the president of the United States will stand with you. My election as president is going to put some backbone in the backs of some mayors and governors I know through the length and breadth of this country.

You had better be thankful for the police and the firemen of this country. If it were not for them, you couldn't even ride in the streets, much less walk in the streets, of our large cities. Yes, the Kerner Commission Report, recently written by Republicans and Democrats, said that you are to blame for the breakdown of law and order, and that the police are to blame. Well, you know, of course, you aren't to blame. They said we have a sick society. Well, we don't have any sick society. We have a sick Supreme Court and some sick politicians in Washington,—that's who's sick in our country. The Supreme Court of our country has ruled that you cannot even say a simple prayer in a public school, but you can send obscene literature through the mail, and recently they ruled that a Communist can work in a defense plant. But when I become your president, we're going to take every Communist out of every defense plant in the United States, I can assure you.

The Kerner Commission report also recommended that the taxes of the American people be raised to pay folks not to destroy the country, and not to work. I never thought the day would come when a

Republican and Democratic report would call for the taxes on the already over-taxed people of our country to pay people not to destroy. It is the most ludicrous and asinine report ever made to a president of our country. I want to tell you folks something. I was fighting the Nazis and Fascists before you were born. I was even shot at by them. I've been shot at by the Nazis—the Nazis and the Fascists. Now the Kerner Commission report—who is it writes these reports, ladies and gentlemen? It's usually some pointed head from one of those multibillion dollar tax-exempt foundations. When they recommend that taxes be raised on you and me, they don't have to pay taxes because they're tax-exempt. When I become the president, I'm going to ask the Congress to remove the tax exemption feature on these multibillion dollar tax-exempt foundations and let them pay taxes like the average citizen of New York pays also. It's estimated that 25 billion dollars goes through tax loopholes that ought to be paid by those able to pay and Senator Robert Kennedy himself said the same thing. So I say that what we ought to do is to remove that tax-exemption feature. And when we do, we can raise the workingman's dependent exemption from $600 to $1200 even in wartime.

Well now, all you television folks get a good picture over there now. Go ahead. You know—now it's all over. Get this camera turned back this way. You know—everywhere we've spoken we've had this same kind of crowd, but the television puts all its footage on a few folks that don't know how to behave in a crowd and make it appear that there are no people supporting you here. And I frankly think the networks are doing that on purpose, myself. I don't think they want to show the support we have here in New York City and throughout the country. Yes sir, but I think they know tonight and have seen something they didn't expect in Madison Square Garden, and I reckon they'll try to explain it away tomorrow, the *New York Times*, and the other papers will. But you just remember that some of these newspapers can fool some of the people some of the time, but they can't fool all the people all the time. You remember that.

We have a comprehensive platform that I hope you get copies of before the election, in which we have dealt with every problem that faces the American people. But let me tell you briefly about foreign policy. The Democrats and the Republicans are always saying: "What do the folks at Madison Square Garden supporting the American Independent Party know about foreign policy?" I ask them: "What do you know about foreign policy? We've had four wars in the last 50 years. We've spent $122 billion of our money on foreign aid. We are bogged down in a no-win war in Southeast Asia, and anarchy in the streets. What do you know about foreign policy? You haven't been so successful in conducting American foreign policy in the last 50 years yourself." I can say this: we are in Vietnam. But General LeMay knows as I know and you know that the strongest deterrent to any further global conflict is superiority in offensive and defensive capabilities of our country. We can never be on a parity nor inferior because when you are superior, you can always go to the negotiating table; you can go to the peace table; you can go to the conference table. The way I would like to see every difference between any nation settled is around the conference table. But as long as there are tensions in the world, we cannot gamble upon the security of this city or this state or this nation by having anything but absolute superiority in the matter of defensive and offensive capabilities.

We are in Vietnam whether you like it or not. I sincerely hope and pray that the conflict is soon over, but we should have learned one thing about our involvement in Southeast Asia—the same thing that Mr. Humphrey now says in his speeches: we should not march alone. I said last year in California that we should never have gone to Vietnam—by ourselves. We should have looked our allies in the face in Western Europe and our non-Communist Asian allies and said to them: it is as much your interest as it is ours and you are going to go with manpower, munitions, and money, and if you don't go and help us in Southeast Asia, and if you don't stop trading with the North Vietnamese who are killing American servicemen, we are not only going to cut off every dime of foreign aid you're getting, but we're going to ask you to pay back all you owe us from World War I right on this very day.

Yes, the average taxpayer in New York doesn't understand his money going to those nations who not only won't support us, but on the other hand actively trade with the North Vietnamese. I'm not saying we must kick our allies out. We need them in Western Europe, and they need us. We need them in non-Communist Asia, and they need us. But NATO countries of Western Europe have 55 million people more than do the United States, and in the future they're going to have to carry their share of the defense burden because we cannot carry it alone. We will not carry it alone, even though we recognize that those things that happen in other parts of the world affect us in this country, they must carry their fair share of not only the manpower commitments, but also the commitments in munitions and money, and I know you agree with that.

I sincerely hope and pray that we have a successful negotiated peace. Well, I'll drown them out, come on. I sincerely hope and pray that we have an honorably negotiated peace to arise out of the Paris peace talks. I know that you pray that, and that the American servicemen can come home. But if we fail diplomatically and politically in Southeast Asia, we're not going to stay there forever, we're not going to see hundreds of American servicemen killed every week for years and months to come. If we do not win diplomatically and politically in Paris, that is, by honorable conclusion of the war, then in my judgment, we ought to end it militarily with conventional weapons and bring the American servicemen home. If we cannot settle it diplomatically and politically, and could not win it militarily with conventional weapons, then I wonder why we're there in the first place? We're going to conclude this war one way or the other either through honorable negotiations or conventional military power.

There's something else we ought to talk about and you see some of it here in the state of New York. We should stop the morale boost for the Communists in our own country. In every state in the union, this treasonable conduct on the part of a few, and their speeches, are printed in Hanoi, Peking, Moscow, and Havana. General Westmoreland said it is prolonging the war, and it is causing New Yorkers and Alabamans to be killed in Southeast Asia. When you ask the Attorney General of our nation: "Why don't you do something about this treasonable conduct" do you know what he says? "We are too busy bussing school children in New York and Los Angeles and we don't have time." We also have some college students who raise money, food, and clothes for the Communists and fly the Viet Cong flag in the name of academic freedom, and free speech. We didn't allow that in World War II; we did not allow for anybody to call for Nazi victory, or Fascist victory.

There is such a thing as legitimate dissent. Senator Robert Kennedy from this state said we should not be in Southeast Asia, and you have a right to say it yourself, if that's what you believe because you don't believe it's in the interests of our country to be there. But if you arise and make a speech the next day and say I long for Communist victory, every average citizen in New York knows that one is dissent and the other is something else. I want to tell you that when I become your president, I'm going to have my Attorney General seek an indictment against any professor calling for Communist victory and stick him in a good jail somewhere. When you drag a few of these college students who are raising money for the Communists and put them in a good jail you'll stop that too, I can asure you. That'll stop them. We're going to destroy academic freedom in this country if we continue to abuse it as it has been abused at this time. Whether you agree with the war or not, we should agree that whatever we say or do should be in the national interests of getting the American servicemen home safely, and that sort of conduct is not conducive to the return of the American servicemen to New York and Alabama.

My friends, let me say this. We can win this election because it only takes a plurality to win when there are three or more running. If we get thirty-four percent of the vote in this state, and the other two get thirty-three percent apiece, then we win the entire electoral vote of the State of New York. That's all it takes. You know this, and that's one reason Mr. Nixon doesn't want to debate. Well, I want to tell Mr. Nixon it's a good thing he doesn't debate because if he ever does, we're going to point out that he's made so many inconsistent statements about so many matters, I would be happy to debate. But he cannot get a debate started.

That's alright. That's alright honey—that's right sweety-pie—oh, that's a he. I thought you were a she. I tell you what, I got. . . .

Well, don't worry what the newspapers say about us. Everything I've said tonight is logical and reasonable and constitutional. Not a single thing have I said tonight that anybody can argue logically with, and that's the reason they call us extremists and want to say we're Fascists. They cannot argue with the logic of the position we take here in Madison Square Garden tonight. They want to say, well, they're evil folks. I want to tell these newspapers something. These large newspapers that think they know more than the average citizen on the street of New York haven't always been right. I remember the time the *New York Times* said that Mao Tse-tung was a good man, and he turned out to be a Communist. I remember when they said that Ben Bella was a good man, and he turned out to be a Communist. When old Castro was in the hills of Cuba, the *New York Times* said he was the Robin Hood of the Caribbean, and they introduced him on national television as the George Washington of Cuba. They were mistaken about Castro.

They [newspapers] are mistaken about our movement, and they are mistaken about the good people of New York State who are here tonight supporting our candidacy because the two national parties (other than our party) have paid no attention to you. But they are paying attention to those who are making the most noise here at Madison Square Garden tonight and every other place in the country. You know that some of those people who make it unsafe for you and me are going to school on your tax money and they are exempt from the draft. Well, I tell you one thing. I'm tired of my tax money going to educate somebody who wants to raise money for the Communists in our country, and that's exactly what a lot of them do on some of the college campuses in this country. I'm certainly not talking about all the college students. You know the few that I'm talking about, and there are some in every state in the union.

Four years ago our movement received thirty-four percent of the vote in Wisconsin, thirty percent in Indiana, and forty-four percent in Maryland. We have won nearly every radio and television poll in every state in the union, so don't pay any attention to the pollsters. They said we were going to get fifteen percent of the Midwest, well, Ohio's part of the Midwest, and we got eighteen percent of the voters in that one state to sign a petition to get us on the ballot, and I would say that for every one who signed a petition in the state of Ohio, there were four more who would have signed had they been given the opportunity. Yes, we got forty-four percent of the vote four years ago in the state of Maryland.

You know, I like to tell this because—if you'll listen to this, I'll tell you a good joke—you've heard it before, but it's very good. Down in the state of Maryland that night four years ago in the presidential primary, I was leading up until about 9:30 with several hundred thousand votes in, and they called the mayor of Baltimore to the television and asked him what he thought about this man from Alabama running first in the presidential primary in our free state. Well, do you know what he said, being a big-time politician? He said: "It's sad; it's sad. We'll never live this down. What has come over the people of the free state of Maryland?" Well, if he had gone out and asked a good cab driver in Baltimore, he could have told him. You vote for me and you are going to be through with all that. Let me tell you now you continue to support our movement until November 5, together we are going to change directions in this country, and we are going to return some sanity to the American government scene. I do appreciate you being here in Madison Square Garden tonight. Thank you very much, ladies and gentlemen.

☆

1972

☆

The first significant event in the scramble for the Democratic nomination to oppose President Nixon can be traced to February 8, 1969. On that day Senator George McGovern was chosen to head a party Reform Commission that would rewrite many of the delegate-selecton rules for the next convention. Closely involved in changing the rules, McGovern was in a position to understand and benefit from them better than any other potential candidate. Thus, since he had briefly been a Presidential candidate following Robert Kennedy's death in 1968, it came as no surprise when McGovern resigned his Commission chairmanship and announced his candidacy for President on January 18, 1971, earlier than any previous serious effort.

McGovern had come from rural South Dakota, served as a combat flyer during World War II, received a Ph.D. in American History and was a teacher for a short time. A skilled political organizer, by the early 1960s he was serving as head of John Kennedy's Food for Peace program before gaining a Senate seat from his conservative home state. His candidacy did not attract special notice in 1971 as a large number of well-known rivals entered the race to compete against Richard Nixon. The acknowledged front runner throughout most of 1971 was Maine Senator Edmund Muskie, who had run as a Vice Presidential candidate with Hubert Humphrey in 1968. Others to enter the race included Humphrey himself, New York Mayor John

Lindsay, Washington Senator "Scoop" Jackson and Alabama Governor George Wallace.

The Democratic primary season would stretch from the opener in New Hampshire to the end in New York on June 20. Due to a lack of a clear theme for his candidacy, a widely reported emotional outburst in defense of his wife against a scurrilous local newspaper, and overconfidence, Muskie won only 46 percent of the New Hampshire vote to McGovern's suprprising 37 percent. The press began hounding Muskie, and his centrist campaign slipped badly in primaries in Florida, Wisconsin, and Pennsylvania.

While Wallace surprised pundits and politicans by winning the Florida primary, and even liberal Dade County, McGovern won Wisconsin and a majority in Massachusetts and attained significant momentum for the nomination. His young staff, headed by future Presidential contender Gary Hart, attracted numerous volunteers to canvass many of the caucus states. Humphrey had won Pennsylvania, Indiana, and West Virginia (the later two in head-on contests with George Wallace) but was narrowly defeated by McGovern in the California primary. Wallace had been removed from consideration for the nomination in May by an assasination attempt that left him paralyzed.

The Democratic Convention in Miami Beach was a rancorous affair. Delegate quotas for blacks and women that had been mandated by McGovern's Reform Commission came under intense criticism. A national television audience saw women and homosexuals advocate platform planks concerning abortion and gay rights that went far beyond previous attempts. McGovern had run his campaign primarily as an opponent of American involvement in the Vietnam War, however, and sought to dampen close identification with other more divisive issues.

At 2:48 in the morning of July 14, 1972, George McGovern finally delivered his acceptance speech to an estimated television audience of only 3,600,000. Internal party wrangling over the Vice Presidential nomination had delayed proceedings to this hour, and commentators laughed at the lack of deference paid to the increasingly dominant medium of television. McGovern's was a forceful and powerful address that broke sharply with the tradition of a bipartisan foreign policy. "Within ninety days of my inauguration," he said, "every American soldier and every American prisoner will be out of the jungle and out of their cells and back home in America where they belong." He attempted to redefine national security as credibility, more schools, and better health care, adding that "if we someday choke on the pollution of our own air, there will be little consolation in leaving behind a dying continent ringed with steel."

McGovern's chances for victory were never great in 1972, but they took a decided turn for the worse by late July when it became known that his Vice Presidential running mate, Senator Thomas Eagleton of Missouri, had previously been hospitalized for mental illness. McGovern's growing aura of indecisiveness was accentuated when he told the press that he was "1,000 percent for Tom Eagleton and [had] no intention of dropping him from the ticket," then finally decided to dump Eagleton because of the political damage caused by the disclosure. McGovern's August 5th speech announcing Sargent Shriver as the new Vice Presidential candidate exhibits his belief in the sharp differences dividing his own candidacy from that of Nixon. Read more carefully, however, it makes clear how Nixon outflanked McGovern as a peace candidate as well as in several other areas.

Nixon easily won renomination at the Republican convention, which was again held in Miami Beach. His administration had achieved a balanced budget in 1969 but was not able to check the growing inflationary spiral nor the mounting unemployment rates. In the summer of 1971 he instituted a ninety-day freeze on all wages, rents, and prices, followed by the creation of a Pay Board and a Price Commission to oversee wage and price increases once the freeze was over.

Nixon's "secret plan" to end the war in Vietnam turned out to be little different from that offered by Humphrey in his Salt Lake City address in 1968. The gradual withdrawal of American forces, combined with a greater fighting role for the South Vietnamese forces, was accompanied by an increasing use of American air power to bomb suspected Viet Cong and North Vietnamese strongholds. A joint U.S.-South Vietnamese invasion of neutral Cambodia on April 30, 1970, to ferret out Communist sanctuaries sparked angry student demonstrations across the nation. It seemed as of 1970 that Nixon had further polarized the nation by relentlessly pursuing the war, although with fewer American ground troops.

By 1972, 96 percent of all American homes had television sets. Nixon had grown more sophisticated in exploiting the power of the media since his poor performance in the 1960 televised debates with Kennedy. As President he largely insulated himself from Administration dissenters, surrounding himself with top aides drawn largely from the world of advertising. Nixon's public rhetoric proved to be sharply at odds with the illegal activities he and Attorney General Mitchell sponsored against Democratic opponents, critical reporters, and television networks. The Watergate break-in at the Democratic Party headquarters in June 1972, however, was largely ignored by the media in the fall campaign. Nixon's breakthrough in thawing relations with China and the Soviet Union included elaborate trips to both countries in 1972. These had been effectively orchestrated for prime-time television coverage in the United States and Nixon emerged to many of the American public as a great peacemaker.

Nixon's renomination acceptance speech, delivered to Republican delegates in Miami Beach in August, chastised the Democrats for "dividing Americans into quotas" and for following a "politics of paternalism, where master planners in Washington make decisions for people." Permissiveness, crime, and narcotics were the targets of an all-out offensive on the part of his Administration, Nixon said. Regarding the war in Vietnam, the President scoffed at the idea of giving amnesty to draft dodgers and was highly critical of the Democrats for proposing huge defense cuts and a "retreat to peace" in Vietnam.

That fall, National Security Adviser Henry Kissinger was negotiating a settlement to the war. On October 26th he told the American people that "peace is at hand." Nixon made a last-minute address on November 2nd, which reinforced the impression that although "there are still some provisions of the agreement which must be clarified" a "peace with honor" could be rapidly expected.

RICHARD M. NIXON

Acceptance Speech

MIAMI BEACH, FLORIDA

August 23, 1972

Mr. Chairman, delegates to this convention, my fellow Americans:

Four years ago, standing in this very place, I proudly accepted your nomination for President of the United States.

With your help and with the votes of millions of Americans, we won a great victory in 1968.

Tonight, I again proudly accept your nomination for President of the United States.

Let us pledge ourselves to win an even greater victory this November in 1972.

I congratulate Chairman Ford. I congratulate Chairman Dole, Anne Armstrong, and the hundreds of others who have laid the foundation for that victory by their work at this great convention.

Our platform is a dynamic program for progress for America and for peace in the world.

Speaking in a very personal sense, I express my deep gratitude to this convention for the tribute you have paid to the best campaigner in the Nixon family—my wife Pat. In honoring her, you have honored millions of women in America who have contributed in the past and will contribute in the future so very much to better government in this country.

Again, as I did last night, when I was not at the convention, I express the appreciation of all of the delegates and of all America for letting us see young America at its best at our convention. As I express my appreciation to you, I want to say that you have inspired us with your enthusiasm, with your intelligence, with your dedication at this convention. You have made us realize that this is a year when we can prove the experts' predictions wrong, because we can set as our goal winning a majority of the new voters for *our* ticket this November.

I pledge to you, all of the new voters in America who are listening on television and listening here in this convention hall, that I will do everything that I can over these next 4 years to make your support be one that you can be proud of because, as I said to you last night, and I feel it very deeply in my heart: Years from now I want you to look back and be able to say that your first vote was one of the best votes you ever cast in your life.

Mr. Chairman, I congratulate the delegates to this convention for renominating as my running-mate the man who has just so eloquently and graciously introduced me, Vice President Ted Agnew.

I thought he was the best man for the job 4 years ago.

I think he is the best man for the job today.

And I am not going to change my mind tomorrow.

Finally, as the Vice President has indicated, you have demonstrated to the Nation that we can have an open convention without dividing Americans into quotas.

Let us commit ourselves to rule out every vestige of discrimination in this country of ours. But my fellow Americans, the way to end discrimination against some is not to begin discrimination against others.

Dividing Americans into quotas is totally alien to the American traditions.

Americans don't want to be part of a quota. They want to be part of America. This Nation proudly calls itself the United States of America. Let us reject any philosophy that would make us the divided people of America.

In that spirit, I address you tonight, my fellow Americans, not as a partisan of party, which would divide us, but as a partisan of principles which can unite us.

Six weeks ago our opponents at their convention rejected many of the great principles of the Democratic Party. To those millions who have been driven out of their home in the Democratic Party, we say come home. We say come home not to another party, but we say come home to the great principles we Americans believe in together.

And I ask you, my fellow Americans, tonight to join us not in a coalition held together only by a desire to gain power. I ask you to join us as members of a new American majority bound together by our common ideals.

I ask everyone listening to me tonight—Democrats, Republicans,

Independents, to join our new majority—not on the basis of the party label you wear in your lapel, but on the basis of what you believe in your hearts.

In asking for your support I shall not dwell on the record of our Administration which has been praised perhaps too generously by others at this convention.

We have made great progress in these past 4 years.

It can truly be said that we have changed America and that America has changed the world. As a result of what we have done, America today is a better place and the world is a safer place to live in than was the case 4 years ago.

We can be proud of that record, but we shall never be satisfied. A record is not something to stand on; it is something to build on.

Tonight I do not ask you to join our new majority because of what we have done in the past. I ask your support of the principles I believe should determine America's future.

The choice in this election is not between radical change and no change. The choice in this election is between change that works and change that won't work.

I begin with an article of faith.

It has become fashionable in recent years to point up what is wrong with what is called the American system. The critics contend it is so unfair, so corrupt, so unjust, that we should tear it down and substitute something else in its place.

I totally disagree. I believe in the American system.

I have traveled to 80 countries in the past 25 years, and I have seen Communist systems, I have seen Socialist systems, I have seen systems that are half Socialist and half free.

Every time I come home to America, I realize how fortunate we are to live in this great and good country.

Every time I am reminded that we have more freedom, more opportunity, more prosperity than any people in the world; that we have the highest rate of growth of any industrial nation; that Americans have more jobs at higher wages than in any country in the world; that our rate of inflation is less than that of any industrial nation; that the incomparable productivity of America's farmers has made it possible for us to launch a winning war against hunger in the United States; and that the productivity of our farmers also makes us the best fed people in the world with the lowest percentage of the family budget going to food of any country in the world.

We can be very grateful in this country that the people on welfare in America would be rich in most of the nations of the world today.

Now, my fellow Americans, in pointing up those things, we do not overlook the fact that our system has its problems.

Our Administration, as you know, has provided the biggest tax cut in history, but taxes are still too high.

That is why one of the goals of our next Administration is to reduce the property tax which is such an unfair and heavy burden on the poor, the elderly, the wage earner, the farmer, and those on fixed incomes.

As all of you know, we have cut inflation in half in this Administration, but we have got to cut it further. We must cut it further so that we can continue to expand on the greatest accomplishment of our new economic policy: For the first time in 5 years wage increases in America are not being eaten up by price increases.

As a result of the millions of new jobs created by our new economic policies, unemployment today in America is less than the peacetime average of the sixties, but we must continue the unparalleled increase in new jobs so that we can achieve the great goal of our new prosperity—a job for every American who wants to work, without war and without inflation. The way to reach this goal is to stay on the new road we have charted to move America forward and not to take a sharp detour to the left, which would lead to a dead end for the hopes of the American people.

This points up one of the clearest choices in this campaign. Our opponents believe in a different philosophy.

Theirs is the politics of paternalism, where master planners in Washington make decisions for people.

Ours is the politics of people—where people make decisions for themselves.

The proposal that they have made to pay $1,000 to every person in America insults the intelligence of the American voters.

Because you know that every politician's promise has a price—the taxpayer pays the bill.

The American people are not going to be taken in by any scheme where Government gives money with one hand and then takes it away with the other.

Their platform promises everything to everybody, but at an increased net in the budget of $144 billion, but listen to what it means to you, the taxpayers of the country. That would mean an increase of 50 percent in what the taxpayers of America pay. I oppose any new spending programs which will increase the tax burden on the already overburdened American taxpayer.

And they have proposed legislation which would add 82 million people to the welfare rolls.

I say that instead of providing incentives for millions of more Americans to go on welfare, we need a program which will provide incentives for people to get off of welfare and to get to work.

We believe that it is wrong for anyone to receive more on welfare than for someone who works. Let us be generous to those who can't work without increasing the tax burden of those who do work.

And while we are talking about welfare, let us quit treating our senior citizens in this country like welfare recipients. They have worked hard all their lives to build America. And as the builders of America, they have not asked for a handout. What they ask for is what they have earned—and that is retirement in dignity and self-respect. Let's give that to our senior citizens.

Now, when you add up the cost of all of the programs our opponents have proposed, you reach only one conclusion: They would destroy the system which has made America number one in the world economically.

Listen to these facts: Americans today pay one-third of all of their income in taxes. If their programs were adopted, Americans would pay over one-half of what they earn in taxes. This means that if their programs are adopted, American wage earners would be working more for the government than they would for themselves.

Once we cross this line, we cannot turn back because the incentive which makes the American economic system the most productive in the world would be destroyed.

Theirs is not a new approach. It has been tried before in countries abroad, and I can tell you that those who have tried it have lived to regret it.

We cannot and we will not let them do this to America.

Let us always be true to the principle that has made America the world's most prosperous nation—that here in America a person should get what he works for and work for what he gets.

Let me illustrate the difference in our philosophies. Because of our free economic system, what we have done is to build a great building of economic wealth and money in America. It is by the far the tallest building in the world and we are still adding to it. Now because some of the windows are broken, they say tear it down and start again. We say, replace the windows and keep building. That is the difference.

Let me turn now to a second area where my beliefs are totally different from those of our opponents.

Four years ago crime was rising all over America at an unprecedented rate. Even our Nation's Capital was called the crime capital of the world. I pledged to stop the rise in crime. In order to keep that pledge, I promised in the election campaign that I would appoint judges to the Federal courts, and particularly to the Supreme Court, who would recognize that the first civil right of every American is to be free from domestic violence.

I have kept that promise. I am proud of the appointments I have made to the courts, and particularly proud of those I have made to the Supreme Court of the United States. And I pledge again tonight, as I did 4 years ago, that whenever I have the opportunity to make more appointments to the courts, I shall continue to appoint judges who share my philosophy that we must strengthen the peace forces as against the criminal forces in the United States.

We have launched an all-out offensive against crime, against narcotics, against permissiveness in our country.

I want the peace officers across America to know that they have the total backing of their President in their fight against crime.

My fellow Americans, as we move toward peace abroad, I ask you to support our programs which will keep the peace at home.

Now, I turn to an issue of overriding importance not only to this election, but for generations to come—the progress we have made in building a new structure of peace in the world.

Peace is too important for partisanship. There have been five Presidents in my political lifetime—Franklin D. Roosevelt, Harry Truman, Dwight Eisenhower, John F. Kennedy, and Lyndon Johnson.

They had differences on some issues, but they were united in their belief that where the security of America or the peace of the world is involved we are not Republicans, we are not Democrats. We are Americans, first, last, and always.

These five Presidents were united in their total opposition to isolation for America and in their belief that the interests of the United States and the interests of world peace require that America be strong enough and intelligent enough to assume the responsibilities of leadership in the world.

They were united in the conviction that the United States should have a defense second to none in the world.

They were all men who hated war and were dedicated to peace.

But not one of these five men and no President in our history believed that America should ask an enemy for peace on terms that would betray our allies and destroy respect for the United States all over the world.

As your President, I pledge that I shall always uphold that proud bipartisan tradition. Standing in this Convention Hall 4 years ago, I pledged to seek an honorable end to the war in Vietnam. We have made great progres toward that end. We have brought over half a million men home and more will be coming home. We have ended America's ground combat role. No draftees are being sent to Vietnam. We have reduced our casualties by 98 percent. We have gone the extra mile, in fact, we have gone tens of thousands of miles trying to seek a negotiated settlement of the war. We have offered a cease-fire, a total withdrawal of all American forces, an exchange of all prisoners of war, internationally supervised free elections with the Communists participating in the elections and in the supervision.

There are three things, however, that we have not and that we will not offer.

We will never abandon our prisoners of war.

Second, we will not join our enemies in imposing a Communist government on our allies—the 17 million people of South Vietnam.

And we will never stain the honor of the United States of America.

Now I realize that many, particularly in this political year, wonder why we insist on an honorable peace in Vietnam. From a political standpoint they suggest that since I was not in office when over a half million American men were sent there, that I should end the war by agreeing to impose a Communist government on the people of South Vietnam and just blame the whole catastrophe on my predecessors.

This might be good politics, but it would be disastrous to the cause of peace in the world. If, at this time, we betray our allies, it will discourage our friends abroad and it will encourage our enemies to engage in aggression.

In areas like the Mideast, which are danger areas, small nations who rely on the friendship and support of the United States would be in deadly jeopardy.

To our friends and allies in Europe, Asia, the Mideast, and Latin America, I say the United States will continue its great bipartisan tradition—to stand by our friends and never to desert them.

Now in discussing Vietnam, I have noted that in this election year there has been a great deal of talk about providing amnesty for those few hundred Americans who chose to desert their country rather than to serve it in Vietnam. I think it is time that we put the emphasis where it belongs. The real heroes are two and one-half million young Americans who chose to serve their country rather than desert it. I say to you tonight, in these times when there is so much of a tendency to run down those who have served America in the past and who serve it today, let us give those who serve in our Armed Forces and those who have served in Vietnam the honor and the respect that they deserve and that they have earned.

Finally, in this connection, let one thing be clearly understood in this election campaign: The American people will not tolerate any attempt by our enemies to interfere in the cherished right of the American voter to make his own decision with regard to what is best for America without outside intervention.

Now it is understandable that Vietnam has been a major concern in foreign policy. But we have not allowed the war in Vietnam to paralyze our capacity to initiate historic new policies to construct a lasting and just peace in the world.

When the history of this period is written, I believe it will be recorded that our most significant contributions to peace resulted from our trips to Peking and to Moscow.

The dialogue that we have begun with the People's Republic of China has reduced the danger of war and has increased the chance for peaceful cooperation between two great peoples.

Within the space of 4 years in our relations with the Soviet Union we have moved from confrontation to negotiation, and then to cooperation in the interest of peace.

We have taken the first step in limiting the nuclear arms race.

We have laid the foundation for further limitations on nuclear weapons and eventually of reducing the armaments in the nuclear area.

We can thereby not only reduce the enormous costs of arms for both our countries, but we can increase the chances for peace.

More than on any other single issue, I ask you, my fellow Americans, to give us the chance to continue these great initiatives that can contribute so much to the future of peace in the world.

It can truly be said that as a result of our initiatives, the danger of war is less today than it was; the chances for peace are greater.

But a note of warning needs to be sounded. We cannot be complacent. Our opponents have proposed massive cuts in our defense budget which would have the inevitable effect of making the United States the second strongest nation in the world.

For the United States unilaterally to reduce its strength with the naive hope that other nations would do likewise would increase the danger of war in the world.

It would completely remove any incentive of other nations to agree to a mutual limitation or reduction of arms.

The promising initiatives we have undertaken to limit arms would be destroyed.

The security of the United States and all the nations in the world who depend upon our friendship and support would be threatened.

Let's look at the record on defense expenditures. We have cut spending in our Administration. It now takes the lowest percentage of our national product in 20 years. We should not spend more on defense than we need. But we must never spend less than we need.

What we must understand is, spending what we need on defense will cost us money. Spending less than we need could cost us our lives or our freedom.

So tonight, my fellow Americans, I say, let us take risks for peace, but let us never risk the security of the United States of America.

It is for that reason that I pledge that we will continue to seek peace and the mutual reduction of arms. The United States, during this period, however, will always have a defense second to none.

There are those who believe that we can entrust the security of America to the good will of our adversaries.

Those who hold this view do not know the real world. We can negotiate limitation of arms and we have done so. We can make agreements to reduce the danger of war, and we have done so.

But one unchangeable rule of international diplomacy that I have learned over many, many years is that, in negotiations between great powers, you can only get something if you have something to give in return.

That is why I say tonight: Let us always be sure that when the President of the United States goes to the conference table, he never has to negotiate from weakness.

There is no such thing as a retreat to peace.

My fellow Americans, we stand today on the threshold of one of the most exciting and challenging eras in the history of relations between nations.

We have the opportunity in our time to be the peacemakers of the world, because the world trusts and respects us, and because the world knows that we shall only use our power to defend freedom, never to destroy it; to keep the peace, never to break it.

A strong America is not the enemy of peace; it is the guardian of peace.

The initiatives that we have begun can result in reducing the danger of arms, as well as the danger of war which hangs over the world today.

Even more important, it means that the enormous creative energies of the Russian people and the Chinese people and the American people and all the great peoples of the world can be turned away from production of war and turned toward production for peace.

In America it means that we can undertake programs for progress at home that will be just as exciting as the great initiatives we have undertaken in building a new structure of peace abroad.

My fellow Americans, the peace dividend that we hear so much about has too often been described solely in monetary terms—how much money we could take out of the arms budget and apply to our domestic needs. By far the biggest dividend, however, is that achieving our goal of a lasting peace in the world would reflect the deepest hopes and ideals of all of the American people.

Speaking on behalf of the American people, I was proud to be able to say in my television address to the Russian people in May: "We covet no one else's territory. We seek no dominion over any other nation. We seek peace not only for ourselves, but for all the people of the world."

This dedication to idealism runs through America's history.

During the tragic War Between the States, Abraham Lincoln was asked whether God was on his side. He replied, "My concern is not whether God is on our side, but whether we are on God's side."

May that always be our prayer for America.

We hold the future of peace in the world and our own future in our hands. Let us reject therefore the policies of those who whine and whimper about our frustrations and call on us to turn inward.

Let us not turn away from greatness.

The chance America now has to lead the way to a lasting peace in the world may never come again.

With faith in God and faith in ourselves and faith in our country, let us have the vision and the courage to seize the moment and meet the challenge before it slips away.

On your television screen last night, you saw the cemetery in Leningrad I visited on my trip to the Soviet Union—where 300,000 people died in the siege of that city during World War II.

At the cemetery I saw the picture of a 12-year-old girl. She was a beautiful child. Her name was Tanya.

I read her diary. It tells the terrible story of war. In the simple words of a child she wrote of the deaths of the members of her family. Zhenya in December. Grannie in January. Then Leka. Then Uncle Vasya. Then Uncle Lyosha. Then Mama in May. And finally—these were the last words in her diary: "All are dead. Only Tanya is left."

Let us think of Tanya and of the other Tanyas and their brothers and sisters everywhere in Russia, in China, in America, as we proudly meet our responsibilities for leadership in the world in a way worthy of a great people.

I ask you, my fellow Americans, to join our new majority not just in the cause of winning an election, but in achieving a hope that mankind has had since the beginning of civilization. Let us build a peace that our children and all the children of the world can enjoy for generations to come.

☆

RICHARD M. NIXON
Campaign Speech
WHITE HOUSE, WASHINGTON, D. C.

November 2, 1972

Good evening:

I am speaking to you tonight from the Library of the White House. This room, like all the rooms in this great house, is rich in history.

Often late at night I sit here thinking of the crises other Presidents have known—and of the trials that other generations of Americans have come through.

I think, too, of the Presidents who will be sitting here a generation from now, and how they will look back on these years. And I think of what I want to accomplish in these years. I would like to share some of those thoughts with you this evening.

Above all, I want to complete the foundations for a world at peace—so that the next generation can be the first in this century to live without war and without the fear of war.

Beyond this, I want Americans—all Americans—to see more clearly and to feel more deeply what it is that makes this Nation of ours unique in history, unique in the world, a nation in which the soul and spirit are free, in which each person is respected, in which the individual human being, each precious, each different, can dare to dream and can live his dreams.

I want progress toward a better life for all Americans—not only in terms of better schools, greater abundance, a cleaner environment, better homes, more attractive communities, but also in a spiritual sense, in terms of greater satisfaction, more kindness in our relations with each other, more fulfillment.

I want each American—-all Americans—to find a new zest in the pursuit of excellence, in striving to do their best and to be their best, in learning the supreme satisfaction of setting a seemingly impossible goal, and meeting or surpassing that goal, of finding in themselves that extra reserve of energy or talent or creativity that they had not known was there.

These are goals of a free people, in a free nation, a nation that lives not by handout, not by dependence on others or in hostage to the whims of others, but proud and independent—a nation of individuals with self-respect and with the right and capacity to make their own choices, to chart their own lives.

That is why I want us to turn away from a demeaning, demoralizing dependence on someone else to make our decisions and to guide the course of our lives.

That is why I want us to turn toward a renaissance of the individual spirit, toward a new vitality of those governments closest to the people, toward a new pride of place for the family and the community, toward a new sense of responsibility in all that we do, responsibility for ourselves and to ourselves, for our communities and to our communities, knowing that each of us, in every act of his daily life, determines what kind of community and what kind of a country we all will live in.

If, together, we can restore this spirit, than 4 years from now America can enter its third century buoyant and vital and young, with all the purpose that marked its beginning two centuries ago.

In these past 4 years, we have moved America significantly toward this goal. We have restored peace at home, and we are restoring peace abroad.

As you know, we have now made a major breakthrough toward achieving our goal of peace with honor in Vietnam. We have reached substantial agreement on most of the terms of a settlement. The settlement we are ready to conclude would accomplish the basic objectives that I laid down in my television speech to the Nation on May 8 of this year:

—the return of all of our prisoners of war, and an accounting for all of those missing in action;
—a cease-fire throughout Indochina; and
—for the 17 million people of South Vietnam, the right to determine their own future without having a Communist government or a coalition government imposed upon them against their will.

However, there are still some issues to be resolved. There are still some provisions of the agreement which must be clarified so that all ambiguities will be removed. I have insisted that these be settled before we sign the final agreement. That is why we refused to be stampeded into meeting the arbitrary deadline of October 31.

Now, there are some who say: "Why worry about the details? Just get the war over!"

Well, my answer is this. My study of history convinces me that the details can make the difference between an agreement that collapses and an agreement that lasts—and equally crucial is a clear understanding by all of the parties of what those details are.

We are not going to repeat the mistake of 1968, when the bombing halt agreement was rushed into just before an election without pinning down the details.

We want peace—peace with honor—a peace fair to all and a peace that will last. That is way I am insisting that the central points be clearly settled, so that there will be no misunderstandings which could lead to a breakdown of the settlement and a resumption of the war.

I am confident that we will soon achieve that goal.

But we are not going to allow an election deadline or any other kind of deadline to force us into an agreement which would be only a temporary truce and not a lasting peace. We are going to sign the agreement when the agreement is right, not one day before. And when the agreement is right, we are going to sign, without one day's delay.

Not only in America, but all around the world, people will be watching the results of our election. The leaders in Hanoi will be watching. They will be watching for the answer of the American people—for your answer—to this question: Shall we have peace with honor or peace with surrender?

Always in the past you have answered "Peace with honor." By giving that same answer once again on November 7 you can help make certain that peace with honor can now be achieved.

In these past 4 years, we have also been moving toward lasting peace in the world at large.

We have signed more agreements with the Soviet Union than were negotiated in all the previous years since World War II. We have established the basis for a new relationship with the People's Republic of China, where one-fourth of all the people in this world live. Our vigorous diplomacy has advanced the prospects for a stable peace in the Middle East. All around the world, we are opening doors to peace, doors that were previously closed. We are developing areas of common interest where there have been previously only antagonisms. All this is a beginning. It can be the beginning of a generation of peace—of a world in which our children can be the first generation in this century to escape the scourge of war.

These next 4 years will set the course on which we begin our third century as a nation. What will that course be? Will it have us turning inward, retreating from the responsibilities not only of a great power but of a great people—of a nation that embodies the ideals man has dreamed of and fought for through the centuries?

We cannot retreat from those responsibilities. If we did America would cease to be a great nation, and peace and freedom would be in deadly jeopardy throughout the world.

Ours is a great and a free nation today because past generations of Americans met their responsibilities. And we shall meet ours.

We have made progress toward peace in the world, toward a new relationship with the Soviet Union and the People's Republic of China, not through naive sentimental assumptions that good will is all that matters, or that we can reduce our military strength because we have no intention of making war and we therefore assume other nations would have no such intention. We have achieved progress through peace for precisely the opposite reasons: because we demonstrated that we would not let ourselves be surpassed in military strength and because we bargained with other nations on the basis of their national interest and ours.

As we look at the real world, it is clear that we will not in our lifetimes have a world free of danger. Anyone who reads history knows that danger has always been part of the common lot of mankind. Anyone who knows the world today knows that nations have not all been suddenly overtaken by some new and unprecedented wave of pure good will and benign intentions. But we can lessen the danger. We can contain it. We can forge a network of relationships and of interdependencies that restrain aggression and that take the profit out of war.

We cannot make all nations the same, and it would be wrong to try. We cannot make all of the world's people love each other. But we can establish conditions in which they will be more likely to live in peace with one another. Tonight I ask for your support as we continue to work toward that great goal.

Here at home, as we look at the progress we have made, we find that we are reaching new levels of prosperity.

We have cut inflation almost in half. The average worker has scored his best gains in 8 years in real spendable earnings. We are creating record numbers of new jobs. We are well on the way to achieving what America has not had since President Eisenhower lived here in the White House: prosperity with full employment, without inflation and without war.

We have lowered the level of violence, and we are finally turning the tide against crime.

I could go on with what we have done—for the environment, for the consumer, for the aging, for the farmer, for the worker, for all Americans —but now we must not look backward to what we have done in the past, but forward to what we will do in the future.

It is traditional for a candidate for election to make all sorts of promises about bold new programs he intends to introduce if elected. This year's Presidential campaign has probably established an all-time record for promises of huge new spending programs for just about anything and everything for everybody imaginable. I have not made such promises in this campaign. And I am not going to do so tonight. Let me tell you why.

In the first place, the sort of bold new programs traditionally promised by candidates are all programs that you—the taxpayer—pay for. The programs proposed by our opponents in this campaign would require a 50-percent increase in Federal taxes in your taxes. I think your taxes are already too high. That is why I oppose any new program which would add to your tax burden.

In the second place, too many campaign promises are just that—campaign promises. I believe in keeping the promises I make, and making only those promises I am confident I can keep. I have promised that I will do all in my power to avoid the need for new taxes. I am not going to promise anything else in the way of new programs that would violate that pledge.

In the third place, my own philosophy of government is not one that looks to new Federal dollars—your dollars—as the solution of every social problem.

I have often said that America became great not because of what government did for people, but because of what people did for themselves. I believe government should free the energies of people to build for themselves and their communities. It should open opportunities, provide incentives, encourage initiative—not stifle initiative by trying to direct everything from Washington.

This does not mean that the Federal Government will abdicate its responsibilities where only it can solve a problem.

It does mean that after 40 years of unprecedented expansion of the Federal Government, the time has come to redress the balance—to shift more people and more responsibility and power back to the States and localities and, most important, to the people, all across America.

In the past 40 years, the size of the Federal budget has grown from $4.6 billion to $250 billion. In that same period, the number of civilian employees of the Federal Government has increased from 600,000 to 2,800,000. And in just the past 10 years the number of Federal grant-in-aid programs has increased from 160 to more than 1,000.

If this kind of growth were projected indefinitely into the future, the result would be catastrophic. We would have an America topheavy with bureaucratic meddling, weighted down by big government, suffocated by taxes, robbed of its soul.

We must not and we will not let this happen to America. That is why I oppose the unrestrained growth of big government in Washington. That is why one of my first priorities in the next 4 years will be to encourage a rebirth and renewal of State and local government. That is why I believe in giving the people in every community a greater say in those decisions that most directly affect the course of their daily lives.

Now, there will be those who will call this negative, who call it a retreat from Federal responsibilities.

I call it affirmative—an affirmation of faith in the people, faith in the individual, faith in each person's ability to choose wisely for himself and for his community.

I call it an affirmation of faith in those principles that made America great, that tamed a continent, that transformed a wilderness into the greatest and strongest and freest nation in the world.

We have not changed. The American people have not grown weak. What has grown weak is government's faith in people. I am determined to see that faith restored.

I am also determined to see another kind of faith restored and strenghtened in America. I speak of the religious faith, the moral and spiritual values that have been so basically a part of our American experience. Man does not live for himself alone, and the strength of our character, the strength of our faith, and the strength of our ideals—these have been the strength of America.

When I think of what America means, I think of all the hope that lies in a vast continent—of great cities and small towns, of factories and farms, of a greater abundance, more widely shared, than the world has ever known, of a constant striving to set right the wrongs that still persist—and I think of 210 million people, of all ages, all persuasions, all races, all stations in life.

More particularly, I think of one person, one child—any child. That child many be black or brown or white, rich or poor, a boy whose family came here in steerage in 1920, or a girl whose ancestors came on the Mayflower in 1620. That one child is America, with a life still ahead, with his eyes filled with dreams, and with the birthright of every American child to a full and equal opportunity to pursue those dreams.

It is for that one child that I want a world of peace and a chance to achieve all that peace makes possible. It is for that one child that I want opportunity, and freedom, and abundance. It is for that one child that I want a land of justice, and order, and a decent respect for the rights and feelings of others.

It is for that one child that I want it said, a generation from now, a century from now, that America in the 1970's had the courage and the vision to meet its responsibilities and to face up to its challenges—to build peace, not merely for our generation but for the next generation; to restore the land, to marshal our resources, not merely for our generation but for the next generation; to guard our values and renew our spirit, not merely for our generation but for the next generation,

It is for that one child that I want these next 4 years to be the best 4 years in the whole history of America.

The glory of this time in our history is that we can do more than ever before—we have the means, we have the skills, we have an increasing understanding of how the great goals that we seek can be achieved.

These are not partisan goals. They are America's goals. That is why I ask you tonight, regardless of party, to join the new American majority next Tuesday in voting for candidates who stand for these goals. That is why I ask for your support—after the election—in helping to move forward toward these goals over the next 4 years.

If we succeed in this task, then that one child—all of our children—can look forward to a life more full of hope, promise, than any generation, in any land, in the whole history of mankind.

Thank you, and good evening.

☆

GEORGE S. McGOVERN

Acceptance Speech

MIAMI BEACH, FLORIDA

July 14, 1972

With a full heart, I accept your nomination. And this afternoon, I crossed the wide Missouri to recommend a running mate of wide vision and deep compassion—Tom Eagleton.

My nomination is all the more precious in that it is the gift of the most open political process in our national history. It is the sweet harvest cultivated by tens of thousands of tireless volunteers—old and young—and funded by literally hundreds of thousands of small contributors. Those who lingered on the edge of despair a brief time ago had been brought into this campaign—heart, hand, head and soul.

I have been the beneficiary of the most remarkable political organization in American history—an organization that gives dramatic proof to the power of love and to a faith that can move mountains.

As Yeats put it: "Count where man's glory most begins and ends, and say, my glory was I had such friends."

This is a nomination of the people, and I hereby dedicate this campaign to the people.

And next January we will restore the government to the people. American politics will never be the same again.

We are entering a new period of important, hopeful change in America comparable to the political ferment released in the eras of Jefferson, Jackson and Roosevelt.

I treasure this nomination especially because it comes after vigorous competition with the ablest men and women our party can offer.

In the months ahead, I covet the help of every Democrat and every Republican and independent who wants America to be the great and good land it can be.

This is going to be a national campaign carried to every part of the nation—North, South, East and West. We are not conceding a single state to Richard Nixon. I want to say to my friend, Frank King, that Ohio may have passed a few times at this convention, but I'm not going to pass Ohio. Governor Gilligan, Ohio may be a little slow counting the votes, but when they come in this November, they are going to show a Democratic victory.

To anyone in this hall or beyond who doubts the ability of Democrats to join together in common cause, I say never underestimate the power of Richard Nixon to bring harmony to Democratic ranks. He is our unwitting unifier and the fundamental issue of this campaign. And all of us together are going to help him recede the pledge he made ten years ago. Next year you won't have Richard Nixon to kick around any more.

We have had our fury and our frustrations in these past months and at this convention.

My old and treasured friend and neighbor, Hubert Humphrey; that gracious and good man from Maine, Ed Muskie; a tough fighter for his beliefs, Scoop Jackson; a brave and spirited woman, Shirley Chisholm; a wise and powerful lawmaker from Arkansas, Wilbur Mills; the man from North Carolina who opened new vistas in education and public excellence, Terry Sanford; the leader who in 1968 combined the travail and the hope of the American spirit, Gene McCarthy.

I was as moved as all of you by the appearance at this convention of the Governor of Alabama, George Wallace, whose votes in the primary showed the depths of discontent in this country, and whose courage in the face of pain and adversity is the mark of a man of boundless will. We all despise the senseless act that disrupted his campaign. Governor, we pray for your speedy and full recovery, so you can stand up and speak out forcefully for all those who see you as their champion.

Well, I frankly welcome the contrast with the smug, dull, and empty event which will take place here in Miami next month. We chose this struggle. We reformed our party and let the people in.

And we stand today not as a collection of backroom strategists, not as a tool of I.T.T. or any other special interest, but as a direct reflection of the public will.

So let our opponents stand on the status quo, while we seek to refresh the American spirit.

Let the opposition collect their $10-million in secret money from the privileged. And let us find one million ordinary Americans who will contribute $25 to this campaign—a McGovern "million-member club" with members who will expect not special favors for themselves but a better land for us all.

In Scripture and in the music of our children we are told: "To everything there is a season, and a time to every purpose under heaven."

And for America, the time has come at last.

This is the time for truth, not falsehood.

In a democratic nation, no one likes to say that his inspiration came from secret arrangements behind closed doors. But in a sense that is how my candidacy began. I am here as your candidate tonight in large part because during four administrations of both parties, a terrible war has been charted behind closed doors.

I want those doors opened, and I want that war closed. And I make these pledges above all others—the doors of government will be open, and that brutal war will be closed.

Truth is a habit of integrity, not a strategy of politics. And if we nurture the habit of candor in this campaign, we will continue to be candid once we are in the White House. Let us say to Americans, as Woodrow Wilson said in his first campaign: "Let me inside [the government] and I will tell you everything that is going on in there."

And this is a time not for death, but for life.

In 1968, Americans voted to bring our sons home from Vietnam in peace—and since then, 20,000 have come home in coffins.

I have no secret plan for peace. I have a public plan.

As one whose heart has ached for 10 years over the agony of Vietnam, I will halt the senseless bombing of Indochina on Inauguration Day.

There will be no more Asian children running ablaze from bombed-out schools.

There will be no more talk of bombing the dikes or the cities of the North.

Within 90 days of my inauguration, every American soldier and every American prisoner will be out of the jungle and out of their cells and back home in America where they belong.

And then let us resolve that never again will we shed the precious young blood of this nation to perpetuate an unrepresentative client abroad.

Let us choose life, not death, this is the time.

This is also the time to turn away from excessive preoccupation overseas to rebuilding our own nation.

American must be restored to her proper role in the world. But we can do that only through the recovery of confidence in ourselves. The greatest contribution America can make to our fellow mortals is to heal our own great but deeply troubled land. We must respond to that ancient command: "Physician, heal thyself."

It is necessary in an age of nuclear power and hostile ideology that we be militarily strong. America must never become a second-rate nation. As one who has tasted the bitter fruits of our weakness before Pearl Harbor, 1941, I give you my sacred pledge that if I become President of the United States, America will keep its defenses alert and fully sufficient to meet any danger. We will do that not only for ourselves, but for those who deserve and need the shield of our strength—our old allies in Europe, and elsewhere, including the people of Israel, who will always have our help to hold their promised land.

Yet we know that for 30 years we have been so absorbed with fear and danger from abroad that we have permitted our own house to fall into disarray. We must now show that peace and prosperity can exist side by side—indeed, each now depends on the other.

National strength includes the credibility of our system in the eyes of our own people as well as the credibility of our deterrent in the eyes of others abroad.

National security includes schools for our children as well as silos for our missiles, the health of our families as much as the size of our bombs, the safety of our streets and the condition of our cities and not just the engines of war.

And if we some day choke on the pollution of our own air, there will be little consolation in leaving behind a dying continent ringed with steel.

Let us protect ourselves abroad and perfect ourselves at home.

This is the time.

And we must make this a time of justice and jobs for all.

For more than three years, we have tolerated stagnation and a rising level of joblessness, with more than five million of our best workers unemployed. Surely this is the most false and wasteful economics.

Our deep need is not for idleness but for new housing and hospitals, for facilities to combat pollution and take us home from work, for products better able to compete on vigorous world markets.

The highest domestic priority of my Administration will be to insure that every American able to work has a job to do. This job guarantee will and must depend upon a reinvigorated private economy, freed at last from the uncertainties and burdens of war.

But it is our commitment that whatever employment the private sector does not provide, the Federal Government will either stimulate, or provide itself. Whatever it takes, this country is going back to work.

America cannot exist with most of our people working and paying taxes to support too many others mired in the demeaning, bureaucratic welfare system. Therefore, we intend to begin by putting millions back to work; and after that is done, we will assure those unable to work an income sufficient to assure a decent life.

Beyond this, a program to put America back to work demands that work be properly rewarded. That means the end of a system of economic controls in which labor is depressed, but prices and corporate profits are the highest in history. It means a system of national health insurance, so that a worker can afford decent health care for himself and his family. It means real enforcement of the laws so that the drug racketeers are put behind bars for good and our streets are once again safe for our families.

Above all, honest work must be rewarded by a fair and just tax system. The tax system today does not reward hard work—it penalizes it. Inherited or invested wealth frequently multiplies itself while paying no taxes at all. But wages earned on the assembly line, or laying bricks, or picking fruit—these hard earned dollars are taxed to the last penny. There is a depletion allowance for oil wells, but no allowance for the depletion of a man's body in years of toil.

The Administration tells us that we should not discuss tax reform in an election year. They would prefer to keep all discussion of the tax code in closed committee rooms, where the Administration, its powerful friends and their paid lobbyists can turn every effort at reform into a new loophole for the rich. But an election year is the people's year to speak—and this year, the people are going to insure that the tax system is changed so that work is rewarded and so that those who derive the highest benefits will pay their fair share, rather than slipping through the loopholes at the expense of the rest of us.

So let us stand for justice and jobs, and against special privilege. This is the time.

We are not content with things as they are. We reject the view of those who say: "America—love it or leave it." We reply: "Let us change it so we can love it the more."

And this is the time. It is the time for this land to become again a witness to the world for what is noble and just in human affairs. It is the time to live more with faith and less with fear—with an abiding confidence that can sweep away the strongest barriers between us and teach us that we truly are brothers and sisters.

So join with me in this campaign, lend me your strength and your support, give me your voice—and together, we will call America home to the founding ideals that nourished us in the beginning.

From secrecy and deception in high places, come home, America.

From a conflict in Indochina which maims our ideals as well as our soldiers, come home, America.

From the entrenchment of special privilege and tax favoritism, come home, America.

From military spending so wasteful that it weakens our nation, come home, America.

From the waste of idle hands to the joy of useful labor, come home, America.

From the prejudice of race and sex, come home, America.

From the loneliness of the aging poor and the despair of the neglected sick, come home, America.

Come home to the affirmation that we have a dream.

Come home to the conviction that we can move our country forward.

Come home to the belief that we can seek a newer world.

For:

> This land is your land,
> This land is my land,
> From California to the New York Island,
> From the Redwood Forest
> To the Gulfstream waters,
> This land was made for you and me.

May God grant us the wisdom to cherish this good land to meet the challenge that beckons us home.

☆

GEORGE S. McGOVERN

Campaign Speech

WASHINGTON, D. C.

August 5, 1972

My fellow citizens:

Last week, as most of you know, Senator Thomas Eagleton withdrew as the Democratic Vice-Presidential nominee. When I learned of his treatment for mental distress, I hoped that his past afflictions would not be allowed to obscure and dominate the public dialogue.

After all, the purpose of psychiatric treatment is to restore the individual to the fullness of his powers. For millions of Americans such treatment has permanently eliminated barriers to a successful life, and who among us has not known the suffering of temporary depression—the feelings which lead many to seek professional help are often similar to these—merely more intense? They can be resolved and overcome and permanently laid to rest.

Senator Eagleton has done this, and his has been no secret victory.

Yet it soon became apparent that a disclosure of psychiatric treatment stirred a powerful sense of uneasiness among many Americans, that this question might obscure and confuse the real choices of this Presidential year, and that could not be permitted.

The scales of judgment did not contain just the careers and ambitions of a few. The issue could not be the medical history of a single man, but whether the American people will turn from the policies of the Nixon Administration to a new leadership whose capacity for thoughtful and constructive change would have their fullest confidence. That is the central issue.

With that decision in the balance and so much more, so many human hopes and so much human anguish, I felt it necessary to pursue my public responsibilities as best I saw them rather than follow the inclinations of my heart. On Tuesday the Democratic National Committee will meet to select a candidate for Vice President. At that time I will recommend the selection of Sargent Shriver as my Presidential running mate.

Mr. Shriver has served with great distinction in a number of high and difficult positions. President Kennedy chose him to organize and direct the Peace Corps, while under President Johnson he was the first director of the Office of Economic Opportunity. He later served as Ambassador to France under both President Johnson and President Nixon. A distinguished business leader, his life has been marked by a special dedication to the needs of the poor and to those who suffer from racial injustice.

I am fully confident of his ability to serve as Vice President of the United States.

And now we can move toward what President Nixon has called the the clearest political choice of the century. I agree with that analysis. It is a choice—this choice of the century between your hopes on one hand and your fears on the other, between today's America and the one you want for your children, between those who believe we must abandon our ideals to present realities and those who wish to shape reality to American ideals.

Four years ago the present Republican Administration assumed the responsibilities of national leaders. They can now be judged, not by their attacks on others but by their own actions. You elected a President who promised to end the war in Vietnam and to halt inflation, an Administration which offered to restore prosperity and replace a welfare system which is unfair both to those it serves and to those who pay for it, and Administration which pledged to make your streets safe, your air cleaner and to reunify a divided and troubled people.

Now they offer four more years of the same men and the same policies which have presided over a continued deterioration of American life.

How can they imagine that this is what you want? Perhaps they think you will accept the claims of success which flow from an election year White House. But they cannot deceive you about the experiences of your own daily lives.

You need no economist to tell you what happens to a week's wages at the supermarket checkout counter, or to the savings of a lifetime when illness strikes. The pronouncements of bureaucratic experts have not removed the fear from your streets or made it easier to send your children to decent schools.

Despite the slogans and pieties of the White House, we are a divided people still. The poor remain still, the jobless remain jobless and we seem to be losing our confidence that difficulties however great can be solved.

Men who must run on such a record are driven to conceal their own failures by trying to awaken your fears. Indeed, they have already begun. This, too, is in the tradition of a party whose nominee predicted that if Franklin Roosevelt were elected, grass would grow in the streets of a hundred cities, the weeds will overrun the fields of millions of farms, their churches and school houses will decay.

But we need not go back that far. In 1960, the Republican nominee said that John Kennedy's domestic policies could only produce cruel inflation, Government interference with every aspect of our economic life, recession or even worse.

But President Nixon did not see his warning fulfilled until his own Administration.

They could not scare the country then, and they will not scare the American people now, for the policies of the Democratic party are a danger only to those who seek power or selfish gain at the expense of the nation's strength and the well-being of its citizens.

And first among those policies that we must pursue is an end to the war in Vietnam. Like President Eisenhower, President Nixon pledged to end the war which he inherited.

Unlike President Eisenhower, he has not kept that pledge in four years. And there is no reason to believe that the President who could not bring peace in four years will be able to produce it in eight years.

After a decade of effort, after spending hundreds of billions of dollars, losing tens of thousand of lives, it is now time to come home.

We have done more than we promised. The rest is up to the people of Southeast Asia.

I will no longer deprive this nation of the honor of bringing peace in order to save the prestige of the warmakers.

I fully understand the dangers of war and the needs of security and adequate defense, but the desire for more money and for new weapons seems to have no limit at all.

We reduce our involvement in Vietnam, and military spending goes on.

We sign an arms control agreement with the Russians, and military spending goes on.

We open up new relations with China, and military spending goes up.

I call for an end to military waste in the defense budget.

My proposed defense budget is actually larger than that of President Eisenhower at the height of the cold war. It is designed like his to satisfy the needs of security rather than the appetites of the military-industrial complex.

It will produce only one white flag when a handful for professionals and industries surrender their claim to money which has wiser and more urgent uses.

And even President Nixon may find it difficult to call us the party of war and the party of surrender in the same campaign.

Our tax reform rests on the simple principle that all citizens should be equally responsible for the burden of taxation. The tax code now fills hundreds of pages. It is riddled with loopholes, special exemptions and shelters, available to those with access to wealth or to legal talent.

Income which is earned on an assembly line or in an office should no longer be more heavily taxed than profits from oil or securities.

Tax reform endangers only those whose ability to avoid taxes has made it necessary for the rest of you to pay more.

Most of us can also agree that our present welfare system must be abolished. Those who can work should have jobs, even if the government must provide them, and all our citizens, those who work and those who cannot, should be assured an adequate income, one which will let them feed and clothe and house their families.

President Nixon himself has proposed an annual guaranteed income. We do not disagree on that principle. But poverty cannot be ended by providing less than people need even for the barest necessities of life. Every worker, and every merchant will do better when poverty gives way to new purchasing power.

These proposals and others will of course be opposed. To the extent opposition is based on misunderstanding or on honest difference of opinion, I will try to clarify the one and debate the other. As for those who attack us in defense of their own power and unjust special privilege, I welcome the struggle. Once we expose the false issues we can perhaps debate more fundamental problems.

We have built the most productive nation in all the history of the world, inhabited by a people of unequal skill and energy. And yet this enormous triumph, this peerless society, is not leading to the rapid enrichment of human life. Factories produce, new buildings go up, technology advances and yet for many Americans life is getting emptier and harder. Work is drained of its real satisfaction while the products of that labor lack the quantities, the qualities which come from pride in their production and concern for the person that will use those products.

Our land is being ravaged while our cities become more painful and more dangerous. Our native impulses toward justice for the unfortunate, the poor and the oppressed seem subdued. It is almost as though we had turned our own creation against ourselves, had forgotten that the purpose of wealth and power is not to increase itself but to enlarge the happiness and well-being of the individual.

It is our task—even our obligation to our children—to seek understanding of these problems and to begin to solve them.

A native poet wrote that, to the pioneers, America was not a place or a way of life but a journey. It was, he said, the stream uncrossed, the promise still untried, the metal sleeping in the mountainside. Now the tracks are cold and the land subdued.

But the chronicle of America, like some great river, sweeps into the future. It cannot be mastered by clinging to threatened banks but only by those who, unafraid and desiring, set out upon powerful and uncertain currents, transforming shifting dangers and change into a trail for a new American journey. This time, not a journey to a distant coast but inward, toward the most powerful aspirations of the human heart.

To make this society, its factories, its institutions, its schools, its government, to serve each person's right to extend all the powers of his humanity to the limits of possibility—that is what Thomas Jefferson meant when he wrote of the pursuit of happiness.

Neither I nor any President can give you this but you can. I do not ask you to believe in me but to believe in yourselves. Yours will be the choice between America's present and those American possibilities between what we are and what we could be.

If those of us seeking positions of leadership can make that choice clear, if we can sweep away illusions and lies and false threats, I have no doubt what will be your answer. It is one Americans have always given before.

For myself, as this campaign begins, I ask only, in the words of Solomon, give me now wisdom and knowledge that I may go out and come in before this people, for who can judge this thy people that is so great.

☆

1976

☆

The Watergate scandal climaxed in August 1974 when Richard Nixon resigned in disgrace from the Presidency. The House Judiciary Committee had voted three counts of impeachment against the President for obstructing justice, abusing presidential power, and violating his constitutional duty to enforce the law by refusing to turn over subpoenaed tapes. This followed the resignation from office of Vice President Spiro Agnew, who had pleaded nolo contendere to a series of charges involving financial corruption. Later exposure of widespread illegal activities by the CIA and the FBI revealed how issues of national security had been exploited for partisan political advantage. It was widely noted that Americans were growing cynical, turning inward, questioning their values, and seeking leaders they could trust. Altogether, this climate made the prospects of a Republican victory in the Bicentennial Year of 1976 seem remote at best.

Long-time Michigan Congressman Gerald Ford had briefly assumed the office of Vice President before becoming President upon Nixon's resignation. Although providing a welcome relief from the gloom of the Nixon White House, Ford soon diminished his own chances for election to the Presidency in 1976 by granting Nixon a full pardon for all offenses. Ford's assertion that he was only seeking to spare the nation further trauma was greeted in the press with great skepticism. Soon thereafter the Congressional elections of 1974 found the Republicans suffering heavy losses.

The new President's troubles mounted as both inflation and a serious recession set in by late 1974. A short-lived Adminstration sponsored public relations campaign featuring WIN (Whip Inflation Now) buttons became the focus of many jokes at the President's expense. Ford used his veto power frequently to oppose Congressional spending and tax reduction plans. The result, however, was that unemployment grew to 9 percent in 1975 and federal deficits burgeoned to a record $60 billion in 1976. To make matters worse for the Administration, by the spring of 1975, after Congress had balked at sending more money to support the South Vietnamese government, the Viet Cong and the North Vietnamese achieved a final military victory.

Ford retained Nixon's Secretary of State Henry Kissinger in office and visited the Soviet Union in the fall of 1974 in order to promote negotiations for another round in the Strategic Arms Limitations Talks begun under his predecessor. To many Republican conservatives, however, Kissinger symbolized the policy of detente, which was becoming increasingly suspect. Ford's choice of Nelson Rockefeller as his Vice Presidential successor was strongly disliked by many Republican conservatives who had long held the former New York Governor to be a prime mover of the liberal wing of the party.

It was in this context that former California Governor Ronald Reagan announced his candidacy in November 1975. The primary season found him making a number of statements that endeared him to the growing sector of Republican conservatives but sounded reminiscent of the ideas espoused in 1964 by Barry Goldwater. This alarmed many potential voters who were otherwise attracted to Reagan's appealing personality. In September 1975, for example, before Reagan entered the race, he made a speech in Chicago that called for authority to have a wide range of social programs transferred back to the states. This change in policy, he said, would save $90 billion and "with such savings, it would be possible to balance the federal budget, make an initial five billion dollar payment on the national debt, and cut the federal personal income tax burden of every American by an average of twenty-three percent." This proposal lay dormant until Ford's managers resurrected it in the winter to force Reagan into providing politically damaging details about budget cuts. Ford himself labeled Reagan's ideas "totally impractical."

The battle between Ford and Reagan turned out to be a close one. While Ford narrowly won New Hampshire, Florida, and Illinois in the early weeks, Reagan bounced back with victories in North Carolina and Texas. The final vote at Kansas City favored Ford over Reagan by a narrow 1187 to 1070. In a private unity meeting with Ford that followed the nomination, Reagan boosted Senator Robert Dole of Kansas for the Vice Presidency. Dole was eventually selected to run but was widely regarded as an overly aggressive campaigner who alienated many voters during his debate against the Democratic Vice Presidential nominee Walter Mondale.

In his acceptance speech on August 19th, President Ford aimed several pointed barbs at the "vote hungry, free spending majority on Capital Hill." Aside from challenging his Democratic Party opponent to debate him, Ford issued no new campaign themes but did deliver what many thought was one of the most effective speeches of his life. He sought to identify himself with the mass of American voters who "pay the taxes and obey the laws. You are the people who make our system work," he intoned. "You are the people who make America what it is. It is from your ranks that I come, and on your side I stand."

A little more than a month before Ford's address, former one-term Georgia Governor Jimmy Carter won the Democratic nomination for President in New York City. Carter's campaign was one of the most startling in all of American History. A naval officer turned peanut farmer and politician, Carter campaigned full time for over a year before the nomination. Noted for his constant smile and his promise that "I will never lie to the American people," Carter possessed a number of capable assistants. These included Gerald Rafshoon, an Atlanta-based advertising executive whose television ads proved effective in early primaries. Being a "born-again" Christian" and seeking to appeal to voters across a wide political spectrum, Carter had the ability to convince voters in small group conversational settings, a skill that proved effective in winning the Iowa caucuses on January 19th.

Rivals for the nomination that year included Senator Birch Bayh of Indiana, Representative Morris Udall of Arizona, former Senator Fred Harris of New Mexico, and Kennedy in-law Sargent Shriver. Carter beat his rivals again in New Hampshire with 30 percent of the vote. He was quickly gaining national exposure. Although the Massachusetts primary found Senator Henry Jackson of Washington beating Carter, the Georgian rebounded in primary victories in Florida and North Carolina against the peripatetic Alabama Governor, George Wallace. By April, when California's Governor Jerry Brown had entered the race, Carter had built up strong momentum that could not be stopped.

On July 15th, Carter told delegates at New York's Madison Square Garden that the United States "has lived through a time of torment. It's now a time for healing. We want to have faith again." The nation could have been spared the "tragedy of Vietnam and Cambodia, the disgrace of Watergate, and the embarrassment of CIA revelations could have been avoided if our government had simply reflected the sound judgment and good common sense and the high moral character of the American people." Choosing liberal Senator Walter Mondale as his running mate, Carter sought to align himself with the pantheon of past Democratic Presidents. He avoided making an issue of the Watergate scandals or the Ford pardon of Nixon.

Carter opened the fall campaign on Labor Day in an unconventional, though symbolic place, President Franklin Roosevelt's "Little White House" in Warm Springs, Georgia. Democrats normally began their fall campaigns in Detroit's Cadillac Square, an important spot to endear them to America's workingmen. But this day Carter was shifting symbols for his nationally televised speech. According to journalist Jules Witcover in his book *Marathon: The Pursuit of the Presidency 1972–1976*:

> The Carter image-enhancers left nothing undone to evoke the memory of Roosevelt. Two of his sons, Franklin, Jr., and James, were on the platform; Graham Jackson, a black accordionist who had been a favorite of FDR's and the subject of a famous photo showing him weeping at the news of Roosevelt's passing, played "Happy Days Are Here Again," which still means FDR to millions of Americans; patients in wheelchairs were up front to hear Carter's speech.

While Carter's speech sought to reinforce Ford's failure to effect national unity and to put people to work, it also called for the decentralization of power.

At first Ford avoided the campaign trail, using what was known as the "Rose Garden" strategy, acting "Presidential" in various appearances at the White House. Nixon had used a similar strategy in 1972. Then on September 15th, Ford delivered a speech to 14,000 people at his alma mater, the University of Michigan. Although hampered by a number of hecklers and the explosion of a cherry bomb, Ford was able to complete his speech. He called for financial assistance to promote "home ownership for every American family that wants to own a home and is willing to work and save for it." He was also highly critical of Carter's repeated pledge to the American people to "trust me." Ford said that "trust is not being all things to all people, but being the same thing to all people."

Carter's ultimate victory in November came after a campaign that featured a debate in which Ford misspoke concerning the fact that

Poland was under Communist domination and Carter's admission in a *Playboy Magazine* interview to having "lust in his heart" for women other than his wife. It was the closest election in the electoral college since 1916, although Carter did edge out Ford by 2 percent in popular votes.

JIMMY CARTER
Acceptance Speech

CHICAGO, ILLINOIS

July 15, 1976

My name is Jimmy Carter, and I'm running for President. It's been a long time since I said those words the first time, and now I've come here, after seeing our great country, to accept your nomination.

I accept it in the words of John F. Kennedy: "With a full and grateful heart—and with only one obligation—to devote every effort of body, mind and spirit to lead our party back to victory and our nation back to greatness."

It's a pleasure to be with all you Democrats and to see that our Bicentennial celebration and our Bicentennial convention has been one of decorum and order without any fights or free-for-alls. Among Democrats, that could only happen once every 200 years.

With this kind of a united Democratic Party, we are ready and eager to take on the Republicans, whichever Republican Party they decide to send against us in November.

1976 will not be a year of politics as usual. It can be a year of inspiration and hope. And it will be a year of concern, of quiet and sober reassessment of our nation's character and purpose—a year when voters have already confounded the experts.

And I guarantee you that it will be the year when we give the government of this country back to the people of this country.

There's a new mood in America.

We have been shaken by a tragic war abroad and by scandals and broken promises at home.

Our people are searching for new voices and new ideas and new leaders.

Although government has its limits and cannot solve all our problems, we Americans reject the view that we must be reconciled to failures and mediocrity, or to an inferior quality of life.

For I believe that we can come through this time of trouble stronger than ever. Like troops who've been in combat, we've been tempered in the fire—we've been disciplined and we've been educated. Guided by lasting and simple moral values, we've emerged idealists without illusions, realists who still know the old dreams of justice and liberty—of country and of community.

This year we have had 30 state primaries, more than ever before, making it possible to take our campaign directly to the people of America—to homes and shopping centers, to factory shift lines and colleges, to beauty parlors, and barber shops, to farmers' markets and union halls.

This has been a long and personal campaign—a kind of humbling experience, reminding us that ultimate political influence rests not with the powerbrokers, but with the people. This has been a time for learning and for the exchange of ideas, a time of tough debate on the important issues facing our country. This kind of debate is part of our tradition, and as Democrats we are heirs to a great tradition.

I have never met a Democratic president, but I've always been a Democrat.

Years ago, as a farm boy sitting outdoors with my family on the ground in the middle of the night, gathered close around a battery radio connected to the automobile battery and listening to the Democratic conventions in far-off cities, I was a long way from the selection process than. I feel much closer to it tonight.

Ours is the party of the man who was nominated by those distant conventions, and who inspired and restored this nation in its darkest hours—Franklin D. Roosevelt.

Ours is the party of a fighting Democrat who showed us that a common man could be an uncommon leader—Harry S. Truman.

Ours is the party of a brave young President who called the young in heart, regardless of age, to seek a New Frontier of national greatness—John F. Kennedy.

And ours is also the party of a great-hearted Texan, who took office in a tragic hour and who went on to do more than any other President in this century to advance the cause of human rights—Lyndon Johnson.

Now our party was built out of the sweatshops of the old Lower East Side, the dark mills of New Hampshire, the blazing hearths of Illinois, the coal mines of Pennsylvania, the hardscrabble farms of the southern coastal plains and the unlimited frontiers of America.

Ours is a party that welcomed generations of immigrants—the Jews, the Irish, the Italians, the Poles, and all the others—enlisted them in its ranks, and fought the political battles that helped bring them into the American mainstream—and they have shaped the character of our party.

That is our heritage. Our party has not been perfect. We've made mistakes and we've been disillusioned. We've seen a wall of leadership and compassion and progress.

Our leaders have fought for every piece of progressive legislation from RFD and REA to Social Security and civil rights. In times of need, the Democrats were there.

But in recent years, our nation has seen a failure of leadership. We've been hurt and we've been disillusioned. We've seen a wall go up that separates us from our own government.

We've lost some precious things that historically have bound our people and our government together.

We feel that moral decay has weakened our country, that it's crippled by a lack of goals and values. And that our public officials have lost faith in us.

We've been a nation adrift too long. We've been without leadership too long. We've had divided and deadlocked government too long. We've been governed by veto too long. We've suffered enough at the hands of a tired and worn-out administration without new ideas, without youth or vitality, without visions, and without the confidence of the American people.

There is a fear that our best years are behind us, but I say to you that our nation's best is still ahead.

Our country has lived through a time of torment. It's now a time for healing.

We want to have faith again!

We want to be proud again!

We *just* want the truth again!

It's time for the people to run the government, and not the other way around.

It's time to honor and strengthen our families and our neighborhoods, and our diverse cultures and customs.

We need a Democratic President and a Congress to work in harmony for a change, with mutual respect for a change, in the open for a change and next year we are going to have that new leadership. You can depend on it.

It's time for America to move and to speak, not with boasting and belligerence, but with a quiet strength—to depend in world affairs not merely on the size of an arsenal but on the nobility of ideas—and to govern at home not by confusion and crisis but with grace and imagination and common sense.

Too many have had to suffer at the hands of a political and economic elite who have shaped decisions and never had to account for mistakes not to suffer from injustice. When unemployment prevails, they never stand in line looking for a job. When deprivation results from a confused and bewildering welfare system, they never do without food or clothing or a place to sleep. When the public schools are inferior or torn by strife, their children go to exclusive private schools. And when the bureaucracy is bloated and confused, the powerful always manage to discover and occupy niches of special influence and privilege. An unfair tax structure serves their needs. And tight secrecy always seems to prevent reform.

All of us must be careful not to cheat each other.

Too often, unholy, self-perpetuating alliances have been formed between money and politics, and the average citizen has been held at arm's length.

Each time our nation has made a serious mistake, the American people have been excluded from the process. The tragedy of Vietnam and Cambodia, the disgrace of Watergate, and the embarrassment of the CIA revelations could have been avoided if our government had simply reflected the sound judgment and good common sense and the high moral character of the American people.

It's time for us to take a new look at our own government, to strip away the secrecy, to expose the unwarranted pressure of lobbyists, to eliminate waste, to release our civil servants from bureaucratic chaos, to provide tough management and always to remember that in any town or city, the mayor, the governor and the President represent exactly the same constituents.

As a governor, I had to deal each day with the complicated and confused and overlapping and wasteful federal government bureaucracy. As President, I want you to help me evolve an efficient, economical, purposeful and manageable government for our nation. Now I recognize the difficulty, but if I'm elected, it's going to be done, and you can depend on it.

We must strengthen the government closest to the people.

Business, labor, agriculture, education, science education, government should not struggle in isolation from one another, but should be able to strive toward mutual goals and shared opportunities.

We should make major investments in people and not in buildings and weapons. The poor, the aged, the weak, the afflicted must be treated with respect and compassion and with love.

Now I have spoken a lot of times this year about love, but love must be aggressively translated into simple justice.

The test of any government is not how popular it is with the powerful, but how honestly and fairly it deals with those who must depend on it.

It's time for a complete overhaul of our income tax system. I still tell you it's a disgrace to the human race. All my life I have heard promises of tax reform, but it never quite happens. With your help, we are finally going to make it happen and you can depend on it.

Here is something that can really help our country.

It's time for universal voter registration.

It's time for a nationwide, comprehensive health program for all our people.

It's time to guarantee an end to discrimination because of race or sex by full involvement in the decision-making processes of government by those who know what it is to suffer from discrimination, and they'll be in the government if I'm elected.

It's time for the law to be enforced. We cannot educate children, we cannot create harmony among our people, we cannot preserve basic human freedom unless we have an orderly society. Now crime and a lack of justice are especially cruel to those who are least able to protect themselves. Swift arrest and trial, and fair and uniform punishment should be expected by anyone who would break our laws.

It's time for our government leaders to respect the law no less than the humblest citizen, so that we can end once and for all a double standard of justice. I see no reason why big shot crooks should be free and the poor ones go to jail.

A simple and a proper function of government is just to make it easy for us to do good and difficult for us to do wrong.

Now as an engineer, a planner and a businessman, I see clearly the value to our nation of a strong system of free enterprise based on increased productivity and adequate wages. We Democrats believe that competition is better than regulation. And we intend to combine strong safeguards for consumers with minimal intrusion of government in our free economic system.

I believe that anyone who is able to work ought to work—and ought to have a chance to work. We'll never end the inflationary spiral, we'll never have a balanced budget, which I am determined to see, as long as we have eight or nine million Americans out of work who cannot find a job.

Now any system of economics is bankrupt if it sees either value or virtue in unemployment. We simply cannot check inflation by keeping people out of work.

The foremost responsibility of any President above all else is to guarantee the security of our nation—a guarantee of freedom from the threat of successful attack or blackmail and the ability with our allies to maintain peace.

But peace is not the mere absence of war. Peace is action to stamp out international terrorism. Peace is the unceasing effort to preserve human rights. And peace is a combined demonstration of strength and good will. We'll pray for peace and we'll work for peace, until we have removed from all nations for all time the threat of nuclear destruction.

America's birth opened a new chapter in mankind's history. Ours was the first nation to dedicate itself clearly to basic moral and philosophical principles:

That all people are created equal and endowed with inalienable rights to life, liberty and the pursuit of happiness; and that the power of government is derived from the consent of the governed.

This national commitment was a singular act of wisdom and courage, and it brought the best and the bravest from other nations to our shores.

It was a revolutionary development that captured the imagination of mankind.

It created the basis for a unique role for America—that of a pioneer in shaping more decent and just relations among people and among societies.

Today, 200 years later, we must address ourselves to that role both in what we do at home and how we act abroad—among people everywhere who have become politically more alert, socially more congested and increasingly impatient with global inequities, and who are now organized as you know, into some 50 different nations.

This calls for nothing less than a sustained architectural effort to shape an international framework of peace within which our own ideals gradually can become a global reality.

Our nation should always derive its character directly from the people and let this be the strength and the image to be presented to the world—the character of the American people.

To our friends and allies I say that what unites us through our common dedication to democracy is much more important than that in which occasionally divides us on economics or politics.

To the nations that seek to free themselves from poverty, I say that America shares your aspirations and extends its hand to you.

To those nation-states that wish to compete with us, I say that we neither fear competition nor see it as an obstacle to wider cooperation.

And to all people I say that after many years America still remains confident and youthful in its commitment to freedom and equality, and we always will be.

During this election year, we candidates will ask you for your votes, and from us will be demanded our vision.

My vision of this nation and its future has been deepened and matured during the 19 months that I have campaigned among you for President.

I've never had more faith in America than I do today.

We have an America that, in Bob Dylan's phrase, is busy being born, not in dying.

We can have an American government that's turned away from scandal and corruption and official cynicism and is once again as decent and competent as any people.

We can have an America that has reconciled its economic needs with its desire for an environment that we can pass on with pride to the next generation.

We can have an America that provides excellence in education to my child and your child and every child.

We can have an America that encourages and takes pride in our ethnic diversity, our religious diversity, our cultural diversity knowing that out of this pluralistic heritage has come the strength and the vitality and the creativity that made us great and will keep us great.

We can have an American government that does not oppress or spy on its own people, but respects our dignity and our privacy and our right to be let alone.

We can have an America where freedom on the one hand and equality on the other hand are mutually supportive and not in conflict, and where the dreams of the nation's first leaders are fully realized in our own day and age.

And we can have an America that harnesses the idealism of the student, the compassion of the nurse or the social worker, the determination of the farmer, the wisdom of a teacher, the practicality of the business leader, the experience of the senior citizen and the hope of a laborer to build a better life for us all, and we can have it and we are gonna have it.

As I've said many times before, we need to have an American President who does not govern with negativism and fear of the future, but with vigor and vision and aggressive leadership—a President who is not isolated from the people, but who shares your pain and shares your dreams, takes his strength and his wisdom and his courage from you.

I see an America on the move again, united, a diverse and vital and tolerant nation, entering our third century with pride and confidence—an America that lives up to the majesty of our Constitution and the simple decency of our people.

This is the America we want.

This is the America that we will have.

We'll go forward from this convention with some differences of opinion, perhaps, but nevertheless united in a calm determination to make our country large and driving and generous in spirit once again, ready to embark on great national deeds. And once again, as brothers and sisters, our hearts will swell with pride to call ourselves Americans.

Thank you very much.

☆

JIMMY CARTER
Campaign Speech
LOS ANGELES, CALIFORNIA

August 30, 1976

Delivered before the Town Hall Forum

During the past week, when the attention of the political world was focused on the events in Kansas City, I spent most of my time at my home in Plains, Georgia, reading, studying national issues, talking with friends and advisers, and trying to sort out my thoughts as I look ahead to the Presidential campaign.

I want to share some of those thoughts with you today and I want to say at the outset that my mood is one of confidence and optimism. Not simply optimism over my own immediate political prospects, but optimism about the future of this country.

I think, and I believe the American people agree, that this is one of our most important elections, that this is one of those elections, as in 1932 and 1960, when we have a chance to break with the past and make a fresh start in our national affairs.

Every election is unique, of course. In 1932 our nation faced an economic disaster, and our people correctly judged that Franklin Roosevelt was the candidate whose personal character and political courage made him best qualified to lead us through that crisis.

In 1960 we faced not an economic crisis but a state of spiritual malaise, a sense of national drift, and the people correctly judged that John Kennedy, with all his youth and vigor, could keep his promise to get the country moving again, as in fact he did.

Today, as we face the election of 1976, I think there is a feeling in the land, much like those of 1932 and 1960, that we face an economic crisis, and that we are drifting and need to get moving again. But there is something more than that. After all we have been through in recent years, we need to have our faith in our government restored. We want to believe once again that our national leaders are honorable and competent and deserving of our trust. For if we cannot believe that, little else matters.

I have thought for some time that this year's campaign was taking place on two distinct levels. At our level, and quite properly, there is policy, and the economy. In many hundreds of public forums I have discussed all these issues with our people for 20 months, and later this month I will make statements on defense and veterans' affairs, agriculture and economics. But today I would like to discuss with you the other level of this year's campaign, the less tangible issue, which is simply the desire of the American people to have faith again in our own government.

We have been through too much in too short a time. Our national nightmare began with the assassination of John Kennedy, and went on to include the assassination of Robert Kennedy, and of Martin Luther King, Jr., and the wounding of George Wallace. We watched the widespread opposition to the war in Vietnam, and the division and bitterness that war caused, and the violence in Chicago in 1968, and the invasion of Cambodia, and the shootings at Kent State, and revelations of official lying and spying and bugging, the resignations in disgrace of both Richard Nixon and Spiro Agnew, and a disclosure that our top security and law enforcement agencies were deliberately and routinely violating the law.

No other generation in American history has ever been subjected to such a battering as this. Small wonder, then, that the politics of 1976 have turned out to be significantly different from years past. I doubt that four years ago or eight years ago a former Southern governor with no national reputation and no Washington experience would have been able to win the Democratic nomination for President. But this year many voters were looking for new leaders, leaders who were not associated with the mistakes of the past.

This is suggested not only by my own campaign, but by the success that Governor Jerry Brown achieved in several of the Democratic primaries. For, however else we may differ, Governors Brown and Reagan and I have in common the fact that we are all outsiders as far as Washington is concerned, and committed to major changes in our nation's government if elected President.

To want a change, to want a fresh start, to want government that is honest and competent again, is not a partisan issue. Democrats and Republicans, liberals and conservatives, all share those fundamental concerns.

In the last analysis, good government is not a matter of being liberal or conservative. Good government is the art of doing what is right, and that is far more difficult. To be liberal or conservative requires only ideology; to do what is right requires sensitivity and wisdom.

I think that most Americans are not very ideological. Most Americans share a deep-seated desire for two goals that might, to an ideological person seem contradictory. We want both progress and preservation.

We want progress because progress is the very essence of our American dream—the belief that each generation, through hard work, can give a better life to its children. And increasingly in this century we have realized that it is a proper function of government to help make that dream come true.

But we do not want reckless change. We want to preserve what is best in our past—our political traditions, our cultural heritage, our physical resources—as guideposts to our future.

To walk the line between progress and preservation, between too much change and too little, is no easy task. It cannot be achieved by the extremists of either side, by those who scorn the past or those who fear the future. It can only be accomplished by leaders who are independent and imaginative and flexible in their thinking, and are guided not by closed minds but by common sense.

That is the kind of leadership the American people are looking for this year, and that is the kind of leadership that, if elected, I intend to provide.

As I have observed the political world in recent years, it has seemed to me that there is a process at work, in both political parties and probably in all nations, by which over a period of time the political leadership becomes isolated from, and different from, the people they are supposed to serve.

It seems almost inevitable that if political leaders stay in power too long, and ride in limousines too long, and eat expensive meals in private clubs too long, they are going to become cut off from the lives and concerns of ordinary Americans. It is almost like a law of nature— as Lord Acton said, power tends to corrupt.

I think this process reached a peak a few years ago, when we had a President who surrounded himself with people who knew everything in the world about merchandising and manipulation and winning elections, and nothing at all about the hopes and fears and dreams of average people.

When government becomes cut off from its people, when its leaders are talking only to themselves instead of addressing reality, then it is time for a process of national self-renewal, time to look outside the existing governing class for new leaders with new ideas. I think that is what happened in the Democratic party this year. I think our party was ready for renewal, for new faces, for a changing of the guard. If the candidate had not been myself, I think we would have chosen someone else who was not part of the old order of things.

My sense is that millions of Americans feel that this is the year in which they will give the system one last chance. They do not want to be disillusioned again. They are going to study the candidates, examine our political records and our personal ability and character, and make a judgment as to which candidate can best restore competence and vision and honesty to our government.

I welcome their scrutiny, and have confidence in their judgment.

Obviously there are some outstanding political leaders in Washington—one of the most outstanding, Senator Mondale, is my running mate—and yet I think our people are correct in seeking leadership from outside Washington, new leadership which can approach the executive branch of government with fresh eyes and an open mind.

As a governor, I have been on the receiving end of our federal programs. Members of Congress may see the new programs on the drawing board, or hear about their theories, but governors and local and state officials deal with the realities. I have wrestled with the unnecessary regulations, and the paperwork and red tape and the overlapping jurisdictions. I know what it is to try to start a state drug-treatment program and have to negotiate with almost a dozen different federal agencies that have separate legal responsibility for the drug problem.

Let me say that, on the basis of my experience, I have never been more serious or more determined in my life than when I promise to carry out a complete reorganization of the executive branch of government.

Let me say also, in case there is any question in anyone's mind, that I am not anti-government. I am anti-waste in government. I don't believe in give-away programs. I don't believe in wasting money. I do believe in tough, competent management, and I have tried to practice it as a naval officer, as a farmer, as a businessman, and as a governor. I also believe in delivering services to those people who need those services in an efficient, economical, and sensitive way. That is not liberal or conservative. It's just good government, and that's what the American people want, and what I intend to provide.

I think the basic issue in this campaign is going to be whether we want government that looks confidently to the future, or government that clings fearfully to the past.

There's a song in the musical "Oklahoma" called "Everything's Up to Date in Kansas City." But I didn't think everything was up to date in Kansas City last week. We kept hearing the same old tired rhetoric about socialism and reckless spending that we've been hearing every four years since the Roosevelt years. I don't think the American people are much impressed by that kind of rhetoric. The American people don't believe that Social Security and Medicare were reckless spending, or that TVA and the minimum wage were socialism. The American people consider the source of those charges, and look at the record, and aren't deceived by the nay-sayers.

One of the real issues in this campaign is going to be President Ford's record of vetoes. It is a record that I cite more in sorrow than in anger, for it is a record of political insensitivity, of missed opportunities, of constant conflict with the Congress, and of national neglect.

In six years as President, Mr. Ford's predecessor vetoed 41 bills that had been passed by Congress. In only two years, Ford has already vetoed 53 bills, about four times as many bills per year as his predecessor—and to be four times as negative as Mr. Ford's predecessor is a remarkable achievement.

What did these vetoes accomplish? Did they save us from wasteful, reckless spending, as the Administration would like us to believe? I think not.

One of the bills President Ford vetoed was the Emergency Employment Act, which would have created nearly two million full and part-time jobs, to help those millions of Americans who have been rendered jobless by Republican economic policies. I think our government has a responsibility to help those people get back to work. When people can't find jobs, we pay the price over and over in increased costs of welfare and unemployment compensation and lost tax revenues.

Congress also passed a bill that would have granted those unemployed homeowners temporary help in meeting their mortgage payments. I think that was a responsible action for Congress to take. But Mr. Ford vetoed the bill.

When people are out of work, they and their children still have to eat, and Congress passed the School Lunch Act, to increase the number of families whose children were eligible for school lunch subsidies. But Mr. Ford vetoed that bill.

I had occasion, very close to home, to see what that kind of veto could mean to the real people who were on the receiving end of it. I know a young teacher who taught a remedial class for first-graders in the Plains Elementary School. Most of the students in this special class happened to be black, and were having a hard time getting started in school because of the devastating poverty in which they had been raised.

Free milk was provided twice a day, in the morning and at lunch, for needy students, but then there was a cutback and the morning milk was eliminated. So the young teacher began using her own money to see that all her students had milk. And when she ran out of money she went to her father and he saw to it that her students had milk every morning.

That is the sort of thing that happens when our leaders ignore the human factor in government, when they think in terms of statistics and economic theories instead of in terms of real human needs.

These leaders are so short-sighted. Doesn't it make more sense to spend money on milk and education today, to help children get a fair start in life, than to spend money on police and courts and jails ten years from now, when those children have grown up untrained for a productive life and turned against a society that treated their needs with indifference?

It has been my experience in government that the most profitable investment is in people, and that is the rule I will follow if I become your President.

There were many other vetoes. Mr. Ford vetoed a bill to provide loans and grants to train nurses. He vetoed a bill to send more doctors to rural areas and inner-city slums where there are far too few doctors. He vetoed a bill to provide job training and college educations for Vietnam veterans, the most unappreciated heroes in our nation's history.

These vetoes haven't helped our economy. They haven't balanced the budget—far from it. They have only contributed to needless human suffering.

An occasional veto may be justified, if legislation is poorly drafted or ill-considered, but 53 vetoes in two years demonstrates a negativism, a dormancy, and a fear of action that can only be harmful to this country. There is something seriously wrong when the members of Congress, all of whom were elected by the people, repeatedly pass legislation the country needs, only to have it vetoed by an appointed President. I believe those men and women in Congress are a great deal closer to the national mood than Mr. Ford has shown himself to be.

We have had enough of government by veto. It is time we had a President who will lead our nation, and who will work in harmony with Congress for a change, with mutual respect for a change, out in the open for a change, so the working families of this country can be represented as well as the rich and the powerful and the special interest groups.

Another major issue this fall is going to be the state of our nation's economy. Republicans have a long tradition of mishandling the economy, one that goes back to Herbert Hoover. Except in election years, when they sometimes manage to make the economy pick up by temporarily adopting Democratic economic programs.

During the Eisenhower, Nixon and Ford Administrations, we had five recessions. Under Kennedy and Johnson we had none. And we all know that recessions are hardest on those people who are weakest, who are poor and uneducated and isolated, who are confused and inarticulate, who are often unemployed and chronically dependent—in short, those members of society whom a good government would be trying hardest to help.

Do you know what the basic Republican anti-inflation policy has been? To put people out of work. Cooling down the economy, they call it, because that sounds nicer. I say to you that any economic policy that sees virtue in unemployment is morally and politically and intellectually bankrupt.

What's more, those policies have been dismal failures. In 1968, the last year of a Democratic administration, the unemployment rate was 3.6%. Today it's more than twice that—about 7.8% and rising. Under Kennedy and Johnson the average annual rate of inflation was 2%. During the Nixon and Ford administrations it has been almost 7%.

With all this human suffering, has the Republican administration balanced the budget? In the last three years, the accumulated deficits are about $160 billion, more than the previous 30 years combined. Under Kennedy and Johnson, the average deficit was less than $4 billion. Under Nixon and Ford the average deficit has been more than $24 billion a year.

In short, the Republican economic policies have not worked, and

I believe they have failed to work because they were the creations of people who put economic theories and special interests ahead of the realities of human need in this country.

There are many other problems and many other issues in this campaign. I have been speaking about the breakdown of the American family, and I mentioned that among young people the second most prevalent cause of death is suicide and that in the past ten years the gonorrhea rate has tripled among children 14 years of age or younger.

I sensed that some people thought I shouldn't use those words, suicide and gonorrhea, because they are ugly words describing unpleasant facts. But there are many unpleasant problems in our society—children who need food, overcrowded jails and mental institutions, inadequate treatment for the young men who were maimed in Vietnam, and the heartbreak and family disintegration that unemployment can bring.

All these are ugly problems and it is a natural human instinct for us to want to tune them out. But we cannot tune them out. We can only succeed in tuning out our own humanity, including those qualities of compassion and concern without which no society, however rich or powerful, can be truly great.

"No man is an island," John Donne wrote many years ago; we are all part of the mainland of humanity. That is still true today, and as American citizens, most of us blessed with a good education and influence in society, we cannot ignore the needs and suffering of our less fortunate fellow citizens—not if we want this nation to remain great.

"Ask not for whom the bell tolls," Donne went on to say; "it tolls for thee."

I think there is a bell tolling for all of us this year.

It is asking us what kind of America we want.

It is asking whether once again an American President can inspire patriotism and pride in all of our people.

It is asking if we can tear down the walls that have divided different races and different religions and different regions in America, and once more be a united nation.

It is asking if we are indeed a tired, worn out, cynical nation, or if we can once more be moved by optimism and hope and love for our fellow human beings.

It is asking if through our democratic system we can once again give this nation a government as competent and as good as our people.

I believe we can. We have lived through a time of torment, and now we are ready for a time of healing. I believe we are ready for new leadership, leaders who come from the people and who speak to the people and who care about the people. I believe we have reached a turning point in our national history, a time of cleansing and rededication, and I promise you I will do all in my power to bring this nation back to the greatness we deserve and that the world expects of us.

Thank you.

☆

GERALD R. FORD
Acceptance Speech
KANSAS CITY, MISSOURI

August 19, 1976

Mr. Chairman, delegates and alternates to this Republican Convention:

I am honored by your nomination, and I accept it with pride, with gratitude, and with a total will to win a great victory for the American people. We will wage a winning campaign in every region of this country, from the snowy banks of Minnesota to the sandy plains of Georgia. We concede not a single State. We concede not a single vote.

This evening I am proud to stand before this great convention as the first incumbent President since Dwight D. Eisenhower who can tell the American people: America is at peace.

Tonight, I can tell you straightaway this Nation is sound, this Nation is secure, this Nation is on the march to full economic recovery and a better quality of life for all Americans.

And I will tell you one more thing. This year the issues are on our side. I am ready, I am eager to go before the American people and debate the real issues face to face with Jimmy Carter. The American people have a right to know firsthand exactly where both of us stand.

I am deeply grateful to those who stood with me in winning the nomination of the party whose cause I have served all of my adult life. I respect the convictions of those who want a change in Washington. I want a change, too. After 22 long years of majority misrule, let's change the United States Congress.

My gratitude tonight reaches far beyond this arena to countless friends whose confidence, hard work, and unselfish support have brought me to this moment. It would be unfair to single out anyone, but may I make an exception for my wonderful family—Mike, Jack, Steve and Susan, and especially my dear wife Betty.

We Republicans have had some tough competition. We not only preach the virtues of competition, we practice them. But tonight we come together not on a battlefield to conclude a cease-fire, but to join forces on a training field that has conditioned us all for the rugged contest ahead.

Let me say this from the bottom of my heart. After the scrimmages of the past few months, it really feels good to have Ron Reagan on the same side of the line.

To strengthen our championship lineup, the convention has wisely chosen one of the ablest Americans as our next Vice President, Senator Bob Dole of Kansas. With his help, with your help, with the help of millions of Americans who cherish peace, who want freedom preserved, prosperity shared, and pride in America, we will win this election.

I speak not of a Republican victory, but a victory for the American people. You at home listening tonight, you are the people who pay the taxes and obey the laws. You are the people who make our system work. You are the people who make America what it is. It is from your ranks that I come and on your side that I stand.

Something wonderful happened to this country of ours the past 2 years. We all came to realize it on the Fourth of July. Together, out of years of turmoil and tragedy, wars and riots, assassinations and wrong-doing in high places, Americans recaptured the Spirit of 1776. We saw again the pioneer vision of our revolutionary founders and our immigrant ancestors. Their vision was of free men and free women enjoying limited government and unlimited opportunity.

The mandate I want in 1976 is to make this vision a reality, but it will take the voices and the votes of many more Americans who are not Republicans to make that mandate binding and my mission possible.

I have been called an unelected President, an accidental President. We may even hear that again from the other party, despite the fact that I was welcomed and endorsed by an overwhelming majority of their elected representatives in the Congress who certified my fitness to our highest office.

Having become Vice President and President without expecting or seeking either, I have a special feeling toward these high offices. To me, the Presidency and the Vice Presidency were not prizes to be won, but a duty to be done.

So, tonight, it is not the power and the glamor of the Presidency that leads me to ask for another 4 years. It is something every hard-working American will understand—the challenge of a job well begun, but far from finished.

Two years ago, on August 9, 1974, I placed my hand on the Bible, which Betty held, and took the same constitutional oath that was administered to George Washington. I had faith in our people, in our institutions, and in myself.

"My fellow Americans," I said, "our long national nightmare is over." It was an hour in our history that troubled our minds and tore at our hearts. Anger and hatred had risen to dangerous levels, dividing friends and families. The polarization of our political order had aroused unworthy passions of reprisal and revenge. Our governmental system was closer to stalemate than at any time since Abraham Lincoln took that same oath of office.

Our economy was in the throes of runaway inflation, taking us head-long into the worst recession since Franklin D. Roosevelt took the same oath. On that dark day I told my fellow countrymen, "I am acutely aware that you have not elected me as your President by your ballots, so I ask you to confirm me as your President with your prayers."

On a marble fireplace in the White House is carved a prayer which John Adams wrote. It concludes, "May none but honest and wise men ever rule under this roof." Since I have resided in that historic house, I have tried to live by that prayer. I faced many tough problems. I probably made some mistakes, but on balance, America and Americans have made an incredible comeback since August 1974. Nobody can honestly say otherwise. And the plain truth is that the great progress we have made at home and abroad was in spite of the majority who run the Congress of the United States.

For 2 years I have stood for all the people against a vote-hungry, free-spending congressional majority on Capitol Hill. Fifty-five times I vetoed extravagant and unwise legislation; 45 times I made those vetoes stick. Those vetoes have saved American taxpayers billions and billions of dollars. I am against the big tax spender and for the little taxpayer.

I called for a permanent tax cut, coupled with spending reductions, to stimulate the economy and relieve hard-pressed middle-income taxpayers. Your personal exemption must be raised from $750 to $1,000. The other party's platform talks about tax reform, but there is one big problem—their own Congress won't act.

I called for reasonable constitutional restrictions on court-ordered busing of schoolchildren, but the other party's platform concedes that busing should be a last resort. But here is the same problem—their own Congress won't act.

I called for a major overhaul of criminal laws to crack down on crime and illegal drugs. The other party's platform deplores America's $90 billion cost of crime. There is the problem again—their own Congress won't act.

The other party's platform talks about a strong defense. Now, here is the other side of the problem—their own Congress did act. They slashed $50 billion from our national defense needs in the last 10 years.

My friends, Washington is not the problem, their Congress is the problem.

You know, the President of the United States is not a magician who can wave a wand or sign a paper that will instantly end a war, cure a recession, or make bureaucracy disappear. A President has immense powers under the Constitution, but all of them ultimately come from the American people and their mandate to him.

That is why, tonight, I turn to the American people and ask not only for your prayers, but also for your strength and your support, for your voice and for your vote. I come before you with a 2-year record of performance, without your mandate. I offer you a 4-year pledge of greater performance with your mandate.

As Governor Al Smith used to say, "Let's look at the record." Two years ago, inflation was 12 percent. Sales were off. Plants were shut down. Thousands were being laid off every week. Fear of the future was throttling down our economy and threatening millions of families.

Let's look at the record since August 1974. Inflation has been cut in half. Payrolls are up. Profits are up. Production is up. Purchases are up. Since the recession was turned around almost 4 million of our fellow Americans have found new jobs or got their old jobs back. This year, more men and women have jobs than ever before in the history of the United States. Confidence has returned and we are in the full surge of sound recovery to steady prosperity.

Two years ago America was mired in withdrawal from Southeast Asia. A decade of Congresses had shortchanged our global defenses and threatened our strategic posture. Mounting tension between Israel and the Arab nations made another war seem inevitable. The whole world watched and wondered where America was going. Did we in our domestic turmoil have the will, the stamina, and the unity to stand up for freedom?

Look at the record since August, 2 years ago. Today, America is at peace and seeks peace for all nations. Not a single American is at war anywhere on the face of this earth tonight.

Our ties with Western Europe and Japan, economic as well as military, were never stronger. Our relations with Eastern Europe, the Soviet Union, and mainland China are firm, vigilant, and forward-looking. Policies I have initiated offer sound progress for the peoples of the Pacific, Africa, and Latin America. Israel and Egypt, both trusting the United States, have taken an historic step that promises an eventual just settlement for the whole Middle East.

The world now respects America's policy of peace through strength. The United States is again the confident leader of the free world. Nobody questions our dedication to peace, but nobody doubts our willingness to use our strength when our vital interests are at stake, and we will.

I called for an up-to-date, powerful Army, Navy, Air Force, and Marines that will keep America secure for decades. A strong military posture is always the best insurance for peace. But America's strength has never rested on arms alone. It is rooted in our mutual commitment of our citizens and leaders in the highest standards of ethics and morality and in the spiritual renewal which our Nation is undergoing right now.

Two years ago, people's confidence in their highest officials, to whom they had overwhelmingly entrusted power, had twice been shattered. Losing faith in the word of their elected leaders, Americans lost some of their own faith in themselves.

Again, let's look at the record since August 1974. From the start, my administration has been open, candid, forthright. While my entire public and private life was under searching examination for the Vice Presidency, I reaffirmed my life-long conviction that truth is the glue that holds government together—not only government but civilization, itself. I have demanded honesty, decency, and personal integrity from everybody in the executive branch of the Government. The House and Senate have the same duty.

The American people will not accept a double standard in the United States Congress. Those who make our laws today must not debase the reputation of our great legislative bodies that have given us such giants as Daniel Webster, Henry Clay, Sam Rayburn, and Robert A. Taft. Whether in the Nation's Capital, the State capital, or city hall, private morality and public trust must go together.

From August of 1974 to August of 1976, the record shows steady progress upward toward prosperity, peace, and public trust. My record is one of progress, not platitudes. My record is one of specifics, not smiles. My record is one of performance, not promises. It is a record I am proud to run on. It is a record the American people—Democrats, Independents, and Republicans alike—will support on November 2.

For the next 4 years I pledge to you that I will hold to the steady course we have begun. But I have no intention of standing on the record alone. We will continue winning the fight against inflation. We will go on reducing the dead weight and impudence of bureaucracy.

We will submit a balanced budget by 1978. We will improve the quality of life at work, at play, and in our homes and in our neighborhoods. We will not abandon our cities. We will encourage urban programs which assure safety in the streets, create healthy environments, and restore neighborhood pride.

We will return control of our children's education to parents and local school authorities. We will make sure that the party of Lincoln remains the party of equal rights. We will create a tax structure that is fair for all our citizens, one that preserves the continuity of the family home, the family farm, and the family business.

We will ensure the integrity of the social security system and improve Medicare so that our older citizens can enjoy the health and the happiness that they have earned. There is no reason they should have to go broke just to get well.

We will make sure that this rich Nation does not neglect citizens who are less fortunate, but provides for their needs with compassion and with dignity. We will reduce the growth and the cost of government and allow individual breadwinners and businesses to keep more of the money that they earn.

We will create a climate in which our economy will provide a meaningful job for everyone who wants to work and a decent standard of life for all Americans. We will ensure that all of our young people have a better chance in life than we had, an education they can use, and a career they can be proud of.

We will carry out a farm policy that assures a fair market price for the farmer, encourages full production, leads to record exports, and eases the hunger within the human family. We will never use the bounty of America's farmers as a pawn in international diplomacy. There will be no embargoes.

We will continue our strong leadership to bring peace, justice, and economic progress where there is turmoil, especially in the Middle East. We will build a safer and saner world through patient negotiations and dependable arms agreements which reduce the danger of conflict and horror of thermonuclear war. While I am President, we will not return to a collision course that could reduce civilization to ashes.

We will build an America where people feel rich in spirit as well as in worldly goods. We will build an America where people feel proud about themselves and about their country.

We will build on performance, not promises; experience, not expediency; real progress instead of mysterious plans to be revealed in some dim and distant future.

The American people are wise, wiser than our opponents think. They know who pays for every campaign promise. They are not afraid of the truth. We will tell them the truth.

From start to finish, our campaign will be credible; it will be responsible. We will come out fighting, and we will win. Yes, we have all seen the polls and the pundits who say our party is dead. I have heard that before. So did Harry Truman. I will tell you what I think. The only polls that count are the polls the American people go to on November 2.

And right now, I predict that the American people are going to say that night, "Jerry, you have done a good job, keep right on doing it."

As I try in my imagination to look into the homes where families are watching the end of this great convention, I can't tell which faces are Republicans, which are Democrats, and which are Independents. I cannot see their color or their creed. I see only Americans.

I see Americans who love their husbands, their wives, and their children. I see Americans who love their country for what it has been and what it must become. I see Americans who work hard, but who are willing to sacrifice all they have worked for to keep their children and their country free.

I see Americans who in their own quiet way pray for peace among nations and peace among themselves. We do love our neighbors, and we do forgive those who have trespassed against us.

I see a new generation that knows what is right and knows itself, a generation determined to preserve its ideals, its environment, our Nation, and the world.

My fellow Americans, I like what I see. I have no fear for the future of this great country. And as we go forward together, I promise you once more what I promised before: to uphold the Constitution, to do what is right as God gives me to see the right, and to do the very best that I can for America.

God helping me, I won't let you down.

Thank you very much.

☆

GERALD R. FORD
Campaign Speech

ANN ARBOR, MICHIGAN

September 17, 1976

Delivered at the University of Michigan

I have come home to Michigan to share with you my views of America in 1976 and my hopes for America in the next four years and beyond.

During the last two years, in the aftermath of a difficult war and a painful ordeal of economic adversity and political crisis, we reached a critical turning point in America's history.

Throughout most of your lives, America has faced turmoil. Some of our most beloved leaders have been assassinated. There was a war we could not either win or end. There were destructive riots on our streets and campuses. We suffered runaway inflation and the worst recession in 40 years. We were betrayed by corruption at the highest levels of government.

Through all of this, we found in ourselves a basic strength which has proven mightier than all our armaments, more precious than our great store of national wealth, and as enduring as our Constitution.

As I said on taking the oath of office as President two years ago, "our long national nightmare is over." In the last two years, the United States of America has made an incredible comeback—and we're not through yet.

In 200 years as a free people, much has changed in our nation but America's basic goals remain the same:

Americans want a job with a good future.

Americans want homes in decent neighborhoods—and schools where our children can get a quality education.

Americans want physical security—safety against war and against crime; safety against pollution in the water we drink and the air that we breathe.

We want medical and hospital care when we are sick, at costs that will not wipe out our savings.

We want the time and opportunity to enlarge our experience through recreation and travel.

We Americans are a proud people. We cherish our inalienable rights: the right to speak our minds—the right to choose the men and women who enact and enforce our laws—the right to stand equal before the law, regardless of sex, age, race or religion—the right as a farmer, businessman, worker and consumer to bargain freely in the economic marketplace—the right to worship as we choose.

It all adds up to the "American dream".

These are the goals which every politician and every citizen has for America. They are not some mystic vision of the future. They are the continuing agenda for action today.

And so, the question in this campaign of 1976 is not "who has the better vision of America." The question is "who will act to make that vision a reality."

The American people are ready for the truth, simple truth, simply spoken, about what the government can do for them and what it cannot and should not do. They will demand specifics—not smiles; performance—not promises.

There are some in this political year who claim that more government, more spending, more taxes and more controls on our lives will solve our problems.

More government is not the solution. Better government is.

It is time we thought of new ways to make government a capable servant and not a meddling master.

Let's get down to cases.

Let's talk about jobs.

Today 88 million Americans are gainfully employed—more than ever before in our history. But that's not good enough.

My immediate goal is two and a half million new jobs every year with emphasis on our youth, especially the minorities. Not demeaning, dead-end jobs paid for out of the Federal Treasury, but permanent jobs with a future generated by the demands of a healthy economy.

Can we do it? We have done it.

We proved once and for all that you can cut inflation in half and add four million new jobs in just 17 months. We did it with tax cuts that allowed Americans to spend more of their own money. We did it with tax incentives that encouraged job production. We did it by letting our free economic system do what it does better than any other system in the world—produce!

But I won't be satisfied until every American who wants a job can find a job.

I am particularly concerned that there are too many young Americans who cannot find a good job, or get the training and experience they need to find a good job.

Americans have long since recognized the importance of assuring that every high school graduate who is willing, able and qualified be able to go to college. We have done so through grants, loans and scholarships.

I believe we can apply this same principle to create a program for young people who choose not to go to college, but want a job at which they can learn a trade, a craft or practical business skills.

Let's put America—all of America—to work!

Once a good job is secured, it's an American tradition to put some of those earnings toward a family home. But nowadays, with interest rates too high, downpayments too high, and even monthly payments often too high—home-ownership is not within the reach of many Americans, particularly young Americans beginning a career or marriage.

My goal is home-ownership for every American family that wants to own a home and is willing to work and save for it.

Here is how I will meet that goal: First—I will continue to pursue economic policies, including tight control of unnecessary Federal spending, which will hold inflation down, reduce interest rates, cut your taxes, increasing your purchasing power and making more funds available for home mortgages.

Second—It's time we did something more about the down-payment requirements which so many people can't afford. I will recommend changes in the FHA law to reduce down-payments on lower and middle-price houses, by up to 50 percent.

Third—I will direct the Department of Housing and Urban Development to accelerate implementation of a new federal guaranty program to lower monthly payments in the early years of home-ownership and gradually increase them as the family income goes up.

A good job. A good home. Now let's talk about the good health we must have to appreciate both. My goal is an America where health care is not only the best in the world—but is both accessible and affordable. But raising Federal taxes by 70 billion dollars a year for a government-dominated national health insurance program is not the way to do it. That path leads to more bureaucracy, more fraud, more taxes and second class medical care.

That's what I'm against. Here's what I'm for:

As our first priority, I have recommended protection against the costs of a catastrophic or prolonged illness for the aged, and the disabled—insuring that never again will they have to pay more than $750 for medical care in any year. People should not have to go broke just to get well.

Next, I proposed to the Congress last spring, a major reform in federal health programs. We should combine sixteen overlapping and confused Federal health programs—including the scandal-ridden Medicaid program—into one $10 billion program that distributes the federal funds more equitably among the states and insures that those who need these services get first class care.

America is still awaiting action by the Congress on this urgently needed legislation.

Now let's turn to an area of special concern to this audience—education.

One of the most urgent problems is to create a climate in every classroom where teachers can teach and students can learn.

Quality education for every young American is my Administration's goal. Major reforms are necessary in the relationship between the national, state and local units of government so that teachers can spend their time teaching instead of filling out Federal forms. Federal aid is necessary, but Federal aggravation should stop.

Nine months ago, I proposed to the Congress that we replace 24 paper-shuffling, educational bureaucracies with a single federal program, which would provide 3.3 billion dollars in direct aid to elementary and secondary schools.

They have not acted. Once again this Congress has shown itself to be sitting dead in the water—addicted to the status quo. The American people deserve better representation than that! They will demand it on November 2.

We must ensure that low-income students have access to higher education.

We must also find ways through the tax system to ease the burden on families who choose to send their children to non-public schools and to help families cope with the expenses of a college education. In my Administration the education needs of America's middle-income families will neither be forgotten nor forsaken.

Education is the key to a better life. The prevention of crime is essential to making our lives secure.

The Constitution demands that we ensure domestic tranquility, and that is what I called for in my crime message to Congress. Most crimes are committed by hardened career criminals who know no other life than the life of crime. The place for those people is not on the streets, but in jail. The rights of a law-abiding society, the rights of the innocent victim of crime, must be fully protected.

And finally, we must give Americans the chance to enjoy America. I have outlined a 1.5 billion dollar program to expand and improve our national park system over the next ten years. This means more national parks, more recreation areas, more wildlife sanctuaries, more urban parks and historic sites. Let's make this America's Bicentennial birthday gift to all of our future generations.

Today America enjoys the most precious gift to all: we are at peace. No Americans are in combat anywhere on earth, and none are being drafted—and I will keep it that way.

We will be as strong as we need to be to keep the peace, to deter aggression, and to protect our national security.

But if our foreign policy is to have public support, it must represent the moral values of the American people.

What is more moral than peace with freedom and security?

As the leader of the free world, America has a special responsibility to explore new paths to peace for all mankind. It is a responsibility we have not shirked.

We have been a force for peace in the Middle East, not only in promoting new agreements, but in building a structure for a more lasting peace.

We have worked for peace with the Soviet Union, not only in resolving our many conflicts, but in building a world where nuclear armaments are brought under control.

We are working for peace in Europe, where the Armies of two major coalitions confront each other.

We will continue to build our relationship with the People's Republic of China, which contributes importantly to peace and stability in the world.

Now, in the face of a new challenge, we are embarked on a mission for peace in southern Africa.

This is the first Administration in America's history to develop a comprehensive, affirmative African policy. This policy has won respect and trust on that troubled continent.

At my direction, Secretary Kissinger is now engaged in an intensive effort to help all the parties—black and white—involved in the mounting crisis in southern Africa, find a peaceful and just solution to their many and complex differences.

The African parties in the very grave and complicated problems of Namibia and Rhodesia have encouraged us to help them in the search for peace and justice. We are also backed in our efforts by our European Allies with traditional bonds to the African Continent. In particular we are working in close collaboration with the United Kingdom which has an historical and legal responsibility in Rhodesia.

Success will depend fundamentally on the cooperation of the parties directly concerned. We will not and we cannot impose solutions, but will depend upon the goodwill and determined efforts of the African parties themselves to achieve negotiated settlements.

We seek no special advantage for ourselves in these negotiations. We do share with the people of Africa these fundamental objectives:

a peaceful outcome; a future of majority rule and minority rights; a prospect of widening human dignity and economic progress; and a unified and an independent Africa free from outside intervention or threat.

The path that leads to these goals is not an easy one. The risks are great. But America's interests and America's moral purpose summon our effort.

Despite the rigors of a great national election, I have persisted in carrying out this new policy toward Africa—not because it is expedient—because it is right.

I pledge to you that under my Administration, American foreign policy will serve the interests of our country and our people—it will be true to our great heritage of the past, fulfill our purposes in the present, and contribute to our best vision of the future.

It is not enough for anyone to say "trust me". Trust must be earned.

Trust is not having to guess what a candidate means.

Trust is leveling with the people before the election about what you're going to do after the election.

Trust is not being all things to all people, but being the same thing to all people.

Trust is not cleverly shading words so that each separate audience can hear what it wants to hear, but saying plainly and simply what you mean and meaning what you say.

I am proud of the maturity of the American people who demand more honesty, truthfulness and candor of their elected representatives.

The American people, particularly its young people, cannot be expected to take pride—or participate—in a system of government that is defiled and dishonored—in the White House or in the halls of Congress.

Personal integrity is not too much to ask of public servants. We should accept nothing less.

As we enter the last seven weeks of this national election, a new poll indicates that as many as 65 million Americans will not vote in November.

Some people have said that they are not excited about any of this year's candidates. Let them be excited about America.

Let them be excited about their own capacity to grow and change—about our Nation's capacity to grow and change—and even about the evolution, with their help, of the candidate of their choice.

In this year of 1976, I stand before you as the last President of America's first 200 years. But with your help, I also intend to be the first President of America's new generation of freedom.

Working together we can build an America that does not merely celebrate history, but writes it—that offers limited government and unlimited opportunity that concerns itself with the quality of life—that proves individual liberty is still the key to mutual achievement and national progress.

And when the history of this era is written, future generations will look back at America in 1976 and say—yes—they were two hundred years old—but they had really only just begun.

☆

1980

☆

The summer of 1979 had been an unfortunate one for President Jimmy Carter. Populist and folksy gestures that had inaugurated his Presidency, such as walking down Pennsylvania Avenue with his family after his inauguration, seemed increasingly hollow to a public grown cynical toward public officials. Having run against Washington, Carter proved unable to work closely with Congressional leaders to fashion a bold national energy policy that a heavily Democratic Congress would accept. Polls showed his approval rating hovering under 30 percent of the American people. Carter presided over an economy experiencing high interest rates as well as an inflation rate that stayed above 10 percent.

In foreign affairs, Carter had negotiated a spectacular breakthrough to peace between Egypt and Israel in 1978 but had accentuated a sense of limits to America's power while holding up human rights as a litmus test for foreign relations. Conservatives blasted his promotion of a Panama Canal Treaty as well as a Strategic Arms Limitation Treaty with the Russians. In a speech in July 1979 he had proclaimed a "crisis of confidence," criticizing Americans for their materialism and lack of respect for social and political institutions. Gasoline prices had soared while shortages became widespread. By July 29th, influential Senator Henry Jackson told CBS that he had "never observed a political situation such as we face now from a

Democratic Party standpoint where the opposition is as pervasive as it is to the President."

Opposition to Carter centered around Massachusetts Senator Edward Kennedy, the youngest brother of the assassinated President. Angered at Carter's chastisement of the American people and his lack of effective leadership, Kennedy announced his candidacy in November, soon to be joined by Governor Jerry Brown of California.

Carter was able to beat both Kennedy and Brown by the time of the Democratic Convention in August for two main reasons. On the on hand, numerous Americans still distrusted Kennedy's response to an accident that had killed a young woman in 1969 at Chappaquidick Island. His candidacy was marred by poor organization, lack of consistent theme, and Kennedy's inability to project himself in a favorable light through television.

More importantly, however, Carter was assisted by the American's public's reaction to the overthrow of the American Embassy in Teheran by militant Islamic students in November. The subsequent hostage crisis did not end until the inauguration of Ronald Reagan in January 1981 and fostered initial bipartisan support for President Carter's handling of the crisis. The invasion of Afghanistan by the Soviet Union in late December increased political pressure to "rearm" American and end America's sense of national impotence. Most Americans supported Carter's assertive response in pulling out of the 1980 Moscow Olympics as well as his call for a grain embargo. A renewed intensity to the Cold War fed a "new patriotism," all of which reverberated into the rhetoric of Presidential politics. Carter was the short-term beneficiary in his battle with Kennedy and Brown, but Ronald Reagan was the final victor come November.

Reagan found himself opposed for the Republican nomination by Senator Howard Baker of Tennessee, Representative John Anderson of Illinois, former CIA head George Bush, and several other candidates. For a while in the winter of 1980 former President Ford considered entering the race to stop Reagan but finally decided against it. Bush surprised many by winning the Iowa caucuses but Reagan rebounded and built up a solid lead so that Bush finally conceded defeat in May.

Representative Anderson gained a lot of media attention and enthusiastic support by liberals for his forthright positions on the issues beginning in the television debate on January 5th among Republican candidates. He was dubbed the "thinking man's candidate" for advocating such measures as a fifty-cent-a-gallon tax on gasoline as a revenue raiser and conservation measure. His impressive strength in the Vermont and Massachusetts primaries added to his winter luster.

After he lost his home state primary in Illinois to Reagan in March, however, Anderson's chances of beating Reagan were nil. Encouraged by media consultant David Garth and others, he soon began to flirt with the idea of running as an independent candidate for President against the expected nominees, Carter and Reagan, whom he regarded as disasters. On April 24th, he finally announced his decision to run on what eventually was called the National Unity Party. Anderson's campaign that fall ultimately gained 6.61 percent of the vote.

Ronald Reagan's vision of America was starkly different from both Anderson's and Carter's. In his acceptance speech at the Republican convention in Detroit he called for a "rebirth of the American tradition of leadership at every level of government and in private life as well." His was the call for an end to American timidity in the international arena and increased military spending to end a "window of vulnerability" that Americans faced in relation to Soviet missile capability. "Adversaries large and small test our will and seek to confound our resolve," he told the delegates and the television audience, "but we are given weakness when we need strength; vacillation when the times demand firmness."

In domestic policy, Reagan endorsed the Kemp-Roth tax cut plan that would reduce the average American's federal tax load by 30 percent over three years and provide new sources of capital for business expansion. He also promised substantially to reduce the federal deficit. In unambiguous language, Reagan ran against the Washington establishment and the federal bureaucracy. Deregulation of industry, he repeated, would unleash the productive potential of America. In his speech before the International Business Council that fall, Reagan was more specific in outlining his economic program to "get America working again."

Carter's acceptance speech at the Democratic Convention was not a rhetorical climax of his fight for the nomination, for he was preceded by Senator Kennedy, who upstaged the President with a moving address. Nonetheless, one can perceive much of Carter's fall political strategy when reading this address. Blasting the Republican tax program for offering "tax rebates for the rich, deprivation for the poor and fierce inflation for the rest of us," Carter drew attention to his own successful negotiation of peace between Israel and Egypt as well as his sensitivity to issues involving women, minorities, and the poor. He foreshadowed the tactics of fear he would use in the fall campaign by ridiculing the "dream world" of his Republican opponents, which America would probably find in reality to be a "nightmare."

The incumbant President's attempt to link Reagan with racism and himself to the politics of compassion and racial harmony would be more forthrightly repeated in his address to a predominantly black audience in Atlanta that September. "You've seen in this campaign the stirrings of hate and the rebirth of code words like "states' rights" in a speech in Mississippi [by Reagan], in a campaign reference to the Ku Klux Klan, relating to the South." Carter made a case in his own home state that his appointment of numerous blacks to important posts in his Administration (such as Andrew Young who had served as U.N. Representative) and proposals for a youth employment bill and a fair housing bill were of major significance for blacks.

Reagan provided tangible proof of the coming of age of the television personality as Presidential candidate. As a former radio announcer, Hollywood actor, speechmaker for General Electric, and Governor of California, Reagan was able to project a quality of being emotionally open and honest with television viewers while concurrently evoking a nostalgia for stricter moral values and uncompromising anti-Communism. He was the major beneficiary of the new strength of evangelical religious groups, such as the Moral Majority, who were aggressively entering politics through the pulpit and television in support of candidates espousing fundamentalist moral positions. A number of conservative political action committees were also channeling large amounts of money into television ads supporting Reagan's candidacy in 1980. Perhaps most significantly, polls showed that, in his televised debate with Carter, Reagan performed more effectively even though the President exhibited greater mastery of the details of campaign issues.

In calling for new leadership and for putting Americans back to work through the expansion of the private sector, Ronald Reagan was in a position to alter the direction of American society in a more radical direction than any President since Reagan's own hero, Franklin Roosevelt.

RONALD REAGAN
Acceptance Speech
DETROIT, MICHIGAN

July 17, 1980

Mr. Chairman, Mr. Vice President to be, this convention, my fellow citizens of this great nation:

With a deep awareness of the responsibility conferred by your trust, I accept your nomination for the presidency of the United States. I do so with deep gratitude, and I think also I might interject on behalf of all of us, our thanks to Detroit and the people of Michigan and to this city for the warm hospitality they have shown. And I thank you for your wholehearted response to my recommendation in regard to George Bush as a candidate for vice president.

I am very proud of our party tonight. This convention has shown to all America a party united, with positive programs for solving the nation's problems; a party ready to build a new consensus with all those across the land who share a community of values embodied in these words: family, work, neighborhood, peace, and freedom.

I know we have had a quarrel or two, but only as to the method of attaining a goal. There was no argument about the goal. As president, I will establish a liaison with the 50 governors to encourage them to eliminate, wherever it exists, discrimination against women. I will monitor federal laws to insure their implementation and to add statutes if they are needed.

More than anything else, I want my candidacy to unify our country; to renew the American spirit and sense of purpose. I want to carry out message to every American, regardless of party affiliation, who is a member of this community of shared values.

Never before in our history have Americans been called upon to face three grave threats to our very existence, any one of which could destroy us. We face a disintegrating economy, a weakened defense and an energy policy based on the sharing of scarcity.

The major issue of this campaign is the direct political personal and moral responsibility of Democratic Party leadership—in the White House and in Congress—for this unprecedented calamity which has befallen us. They tell us they have done the most that humanly could be done. They say that the United States has had its day in the sun; that our nation has passed its zenith. They expect you to tell your children that the American people no longer have the will to cope with their problems; that the future will be one of sacrifice and few opportunities.

My fellow citizens, I utterly reject that view. The American people, the most generous on earth, who created the highest standard of living, are not going to accept the notion that we can only make a better world for others by moving backwards ourselves. Those who believe we *can* have no business leading the nation.

I will not stand by and watch this great country destroy itself under mediocre leadership that drifts from one crisis to the next, eroding our national will and purpose. We have come together here because the American people deserve better from those to whom they entrust our nation's highest offices, and we stand united in our resolve to do something about it.

We need a rebirth of the American tradition of leadership at every level of government and in private life as well. The United States of America is unique in world history because it has a genius for leaders—many leaders—on many levels. But, back in 1976, Mr. Carter said, "Trust me." And a lot of people did. Now, many of those people are out of work. Many have seen their savings eaten away by inflation. Many others on fixed incomes, especially the elderly, have watched helplessly as the cruel tax of inflation wasted away their purchasing power. And, today, a great many who trusted Mr. Carter wonder if we can survive the Carter policies of national defense.

"Trust me" government asks that we concentrate our hopes and dreams on one man; that we trust him to do what's best for us. My view of government places trust not in one person or one party, but in those values that transcend persons and parties. The trust is where it belongs—in the people. The responsibility to live up to that trust is where it belongs, in their elected leaders. That kind of relationship, between the people and their elected leaders, is a special kind of compact.

Three hundred and sixty years ago, in 1620, a group of families dared to cross a mighty ocean to build a future for themselves in a new world. When they arrived at Plymouth, Massachusetts, they formed what they called a "compact"; an agreement among themselves to build a community and abide by its laws.

The single act—the voluntary binding together of free people to live under the law—set the pattern for what was to come.

A century and a half later, the descendants of those people pledged their lives, their fortunes and their sacred honor to found this nation. Some forfeited their fortunes and their lives; none sacrificed honor.

Four score and seven years later, Abraham Lincoln called upon the people of all America to renew their dedication and their commitment to a government of, for and by the people.

Isn't it once again time to renew our compact of freedom; to pledge to each other all that is best in our lives; all that gives meaning to them—for the sake of this, our beloved and blessed land?

Together, let us make this a new beginning. Let us make a commitment to care for the needy; to teach our children the values and the virtues handed down to us by our families; to have the courage to defend those values and the willingness to sacrifice for them.

Let us pledge to restore, in our time, the American spirit of voluntary service, of cooperation, of private and community initiative; a spirit that flows like a deep and mighty river through the history of our nation.

As your nominee, I pledge to restore to the federal government the capacity to do the people's work without dominating their lives. I pledge to you a government that will not only work well, but wisely; its ability to act tempered by prudence, and its willingness to do good balanced by the knowledge that government is never more dangerous than when our desire to have it help us blinds us to its great power to harm us.

The first Republican president once said, "While the people retain their virtue and their vigilance, no administration by any extreme of wickedness or folly can seriously injure the government in the short space of four years."

If Mr. Lincoln could see what's happened in these last three-and-a-half years, he might hedge a little on that statement. But, with the virtues that are our legacy as a free people and with the vigilance that sustains liberty, we still have time to use our renewed compact to overcome the injuries that have been done to America these past three-and-a-half years.

First, we must overcome something the present administration has cooked up: a new and altogether indigestible economic stew, one part inflation, one part high unemployment, one part recession, one part runaway taxes, one part deficit spending and seasoned by an energy crisis. It's an economic stew that has turned the national stomach.

Ours are not problems of abstract economic theory. Those are problems of flesh and blood; problems that cause pain and destroy the moral fiber of real people who should not suffer the further indignity of being told by the government that it is all somehow their fault. We do not have inflation because—as Mr. Carter says—we have lived too well.

The head of a government which has utterly refused to live within its means and which has, in the last few days, told us that this year's deficit will be $60 billion, dares to point the finger of blame at business and labor, both of which have been engaged in a losing struggle just trying to stay even.

High taxes, we are told, are somehow good for us, as if, when government spends our money it isn't inflationary, but when we spend it, it is.

Those who preside over the worst energy shortage in our history tell us to use less, so that we will run out of oil, gasoline and natural gas a little more slowly. Conservation is desirable, of course, for we must not waste energy. But conservation is not the sole answer to our energy needs.

America must get to work producing more energy. The Republican program for solving economic problems is based on growth and productivity.

Large amounts of oil and natural gas lay beneath our land and off our shores, untouched because the present administration seems to believe the American people would rather see more regulation, taxes and controls than more energy.

Coal offers great potential. So does nuclear energy produced under rigorous safety standards. It could supply electricity for thousands of industries and millions of jobs and homes. It must not be thwarted by a tiny minority opposed to economic growth which often finds friendly ears in regulatory agencies for its obstructionist campaigns.

Make no mistake. We will not permit the safety of our people or our environmental heritage to be jeopardized, but we are going to reaffirm that the economic prosperity of our people is a fundamental part of our environment.

Our problems are both acute and chronic, yet all we hear from those in positions of leadership are the same tired proposals for more government tinkering, more meddling and more control—all of which led us to this state in the first place.

Can anyone look at the record of this administration and say, "Well done?" Can anyone compare the state of our economy when the Carter administration took office with where we are today and say, "Keep up the good work?" Can anyone look at our reduced standing in the world today and say, "Let's have four more years of this?"

I believe the American people are going to answer these questions the first week of November and their answer will be, "No—we've had enough." And, then it will be up to us—beginning next January 20th—to offer an administration and congressional leadership of competence and more than a little courage.

We must have the clarity of vision to see the difference between what is essential and what is merely desirable, and then the courage to bring our government back under control and make it acceptable to the people.

It is essential that we maintain both the forward momentum of economic growth and the strength of the safety net beneath those in society who need help. We also believe it is essential that the integrity of all aspects of Social Security be preserved.

Beyond these essentials, I believe it is clear our federal government is overgrown and overweight. Indeed, it is time for our government to go on a diet. Therefore, my first act as chief executive will be to impose an immediate and thorough freeze on federal hiring. Then, we are going to enlist the very best minds from business, labor and whatever quarter to conduct detailed review of every department, bureau and agency that lives by federal appropriations. We are also going to enlist the help and ideas of many dedicated and hard-working government employees at all levels who want a more efficient government as much as the rest of us do. I know that many are demoralized by the confusion and waste they confront in their work as a result of failed and failing policies.

Our instructions to the groups we enlist will be simple and direct. We will remind them that government programs exist at the sufferance of the American taxpayer and are paid for with money earned by working men and women. Any program that represents a waste of their money—a theft from their pocketbooks—must have that waste eliminated or the program must go—by executive order where possible; by congressional action where necessary. Everything that can be run more effectively by state and local government we shall turn over to state and local government, along with the funding sources to pay for it. We are going to put an end to the money merry-go-round where our money becomes Washington's money, to be spent by the states and cities exactly the way the federal bureaucrats tell them to.

I will not accept the excuse that the federal government has grown so big and powerful that it is beyond the control of any president, any administration or Congress. We are going to put an end to the notion that the American taxpayer exists to fund the federal government. The federal government exists to *serve* the American people. On January 20th, we are going to re-establish that truth.

Also on that date we are going to initiate action to get substantial relief for our taxpaying citizens and action to put people back to work. None of this will be based on any new form of monetary tinkering or fiscal sleight-of-hand. We will simply apply to government the common sense we all use in our daily lives.

Work and family are at the center of our lives; the foundation of our dignity as a free people. When we deprive people of what they have earned, or take away their jobs, we destroy their dignity and undermine their families. We cannot support our families unless there are jobs; and we cannot have jobs unless people have both money to invest and the faith to invest it.

These are concepts that stem from an economic system that for more than two hundred years has helped us master a continent, create a previously undreamed of prosperity for our people and has fed millions of others around the globe. That system will continue to serve us in the future if our government will stop ignoring the basic values on which it was built and stop betraying the trust and good will of the American workers who keep it going.

The American people are carrying the heaviest peacetime tax burden in our nation's history—and it will grow even heavier, under present law, next January. We are taxing ourselves into economic exhaustion and stagnation, crushing our ability and incentive to save, invest and produce.

This must stop. We *must* halt this fiscal self-destruction and restore sanity to our economic system.

I have long advocated a 30 percent reduction in income tax rates over a period of three years. This phased tax reduction would begin with a 10 percent "down payment" tax cut in 1981, which the Republicans and Congress and I have already proposed.

A phased reduction of tax rates would go a long way toward easing the heavy burden on the American people. But, we should not stop here.

Within the context of economic conditions and appropriate budget priorities during each fiscal year of my presidency, I would strive to go further. This would include improvement in business depreciation taxes so we can stimulate investment in order to get plants and equipment replaced, put more Americans back to work and put our nation back on the road to being competitive in world commerce. We will also work to reduce the cost of government as a percentage of our gross national product.

The first task of national leadership is to set honest and realistic priorities in our policies and our budget and I pledge that my administration will do that.

When I talk of tax cuts, I am reminded that every major tax cut in this century has strengthened the economy, generated renewed productivity and ended up yielding new revenues for the government by creating new investment, new jobs and more commerce among our people.

The present administration has been forced by us Republicans to play follow-the-leader with regard to a tax cut. But, in this election year we must take with the proverbial "grain of salt" any tax cut proposed by those who have given us the greatest tax *increase* in our history.

When those in leadership give us tax increases and tell us we must also do with less, have they thought about those who have always had less—especially the minorities? This is like telling them that just as they step on the first rung of the ladder of opportunity, the ladder is being pulled out from under them. That may be the Democratic leadership's message to the minorities, but it won't be ours. Our message will be: we have to move ahead, but we're not going to leave anyone behind.

Thanks to the economic policies of the Democratic Party, millions of Americans find themselves out of work. Millions more have never even had a fair chance to learn new skills, hold a decent job, or secure for themselves and their families a share in the prosperity of this nation.

It is time to put America back to work; to make our cities and towns resound with the confident voices of men and women of all races, nationalities and faiths bringing home to their families a decent paycheck they can cash for honest money.

For those without skills, we'll find a way to help them get skills.

For those without job opportunities we'll stimulate new opportunities, particularly in the inner cities where they live.

For those who have abandoned hope, we'll restore hope and we'll welcome them into a great national crusade to make America great again!

When we move from domestic affairs and cast our eyes abroad, we see an equally sorry chapter on the record of the present administration.

—A Soviet combat brigade trains in Cuba, just 90 miles from our shores.

—A Soviet army of invasion occupies Afghanistan, further threatening our vital interests in the Middle East.

—America's defense strength is at its lowest ebb in a generation, while the Soviet Union is vastly outspending us in both strategic and conventional arms.

—Our European allies, looking nervously at the growing menace from the East, turn to us for leadership and fail to find it.

—And, incredibly more than 50 of our fellow Americans have been held captive for over eight months by a dictatorial foreign power that holds us up to ridicule before the world.

Adversaries large and small test our will and seek to confound our resolve, but we are given weakness when we need strength; vacillation when the times demand firmness.

The Carter administration lives in the world of make-believe. Every day, drawing up a response to that day's problems, troubles, regardless of what happened yesterday and what will happen tomorrow.

The rest of us, however, live in the real world. It is here that disasters are overtaking our nation without any real response from Washington.

This is make-believe, self-deceit and—above all—transparent hypocrisy.

For example, Mr. Carter says he supports the volunteer army, but he lets military pay and benefits slip so low that many of our enlisted personnel are actually eligible for food stamps. Re-enlistment rates drop and, just recently, after he fought all week *against* a proposal to increase the pay of our men and women in uniform, he helicoptered out to our carrier, the *U.S.S. Nimitz*, which was returning from long months of duty. He told the crew that he advocated better pay for them and their comrades! Where does he really stand, now that he's back on shore?

I'll tell you where I stand. I do *not* favor a peacetime draft or registration, but I do favor pay and benefit levels that will attract and keep highly motivated men and women in our volunteer forces and an active reserve trained and ready for an instant call in case of an emergency.

There may be a sailor at the helm of the ship of state, but the ship has no rudder. Critical decisions are made at times almost in comic fashion, but who can laugh? Who was not embarrassed when the administration handed a major propaganda victory in the United Nations to the enemies of Israel, our staunch Middle East ally for three decades, and then claim that the American vote was a "mistake," the result of a "failure of communication" between the president, his secretary of state and his U.N. ambassador?

Who does not feel a growing sense of unease as our allies, facing repeated instances of an amateurish and confused administration, reluctantly conclude that America is unwilling or unable to fulfill its obligations as leader of the free world?

Who does not feel rising alarm when the question in any discussion of foreign policy is no longer, "Should we do something?", but "Do we have the capacity to do *anything?*"

The administration which has brought us to this state is seeking your endorsement for four more years of weakness, indecision, mediocrity and incompetence. No American should vote until he or she has asked, is the United States stronger and more respected now than it was three-and-a-half years ago? Is the world today a safer place in which to live?

It is the responsibility of the president of the United States, in working for peace, to insure that the safety of our people cannot successfully be threatened by a hostile foreign power. As president, fulfilling that responsibility will be my Number One priority.

We are not a warlike people. Quite the opposite. We always seek to live in peace. We resort to force infrequently and with great reluctance—and only after we have determined that it is absolutely necessary. We are awed—and rightly so—by the forces of destruction at loose in the world in this nuclear era. But neither can we be naive or foolish. Four times in my lifetime America has gone to war, bleeding the lives of its young men into the sands of beachheads, the fields of Europe and the jungles and rice paddies of Asia. We know only too well that war comes not when the forces of freedom are strong, but when they are weak. It is then that tyrants are tempted.

We simply cannot learn these lessons the hard way again without risking our destruction.

Of all the objectives we seek, first and foremost is the establishment of lasting world peace. We must always stand ready to negotiate in good faith, ready to pursue any reasonable avenue that holds forth the promise of lessening tensions and furthering the prospects of peace. But let our friends and those who may wish us ill take note: the United States has an obligation to its citizens and to the people of the world never to let those who would destroy freedom dictate the future course of human life on this planet. I would regard my election as proof that we have renewed our resolve to preserve world peace and freedom. This nation will once again be strong enough to do that.

This evening marks the last step—save one—of a campaign that has taken Nancy and me from one end of this great land to the other, over many months and thousands of miles. There are those who question the way we choose a president; who say that our process imposes difficult and exhausting burdens on those who seek the office. I have not found it so.

It is impossible to capture in words the splendor of this vast continent which God has granted as our portion of his creation. There are no words to express the extraordinary strength and character of this breed of people we call Americans.

Everywhere we have met thousands of Democrats, Independents and Republicans from all economic conditions and walks of life bound together in that community of shared values of family, work, neighborhood, peace and freedom. They are concerned, yes, but they are not frightened. They are disturbed, but not dismayed. They are the kind of men and women Tom Paine had in mind when he wrote—during the darkest days of the American Revolution—"We have it in our power to begin the world over again."

Nearly one-hundred-and-fifty years after Tom Paine wrote those words, an American president told the generation of the Great Depression that it had a "rendezvous with destiny." I believe this generation of Americans today has a rendezvous with destiny.

Tonight, let us dedicate ourselves to renewing the American compact. I ask you not simply to "Trust me," but to trust your values—our values—and to hold me responsible for living up to them. I ask you to trust that American spirit which knows no ethnic, religious, social, political, regional or economic boundaries; the spirit that burned with zeal in the hearts of millions of immigrants from every corner of the earth who came here in search of freedom.

Some say that spirit no longer exists. But I have seen it—I have felt it—all across the land; in the big cities, the small towns and in rural America. The American spirit is still there, ready to blaze into life if you and I are willing to do what has to be done; the practical, down-to-earth things that will stimulate our economy, increase productivity and put America back to work.

The time is *now* to resolve that the basis of a firm and principled foreign policy is one that takes the world as it is and seeks to change it by leadership and example; not by harangue, harassment or wishful thinking.

The time is *now* to say that while we shall seek new friendships and expand and improve others, we shall not do so by breaking our word or casting aside old friends and allies.

And, the time is *now* to redeem promises once made to the American people by another candidate, in another time and another place. He said, ". . . For three long years I have been going up and down this country preaching that government—federal, state and local—costs too much. I shall not stop that preaching. As an immediate program of action, we must abolish useless offices. We must eliminate unnecessary functions of government. . . . we must consolidate subdivisions of government and, like the private citizen, give up luxuries which we can no longer afford.

"I propose to you, my friends, and through you that government of all kinds, big and little be made solvent and that the example be set by the president of the United States and his Cabinet."

So said Franklin Delano Roosevelt in his acceptance speech to the Democratic National Convention in July 1932.

The time is *now*, my fellow Americans, to recapture our destiny, to take it into our own hands. But, to do this will take many of us, working together. I ask you tonight to volunteer your help in this cause so we can carry our message throughout the land.

Yes, isn't *now* the time that we, the people, carried out these unkept promises? Let us pledge to each other and to all America on this July day 48 years later, we intend to do *just that*.

I have thought of something that is not part of my speech and I'm worried over whether I should do it.

Can we doubt that only a Divine Providence placed this land, this island of freedom, here as a refuge for all those people in the world who yearn to breathe freely: Jews and Christians enduring persecution behind the Iron Curtain, the boat people of Southeast Asia, of Cuba and Haiti, the victims of drought and famine in Africa, the freedom fighters of Afghanistan and our own countrymen held in savage captivity.

I'll confess that I've been a little afraid to suggest what I'm going to suggest—I'm more afraid not to—that we begin our crusade joined together in a moment of silent prayer. God bless America.

☆

RONALD REAGAN
Campaign Speech
CHICAGO, ILLINOIS

September 9, 1980

Delivered before the International Business Council

Almost two months ago, in accepting the Presidential nomination of my party, I spoke of the historically unique crisis facing the United States. At that time I said:

> Never before in our history have Americans been called upon to face three grave threats to our very existence, any one of which could destroy us. We face a disintegrating economy, a weakened defense and an energy policy based on the sharing of scarcity.

Now since I first spoke those words, no action has been taken by President Carter to change this grave, unprecedented situation.

In fact, during the last few months the overall economic situation in the United States has deteriorated markedly. The cumulative effect of the economic policies the Carter Administration has followed over the last three and one-half years has damaged our economy much more than virtually anyone could have foreseen. Interest rates and inflation have become unconscionably high. Almost two million Americans have lost their jobs this year alone. And the tax burden continues to steadily increase.

In effect, Mr. Carter's economic failures are an assault on the hopes and dreams of millions of American families.

They are essentially an unprecedented failure of Presidential leadership that strikes at the very heart of every American family, every factory, every farm, every community.

Make no mistake about it: what Mr. Carter has done to the American economy is not merely a matter of lines and graphs on a chart. Individuals and families are being hurt and hurt badly. Factories are empty; unemployment lines are full.

Every American family has felt what the Carter inflation means to hopes for a better life. Every visit to the supermarket reminds us of what Mr. Carter's policies have done. We pay the price of Carter's inflation every time we buy food or clothing or other essentials.

We are dealing with an unprecedented crisis that takes away not only wages and savings, but hopes and dreams.

And what is his response to this tragedy?

Words. And more words.

Two weeks ago, he gave us his latest in a series of economic policy shifts. This one is the fifth "new economic program" in the last three and one-half years. It contains rhetoric that Mr. Carter apparently hopes will lead us to believe he has finally discovered free enterprise.

Hearing him and members of his Administration use the language of free enterprise reminds me of one of the stories of Mark Twain. He had a habit of using very foul language, which distressed his wife to no end. She decided on a form of shock treatment to cure him of his habit. One day he came home, and she stood in front of him and recited every word of the salty language she had ever heard him use. He listened patiently and when she was finished, said: "My dear, you have the words all right, you just don't have the tune."

I'd like to speak to you today about a new concept of leadership, one that has both the words and the music. One based on faith in the American people, confidence in the American economy, and a firm commitment to see to it that the Federal Government is once more responsive to the people.

That concept is rooted in a strategy for growth, a program that sees the American economic system as it is—a huge, complex, dynamic system which demands not piecemeal Federal packages, or pious hopes wrapped in soothing words, but the hard work and concerted programs necessary for real growth.

We must first recognize that the problem with the U.S. economy is swollen, inefficient government, needless regulation, too much taxation, too much printing-press money. We don't need any more doses of Carter's eight- or 10-point programs to "fix" or fine tune the economy. For three and one-half years these ill-thought-out initiatives have constantly sapped the healthy vitality of the most productive economic system the world has ever known.

Our country is in a downward cycle of progressive economic deterioration that must be broken if the economy is to recover and move into a vigorous growth cycle in the 1980's.

We must move boldly, decisively and quickly to control the runaway growth of Federal spending, to remove the tax disincentives that are throttling the economy, and to reform the regulatory web that is smothering it.

We must have and I am proposing a new strategy for the 1980's.

Only a series of well-planned economic actions, taken so that they complement and reinforce one another, can move our economy forward again.

We must keep the rate of growth of government spending at reasonable and prudent levels.

We must reduce personal income tax rates and accelerate and simplify depreciation schedules in an orderly, systematic way to remove disincentives to work, savings, investment and productivity.

We must review regulations that affect the economy and change them to encourage economic growth.

We must establish a stable, sound and predictable monetary policy.

And we must restore confidence by following a consistent national economic policy that does not change from month to month.

I am asked: 'Can we do it all at once?' My answer is: 'We must.'

I am asked: 'Can we do it immediately?' Well, my answer is: 'No, it took Mr. Carter three and one-half years of hard work to get us into this economic mess. It will take time to get us out.'

I am asked: 'Is it easy?' Again, my answer is: 'No. It is going to require the most dedicated and concerted peacetime action ever taken by the American people for their country.'

But we can do it, we must do it, and I intend that we will do it.

We must balance the budget, reduce tax rates and restore our defenses.

These are the challenges. Mr. Carter says he can't meet these challenges; that he can't do it. I believe him. He can't. But, I refuse to accept his defeatist and pessimistic view of America. I know we can do these things, and I know we will.

But don't just take my word for it. I have discussed this with any number of distinguished economists and businessmen, including such men as George Schultz, William Simon, Alan Greenspan, Charles Walker and James Lynn. The strategy is based on solid economic principles and basic experience in both government and the marketplace. It has worked before and will work again.

Let us look at how we can meet this challenge.

One of the most critical elements of my economic program is the control of government spending. Waste, extravagance, abuse and outright fraud in Federal agencies and programs must be stopped. The billions of the taxpayers' dollars that are wasted every year throughout hundreds of Federal programs, and it will take a major, sustained effort over time to effectively counter this.

Federal spending is now projected to increase to over $900 billion a year by fiscal year 1985. But, through a comprehensive assault on waste and inefficiency, I am confident that we can squeeze and trim

2 percent out of the budget in fiscal year 1981, and that we will be able to increase this gradually to 7 percent of what otherwise would have been spent in fiscal year 1985.

Now this is based on projections that have been made by groups in the government. Actually I believe we can do even better. My goal will be to bring about spending reductions of 10 percent by fiscal year 1984.

Crucial to my strategy of spending control will be the appointment to top government positions of men and women who share my economic philosophy. We will have an administration in which the word from the top isn't lost or hidden in the bureaucracy. That voice will be heard because it is a voice that has too long been absent from Washington—it is the voice of the people.

I will also establish a citizen's task force, as I did in California, to rigorously examine every department and agency. There is no better way to bring about effective government than to have its operations scrutinized by citizens dedicated to that principle.

I already have as part of my advisory staff a Spending Control Task Force, headed by my good friend and former director of the Office of Management and Budget, Caspar Weinberger, that will report on additional ways and techniques to search out and eliminate waste, extravagance, fraud and abuse in Federal programs.

This strategy for growth does not require altering or taking back necessary entitlements already granted to the American people. The integrity of the Social Security System will be defended by my administration and its benefits will once again be made meaningful.

This strategy does require restraining the Congressional desire to "add-on" to every old program and to create new programs funded by deficits.

This strategy does require that the way Federal programs are administered will be changed so that we can benefit from the savings that will come about when, in some instances, administrative authority can be moved back to the states.

The second major element of my economic program is a tax rate reduction plan. This plan calls for an across-the-board, three-year reduction in personal income tax rates—10 percent in 1981, 10 percent in 1982 and 10 percent in 1983. My goal is to implement three reductions in a systematic and planned manner.

More than any single thing, high rates of taxation destroy incentive to earn, to save, to invest. And they cripple productivity, lead to deficit financing and inflation, and create unemployment.

We can go a long way toward restoring the economic health of this country by establishing reasonable, fair levels of taxation.

But even the extended tax rate cuts which I am recommending

still leave too high a tax burden on the American people. In the second half of the decade ahead we are going to need, and we must have, additional tax rate reductions.

Jimmy Carter says it can't be done. In fact, he says it shouldn't be done. He favors the current crushing tax burden because it fits into his philosophy of government as the dominating force in American economic life.

Official projections of the Congressional Budget Office show that by fiscal year 1985, if the current rates of taxation are still in effect, Federal tax revenues will rise to over $1 trillion a year.

Surely Jimmy Carter isn't telling us that the American people can't find better things to do with all that money than see it spent by the Federal Government.

Assuming a continuation of current policies in government, Congressional projections show a huge and growing potential surplus by 1985. These surpluses can be used in two basic ways: one, to fund additional government programs, or, two, to reduce tax rates.

That choice should be up to the American people.

The most insidious tax increase is the one we must pay when inflation pushes us into higher tax brackets. As long as inflation is with us, taxes should be based on real income. Federal personal income taxes should be based on real income. Federal personal income taxes should be indexed to compensate for inflation, once tax rates have been reduced.

We also need faster, less complex depreciation schedules for business. Outdated depreciation schedules now prevent many industries, especially steel and auto, from modernizing their plants. And faster depreciation would allow these companies to generate more capital internally, permitting them to make the investment necessary to create new jobs, and to become more competitive in world markets.

Another vital part of this strategy concerns government regulation. The subject is so important and so complex that it deserves a speech in itself—and I plan to make one soon. For the moment, however, let me say this:

Government regulation, like fire, makes a good servant but a bad master. No one can argue with the intent of this regulation—to improve health and safety and to give us cleaner air and water—but too often regulations work against rather than for the interests of the people. When the real take-home pay of the average American worker is declining steadily, and 8 million Americans are out of work, we must carefully re-examine our regulatory structure to assess to what degree regulations have contributed to this situation. In my administration there should and will be a thorough and systematic review of the thousands of Federal regulations that affect the economy.

Along with spending control, tax reform and deregulation, a sound, stable and predictable monetary policy is essential to restoring economic health. The Federal Reserve Board is, and should remain, independent of the Executive Branch of government. But the President must nominate those who serve on the Federal Reserve Board. My appointees will share my commitment to restoring the value and stability of the American dollar.

A fundamental part of my strategy for economic growth is the restoration of confidence. If our business community is going to invest and build and create new, well-paying jobs, they must have a future free from arbitrary, government action. They must have confidence that the economic "rules-of-the-game" won't be changed suddenly or capriciously.

In my administration, a national economic policy will be established, and we will begin to implement it, within the first ninety days.

Thus, I envision a strategy encompassing many elements—none of which can do the job alone, but all of which together can get it done. This strategy depends for its success more than anything else on the will of the people to regain control of their government.

It depends on the capacity of the American people for work, their willingness to do the job, their energy and their imagination.

This strategy of economic growth includes the growth that will come from the cooperation of business and labor based on their knowledge that government policy is directed toward jobs, toward opportunity, toward growth.

We are not talking here about some static, lifeless econometric model—we are talking about the greatest productive economy in human history, an economy that is historically revitalized not by government but by people free of government interference, needless regulations, crippling inflation, high taxes and unemployment.

Does Mr. Carter really believe that the American people are not capable of rebuilding our economy? If he does, that is even one more reason—along with his record—that he should not be President.

When such a strategy is put into practice, our national defense needs can be met because the productive capacity of the American people will provide the revenues needed to do what must be done.

All of this demands a vision. It demands looking at government and the economy as they exist and not as words on paper, but as institutions guided by our will and knowledge toward growth, restraint and effective action.

When Mr. Carter first took office, he had sufficient budget flexibility to achieve these goals. But he threw away the opportunity to generate new economic growth and to strengthen national security.

Now the damage done to the economy by his misguided policies will make the achievement of these crucial objectives far more difficult.

Nevertheless, this nation cannot afford to back away from any of these goals. We cannot allow tax burdens to continue to rise inordinately, inflation to take a stronger hold, or allow our defenses to deteriorate further—without severe consequences.

This task is going to be difficult but our goals are optimistic—as they should be. Success is going to take time, as well as work.

There is only one phrase to describe the last three years and eight months. It has been an American tragedy.

It isn't only that Mr. Carter has increased Federal spending by 58 percent in four years, or that taxes in his 1981 budget are double what they were in 1976, the equivalent of a tax increase on an average family of four of more than $5,000.

The tragedy lies as much in what Mr. Carter has failed to do as in what he has done.

He has failed to lead.

Mr. Carter had a chance to govern effectively. He had a sound economic base with an inflation rate of 4.8 percent when he took office.

But he has failed. His failure was rooted in his view of government, in his view of the American people.

Yet he wants this dismal view to prevail for four more years.

The time has come for the American people to reclaim their dream. Things don't have to be this way. We can change them. We must change them. Mr. Carter's American tragedy must and can be transcended by the spirit of the American people, working together.

Let's get America working again.

The time is now.

☆

JIMMY CARTER
Acceptance Speech

NEW YORK CITY

August 14, 1980

Fellow Democrats, fellow citizens:

I thank you for the nomination you've offered me. And I especially thank you for choosing as my running mate the best partner any president ever had—Fritz Mondale.

With gratitude and with determination, I accept your nomination.

And I am proud to run on a progressive and sound platform that you have hammered out at this convention.

Fritz and I will mount a campaign that defines the real issues— a campaign that responds to the intelligence of the American people— a campaign that talks sense—and we're going to beat, whip the Republicans in November.

We'll win because we are the party of a great president who knew how to get re-elected—Franklin D. Roosevelt. And we're the party of a courageous fighter who knew how to "give 'em hell"—Harry Truman. And as Truman said, he just told the truth and they thought it was hell.

And we're the party of a gallant man of spirit—John Fitzgerald Kennedy. And we're the party of a great leader of compassion—Lyndon Baines Johnson.

And the party of a great man who should have been president and would have been one of the greatest presidents in history—Hubert Horatio Hornblower—Humphrey. I have appreciated what this convention has said about Senator Humphrey, a great man who epitomized the spirit of the Democratic Party, and I would like to say that we're also the party of Governor Jerry Brown and Senator Edward M. Kennedy.

I'd like to say a personal word to Senator Kennedy. Ted, you're a tough competitor and a superb campaigner and I can attest to that. Your speech before this convention was a magnificent statement of what the Democratic Party is and what it means to the people of this country—and why a Democratic victory is so important this year. I reach out to you tonight and I reach out to all those who have supported you in your valiant and passionate campaign.

Ted, your party needs—and I need—you and your idealism and dedication working for us. There is no doubt that even greater service lies ahead of you—and we are grateful to you and to have your strong partnership now in the larger cause to which your own life has been dedicated.

I thank you for your support. We'll make great partners this fall in whipping the Republicans.

We're Democrats and we have had our differences, but we share a bright vision of America's future—a vision of good life for all our people—a vision of a secure nation, a just society, a peaceful world, a strong America—confident and proud and united.

And we have a memory of Franklin Roosevelt forty years ago when he said that there are times in our history when concerns over our personal lives are overshadowed by concern for "what will happen to the country we have known." This is such a time—and I can tell you that the choice to be made this year can transform our own personal lives and the life of our country as well.

During the last presidential campaign, I crisscrossed this country and I listened to thousands and thousands of people—housewives and farmers, teachers and small-business leaders, workers and students, the elderly and the poor—people of every race and every background and every walk of life. It was a powerful experience—a total immersion in the human reality of America.

And I have now had another kind of total immersion—being president of the United States of America. Let me talk for a moment about what that job is like—and what I have learned from it.

I've learned that only the most complex and difficult tasks come before me in the Oval Office. No easy answers are found there—because no easy questions come there.

I've learned that for a president experience is the best guide to the right decisions. I'm wiser tonight than I was four years ago.

And I have learned that the presidency is a place of compassion. My own heart is burdened for the troubled Americans. The poor and the jobless and the afflicted—they've become part of me. My thoughts and my prayers for our hostages in Iran are as though they were my own sons and daughters.

The life of every human being on Earth can depend on the experience and judgment and vigilance of the person in the Oval Office. The president's power for building and his power for destruction are awesome. And the power is greatest exactly where the stakes are highest—in matters of war and peace.

And I have learned something else—something that I have come to see with extraordinary clarity. Above all, I must look ahead—because the president of the United States is the steward of the nation's destiny.

He must protect our children—and the children they will have—and the children of generations to follow. He must speak and act for them. That is his burden—and his glory.

And that is why a president cannot yield to the short-sighted demands, no matter how rich or powerful the special interests might be that make those demands. And that is why the president cannot bend to the passions of the moment, however popular they might be. And that is why the president must sometimes ask for sacrifice when his listeners would rather hear the promise of comfort.

The president is a servant of today. But his true constituency is the future. That is why the election of 1980 is so important.

Some have said it makes no difference who wins this election. They are wrong.

This election is a stark choice between two men, two parties, two sharply different pictures of what America is and what the world is. But it is more than that.

It is a choice between two futures. The year 2000 is less than 20 years away—just four presidential elections after this one. Children born this year will come of age in the 21st century.

The time to shape the world of the year 2000 is now. The decisions of the next few years will set our course, perhaps an irreversible course—and the most important of all choices will be made by the American people at the polls less than three months from tonight.

The choice could not be more clear—nor the consequences more crucial.

In one of the futures we can choose—the future that you and I have been building together—I see security and justice and peace.

I see a future of economic security—security that will come from tapping our own great resources of oil and gas, coal and sunlight—and from building the tools, the technology and factories for a revitalized economy based on jobs and stable prices for everyone.

I see a future of justice—the justice of good jobs, decent health care, quality education, and the full opportunity for all people, regardless of color or language or religion; the simple human justice of equal rights for all men—and for all women, guaranteed equal rights at last—under the Constitution of the United States of America.

And I see a future of peace—a peace born of wisdom and based on the fairness toward all countries of the world—a peace guaranteed both by American military strength and by American moral strength as well.

That is the future I want for all people—a future of confidence and hope and a good life. It is the future America must choose—and with your help and with your commitment, it is the future America will choose.

But there is another possible future.

In that other future, I see despair—the despair of millions who would struggle for equal opportunity and a better life—and struggle alone.

And I see surrender—the surrender of our energy future to the merchants of oil; the surrender of our economic future to a bizarre program of massive tax cuts for the rich, service cuts for the poor and massive inflation for everyone.

And I see risk—the risk of international confrontation; the risk of an uncontrollable, unaffordable, and unwinnable nuclear arms race.

No one, Democrat or Republican leader, consciously seeks such a future. And I do not claim that my opponent does. But I do question the disturbing commitments and policies already made by him and by those with him who have now captured control of the Republican Party.

The consequences of those commitments and policies would drive us down the wrong road. It's up to all of us to make sure America rejects this alarming, and even perilous, destiny.

The only way to build a better future is to start with realities of the present. But while we Democrats grapple with the real challenges of a real world, others talk about a world of tinsel and make-believe.

Let's look for a moment at their make-believe world.

In their fantasy America, inner-city people and farm workers and laborers do not exist. Women, like children, are to be seen but not heard. The problems of working women are simply ignored. The elderly do not need Medicare. The young do not need more help in getting a better education. Workers do not require the guarantee of a healthy and a safe place to work.

In their fantasy world, all the complex global changes of the world since World War II have never happened. In their fantasy America, all problems have simple solutions. Simple—and wrong.

It is a make-believe world. A world of good guys and bad guys, where some politicians shoot first and ask questions later.

No hard choices. No sacrifice. No tough decisions. It sounds too good to be true—and it is.

The path of fantasy leads to irresponsibility. The path of reality leads to hope and peace. The two paths could not be more different. Nor could the futures to which they lead.

Let's take a hard look at the consequences of our choice.

You and I have been working toward a secure future by rebuilding our military strength—steadily, carefully and responsibly. The Republicans talk about military strength—but they were in office for eight out of the last 11 years—and in the face of a growing Soviet threat they steadily cut real defense spending by more than a third.

We've reversed the Republican decline in defense. Every year since I've been president, we've had real increases in our commitment to a stronger nation—increases which are prudent and rational. There is no doubt that the United States of America can meet any threat from the Soviet Union.

Our modernized strategic forces, a revitalized NATO, the Trident submarine, the cruise missile, Rapid Deployment Force—all these guarantee that we will never be second to any nation. Deeds, not words—fact, not fiction.

We must and we will continue to build our own defenses. We must and we will continue to seek balanced reductions in nuclear arms.

The new leaders of the Republican Party, in order to close the gap between their rhetoric and their record, have now promised to launch an all-out nuclear arms race. This would negate any further effort to negotiate a strategic arms limitation agreement.

There can be no winners in such an arms race—and all the people of the Earth can be the losers.

The Republican nominee advocates abandoning arms control policies which have been important and supported by every Democratic president since Harry Truman and also by every Republican president since Dwight D. Eisenhower. This radical and irresponsible course would threaten our security—and could put the whole world in peril.

You and I must never let this come to pass.

It's simple to call for a new arms race. But when armed aggression threatens world peace, tough-sounding talk like that is not enough. A president must act—responsibly.

When Soviet troops invaded Afghanistan, we moved quickly to take action. I suspended some grain sales to the Soviet Union. I called for draft registration. We joined wholeheartedly with the Congress. And I joined wholeheartedly with the Congress and with the U.S. Olympics Committee and led more than 60 other nations in boycotting the big propaganda show in Russia—the Moscow Olympics.

The Republican leader opposed two of these forceful but peaceful actions and he waffled on the third. But when we asked him what he would do about aggression in Southwest Asia, he suggested blockading Cuba. Even his running mate wouldn't go along with that.

He doesn't seem to know what to do with the Russians. He's not sure if he wants to feed them or play with them or fight with them.

As I look back on my first term, I'm grateful that we've had a country with a full four years of peace. And that's what we're going to have for the next four years—peace.

It's only common sense that if America is to stay secure and at peace, we must encourage others to be peaceful as well.

As you know, we've helped in Zimbabwe-Rhodesia, where we stood firm for racial justice and democracy. And we have also helped in the Middle East. Some have criticized the Camp David accords and they've criticized some delays in the implementation of the Middle East peace treaty.

Well, before I became president there was no Camp David accord and there was no Middle East peace treaty. Before Camp David, Israel and Egypt were poised across barbed wire, confronting each other with guns and tanks and planes. But afterward, they talked face-to-face with each other across a peace table—and they also communicated through their own ambassadors in Cairo and Tel Aviv.

Now that's the kind of future we're offering—of peace to the Middle East if the Democrats are re-elected in the fall.

I am very proud that nearly half the aid that our country has ever given to Israel in the 32 years of her existence has come during my administration. Unlike our Republican predecessors, we have never stopped nor slowed that aid to Israel. And as long as I am president, we will never do so. Our commitment is clear: security and peace for Israel; peace for all the peoples of the Middle East.

But if the world is to have a future of freedom as well as peace, America must continue to defend human rights.

Now listen to this: The new Republican leaders oppose our human rights policy. They want to scrap it. They seem to think it's naive for America to stand up to freedom and—for freedom and democracy. Just what do they think we should stand up for?

Ask the former political prisoners who now live in freedom if we should abandon our stand on human rights.

Ask the dissidents in the Soviet Union about our commitment to human rights.

Ask the Hungarian-Americans, ask the Polish-Americans. Listen to Pope John Paul II.

Ask those who are suffering for the sake of justice and liberty around the world.

Ask the millions who've fled tyranny if America should stop speaking out for human principles.

Ask the American people. I tell you that as long as I am president, we will hold high the banner of human rights, and you can depend on it.

Here at home the choice between the two futures is equally important.

In the long run, nothing is more crucial to the future of America than energy—nothing was so disastrously neglected in the past.

Long after the 1973 Arab oil embargo, the Republicans in the White House had still done nothing to meet the threat to national security of our nation. Then, as now, their policy was dictated by the big oil companies.

We Democrats fought hard to rally our nation behind a comprehensive energy program and a good program—a new foundation for challenging and exciting progress. Now, after three years of struggle, we have that program.

The battle to secure America's energy future has been fully and finally joined. Americans have cooperated with dramatic results.

We've reversed decades of dangerous and growing dependence on foreign oil. We are now importing 20 percent less oil. That is one and a half million barrels of oil every day less than the day I took office.

And with our new energy policy now in place, we can discover more, produce more, create more, and conserve more energy—and we will use American resources, American technology, and millions of American workers to do it with.

Now what do the Republicans propose?

Basically their energy program has two parts.

The first part is to get rid of almost everything that we've done for the American public in the last three years.

They want to reduce or abolish the synthetic fuels program. They want to slash the solar energy incentives, the conservation programs, aid to mass transit, aid to the elderly Americans to help pay their fuel bills.

They want to eliminate the fifty-five mile speed limit. And while they're at it, the Republicans would like to gut the Clean Air Act. They never liked it to begin with.

That's one part of the program.

The other part is worse.

To replace what we have built, this is what they propose: to destroy the windfall profits tax, and to "unleash" the oil companies and let them solve the energy problem for us.

That's it. That's the whole program. There is no more.

Can this nation accept such an outrageous program? No! We Democrats will fight it every step of the way, and we'll begin tomorrow morning with the campaign for re-election in November.

When I took office, I inherited a heavy load of serious economic problems besides energy—and we've met them all head-on. We've slashed government regulation and put free enterprise back into the airlines, the trucking and the financial systems of our country—and we're now doing the same thing for the railroads. This is the greatest change in the relationship between government and business since the New Deal.

We've increased our exports dramatically. We've reversed the decline in the basic research and development. And we have created more than 8 million new jobs—the biggest increase in the history of our country.

But the road's bumpy, and last year's skyrocketing OPEC price increases have helped to trigger a worldwide inflation crisis.

We took forceful action, and interest rates have now fallen, the dollar is stable and, although we still have a battle on our hands, we are struggling to bring inflation under control.

We are now at a critical turning point in our economic history. Because we made the hard decisions—because we guided our economy through a rough but essential period of transition—we have laid the groundwork for a new economic age.

Our economic renewal program for the 1980s will meet our immediate need for jobs by attacking the very same long-term problems that caused unemployment and inflation in the first place. It will move America simultaneously towards our five great economic goals—lower inflation, better productivity, revitalization of American industry, energy security and jobs.

It is time to put all America back to work—not in make work, but in real work.

There is real work in modernizing American industry and creating new industries for America.

Here are just a few things we will build together:

New industries to turn our coal and shale and farm products into fuel for our cars and trucks, and to turn the light of the sun into heat and electricity for our homes.

A modern transportation system for railbeds and ports to make American coal into a powerful rival of OPEC oil;

Industries that will provide the convenience of communications and futuristic computer technology to serve millions of American homes, offices and factories;

Job training for workers displaced by economic changes;

New investment pinpointed in regions and communities where jobs are needed most;

Better mass transit in our cities and between cities;

And a whole new generation of American jobs to make homes and vehicles and buildings that will house us and move us in comfort—with a lot less energy.

This is important, too: I have no doubt that the ingenuity and dedication of the American people can make every single one of these things happen. We are talking about the United States of America—and those who count this country out as an economic superpower are going to find out just how wrong they are.

We are going to share in the exciting enterprise of making the 1980s a time of growth for America.

The Republican tax program offers rebates to the rich, deprivation for the poor and fierce inflation for all of us. Their party's own vice presidential nominee said that "Reagan-Kemp-Roth" would result in an inflation rate of more than 30 percent. He called it "voodoo economics." He suddenly changed his mind toward the end of the Republican convention, but he was right the first time.

Along with this gigantic tax cut, the new Republican leaders promise to protect retirement and health programs, and to have massive increases in defense spending.

And they claim they can balance the budget.

If they are serious about these promises—and they say they are—then a close analysis shows that the entire rest of the government would have to be abolished—everything from education to farm programs, from the G.I. Bill to the night watchman at the Lincoln Memorial. And the budget would still be in the red.

The only alternative would be to build more printing presses to print cheap money. Either way the American people lose. But the American people will not stand for it.

The Democratic Party has always embodied the hope of our people for justice, opportunity and a better life. And we've worked in every way possible to strengthen the American family, to encourage self-reliance, and to follow the Old Testament admonition: "Defend the poor and fatherless: give justice to the afflicted and needy." (Psalms 82:3)

We have struggled to assure that no child in America ever goes to bed hungry, that no elderly couple in America has to live in a substandard home, and that no young person in America is excluded from college because the family is poor.

What have the Republicans proposed? Just an attack on everything we have done in the achievement in social justice and decency that we've won in the last 50 years—ever since Franklin Delano Roosevelt's first term. They would make Social Security voluntary. They would reverse our progress on the minimum wage, full employment laws, safety in the work place and a healthy environment.

Lately, as you know, the Republicans have been quoting Democratic presidents, but who can blame them? Would you rather quote Herbert Hoover or Franklin Delano Roosevelt? Would you rather quote Richard Nixon or John Fitzgerald Kennedy?

The Republicans have always been the party of privilege, but this year their leaders have gone even further. In their platform, they have repudiated the best traditions of their own party.

Where is the conscience of Lincoln in the party of Lincoln? What's become of that traditional Republican commitment to fiscal responsibility? What's happened to their commitment to a safe and sane arms control?

Now I don't claim perfection for the Democratic Party. I don't claim that every decision that we have made has been right or popular. Certainly they've not all been easy. But I will say this:

We've been tested under fire. We've neither ducked nor hidden. And we've tackled the great, central issues in our time, the historic challenges of peace and energy which had been ignored for years.

We've made tough decisions and we've taken the heat for them. We've made mistakes and we've learned from them. So we have built the foundation now for a better future.

We've done something else—perhaps even more important. In good times and bad, in the valleys and on the peaks, we've told people the truth—the hard truth—the truth that sometimes hurts.

One truth that we Americans have learned is that our dream has been earned for progress and for peace. Look what our land has been through within our own memory—a great depression, a world war, the technological explosion, the civil rights revolution, the bitterness of Vietnam, the shame of Watergate, the twilight peace of nuclear terror.

Through each of these momentous experiences we've learned the hard way about the world and about ourselves. For we've matured and we've grown as a nation. And we've grown stronger.

We've learned the uses and the limitations of power. We've learned the beauty and responsibility of freedom. We've learned the value and the obligation of justice— and we have learned the necessity of peace.

Some would argue that to master these lessons is somehow to limit our potential. That is not so. A nation which knows its true strengths, which sees its true challenges, which understands legitimate constraints—that nation, our nation—is far stronger than one which takes refuge in wishful thinking or nostalgia.

The Democratic Party—the American people—have understood these fundamental truths.

All of us can sympathize with the desire for easy answers. There's often the temptation to substitute idle dreams for hard reality.

The new Republican leaders are hoping that our nation will succumb to that temptation this year. But they profoundly misunderstand and underestimate the character of the American people.

There weeks after Pearl Harbor, Winston Churchill came to North America—and he said:

"We've not journeyed all this way across the centuries, across the oceans, across the mountains, across the prairies because we are made of sugar candy."

We Americans have courage.

Americans have always been on the cutting edge of change. We've always looked forward with anticipation and confidence. I still want the same thing that all of you want—a self-reliant neighborhood and strong families; work for the able-bodied and good medical care for the sick; opportunity for our youth and dignity for our old; equal rights and justice for all people.

I want teachers eager to explain what a civilization really is—and I want students to understand their own needs and their own aims, but also the needs and yearnings of their neighbors. I want women free to pursue without limit the full life of what they want for themselves.

I want our farmers growing crops to feed our nation and the world, secure in the knowledge that the family farm will thrive and with a fair return on the good work they do for all of us. I want workers to see meaning in the labor they perform—and work enough to guarantee a job for every worker in this country.

And I want the people in business free to pursue with boldness and freedom new ideas. And I want minority citizens fully to join the mainstream of American life, and I want from the bottom of my heart to remove the blight of racial and other discrimination from the face of our nation, and I'm determined to do it.

I need for all of you to join me in fulfilling that vision. The choice—the choice between the two futures—could not be more clear. If we succumb to a dream world, then we'll wake up to a nightmare. But if we start with reality and fight to make our dreams a reality—then Americans will have a good life, a life of meaning and purpose in a nation that's strong and secure.

Above all, I want us to be what the founders of our nation meant us to become—the land of freedom, the land of peace, and the land of hope.

Thank you very much.

☆

JIMMY CARTER
Campaign Speech
ATLANTA, GEORGIA

September 16, 1980

Speaking at a meeting with Southern black leaders

Thank you, Andy and Mayor Jackson, Congressman Parren Mitchell, my friend, Cameron Alexander, Reverend Dr. Roberts, Coretta King, Daddy King:

I was going to describe to you in my opening remarks how far we've come, but I think Maynard Jackson did it better than anyone that I know when he, as a black mayor, referred to a white President as a Georgia boy [*Laughter*] I think he pretty well wrapped it up, don't you? [*Laughter*] And I can actually say it gave me a warm feeling to hear it.

As I was coming in the church a while ago, I was asked a question by a newsman about the importance of this meeting, and I've been thinking about it since I decided to come down here. Several mentioned this. I could not improve on the speeches that have been made so far, and I wish I could sit in on the speeches after I leave—[*laughter*]—because there are some things that are going to be said that I would really like to hear. But I'll depend on you all to give me a report.

If it hadn't been for Daddy King and his beloved wife, I would not be President. Had they not had their son, Martin Luther King, Jr., I would not be President. Had he not been a man of courage and vision and tenacity and faith, I would not be President. And had it not been for the people in this audience—I started to say congregation—I would not be President. You all had confidence in me in 1976, when very few people knew who I was, and there was an actual stigma attached to a Southern white politician, a Georgia Governor, that you helped to remove.

I have had continual need for you. Once during the campaign I made a remark about ethnic purity, and it almost crippled me fatally. I didn't know what to do. I got a call from Andy, and I got a call from Daddy King; I got a call from many of you. And I decided to come home to Atlanta, had a rally in the downtown square. Four or five thousand people came. All I wanted to do was what happened. I got on the stage, in front of the TV cameras, and Daddy King held my hand. And the people all over the nation saw it, and it healed the wound that I had done to myself. So, I'm aware of the importance of this meeting, and what was said at the very beginning by Jesse Hill is accurate.

This meeting this morning could very well decide the outcome of this election and, more importantly, but significantly, the future of this country. When my Presidency has not always satisfied every one of you—and I acknowledge that's a fact—my phone has been open to you and others that are not here this morning. And you have never failed to use it. I get quick telephone calls, and they're returned. But if my opponent should be elected, you're going to have a hard time getting a telephone call answered at the White House. And if my opponent is elected, I doubt that there will ever be a Martin Luther King, Jr., holiday. And there ought to be one in this country.

Daddy King is a great politician. He's a great preacher. He's a great family man. Now he's become a great author. He's just written an autobiography, and I hope you all buy it and read it. I was hoping he'd give me a copy; he hasn't done it yet. I'll have to buy one like you will. [*Laughter*] But in the end he says that, "I was put here, as the old folks say, on a purpose." Maybe I was elected President on a purpose. Our country was created on a purpose. Freedom was born in the human breast on a purpose. Courage was created among human beings on a purpose. And we have an obligation to carry out that purpose.

I know that Daddy King's son once said, "Man . . . is not very flotsam and jetsam in the river of life, but he's the child of God." And it's important that in this nation at least, as an example for all the rest of the world, that politicians don't forget that. That worth of an individual human being in the eyes of God and in the eyes of one's fellow human beings—that's been forgotten in the past.

In this region for too long, politicians who hoped to be elected to the office of country commissioner or mayor or Governor or Congressman or Senator had to divide blacks from whites and had to blame the poverty that afflicted our nation among white people on the black people and vice versa. But it wasn't necessary to talk to blacks much, because they didn't have the right to vote. And there are some people sitting here who helped pave the way for those rights, which must be protected and preserved—John Lewis, in the audience, Joe Lowry—I'm going to visit him right after I leave here at Martin's headquarters—and Daddy King.

Back in the early thirties, Daddy King decided, according to his book, that he needed to have the right to vote for President, because the President's decision affected his life and the life of people he loved. He went to the county courthouse here. There were two elevators: one for white folks, one for colored folks; had signs above them so you wouldn't make a mistake. One of them was working up to the registrar's office. I don't think you need to think long to figure out which one was working. So, Daddy King said, "Well, I'll just walk up the stairs." When he approached the stairs, there was a policeman standing there, and a sign was there, by the stairs, that said, "White Only." He kept going back time after time after time, day after day.

Eventually the "colored" elevator was working, and he was able to get to the registrar's office. The registrar told him about the poll tax. Daddy King was willing to pay the poll tax, but he found that you didn't have to pay it not just for only yourself but for all your ancestors who had lived in Georgia and hadn't paid their poll tax. And finally, that obstacle was removed by the Federal Government.

And Daddy King went back as a young man, and they explained that there were 30 questions he had to answer, questions that a political science professor at the University of Georgia could not answer. They were still on the books when I became State senator. That first speech I made in the State senate was to do away with those 30 questions. And in Daddy King's book, he said a lot of black people learned a lot about government trying to answer those 30 questions. It's paying off now.

He never dreamed that eventually his son would be a world hero and that we would have black mayors in Atlanta and Detroit, Los Angeles, many other great cities—Birmingham now—many other great cities around this country. He never dreamed that his granddaughter would be in the Georgia legislature, that his daughter-in-law would serve at the United Nations, that Andy Young would be the spokesman for this country, among more than 150 nations on Earth, and would spread the Gospel that was preached on this pulpit thoughout the world and that politicians who lead other nations would listen and would say, "So that's what the United States is. I was getting the wrong impression when Richard Nixon was the President."

These changes have been made. We've come a long way. We haven't yet reached the Promised Land that was spelled out so clearly for us by Martin Luther King, Jr., and by many of you who were also very courageous and very tenacious in spite of the most difficult possible obstacles.

We're no longer divided, white from blacks. We no longer see so many of our babies die, black and white. We no longer see so many of our young people leave the South because there was no alternative, black and white. We no longer see the devastation of poverty and disease and discrimination sweep through our communities, both black and white. We've made progress. We still have a long way to go.

I've appointed all those people that Andy described, and I can tell you this: I have not had to lower the standards of quality and excellence and commitment in order to do it. I haven't done them a favor; they've done me a favor. And I'm not through yet. We've got a lot of other appointments to make.

We've had economic difficulties the last few years, as Andy pointed out. But in spite of those obstacles, we've added 8½ million new jobs to the American economy. Employment among black people has gone up 22 percent in the last 3½ years. 1.3 million of those new jobs are held by black people; another million by people who speak Spanish. We've focused those jobs on those that need them most and the plans for the future are much greater than that. And our nation hasn't suffered. These are not make-work jobs created in Government. These are permanent jobs, solid jobs, career jobs.

We've got a proposal in Congress now to add two more billion dollars to put our young people to work, because we've got so far to go in that respect—a way to tie together the high school graduates and the trade school graduates with the jobs available in that community and make sure they know how to hold a job when they get there and to help tide over that salary payment for those few months as they become qualified. It's going to meld together labor and education now, for a change, and we'll have a much brighter future because of it.

We've solved to a great degree the problem of not having an energy policy. And we'll have $88 billion in the future to have help for poor people to pay their energy bills and to have a better transportation system to get to and from work and to create new technology and an exciting life and dynamic life for our country, to rebuild America's industry and to give our workers tools with which to be more productive. And we are opening up the world, now and in the future, for additional trade.

I was in a little steel mill last week in Perth Amboy, New Jersey, the most modern steel mill in the world. The workers there produce more steel per year, each worker, than any other place in the world, and they are selling steel rods to China cheaper, halfway around the world, than Japan can make them and ship them a couple of hundred miles across the China Sea. It's the kind of thing we can do.

That valuable relationship with a billion people in China and millions of people in Zimbabwe and other areas of the world that are now our friends is very valuable to everyone here. One of the most emotional meetings I have ever had was with Prime Minister Mugabe in the East Room of the White House just a few days ago—the new Prime Minister of Zimbabwe. This was a terrible political struggle—Parren Mitchell and Andy Young know it—because of tremendous pressures from an ill-informed American public, concentrated on me in the Oval Office, not to stand for democracy, not to stand for majority rule, not to stand for the elimination of racial discrimination all the way over in the dark continent of Africa. But with your help we stood firm, and now there's a freedom there and a democracy there and a majority rule there that's an inspiration to the entire world. And I'm proud that Andy Young was there to help us make this come true.

You've seen in this campaign the stirrings of hate and the rebirth of code words like "States rights" in a speech in Mississippi, in a campaign reference to the Ku Klux Klan, relating to the South. That is a message that creates a cloud on the political horizon. Hatred has no place in this country. Racism has no place in this country. Daddy King says in his book, "Nothing that a man does makes him lower than when he allows himself to hate anyone. Hatred is not needed," he says, "to stamp out evil. Despite what some people have been taught, people can accomplish all things God wills in this world. Hate cannot."

Just briefly, let's look to the future. I see a future for this country to be strong, to be united, to be confident, to be inspired, to be even more free, to be employed in useful work, to be well educated, to be united, to be filled with love and compassion one from another. I see a future in this country where those that fought hard to achieve civil rights will continue, in the Federal Government and all other governments, to administer the very laws that they were willing to risk their lives to achieve.

I see a Federal court system that's filled not only with a desire for justice but a desire for understanding of the special deprivation of justice that still prevails in this country against those who are poor or inarticulate or not well organized or not well educated. We've got a long way to go in the Federal courts where, still, money available to have competent lawyers is an obstacle to true justice. But whenever I appoint a black judge or Hispanic judge or even a woman judge, I know that they not only have committed in their own hearts a vision of what this nation ought to be but a special knowledge of the effects of past discrimination that are still there as a means to prevent equality of opportunity.

And I see an America where young people don't have to worry about employment. I don't know of anything that's more devastating to a nation than to have a 17- or 18- or a 19- or a 20-year-old young person, having struggled through high school, sometimes at great sacrifice to the family, having been given talent and ability and ambition and hope by God, week after week after week not be able to find a way to use their talent or that ability—it becomes a matter of loss of self-respect and then following that, discouragement and despair and then alienation and then a sense of lashing out at the system that deprived that young person of a chance to be useful in God's world. We've got to continue that effort, and that is still a question in doubt. We have a youth bill in the Congress right now, a $2 billion youth bill to create that kind of opportunity for many of our young people.

And we've got another bill in the Congress that hasn't yet been passed, that many of you have worked to achieve, to create fair housing implementation. We had a fair housing bill passed in 1968. It hasn't been implemented. It's passed the House; it's in doubt in the Senate. I had a long conversation with Senator Kennedy yesterday on Air Force One, coming back from Texas. He said, "Mr. President, we've got to work together to get that bill through the Senate. It's now come out of my committee, and we'll be marshaling our forces to get that fair housing bill passed." He and I agreed on the phone it's the greatest civil rights legislation in the last 10 years.

You've not yet been adequately marshaled to put those Senators on the record. And I'd like to ask you this morning, if you don't do anything else in the Congress, to help get that fair housing bill passed. It's important to the future of our country to eliminate the last legal impediment of the right of our people to have equal opportunity by choosing where they want to live. This is extremely important.

And the last point I want to make to you is this: Andy Young, Don McHenry, Pat Harris, Eleanor Holmes Norton, Drew Days, Clifford Alexander, many others are now working with me in the Federal Government. I consider all of you to be my partners, as well. I know the importance among those who look to you for leadership for your voice to be heard in shaping our nation's future. The decision is going to be made on November the 4th about what kind of future we will have.

And I ask you to study the platform of the Republican Party. It's not going to be possible in my judgment, although I hope I'm wrong, for me to face head on in a public debate Governor Reagan, the Republican nominee. He's now been deprived by his staff of the opportunity to speak out on the issues. He didn't do too well with the Ku-Klux Klan or China, as you know. [*Laughter*] He was making some progress on evolution, but he cut that off. But it's going to be hard for the people to understand what this election is all about unless you tell them. And collectively, this group in this room can remember what happened to Daddy King and his son and many of those you love as they struggled for the right to vote and how important it is for people to register and take advantage of that right, that cost so much, which is so easily ignored.

And I see a nation at peace. Peace is not something that comes to the timid or to the weak. Our nation is strong—strongest on earth. Militarily, economically, politically, morally, ethically, our nation is the strongest on earth. And if we are strong, the weak need not have so much fear. And if we are at peace, then the world has a much better chance to stay at peace.

If we abandon the commitment to control nuclear weapons—which has been a part of the administration of every President, Democratic or Republican, since the time of Eisenhower and Truman—as has been advocated by the Republican nominee, then the chances for the avoiding of a nuclear war in the future will be severely reduced. I'm not predicting war, but I tell you that it's very important for us to stay strong and at the same time search for peace with the Soviet Union and with every other union or nation on earth that wants to avoid a nuclear holocaust.

I'll do my part. The Vice President could make the same speech to you that I've made this morning, and you would have confidence that he was speaking from the heart. You know that. And my Cabinet officers—Andy and all of you know them—have the same philosophy that I have, and those that I've appointed to major positions in the Federal courts, and otherwise, share my commitment that I've described to you so briefly this morning. And all of us will do our part. But I have to tell you that the most important factor is what you do and others like you who are not running for office—at least not running for President, thank goodness.

But you see the importance of the outcome of this election. We are indeed talking about two paths to the future. And I believe that our path, your path, is the one that must prevail, but it can very well not prevail, unless you do your share.

You remember 1968, how a divided Democratic Party deprived Hubert Humphrey of a chance to serve as President and put Richard Nixon in the White House. A few votes, a few more speeches, a few more radio tapes and TV advertisements could have prevented the Nixon administration taking place. That's what we face this year.

Our party has been remarkably unified since the convention. Senator Kennedy is campaigning for me and with me. We'll be together on the 22d in Los Angeles, raising money. But that unity is not enough unless there's enthusiasm and a commitment and a sacrificial spirit to help me solve these difficult issues, for which there are no easy answers, now and in the next 4 years.

You've got a friend in the Oval Office, and if you'll help me, I'll be there as your friend for the next 4 years.

Thank you very much.

☆

JOHN B. ANDERSON
Campaign Speech
WASHINGTON, D.C.

April 24, 1980

I have chosen, after careful deliberation, to pursue an independent course toward the Presidency of the United States.

I will not run as a candidaate of a third party. I will pursue an independent candidacy.

Therefore, I am announcing my withdrawal from the race for the Republican nomination for President.

I do so with gratitude in my heart for the countless Americans who have offered me their support, their hard work, and their hopes.

I am also grateful for those who have exercised their precious right of franchise, and chosen to cast a ballot for my cadidacy on the Republican line in the six primaries I have actively contested.

But I am not leaving any of the people I have mentioned.

I am inviting their continued support of me and my independent candidacy.

I have chosen this course of action because it is now clear that I cannot attain a majority of the delegates who will be attending the Republican national convention in July.

Therefore, it is with deep appreciation that I am releasing from any further obligation those men and women who have been elected as convention delegates pledged to support my candidacy.

At the same time, I have directed my campaign committee to return matching Federal election funds which have not been expended as determined by the Federal Election Commission.

In the course of making these decisions, I have consulted first with members of my family. I have also listened carefully to the advice and suggestions of many friends and counselors.

And I have done something else. I have gone back to reconsider the reasons that led me at the very outset, some ten months ago, to declare my intention to seek the Presidency.

What I have concluded is that in the intervening time my initial motivations to seek the Presidency have been reinforced.

I was convinced then, and I remain convinced now, that our nation is adrift in what Churchill would have called a gathering storm.

Since last June the signs that America is beset by a crisis of governance, and one of truly alarming proportions, have multiplied.

It is a crisis which manifests itself in what the President himself now concedes is an economic recession of unknown depth and duration.

Individual and business bankruptcies are approaching historic levels.

Unemployment is increasing.

The spendable income of the average worker is steadily declining.

Home ownership, once a part of the dream of the good life in America, is now fast exceeding the reach of many of our citizens because of a chronic inflation abetted by high interest rates.

Our basic industries are no longer in the robust and vigorous shape that once defined the American economy and made it a model for the world.

Instead, factory gates are closing shut, and hundreds of thousands of workers are finding themselves thrown into the swelling ranks of the unemployed and discontented.

The source of the problem is plain to see: the current administration has demonstrated a total inability to chart a clear, commonsense economic policy that is capable of arresting our domestic economic decline.

The Carter Administration's failures in this regard have contributed to a growing sense of unease in the international community. There is rising concern that America, unable to deal with its domestic problems, is finally destined to relinquish her role as a leader in world affairs

But I know something that the international community does not know. I know that the heart of America is still beating strong and that there is will and determination among our people.

Our national image of self-doubt and confusion does not stem from the fact that our people have lost confidence in themselves or in the inherent strengths of our nation.

Rather, it is because our people have grown to mistrust the motives and the abilities of our national leadership. Our people have come to doubt that they are being told the real truths about their nation's condition. And they have acquired a skepticism that President Carter will do what needs to be done.

America can no longer afford those who are more interested in perpetuating their political power than in perpetuating the ideal for which everyday Americans continue to strive.

And America will not tolerate a President who puts his finger to the prevailing political winds, rather than to the pulse of an anxious nation.

If a great nation, and we are a great nation, is to repair itself, then its leaders must recognize that the old sophistries can no longer substitute for the plain unvarnished truths.

How can a proud and seemingly affluent society justify unemployment rates ranging up to 40% for many of its young people?

How can a proud and seemingly affluent society justify dampening the hopes of millions of its people for educational opportunities, and dampen their hopes for providing their children with the very advantages enjoyed by the parents?

We cannot and we must not be satisified with anything less than a total review of all the economic policies which have produced the situation, where a great industrial society is revealed as obsolescent, it workers declining in productivity, its exports losing their competitive edge in world markets.

The major premise of my campaign has been that America must build a new ethic of sacrifice and sharing, of conservation and saving, if we are to begin the process needed to restore a sound economy and maintain a stable democratic society.

It is my profound belief that only when we accomplish that basic goal will we recover our traditional prestige and influence in world affairs.

I have offered specific blueprints.

I have suggested that we must have an energy policy geared to the immediate objective of reducing our consumption of imported oil. This gluttony robs our national treasury of $100-billion annually, and offers our foreign policy and national security as hostage to erratic foreign leaders and uncertain events abroad.

To redress this problem will require a willingness to tax ourselves, rather than to permit OPEC to levy taxes upon our economy in the form of higher and higher prices.

I have suggested an income policy to replace the present charade of government efforts to restrain wage and price increases.

I have stated that rather than simply promising everyone an across-the-board reduction in taxes—during a period of unprecedented inflation—we must search out those specific tax reductions which will achieve the savings and investment required to rebuild our economy.

The people of America are ready for a President who will inspire the hope for our revitalization, and the people of America are ready to do their part to accomplish our revitalization.

We must put to rest the notion that as a nation of individuals we are locked in mindless competion for a bigger share of our nation's prosperity—without regard for the greater goal of a healthy, more just, and equitable society.

It is my fundamental belief that such a vision can be communicated to 225-million Americans and out of that vision will emerge a strong, confident and self-reliant nation.

Against that background, I want to turn to the rationale of my independent candidacy because the nation has right to know what it means.

Lest anybody misunderstand, I have been a member of the Republican party for 30 years.

I will continue my membership in that party.

It is obvious that this is a most serious step, and that it is a step fraught with obstacles.

But on balance, the obstacles pale when one considers that too many people in our nation are disillusioned with the prospective choices our party structures are offering.

The result is frustration, apathy and despair.

The danger is that a significant portion of the nation may choose not to participate in the political process in November of 1980.

Yet the electoral decision taken at that time will determine the course of our nation for decades to come.

There is current statistical evidence that virtually one-half of potential voters are dissatisfied with a choice between President Carter and Ronald Reagan.

That figure takes on added significance when you consider that since 1960 the number of eligible voters who cast their ballots has steadily declined to 53%.

It seems likely that voter apathy will increase unless an alternative is available in 1980.

I believe that growing disaffection with the political process poses a far greater threat to the stability of our democratic institutions than what some are sure to charge is an oblique, perhaps frontal, attack on the two-party system.

An independent candidacy, distinguished from a third party candidacy, is an effort to broaden the choice available to millions of potential voters who simply do not participate in party primaries and caucuses.

The evidence is clear that an independent candidacy would provide a choice for those three-quarters of all eligible American voters who do not participate in party primaries or caucuses.

I also believe that an independent candidacy, unfettered by party positions, would vastly increase the likelihood that a thorough, dispassionate discussion of the host of complex issues confronting the nation and the world will take place.

Rather than simply engaging in the conventional partisan jousting to score debating points, it will become possible to conduct a positive effort to articulate positions and policies capable of leading our country into a new era of growth and achievement.

This will obviously require a willingness to communicate some harsh and even unpalatable truths and pose choices that will not be simple or easy.

I strongly disagree with those who claim that my intended action to run an independent candidacy places me in the role of a so-called spoiler.

It does not "spoil" the political process when I seek to involve in that process young people and others who in the past, and even now, consider our democractic system irrelevant to their lives.

And it does not "spoil" the political process to recognize the crisis facing us, and to provide the American people with new and alternative ideas.

There is still another consideration relating to my independent candidacy.

Public opinion polls show that I would receive between 18 and 21 percent of the vote if the election were held today, with President Carter and Ronald Reagan each falling within the 30–40 percent range.

However, 50% of the public still has little information about me, about my ideas for a revitalized America.

I can reach out and touch those people.

And that is where my campaign will succeed.

In the coming weeks, I will have to ascertain that my candidacy can overcome the numerous legal obstacles that stand in the way of an independent candidacy.

However, I am confident the legal obstacles will be overcome and that, indeed, I will remain as an independent candidate, through Election Day.

It will also be necessary in the coming weeks to ascertain that my candidacy can gather the financial and political support necessary to mount a challenge that will prevail.

I have authorized an exploratory group to begin the process of placing my name on as many states' ballots as possible, and to take steps to challenge the laws in those states which restrict access to the ballot.

In summation, I intend to pursue an independent candidacy because our nation faces a crisis and because we need alternatives.

A new national unity is required to recognize the profound problems before us, and to face up to the serious new approaches required to overcome those problems.

It is a time for patriotism, not partisanship.

It is a time for vision, not nostalgia.

It is a time for honesty and boldness.

I believe that our people are tired of evasion and postponement.

I believe there is a new willingness to accept sacrifice, to accept discipline, to accept unpleasant truths.

It is a willingness that remains only to be invited.

Our nation needs a choice in November.

Not just a choice among candidates.

I mean a choice of course for the nation.

I want to offer that choice.

And I believe the American people will want to respond.

☆

1984

☆

Ronald Reagan surprised most pundits and pollsters by the large size of his victory over incumbent President Jimmy Carter in the 1980 election. Reagan's skill as a persuader of the public through adroit use of public relations and television, along with the new Republican control of the Senate, both aided in the passage of a program labeled the "Reagan Revolution." Unprecedented budget cuts in social services and dramatic increases in appropriations for the Defense Department were combined with steep tax cuts aimed at stimulating economic expansion. Critics charged that the tax cuts favored the wealthy while the Census Bureau reported that 15.2 percent of the population lived in poverty, an increase of 13 percent since 1980.

The new President had promised in his 1980 campaign addresses that his economic program would expand the economy to the extent that the bulging federal deficit would be eliminated. By 1982, however, the United States experienced a sharp recession, which pushed unemployment rates to 10.7 percent and led to a political resurgence by Democrats in the congressional elections. The projected budget deficit for 1984 hovered around the $200 billion mark, looming as a potential political problem for the man who had earlier railed against the much lower Carter deficits.

Reagan also challenged the broad consensus on civil rights that had persisted since the mid 1960s. He threw government support against both affirmative-action efforts and school busing that attempted to redress past discrimination. Early in his Administration, however, he achieved an historic milestone when he chose the first woman, Sandra Day O'Connor, to sit on the U.S. Supreme Court. While some fundamentalist conservatives such as Moral Majority head Rev. Jerry Falwell opposed the O'Connor nomination and were disappointed by the lack of federal action limiting abortions and by inaction on other issues on their legislative agenda, most continued strongly to support Reagan.

Having warned that America faced a "window of vulnerability" vis à vis Russian offensive weapons, the new Administration sponsored a five-year $1.7 trillion military budget that increased pressure on the federal debt. Reagan and his Defense Department Secretary Caspar Weinberger increased the Administration's commitments to the *contra* movement fighting the Marxist government of Nicaragua. The United States also provided significant military aid and direction in the war against insurgents by the government of El Salvador. These American commitments overseas were the targets of investigations by House Democrats and the news media, which frequently raised the specter of a "new" Vietnam. But few demonstrations against American policy erupted. In fact, public opinion polls showed wide approval of the President's use of American troops in overthrowing the Marxist regime in Grenada in the fall of 1979.

Another controversy developed in the Middle East after the Reagan Administration landed U.S. troops in war-torn Lebanon to police a cease-fire agreement. The mission of the troops seemed unclear in a country torn by diverse factions. Further debate arose after lax security around the American barracks resulted in the death by bombing of 241 American soliders. But this issue did not become central to the 1984 campaign because Reagan finally agreed on the gradual withdrawal of American troops.

Yet due to the wide attraction by Americans to the personality of Reagan, such adversities as that which had taken place in Lebanon, the severe recession, Reagan's periodic verbal gaffes, or even a variety of scandals involving Administration officials, never seemed to damage severely the President's public opinion ratings. By early 1984, the economy was quickly recovering from the recession and Reagan proclaimed in his State of the Union address that "America is back, standing tall."

Walter Mondale began to plan for his run for the Presidency soon after his defeat for the Vice Presidency in 1980. Securing early endorsements from the leadership of the AFL-CIO and numerous prominent Democrats, he gathered a skilled team of political operatives about him and built a large financial war chest. Crucial also to Mondale's enviable position was Edward Kennedy's firm announcement that he would not run for President in 1984. Others who did enter the Democratic field included Ohio Senator and former astronaut John Glenn, Colorado Senator Gary Hart, Calfornia Senator Alan Cranston, and former Democratic Presidential nominee George McGovern. Chicago's magnetic black preacher Jesse Jackson also became a candidate, seeking what he called a "rainbow coalition" of progressive whites, Hispanics, women, and blacks who were dissatisfied with the conservatism of the other Democrats.

After finishing a surprising second to Mondale in the Iowa caucuses, Hart pulled an upset victory in New Hampshire, and the primary season quickly boiled down to a three-man race among Mondale, Hart, and Jackson. The Colorado Senator was widely pictured as the candidate with "new ideas," attractive to young urban professionals who associated Mondale with the stale interest-group politics of the New Deal era and the failures of the Carter Administration. Jackson rallied an unprecedented number of black voters (but few whites) in a number of primaries in both the North and South, even coming within a percentage point of beating Hart in the New York primary and winning the Louisiana primary.

Yet after the final week of primaries in early June, with Mondale victorious in New Jersey and Hart winning California, a narrow convention victory for the exhausted Mondale seemed inevitable. To add dramatic as well as political appeal to his candidacy, Mondale announced on July 12th that he had selected Representative Geraldine Ferraro of New York as the first woman Vice Presidential candidate of a major party in American history.

The Democrats met in San Francisco and heard effective unity speeches from defeated candidate Jesse Jackson as well as the party keynoter, New York Governor Mario Cuomo. In his acceptance speech, Mondale tacitly accepted the proposition that the country had become more conservative in the past few years. He did roundly criticize Reagan for savaging Social Security and Medicare as well as creating $200 billion deficits. "What we have today is a government of the rich, by the rich, and for the rich . . ." Further, he warned, "we are living on borrowed money and borrowed time." Another significant appeal of Mondale's was to those Americans who had expressed deep concern about the Reagan Administration's inability to negotiate a nuclear weapons agreement with the Soviet Union. "Why can't we meet in summit conferences with the Soviet Union at least once a year?" he asked. "Why can't we reach agreements to save this earth?"

The Republicans met at Dallas in August and renominated Reagan and Vice President George Bush without opposition. On the 23rd, Reagan told the delegates that "America is presented with the clearest political choice of half a century." It was not a choice between right and left, he said, but one of downward versus upward social mobility. He condemned his opponents for "lump[ing] people [together] by groups or special interests" and for abandoning many of the principles enunciated in the Democratic Platform of 1932. Inflation, which had dropped dramatically under Reagan's leadership, had been "a deliberate part of [the Carter Administration's] official economic policy, needed, they said, to maintain prosperity." Reagan's speech reflected his desire to avoid accentuating his conservative positions on a number of moral issues that might alienate him from many watching him on television.

While early expectations of Ferraro's appeal to women voter's was optimistic, August found the Democrats badly damaged by revelations about her incomplete financial-disclosure forms and the business dealings of her husband. She was also publicly criticized by the Archbishop of New York for her position favoring free choice on abortions and frequently heckled by antiabortionist demonstrators around the country.

Despite a poor performance against Mondale in the first debate in Louisville, Kentucky, Reagan kept his wide lead in the polls throughout the campaign. His television advertising effectively sought to evoke an upbeat mood about the well-being of the country under the Reagan Presidency. The popularity of a nuclear freeze (which the President opposed) and the perception of Reagan as more prone to get America into a war was effectively countered in September. The President met with Soviet Foreign Minister Andrei Gromyko, thus dampening criticism for his failure to meet with the Soviet leadership during his Administration. Then Reagan used the United Nations as an effective political forum for his campaign by delivering a speech on September 24 that cited various American efforts to promote peace and called for "lifting the dread of nuclear war from the peoples of the Earth."

The next day, at George Washington University, Mondale delivered a rebuttal to Reagan's U.N. address that was uncharacteristically sharp and well received by the 1,500 students. He welcomed the President's "soothing new tone" but lashed out at Reagan's hypocrisy in playing the peacemaker during the campaign when he had measurably increased world tensions during the first three years of his Administration. "This crowd doesn't want you to think about the stakes in this contest," Mondale asserted. "They want to trivialize it."

RONALD REAGAN
Acceptance Speech

DALLAS, TEXAS

August 23, 1984

Mr. Chairman, Mr. Vice President, delegates to this convention, fellow citizens:

In 75 days, I hope we enjoy a victory that is the size of the heart of Texas. Nancy and I extend our deep thanks to the Lone Star State and the "Big D," the city of Dallas, for all their warmth and hospitality.

Four years ago I did not know precisely every duty of this office, and not too long ago, I learned about some new ones from the first graders of Corpus Christi School in Chambersburg, Pa. Little Leah Kline was asked by her teacher to describe my duties. She said: "The President goes to meetings. He helps the animals. The President gets frustrated. He talks to other Presidents."

How does wisdom begin at such an early age? Tonight, with a full heart and deep gratitude for your trust, I accept your nomination for the Presidency of the United States.

I will campaign on behalf of the principles of our party which lift America confidently into the future.

America is presented with the clearest political choice of half a century. The distinctions between our two parties and the different philosophy of our political opponents are at the heart of this campaign and America's future.

I've been campaigning long enough to know that a political party and its leadership can't change their colors in four days. We won't, and no matter how hard they tried, our opponents didn't in San Francisco.

We didn't discover our values in a poll taken a week before the convention. And we didn't set a weathervane on top of the Golden Gate Bridge before we started talking about the American family.

The choices this year are not just between two different personalities, or between two political parties. They are between two different visions of the future, two fundamentally different ways of governing—their government of pessimism, fear, and limits, or ours of hope, confidence, and growth.

Their government sees people only as members of groups. Ours serves all the people of America as individuals. Theirs lives in the past, seeking to apply the old and failed policies to an era that has passed them by. Ours learns from the past and strives to change by boldly charting a new course for the future.

Theirs lives by promises, the bigger, the better. We offer proven, workable answers.

Our opponents began this campaign hoping that America has a poor memory. Well, let's take them on a little stroll down memory lane and remind them of how a 4.8 percent inflation rate in 1976 became back-to-back years of double-digit inflation, the worst since World War I, punishing the poor and the elderly, young couples striving to start their new lives, and working people struggling to make ends meet.

Inflation was not some plague borne on the wind, it was a deliberate part of their official economic policy needed, they said, to maintain prosperity. They didn't tell us that with it would come the highest interest rates since the Civil War.

As average monthly mortgage payments more than doubled, home building nearly ground to a halt, and tens of thousands of carpenters were thrown out of work. And who controlled both houses of the Congress and the executive branch at the time? Not us.

Campaigning across America in 1980, we saw evidence everywhere of industrial decline. And in rural America, farmers' costs were driven up by inflation, they were devastated by a wrong-headed grain embargo, and were forced to borrow money at exorbitant interest rates just to get by. And, many of them didn't get by. Farmers have to fight insects, weather, and the marketplace—they shouldn't have to fight their own Government.

The high interest rates of 1980 were not talked about in San Francisco.

But now, about taxes. They were talked about in San Francisco. Will Rogers once said he never met a man he didn't like. If I could paraphrase, our friends in the other party have never met a tax they didn't like, or hike. Under their policies, tax rates have gone up three times as much for families with children as they have for everyone else over these past three decades. In just the five years before we came into office, taxes roughly doubled.

Some who spoke so loudly in San Francisco of fairness were among those who brought about the biggest single, individual tax increase in our history in 1977, calling for a series of increases in the Social Security payroll tax and in the amount of pay subject to the tax. The bill they passed called for two additional increases between now and 1990, increases that bear down hardest on those at the lower income levels.

The Census Bureau confirms that, because of the tax laws we inherited, the number of households at or below the poverty level paying Federal income tax more than doubled between 1980 and 1982. Well, they received some relief in 1983 when our across-the-board cut was fully in place, and they'll get more help when indexing goes into effect this January. Our opponents have repeatedly advocated eliminating indexing. Would that really hurt the rich? No, because the rich are already in top brackets. But those working men and women who depend on a cost-of-living adjustment to keep abreast of inflation would find themselves pushed into a higher tax bracket and would not keep even with inflation because they'd be paying a higher income tax. That's "bracket creep" and our opponents are for it; we're against it.

It is up to us to see that all our fellow citizens understand that confiscatory taxes, costly social experiments and economic tinkering were not just the policies of a single administration. For the 26 years prior to January 1981, the opposition party controlled both houses of Congress. Every spending bill and every tax for more than a quarter of a century has been of their doing.

About a decade ago, they said Federal spending was out of control, so they passed a Budget Control Act, and in the next five years, ran up deficits of $260 billion.

In 1981 we gained control of the Senate and the executive branch. With the help of some concerned Democrats in the House we started a policy of tightening the Federal budget instead of the family budget. A task force chaired by Vice President George Bush, the finest Vice President this country has ever had, eliminated unnecessary regulations that had been strangling business and industry.

While we have our friends down memory lane, maybe they'd like to recall a gimmick they designed for their 1976 campaign. As President Ford told us the night before last, adding the unemployment and inflation rates, they got what they called a misery index—in '76 it came to 12½ percent. They declared the incumbent had no right to seek re-election with that kind of misery index.

Four years ago in the 1980 election, they didn't mention the misery index. Possibly because it was then over 20 percent.

And do you know something? They won't mention it in this election either; it's down to 11.6 and dropping.

By nearly every measure, the position of poor Americans worsened under the leadership of our opponents. Teen-age drug use, out-of-wedlock births and crime increased dramatically. Urban neighborhoods and schools deteriorated. Those whom Government intended to help discovered a cycle of dependency that could not be broken. Government became a drug, providing temporary relief, but addiction as well.

And let's get some facts on the table that our opponents don't want to hear. The biggest annual increase in poverty took place between 1978 and 1981: over 9 percent each year. In the first two years of our Administration, that annual increase fell to 5.3 percent. And 1983 was the first year since 1978 that there was no appreciable increase in poverty at all.

Pouring hundreds of billions of dollars into programs in order to make people worse off was irrational and unfair.

It was time we ended this reliance on the Government process and renewed our faith in the human process.

In 1980, the people decided with us that the economic crisis was not caused by the fact that they lived too well. Government lived too well.

It was time for tax increases to be an act of last resort, not of first resort.

The people told the liberal leadership in Washington, "Try shrinking the size of Government before you shrink the size of our paychecks."

Our country was also in serious trouble abroad. We had aircraft that couldn't fly and ships that couldn't leave port. Many of our military were on food stamps because of meager earnings, and re-enlistments were down. Ammunition was low, and spare parts were in short supply.

Many of our allies mistrusted us. In the four years before we took office, country after country fell under the Soviet yoke; since January 20, 1981, not one inch of soil has fallen to the Communists.

But worst of all, Americans were losing the confidence and optimism about the future that has made us unique in the world. Parents were beginning to doubt that their children would have the better life that has been the dream of every American generation.

We can all be proud this pessimism is ended. America is coming back and is more confident than ever about the future.

Tonight, we thank the citizens of the United States, whose faith, and unwillingness to give up on themselves or this country, saved us all.

Together, we began the task of controlling the size and activities of the Government by reducing the growth of its spending while passing a tax program to provide incentives to increase productivity for both workers and industry. Today, a working family earning $25,000 has about $2,900 more in purchasing power than if tax and inflation rates were still at 1980 levels.

Today, of all of the major industrial nations of the world, America has the strongest economic growth; one of the lowest inflation rates; the fastest rate of job creation; six-and-a-half million jobs in the last year-and-a-half; a record 600,000 business incorporations in 1983; and the largest increase in real after-tax personal income since World War II. We're enjoying the highest level of business investment in history and America has renewed its leadership in developing the vast new opportunities in science and high technology.

America is on the move again, and expanding towards new eras of opportunity for everyone. We're accused of having a secret. Well, if we have, it is that we're going to keep the mighty engine of this nation revved up. And that means a future of sustained economic growth without inflation that's going to create for our children and grandchildren a prosperity that finally will last.

Today, our troops have newer and better equipment, and their morale is higher. The better armed they are, the less likely it is they will have to use that equipment. But if, heaven forbid, they are ever called upon to defend this nation, nothing would be more immoral than asking them to do so with weapons inferior to those of any possible opponent.

We have also begun to repair our valuable alliances, especially our historic NATO alliance. Extensive discussions in Asia have enabled us to start a new round of diplomatic progress there. In the Middle East, it remains difficult to bring an end to historic conflicts, but we are not discouraged. And we shall always maintain our pledge never to sell out one of our closest friends, the State of Israel.

Closer to home, there remains a struggle for survival for free Latin American states. Allies of ours, they valiantly struggle to prevent Communist takeovers fueled massively by the Soviet Union and Cuba. Our policy is simple: We are not going to betray our friends, reward the enemies of freedom, or permit fear and retreat to become American policies, especially in this hemisphere. None of the four wars in my lifetime came about because we were too strong. It is weakness that invites adventurous adversaries to make mistaken judgments.

America is the most peaceful, least warlike nation in modern history. We are not the cause of all the ills of this world. We are a patient and generous people. But for the sake of our freedom and that of others, we cannot permit our reserve to be confused with a lack of resolve.

Ten months ago, we displayed this resolve in a mission to rescue American students on the imprisoned island of Grenada. Democratic candidates have suggested that this could be likened to the Soviet invasion of Afghanistan, the crushing of human rights in Poland or the genocide in Cambodia. Could you image Harry Truman, John Kennedy, Hubert Humphrey, or Scoop Jackson making such a shocking comparison?

Nineteen of our fine young men lost their lives on Grenada, and to even remotely compare their sacrifice to the murderous actions taking place in Afghanistan is unconscionable.

There are some obvious and important differences. First, we were invited in by six East Caribbean states. Does anyone seriously believe the people of Eastern Europe, or Afghanistan invited the Russians? Second, there are hundreds of thousands of Soviets occupying captive nations across the world. Today, our combat troops have come home, our students are safe and freedom was all we left behind in Grenada.

There are some who have forgotten why we have a military. It's not to promote war. It's to be prepared for peace. There is a sign over the entrance to Fairchild Air Force base in Washington State that says it all: "Peace is our profession."

Our next Administration is committed to completing the unfinished agenda we have placed before the Congress and the nation. It is an agenda which calls upon the national Democratic leadership to cease its obstructionist ways.

We have heard a lot about deficits this year from those on the other side of the aisle. Well, they should be experts on budget deficits. They've spent most of their political careers creating deficits. For 42 of the last 50 years, they've controlled both houses of the Congress. And for almost all of those 50 years, deficit spending has been their deliberate policy. Now, however, they call for an end to deficits, calling them ours, yet at the same time the leadership of their party resists our every effort to bring Federal spending under control.

For three years straight they have prevented us from adopting a balanced budget amendment to the Constitution. We will continue to fight for that amendment mandating that Government spend no more than Government takes in, and for the right of a President to veto items in appropriations bills without having to veto the entire bill. There is no better way than the line-item veto, now used by Governors in 43 states, to cut out waste in government. I know, as a governor, I made such vetoes over 900 times.

Their candidate, it would appear, has only recently found deficits alarming. Nearly 10 years ago he insisted that a $52 billion deficit should be allowed to get much bigger in order to lower unemployment and said we sometimes "need a deficit in order to stimulate the economy."

As Senator, he voted to override President Ford's veto of billions of dollars in spending bills and then voted no on a proposal to cut the 1976 deficit in half.

Was anyone surprised by his pledge to raise your taxes next year if given the chance? In the Senate, he voted time and again for new taxes, including a 10 percent income tax surcharge and higher taxes on certain consumer items. He also voted against cutting the excise tax on automobiles.

And he was part and parcel of the biggest single individual tax increase in history, the Social Security payroll tax of 1977. It tripled the maximum tax and still didn't make the system solvent.

If our opponents were as vigorous in supporting our voluntary prayer amendment as they are in raising taxes, maybe we could get the Lord back in our schoolrooms and get the drugs and violence out.

Something else illustrates the nature of the choice Americans must make. While we've been hearing a lot of tough talk on crime from our opponents, the House Democratic leadership continues to block a critical anticrime bill that passed the Republican Senate by a 91–1 vote. Their burial of this bill means you and your families will have to wait for even safer homes and streets.

There is no longer any good reason to hold back passage of tuition tax credit legislation. Millions of average parents pay their full share of taxes to support public schools while choosing to send their children to parochial or other independent schools. Doesn't fairness dictate that they should have some help in carrying this double burden?

When we talk of the plight of our cities, what would help more than our enterprise zones bill which provides tax incentives for private industry to help rebuild and restore decayed areas in 75 sites all across America? If they really wanted a future of boundless new opportunities for our citizens, why have they buried enterprise zones in committee?

Our opponents are openly committed to increasing your tax burden. We are committed to stopping them, and we will.

They call their policy the "new realism," but their "new realism" is just the "old liberalism." They will place higher and higher taxes on small businesses, family farms and every other working family so that government may once again grow at the people's expense. We could say they spend money like drunken sailors but that would be unfair to drunken sailors. The sailors are spending their own money.

Our tax policies are and will remain prowork, progrowth and profamily. We intend to simplify the entire tax system; to make taxes more fair, easier to understand and, most important, to bring the tax rates of every American further down, not up. If we bring them down far enough, growth will continue strong; the underground economy will shrink; the world will beat a path to our door; no one will be able to hold America back; and the future will be ours.

Another part of our future, the greatest challenge of all, is to reduce the risk of nuclear war by reducing the levels of nuclear arms. I have addressed parliaments in Europe and Asia during these last three and a half years declaring that a nuclear war cannot be won and must never be fought. Those words were greeted with spontaneous applause.

There are only two nations who by their agreement can rid the world of those doomsday weapons, the United States of America and the Soviet Union. For the sake of our children and the safety of this earth, we ask the Soviets, who have walked out of our negotiations, to join us in reducing and, yes, ridding the earth of this awful threat.

When we leave this hall tonight, we begin to place these clear choices before our fellow citizens. We must not let them be confused by those who still think that G.N.P. stands for gross national promises.

But after the debates, position papers, speeches, conventions, television commercials, primaries, caucuses, and slogans—after all this, is there really any doubt at all about what will happen if we let them win this November?

—Is there any doubt that they will raise our taxes?

—That they will send inflation into orbit again?

—That they will make Government bigger than ever and deficits even worse?

—Raise unemployment?

—Cut back our defense preparedness?

—Raise interest rates?

—Make unilateral and unwise concessions to the Soviet Union? And all in the name of compassion.

It's what they've done to America in the past. But if we do our job right, they won't be able to do it again.

In 1980 we asked the people of America: Are you better off than you were four years ago?

The people answered by choosing us to bring about a change. We have every reason now, four years later, to ask that same question again, for we have made a change and the American people joined us and helped us.

Let us ask for their help again to renew the mandate of 1980, to move us further forward on the road we presently travel, the road of common sense; of people in control of their own destiny; the road leading to prosperity and economic expansion in a world at peace.

As we ask for their help, we should also answer the central questions of public service: Why are we here? What do we believe in? Well for one thing, we are here to see that Government continues to serve the people and not the other way around. Yes, Government should do all that is necessary, but only that which is necessary.

We don't lump people by groups or special interests. And, let me add, in the party of Lincoln, there is no room for intolerance and not even a small corner for anti-Semitism or bigotry of any kind. Many people are welcome in our house, but not the bigots.

We believe in the uniqueness of each individual. We believe in the sacredness of human life. For some time now we have all fallen into a pattern of describing our choice as left or right. It has become standard rhetoric in discussions of political philosophy. But is that an accurate description of the choice before us?

Go back a few years to the origin of the terms and see where left or right would take us if we continued far enough in either direction. One would take us to Communist totalitarianism, the other to the totalitarianism of Hitler.

Isn't our choice really not one of left or right, but of up or down: down through statism, the welfare state, more and more government largesse, accompanied always by more government authority, less individual liberty and ultimately totalitarianism, always advanced as for our own good. The alternative is the dream conceived by our Founding Fathers, up, up to the ultimate in individual freedom consistent with an orderly society.

We don't celebrate dependence day on the Fourth of July, we celebrate Independence Day. The right of each individual to be recognized as unique, possessed of dignity and the sacred right to life, liberty, and the pursuit of happiness. At the same time, with our independence goes a generosity of spirit more evident here than in almost any other part of the world. Recognizing the equality of all men and women, we are able and willing to lift the weak, cradle those who hurt and nurture the bonds that tie us together as one nation under God.

Finally, we are here to shield our liberties, not just for now or for a few years, but forever.

Could I share a personal thought with you? Tonight is special for me. It is the last time, of course, that I address you under these same circumstances. I hope you'll invite me back to future conventions.

Nancy and I will be forever grateful for the honor you have done for us, for the opportunity to serve and for your friendship and trust.

I began political life as a Democrat, casting my first vote in 1932 for Franklin Delano Roosevelt. That year, the Democrats called for a 25 percent reduction in the cost of Government by abolishing useless commissions and offices and consolidating departments and bureaus, and giving more authority to state governments.

As the years went by and those promises were forgotten, did I leave the Democratic Party or did the leadership of the party leave not just me but millions of patriotic Democrats who believed in the principles and philosophy of that platform? One of the first to declare this was so was a former Democratic nominee for President, Al Smith, the Happy Warrior, who went before our nation in 1936 to say he could no longer follow his party's leadership, and that he was "taking a walk."

As Democratic leaders have taken their party further and further away from its first principles, it's no surprise that so many responsible Democrats feel that our platform is closer to their views, and we welcome them to our side.

Four years ago we raised a banner of gold colors, no pale pastel. We proclaimed a dream of an America that would be "a shining city on a hill."

We promised we'd reduce the growth of the Federal Government, and we have. We said we intended to reduce interest rates and inflation, and we have. We said we would reduce taxes to provide incentives for individuals and business to get our economy moving again, and we have. We said there must be jobs with a future for our people, not government make-work programs. And, in the last 19 months, six and a half million new jobs in the private sector have been created. We said we would once again be respected throughout the world, and we are. We said we would restore our ability to protect our freedom on land, sea and in the air, and we have.

We bring to the American citizens in this election year a record of accomplishment and the promises of continuation.

We came together in a "national crusade to make America great again," and to make "a new beginning."

Now, it's all coming together. With our beloved nation at peace, we are in the midst of a springtime of hope for America. Greatness lies ahead of us.

Holding the Olympic games here in the United States began defining the promise of this season.

All through the spring and summer, we marveled at the journey of the Olympic torch as it made its passage, east to west. Over 9,000 miles, by some 4,000 runners, that flame crossed a portrait of our nation.

From our Gotham City, New York, to the cradle of liberty, Boston, across the lovely Appalachian springtime, to the city of the big shoulders, Chicago. Moving south towards Atlanta, over to St. Louis past its Gateway Arch, across wheat fields into the stark beauty of the Southwest and then up into the still snowcapped Rockies. After circling the greening Northwest, it came down to California, across the Golden Gate and finally into Los Angeles.

All along the way, that torch became a celebration of America. And, we all became participants in the celebration.

Each new story was typical of this land of ours. There was Ansel Stubbs, a youngster of 99, who passed the torch in Kansas to 4-year-old Katie Johnson. In Pineville, Ky., it came at 1:00 A.M., so hundreds of people lined the streets with candles. At Tupelo, Miss., at 7:00 A.M. on a Sunday morning, a robed church choir sang "God Bless America" as the torch went by.

That torch went through the Cumberland Gap, past the Martin Luther King Jr. Memorial, down the Santa Fe Trail and alongside Billy the Kid's grave.

In Richardson, Tex., it was carried by a 14-year-old boy in a special wheelchair. In West Virginia, the runner came across a line of deaf children and let each one pass the torch for a few feet, and at the end those youngsters' hands talked excitedly in sign language. In more than one place, crowds spontaneously began singing "America the Beautiful" or "The Battle Hymn of the Republic."

And then, in San Francisco, a Vietnamese immigrant, his little son held on his shoulders, dodged photographers and police motorcycles to cheer a 19-year-old black man pushing an 88-year-old white woman in a wheelchair as she carried the torch.

My friends, that's America.

We cheered in Los Angeles as the flame was carried in and the giant Olympic torch burst into a billowing fire in front of the teams, the youth of 140 nations assembled on the floor of the Coliseum. And in that moment, maybe you were struck as I was with the uniqueness of what was taking place before 100,000 people in the stadium, most of them citizens of our country, and over a billion worldwide watching on television. There were athletes representing 140 countries here to compete in the one country in all the world whose people carry the bloodlines of all those 140 countries and more. Only in the United States is there such a rich mixture of races, creeds, and nationalities, only in our melting pot.

And that brings to mind another great torch, the one that greeted so many of our parents and grandparents. Just this past Fourth of July, the torch atop the Statue of Liberty was hoisted down for replacement. We can be forgiven for thinking maybe it was just worn out from lighting the way to freedom for 17 million new Americans. So now we'll put up a new one.

The poet called Miss Liberty's torch the "lamp beside the golden door." The golden door, that was the entrance to America and it still is. And now you really know why we are here tonight.

The glistening hope of that lamp is still ours. Every promise, every opportunity is still golden in this land. And through that golden door our children can walk into tomorrow with the knowledge that no one can be denied the promise that is America.

Her heart is full; her door is still golden, her future bright. She has arms big enough to comfort and strong enough to support. For the strength in her arms is the strength of her people. She will carry on in the 80's unafraid, unashamed and unsurpassed.

In this springtime of hope, some lights seem eternal; America's is.

Thank you, God bless you, and God bless America.

☆

RONALD REAGAN
Campaign Speech
NEW YORK CITY

September 24, 1984

Addressing the 39th session of the United Nations General Assembly

Mr. President, Mr. Secretary General, distinguished Heads of State, Ministers, Representatives, and guests—first of all, I wish to congratulate President Lusaka on his election as President of the General Assembly. I wish you every success, Mr. President, in carrying out the responsibilities of this high international office.

It's an honor to be here, and I thank you for your gracious invitation. I would speak in support of the two great goals that led to the formation of this organization, the cause of peace and the cause of human dignity.

The responsibility of this Assembly, the peaceful resolution of disputes between peoples and nations, can be discharged successfully only if we recognize the great common ground upon which we all stand—our fellowship as members of the human race, our oneness as inhabitants of this planet, our place as representatives of billions of our countrymen whose fondest hope remains the end to war and to the repression of the human spirit. These are the important central realities that bind us, that permit us to dream of a future without the antagonisms of the past. Just as shadows can be seen only where there is light, so too can we overcome what is wrong only if we remember how much is right. And we will resolve what divides us only if we remember how much more unites us.

This chamber has heard enough about the problems and dangers ahead. Today, let us dare to speak of a future that is bright and hopeful and can be ours only if we seek it. I believe that future is far nearer than most of us would dare to hope.

At the start of this decade, one scholar at the Hudson Institute noted that mankind also had undergone enormous changes for the better in the past two centuries—changes which aren't always readily noticed or written about.

"Up until 200 years ago, there were relatively few people in the world," he wrote. "All human societies were poor. Disease and early death dominated most people's lives. People were ignorant and largely at the mercy of the forces of nature."

"Now," he said, "we are somewhere near the middle of a process of economic development. At the end of that process, almost no one will live in a country as poor as the richest country of the past. There will be many more people . . . living long, healthy lives with immense knowledge and more to learn than anybody has time for." They will be "able to cope with the forces of nature and almost indifferent to distance."

Well, we do live today, as the scholar suggested, in the middle of one of the most important and dramatic periods in human history—one in which all of us can serve as catalysts for an era of world peace and unimagined human freedom and dignity.

And today I would like to report to you, as distinguished and influential members of the world community, on what the United States has been attempting to do to help move the world closer to this era. On many fronts enormous progress has been made, and I think our efforts are complemented by the trend of history.

If we look closely enough, I believe we can see all the world moving toward a deeper appreciation of the value of human freedom in both its political and economic manifestations. This is partially motivated by a worldwide desire for economic growth and higher standards of living. And there's an increasing realization that economic freedom is a prelude to economic progress and growth—and is intricately and inseparably linked to political freedom.

Everywhere, people in governments are beginning to recognize that the secret of a progressive new world is to take advantage of the creativity of the human spirit; to encourage innovation and individual enterprise; to reward hard work; and to reduce barriers to the free flow of trade and information.

Our opposition to economic restrictions and trade barriers is consistent with our view of economic freedom and human progress. We believe such barriers pose a particularly dangerous threat to the developing nations, and their chance to share in world prosperity through expanded export markets. Tomorrow at the International Monetary Fund, I will address this question more fully, including America's desire for more open trading markets throughout the world.

This desire to cut down trade barriers, and our open advocacy of freedom as the engine of human progress are two of the most important ways the United States and the American people hope to assist in bringing about a world where prosperity is commonplace, conflict an aberration, and human dignity and freedom a way of life.

Let me place these steps more in context by briefly outlining the major goals of American foreign policy, and then exploring with you the practical ways we're attempting to further freedom and prevent war: By that I mean, first, how we have moved to strengthen ties with old allies and new friends; second, what we're doing to help avoid the regional conflicts that could contain the seeds of world conflagration; and third, the status of our efforts with the Soviet Union to reduce the level of arms.

Let me begin with a word about the objectives of American foreign policy, which have been consistent since the post-war era, and which fueled the formation of the United Nations and were incorporated into the UN Charter itself.

The UN Charter states two overriding goals: "to save succeeding generations from the scourge of war, which twice in our lifetime has brought untold sorrow to mankind," and "to reaffirm faith in fundamental human rights, in the dignity and worth of the human person, in the equal rights of men and women and of nations large and small."

The founders of the United Nations understood full well the relationship between these two goals. And I want you to know that the government of the United States will continue to view this concern for human rights as the moral center of our foreign policy. We can never look at anyone's freedom as a bargaining chip in world politics. Our hope is for a time when all the people of the world can enjoy the blessings of personal liberty.

But I would like also to emphasize that our concern for protecting human rights is part of our concern for protecting the peace.

The answer is for all nations to fulfill the obligations they freely assumed under the Universal Declaration of Human Rights. It states: "The will of the people shall be the basis of the authority of government; this will shall be expressed in periodic and genuine elections." The Declaration also includes these rights: "to form and to join trade unions," "to own property alone as well as in association with others," "to leave any country including his own and to return to his country," and to enjoy "freedom of opinion and expression." Perhaps the most graphic example of the relationship between human rights and peace is the right of peace groups to exist and to promote their views. In fact, the treatment of peace groups may be a litmus test of government's true desire for peace.

In addition to emphasizing this tie between the advocacy of human rights and the prevention of war, the United States has taken important steps, as I mentioned earlier, to prevent world conflict. The starting point and cornerstone of our foreign policy is our alliance and partnership with our fellow democracies. For 35 years, the North Atlantic Alliance has guaranteed the peace in Europe. In both Europe and Asia, our alliances have been the vehicle for a great reconciliation among nations that had fought bitter wars in decades and centuries past. And here in the Western Hemisphere, north and south are being lifted on the tide of freedom and are joined in a common effort to foster peaceful economic development.

We're proud of our association with all those countries that share our commitment to freedom, human rights, the rule of law and international peace. Indeed, the bulwark of security that the democratic alliance provides is essential and remains essential to the maintenance of world peace. Every alliance involves burdens and obligations, but these are far less than the risks and sacrifices that will result if the peace-loving nations were divided and neglectful of their common security. The people of the United States will remain faithful to their commitments.

But the United States is also faithful to its alliances and friendships with scores of nations in the developed and developing worlds with differing political systems, cultures and traditions. The development of ties between the United States and China, a significant global event of the last dozen years, shows our willingness to improve relations with countries ideologically very different from ours.

We're ready to be the friend of any country that is a friend to us and a friend of peace. And we respect genuine nonalignment. Our own nation was born in revolution. We helped promote the process of decolonization that brought about the independence of so many members of this body. And we're proud of that history.

We're proud, too, of our role in the formation of the United Nations and our support of this body over the years. And let me again emphasize our unwavering commitment to a central principle of the United Nations system—the principle of universality, both here and in the United Nations' technical agencies around the world. If universality is ignored, if nations are expelled illegally, then the UN itself cannot be expected to succeed.

The United States welcomes diversity and peaceful competition. We do not fear the trends of history. We are not ideologically rigid. We do have principles, and we will stand by them. But we will also seek the friendship and goodwill of all, both old friends and new.

We've always sought to lend a hand to help others. From our relief efforts in Europe after World War I, to the Marshall Plan and massive foreign assistance programs after World War II. Since 1946, the United States has provided over $115 billion in economic aid to developing countries, and today, provides about one-third of the nearly $90 billion in financial resources, public and private, that flows to the developing world. And the U.S. imports about one-third of the manufactured exports of the developing world.

But any economic progress as well as any movement in the direction of greater understanding between the nations of the world are, of course, endangered by the prospect of conflict at both the global and regional level. In a few minutes, I will turn to the menace of conflict on a worldwide scale and discuss the status of negotiations between the United States and the Soviet Union. But permit me first to address the critical problem of regional conflicts, for history displays tragic evidence that it is these conflicts which can set off the sparks leading to worldwide conflagration.

In a glass display case across the hall from the Oval Office at the White House there is a gold medal—the Nobel Peace Prize won by Theodore Roosevelt for his contribution in mediating the Russo-Japanese War in 1905. It was the first such prize won by an American, and it's part of a tradition of which the American people are very proud—a tradition that is being continued today in many regions of the globe.

We're engaged, for example, in diplomacy to resolve conflicts in Southern Africa, working with the Front Line States and our partners in the Contact Group. Mozambique and South Africa have reached an historic accord on non-aggression and cooperation. South Africa and Angola have agreed on a disengagement of forces from Angola, and the groundwork has been laid for the independence of Namibia, with virtually all aspects of Security Council Resolution 435 agreed upon. Let me add that the United States considers it a moral imperative that South Africa's racial policies evolve peacefully but decisively toward a system compatible with basic norms of justice, liberty, and human dignity.

I'm pleased that American companies in South Africa, by providing equal employment opportunities, are contributing to the economic advancement of the black population. But, clearly, much more must be done.

In Central America, the United States has lent support to a diplomatic process to restore regional peace and security. We have committed substantial resources to promote economic development and social progress.

The growing success of democracy in El Salvador is the best proof that the key to peace lies in a political solution. Free elections brought into office a government dedicated to democracy, reform, economic progress and regional peace.

Regrettably, there are forces in the region eager to thwart democratic change—but these forces are now on the defensive. The tide is turning in the direction of freedom. We call upon Nicaragua, in particular, to abandon its policies of subversion and militarism, and to carry out the promises it made to the Organization of American States to establish democracy at home.

The Middle East has known more than its share of tragedy and conflict for decades, and the United States has been actively involved in peace diplomacy for just as long. We consider ourselves a full partner in the quest for peace. The record of the 11 years since the October war shows that much can be achieved through negotiations; it also shows that the road is long and hard.

Two years ago, I proposed a fresh start toward a negotiated solution to the Arab-Israeli conflict. My initiative of September 1st, 1982, contains a set of positions that can serve as a basis for a just and lasting peace. That initiative remains a realistic and workable approach, and I am committed to it as firmly as on the day I announced it. And the foundation stone of this effort remains Security Council Resolution 242, which in turn was incorporated in all its parts in the Camp David Accords.

The tragedy of Lebanon has not ended. Only last week, a despicable act of barbarism by some who are unfit to associate with humankind reminded us once again that Lebanon continues to suffer. In 1983, we helped Israel and Lebanon reach an agreement that, if implemented, could have led to the full withdrawal of Israeli forces in the context of the withdrawal of all foreign forces. This agreement was blocked, and the long agony of the Lebanese continues. Thousands of people are still kept from their homes by continuous violence, and are refugees in their own country. The once flourishing economy of Lebanon is near collapse. All of Lebanon's friends should work together to help end this nightmare.

In the Gulf, the United States has supported a series of Security Council resolutions that call for an end to the war between Iran and Iraq that has meant so much death and destruction and put the world's economic well-being at risk. Our hope is that hostilities will soon end, leaving each side with its political and territorial integrity intact, so that both may devote their energies to addressing the needs of their people and a return to relationships with other states.

The lesson of experience is that negotiations work. The peace treaty between Israel and Egypt brought about the peaceful return of the Sinai, clearly showing that the negotiating process brings results when the parties commit themselves to it. The time is bound to come when the same wisdom and courage will be applied with success to reach peace between Israel and all of its Arab neighbors in a manner that assures security for all in the region, the recognition of Israel and a solution to the Palestinian problem.

In every part of the world, the United States is similarly engaged in peace diplomacy as an active player or a strong supporter.

In Southeast Asia, we have backed the efforts of ASEAN to mobilize international support for a peaceful resolution of the Cambodian problem, which must include the withdrawal of Vietnamese forces and the election of a representative government. ASEAN's success in promoting economic and political development has made a major contribution to the peace and stability of the region.

In Afghanistan, the dedicated efforts of the Secretary General and his representatives to find a diplomatic settlement have our strong support. I assure you that the United States will continue to do everything possible to find a negotiated outcome which provides the Afghan people with the right to determine their own destiny, allows the Afghan refugees to return to their own country in dignity and protects the legitimate security interests of all neighboring countries.

On the divided and tense Korean peninsula, we have strongly backed the confidence-building measures proposed by the Republic of Korea and by the UN Command at Panmunjon. These are an important first step toward peaceful reunification in the long term.

We take heart from progress by others in lessening the tensions, notably the efforts by the Federal Republic to reduce barriers between the two German states.

And the United States strongly supports the Secretary General's efforts to assist the Cypriot parties in achieving a peaceful and reunited Cyprus.

The United States has been and will always be a friend of peaceful solutions. This is no less true with respect to my country's relations with the Soviet Union.

When I appeared before you last year, I noted that we cannot count on the instinct for survival alone to protect us against war. Deterrence is necessary but not sufficient. America has repaired its strength; we have invigorated our alliances and friendships. We are ready for constructive negotiations with the Soviet Union.

We recognize that there is no sane alternative to negotiations on arms control and other issues between our two nations, which have the capacity to destroy civilization as we know it. I believe this is a view shared by virtually every country in the world and by the Soviet Union itself.

And I want to speak to you today on what the United States and the Soviet Union can accomplish together in the coming years, and the concrete steps that we need to take.

You know, as I stand here and look out from this podium, there in front of me, I can see the seat of the representative from the Soviet Union. And not far from that seat, just over to the side, is the seat of the representative from the United States. In this historic assembly hall, it's clear there's not a great distance between us. Outside this room, while there still will be clear differences, there's every reason why we should do all that is possible to shorten that distance. And that's why we're here. Isn't that what this organization is all about?

Last January 16th, I set out three objectives for U.S.-Soviet relations that can provide an agenda for our work over the months ahead. First, I said, we need to find ways to reduce, and eventually, to eliminate the threat and use of force in solving international disputes. Our concern over the potential for nuclear war cannot deflect us from the terrible human tragedies occurring every day in the regional conflicts I just discussed. Together, we have a particular responsibility to contribute to political solutions to these problems, rather than to exacerbate them through the provision of even more weapons.

I propose that our two countries agree to embark on periodic consultations at policy level about regional problems. We will be prepared, if the Soviets agree, to make senior experts available at regular intervals for in-depth exchanges of views. I've asked Secretary Shultz to explore this with Foreign Minister Gromyko. Spheres of influence are a thing of the past. Differences between Americans and Soviet interests are not. The objectives of this political dialogue will be to help avoid miscalculation, reduce the potential risk of U.S.-Soviet confrontation, and help the people in areas of conflict to find peaceful solutions.

The United States and the Soviet Union have achieved agreements of historic importance on some regional issues. The Austrian State Treaty and the Berlin Accords are notable and lasting examples. Let us resolve to achieve similar agreements in the future.

Our second task must be to find ways to reduce the vast stockpiles of armaments in the world. I am committed to redoubling our negotiating efforts to achieve real results. In Geneva, a complete ban on chemical weapons; in Vienna, real reductions to lower and equal levels in Soviet and American, Warsaw Pact and NATO conventional forces; in Stockholm, concrete practical measures to enhance mutual confidence, to reduce the risk of war, and to reaffirm commitments concerning non-use of force. In the field of nuclear testing, improvements in verification essential to ensure compliance with the Threshold Test Ban and Peaceful Nuclear Explosions agreements; and in the field of non-proliferation, close cooperation to strengthen the international institutions and practices aimed at halting the spread of nuclear weapons, together with redoubled efforts to meet the legitimate expectations of all nations that the Soviet Union and the United States will substantially reduce their own nuclear arsenals.

We and the Soviets have agreed to upgrade out hotline communications facility, and our discussions of nuclear non-proliferation in recent years have been useful to both sides. We think there are other possibilities for improving communications in this area that deserve serious exploration.

I believe the proposal of the Soviet Union for opening U.S.-Soviet talks in Vienna provided an important opportunity to advance these objectives. We've been prepared to discuss a wide range of issues of concern to both sides, such as the relationship between defensive and offensive forces and what has been called the militarization of space. During the talks we would consider what measures of restraint both sides might take while negotiations proceed. However, any agreement must logically depend on our ability to get the competition in offensive arms under control and to achieve genuine stability at substantially lower levels of nuclear arms.

Our approach in all these areas will be designed to take into account concerns the Soviet Union has voiced. It will attempt to provide a basis for an historic breakthrough in arms control. I'm disappointed we were not able to open our meeting in Vienna earlier this month, on the date originally proposed by the Soviet Union. I hope we can begin these talks by the end of the year, or shortly thereafter.

The third task I set in January was to establish a better working relationship between the Soviet Union and the United States, one marked by greater cooperation and understanding. We've made some modest progress. We have reached agreements to improve our hotline, extend our 10-year economic agreement, enhance consular cooperation and explore coordination of search and rescue efforts at sea.

We've also offered to increase significantly the amount of U.S. grain for purchase by the Soviets, and to provide the Soviets a direct fishing allocation off U.S. coasts. But there's much more we could do together. I feel particularly strongly about breaking down the barriers between the peoples of the United States and the Soviet Union, and between our political, military and other leaders.

Now, all of these steps that I've mentioned, and especially the arms control negotiations, are extremely important to a step-by-step process toward peace. But let me also say that we need to extend the arms control process to build a bigger umbrella under which it can operate—a road map, if you will, showing where, during the next 20 years or so, these individual efforts can lead. This can greatly assist step-by-step negotiations and enable us to avoid having all our hopes or expectations—ride on any single set or series of negotiations. If progress is temporarily halted at one set of talks, this newly established framework for arms control could help us take up the slack at other negotiations.

Today, to the great end of lifting the dread of nuclear war from the peoples of the earth, I invite the leaders of the world to join in a new beginning. We need a fresh approach to reducing international tensions. History demonstrates that—beyond controversy that just as the arms competition has its root in political suspicions and anxieties, so it can be channeled in more stabilizing directions and eventually be eliminated, if those political suspicions and anxieties are addressed as well.

Toward this end, I will suggest to the Soviet Union that we institutionalize regular ministerial or cabinet-level meetings between our two countries on the whole agenda of issues before us, including the problem of needless obstacles to understanding. To take but one idea for discussion: In such talks, we could consider the exchange of outlines of five-year military plans for weapons development and our schedules of intended procurement. We would also welcome the exchange of observers at military exercises and locations. And I propose that we find a way for Soviet experts to come to the United States nuclear test site and for ours to go to theirs to measure directly the yields of tests of nuclear weapons. We should work toward having such arrangements in place by next spring. I hope that the Soviet Union will cooperate in this undertaking and reciprocate in a manner that will enable the two countries to establish the basis for verification for effective limits on underground nuclear testing.

I believe such talks could work rapidly toward developing a new climate of policy understanding, one that is essential if crises are to be avoided and real arms control is to be negotiated. Of course, summit meetings have a useful role to play. But they need to be carefully prepared, and the benefit here is that meetings at the ministerial level would provide the kind of progress that is the best preparation for higher-level talks between ourselves and the Soviet leaders.

How much progress we will make and at what pace, I cannot say. But we have a moral obligation to try and try again.

Some may dismiss such proposals and my own optimism as simplistic American idealism. And they will point to the burdens of the modern world and to history. Well, yes, if we sit down and catalog year by year, generation by generation, the famines, the plagues, the wars, the invasions mankind has endured, the list will grow so long, and the assault on humanity so terrific that it seems too much for the human spirit to bear.

But isn't this narrow and shortsighted, and not at all how we think of history? Yes, the deeds of infamy or injustice are all recorded, but what shines out from the pages of history is the daring of the dreamers and the deeds of the builders and the doers. These things make up the stories we tell and pass on to our children. They comprise the most enduring and striking fact about human history: that through the heartbreak and tragedy man has always dared to perceive the outline of human progress, the steady growth in not just the material wellbeing, but the spiritual insight of mankind.

"There have been tyrants and murderers, and for a time they can seem invincible. But in the end, they always fail. Think on it . . . always. All through history, the way of truth and love has always won." That was the belief and the vision of Mahatma Gandhi. He described that, and it remains today a vision that is good and true.

"All is gift," is said to have been the favorite expression of another great spiritualist, a Spanish soldier who gave up the ways of war for that of love and peace. And if we're to make realities of the two great goals of the United Nations Charter—the dreams of peace and human dignity—we must take to heart these words of Ignatius Loyola; we must pause long enough to contemplate the gifts received from Him who made us: the gift of life, the gift of this world, the gift of each other.

And the gift of the present. It is this present, this time that now we must seize. I leave you with a reflection from Mahatma Gandhi, spoken with those in mind who said that the disputes and conflicts of the modern world are too great to overcome; it was spoken shortly after Gandhi's quest for independence had taken him to Britain.

"I am not conscious of a single experience throughout my three months' stay in England and Europe," he said, "that made me feel that after all East is East and West is West. On the contrary, I have been convinced more than ever that human nature is much the same, no matter under what clime it flourishes, and that if you approached people with trust and affection, you would have ten-fold trust and thousand-fold affection returned to you."

For the sake of a peaceful world, a world where human dignity and freedom is respected and enshrined, let us approach each other with ten-fold trust and thousand-fold affection. A new future awaits us. The time is here, the moment is now.

One of the founding fathers of our nation, Thomas Paine, spoke words that apply to all of us gathered here today—they apply directly to all sitting here in this room—he said, "We have it in our power to begin the world over again."

Thank you. God bless you.

☆

WALTER F. MONDALE
Acceptance Speech

SAN FRANCISCO, CALIFORNIA

July 19, 1984

Thank you. Thank you very much. [Repeated several times in acknowledging applause.] My fellow Democrats, my fellow Americans:

I accept your nomination.

Behind us now is the most wide-open race in political history.

It was noisy—but our voices were heard. It was long—but our stamina was tested. It was hot—but the heat was passion, and not anger. It was a roller coaster—but it made me a better candidate, and it will make me a stronger President of the United States.

I do not envy the drowsy harmony of the Republican Party. They squelch debate; we welcome it. They deny differences; we bridge them. They are uniform; we are united. They are a portrait of privilege; and we are a mirror of America.

Just—just look at us here tonight: black and white, Asian and Hispanic, native and immigrant, young and old, urban and rural, male and female—from yuppy to lunchpail, from sea to shining sea we are all here tonight in this convention, speaking for America.

And when we—and when we in this hall speak for America, it is America that is speaking.

When we speak of family, the voice is Mario Cuomo's.

When we speak of change, the words are Gary Hart's.

When we speak—when we speak of hope, the fire is Jesse Jackson's.

When we speak of caring, the spirit is Ted Kennedy's.

When we speak of patriotism, the strength is John Glenn's.

And when we speak of the future, the message is Geraldine Ferraro.

And now we leave San Francisco—together.

And over the next hundred days, in every word we say, in every life we touch, we will be fighting for the future of America.

Joan and I are parents of three wonderful children who will live much of their lives in the 21st Century. This election is a referendum on their future—and on ours. So tonight I want to speak to the young people of American—and to their parents and to their grandparents.

I'm Walter Mondale. You may have heard of me—but you may not really know me. I grew up in the farm towns of southern Minnesota. My dad was a preacher, and my mom was a music teacher. We never—we never had a dime. But we were rich in the values that are important. And I've carried those values with me ever since.

They taught me to work hard; to stand on my own; to play by the rules; to tell the truth; to obey the law; to care for others; to love our country; and to cherish our faith.

My story isn't unique.

In the last few weeks, I've deepened my admiration for someone who shares those same values. Her immigrant father loved our country. Her widowed mother sacrificed for her family. And her own career is an American classic: Doing your work. Earning your way. Paying your dues. Rising on merit.

My Presidency will be about those values. And my—my Vice President will be Geraldine Ferraro.

Tonight, we open a new door to the future. Mr. Reagan calls it "tokenism." We call it America.

Ever since I graduated from Elmore High, I've been a Democrat. I was the Attorney General of my state; then a United States Senator. And then an honest, caring man—Jimmy Carter—picked me as running mate and in 1976 I was elected Vice President. Then in 1980, Ronald Reagan beat the pants off us.

So tonight, I want to say something to those of you across the country who voted for Ronald Reagan—Republicans, independents, and yes, some Democrats.

I heard you. And our party heard you.

After we lost, we didn't tell the American people that they were wrong. Instead, we began asking you what our mistakes had been.

And for four years, I listened to all of the people of our country. I traveled everywhere. It seemed like I had visited every acre of America.

It wasn't easy. I remember late one night, as I headed from a speech in one city to a hotel a thousand miles away, a friend of mine came up to me and said: "Fritz, I just saw you on TV. Are those bags under your eyes natural?" And I said: "No, I got them the old-fashioned way. I earned them."

To the thousands of Americans who welcomed me into your homes and into your businesses, your churches and your synagogues: I thank you.

You confirmed my belief in our country's values. And you helped me learn and grow.

So tonight we come to you with a new realism: ready for the future, and recapturing the best in our tradition.

We know that America must have a strong defense, and a sober view of the Soviets.

We know that government must be as well-managed as it is well-meaning.

We know that a healthy, growing private economy is the key to the future.

We know that Harry Truman spoke the truth when he said: A President . . . has to be able to say "yes" and "no" but mostly "no."

Look at our platform. There are no defense cuts that weaken our security; no business taxes that weaken our economy; no laundry lists that raid our Treasury.

We are wiser, stronger, and we are focused on the future. If Mr. Reagan wants to rerun the 1980 campaign: fine. Let them fight over the past. We're fighting for the American future—and that's why we're going to win this campaign.

One last word—one last word to those of you who voted for Mr. Reagan.

I know what you were saying. But I also know what you were NOT saying.

You did not vote for $200 billion deficits.

You did not vote for an arms race.

You did not vote to turn the heavens into a battleground.

You did not vote to savage Social Security and Medicare.

You did not vote to destroy family farming.

You did not vote to trash the civil rights laws.

You did not vote to poison the environment.

You did not vote to assault the poor, the sick, and the disabled.

And you did not vote to pay 50 bucks for a 50-cent lightbulb.

Four years ago—four years ago, many of you voted for Mr. Reagan because he promised that you'd be better off. And today, the rich are better off. But working Americans are worse off, and the middle class is standing on a trap door.

Lincoln once said that ours is to be a government of the people, by the people, and for the people. But what we have today is a government of the rich, by the rich, and for the rich and we're going to make a change in November.

Look at the record: First, there was Mr. Reagan's tax program. And what happened was this, he gave each of his rich friends enough tax relief to buy a Rolls-Royce—and then he asked your family to pay for the hub caps.

Then they looked the other way at the ripoffs; soaring utility bills, phone bills, medical bills.

Then they crimped our future. They let us be routed in international competition, and now the help-wanted ads are full of listings for executives, and for dishwashers—but not much in between.

Then they socked it—then they socked it to the workers. They encouraged executives to vote themselves huge bonuses—while using King Kong tactics to make workers take Hong Kong wages.

Mr. Reagan—Mr. Reagan—Mr. Reagan believes that the genius of America is in the boardrooms and exclusive country clubs. I believe that greatness can be found in the men and women who built our nation; do its work; and defend our freedom.

If this Administration has a plan for a better future, they're keeping it a secret.

Here's the truth about the future: We are living on borrowed money and borrowed time. These deficits hike interest rates, clobber exports, stunt investment, kill jobs, undermine growth, cheat our kids, and shrink our future.

Whoever is inaugurated in January, the American people will have to pay Mr. Reagan's bills. The budget will be squeezed. Taxes will go up. And anyone who says they won't is not telling the truth to the American people.

I mean business. By the end of my first term, I will reduce the Reagan budget deficit by two-thirds.

Let's tell the truth. That must be done—it must be done. Mr. Reagan will raise taxes, and so will I. He won't tell you. I just did.

There's another difference. When he raises taxes, it won't be done fairly. He will sock it to average-income families again, and he'll leave his rich friends alone. And I won't stand for it and neither will you and neither will the American people.

To the corporations and the freeloaders who play the loopholes and pay no taxes, my message is: Your free ride is over.

To the Congress, my message is: We must cut spending and pay as we go. If you don't hold the line, I will. That's what the veto is for.

Now that's my plan to cut the deficit. Mr. Reagan is keeping his plan secret until after the election. That's not leadership; that's salesmanship and I think the American people know the difference.

I challenge—tonight—I challenge Mr. Reagan to put his plan on the table next to mine—and then let's debate it on national television before the people of this country. Americans want the truth about their future. They're entitled to it. And they want the truth now—not after the election.

When the American economy leads the world, the jobs are here. The prosperity is here and the future is here for our children. But that's not what's happening today. This is the worst trade year in American history. Three million of our best jobs have gone overseas.

Mr. Reagan has done nothing about it. They have no plan to get our competitive edge back; but we do.

We will cut the deficits, reduce interest rates, make our exports affordable, and make America No. 1 again in the world economy.

We will launch a renaissance in education, in science and learning. A mind is a terrible thing to waste. And this must be the best-educated generation in American history and I will lead our nation forward to the best system that this nation has ever seen. We must do it. We must do it.

It is time for America to have a season of excellence. Parents must turn off that television; students must do their homework; teachers must teach. And America must compete. We'll be number one if we will follow those rules. Let's get with it in America again.

To big companies that send our best jobs overseas, my message is: We need those jobs here at home. And our country won't help your business—unless your business helps our country.

To countries that close their markets to us, my message is: We will not be pushed around any more. We will have a President who stands up for American workers and American businesses and American farmers and international trade.

When I grew up, and people asked us to imagine the future, we were full of dreams. But a few months ago, when I visited a grade school class in Texas and asked the children to imagine the future, they talked to me about nuclear war.

Lately, as we've neared the election, this Administration has begun to talk about a safer world. There's a big difference: As President, I will work for peace from my first day in office and not from my first day of campaigning for re-election.

As President, I will reassert American values. I'll press for human rights in Central America, and for the removal of all foreign forces from the region. And in my first hundred days, I will stop the illegal war in Nicaragua.

We know the deep differences with the Soviets. And America condemns their repression of dissidents and Jews, their suppression of Solidarity, their invasion of Afghanistan, their meddling around the world.

But the truth is that between us, we have the capacity to destroy the planet. Every President since the bomb has gone off has understood that. Every other President talked with the Soviets and negotiated arms control: Why has this Administration failed? Why haven't they tried? Why can't they understand the cry of Americans and human beings for sense and sanity in control of these God-awful weapons? Why? Why?

Why can't we meet in summit conferences with the Soviet Union at least once a year? Why can't we reach agreements to save this Earth? The truth is, we can.

President Kennedy was right when he said: We must never negotiate out of fear. But we must never fear to negotiate. For the sake of civilization, we must negotiate a mutual, verifiable nuclear freeze before these weapons destroy us all.

The second term of the Mondale-Ferraro administration will begin in 1989.

By the start of the next decade, I want to ask our children their dreams, and hear not one word about nuclear nightmares.

By the start of the next decade, I want to walk into any classroom in America and talk to some of the brightest teachers and students, and have them tell me: "I want to be a teacher."

By the start of the next decade, I want to walk into any public health clinic in America and hear the doctor say, "We haven't seen a hungry child this year."

By the start of the next decade, I want to walk into any store in America; and I want to pick up the best product, of the best quality, and the best price; turn it over; and read, "Made in the U.S.A."

By the start of the next decade, I want to meet with the most successful business leaders anywhere in America, and see as many minorities and women in that room as I see in this room here tonight.

By the start of the next decade, I want to point to the Supreme Court and say, "Justice is in good hands."

Before the start of the next decade, I want to go to my second inaugural, and raise my right hand, and swear to "preserve, protect and defend" the Constitution that contains the equal rights amendment.

My friends, America is a future that each generation must enlarge; a door each generation must open; a promise that each generation must keep.

For the rest of my life, I want to talk to young people about their future.

And whatever their race, whatever their religion, whatever their sex, I want to hear some of them say what I say—with joy and reverence—tonight: "I want to be President of the United States."

Thank you.

☆

WALTER F. MONDALE
Campaign Speech
WASHINGTON, D.C.

September 25, 1984

Delivered at George Washington University

Yesterday in New York, Mr. Reagan addressed the United Nations General Assembly on the subject of foreign policy.

We all welcome the soothing new tone.

Gone is the talk of nuclear warning shots. Gone is winnable nuclear war. Gone is the evil empire. After four years of sounding like Ronald Reagan, six weeks before the election he's trying to sound like—Walter Mondale.

The new Reagan supports economic aid to the developing world. The old Reagan slashed it.

The new Reagan wants to help settle regional conflicts. The old Reagan ignored them, or made them worse.

The new Reagan praises international law. The old Reagan jumped bail from the World Court.

The new Reagan criticizes South Africa. The old Reagan cozied up to apartheid.

The new Reagan calls for peace in Central America. The old Reagan launched an illegal war in Nicaragua.

The new Reagan talks about the Camp David process. The old Reagan torpedoed it with the Reagan Plan.

The new Reagan worries about soaring arms sales. The old Reagan sold almost anything to nearly everyone.

The new Reagan warns about nuclear proliferation. The old Reagan said it was none of our business, and opened the sluice-gates on materials to make the bomb.

The new Reagan proposes regular consultation with Soviet experts. The old Reagan is the first American President since Hoover not to meet with his Soviet counterpart.

The new Reagan says we can remove the political suspicions that feed the arms race. The old Reagan told us the Soviet buildup stems from their inherent drive for world domination.

The new Reagan says, "There is no sane alternative to negotiations on arms control." The old Reagan called for a margin of nuclear superiority and for prevailing in a nuclear war.

This Presidential sea-change raises a crucial question: How can the American people tell which Reagan would be President if he's re-elected?

To those who welcome the new Reagan, I say this: My Dad was a Methodist minister, and he once told me, "Son, be skeptical of death-bed conversions." I asked why. And he said, "Because sometimes they get well."

Nineteen months ago, I announced my candidacy for President. Six weeks from today, the voters will make their decision.

It is no secret that I'm the underdog in this race. And when a candidate is behind, he gets a lot of advice.

I have been told to attack Mr. Reagan personally—My answer is no. I did not enter this race to tear down a person. I entered it to fight for our future.

I have been advised to ignore issues—to choose slogans over substance. My answer is no. There is a big distance between Pennsylvania Avenue and Madison Avenue. And there ought to be a big difference between a Presidential election and a pep rally.

I have been counseled to cut loose from my history—to desert the forgotten Americans I have always fought for. My answer is no. I would rather lose a race about decency than win one about self-interest. I would rather fight for the heart and soul of America—than fight for the bonuses of the Fortune 500.

When the true story of this election is written, I suspect it will not be about me, or about Mr. Reagan—but about you.

Your generation will decide this race. You will live with its consequences. And you will shape the American landscape for the rest of the century.

You have probably heard the conventional wisdom about your generation.

You are said to be self-content, materialistic, and devoid of social commitment.

You are supposed to have no sense of history.

You are accused of having an attention span no longer than a television commercial.

That's quite an indictment. I don't believe it. But suppose some people did.

Imagine a Presidential campaign based on those assumptions about your generation.

Believing you to be selfish, they would pander to your supposed greed.

Their message would be: Be glad for what you have—and be blind to those who have little.

Believing you to have no memory, they would exploit your alleged amnesia.

Their message would be: History is bunk. Republicans are Democrats. And in 1984, the year of Orwell and doublespeak, the MX missile is renamed the "Peacekeeper."

Believing you to be shallow, they would manipulate your rumored gullibility.

Their message would be all sizzle, and no substance; all happy-talk, and no straight talk; all blue skies, and no blue print; all television, and no vision.

I do not know which is worse—the emptiness of such a campaign, or the cynicism about the American people that it implies.

I do not know which is more damning—their contempt for the issues, or their condescension toward our people.

They underestimate you. They're betting that Americans are not smart. That's a bad bet.

Watch them maneuver.

For four years, they failed to reach a single arms control agreement with the Soviets. They proposed to extend the arms race into the heavens.

But now, six weeks before the election, they talk of arms control, they dust the conference table—and they brag about blunting an issue.

For four years, they failed to make the world safer. The Soviets have reached into Lebanon. Kadafi has reached into Morocco. Human rights is losing in the Philippines. In Central America, our country is sliding toward war.

But now, six weeks before the election, they talk of peace, they bow toward diplomacy—and they boast about changing an image.

For four years, they racked up the biggest deficit in world history. They let us be routed in international trade. They watched basic industry decline. They put our farmers through the worst recession since the Depression.

But now, six weeks before the election, they reel out a few band-aids; they phony up their deficit numbers; they're silent on budget and tax plans; they gloat about this temporary recovery—and they crow about ducking an issue.

For a generation, my opponent fought Democrats tooth and nail. He campaigned for Richard Nixon in 1960. He fought Kennedy on arms control. He fought Johnson on civil rights. He fought Humphrey on Medicare.

But now, six weeks before the election, he lards his speeches with Roosevelt quotes. He gives a medal to Hubert Humphrey. He invokes Truman in Missouri. He invokes Kennedy in Connecticut. And he asks Democrats to become Republicans—as if it didn't matter.

But it does. Take a second look at the Republican home you're being sold, and the platform it's built on.

Do you really want to join a party that intends to put government between you and the most private choices of your life?

Do you really want women to be paid less than men for the same work?

Do you really want politicians to choose prayers for your children?

Do you really want to get us deeper into war in Central America?

Do you really believe there are winners in a nuclear war?

Now some people have declared this election over. They've announced a Republican landslide. In other words, they're telling you, your vote won't count. Your voice doesn't matter.

This crowd doesn't want you to think about the stakes in this contest. They want to trivialize it.

That is arrogance. We are in an American Presidential election. This is a season for passion and principle.

This election is not about jelly-beans and pen pals. It is about toxic dumps that give cancer to our children.

This election is not about country music and birthday cakes. It is about old people who can't pay for medicine.

This election is not about the Olympic torch. It is about the civil rights laws that opened athletics to women and minorities who won those gold medals.

This election is not about sending a teacher into space. It is about improving teaching and learning here on earth.

This election is not about the size of my opponent's crowds. It is about the size of his deficits.

This election is not about Republicans sending hecklers to my rallies. It is about Jerry Falwell picking Justices for the Supreme Court.

This election is not about my standing in the polls. It is about my stand against the illegal war in Nicaragua.

This election is not about slogans, like "standing tall." It is about specifics, like the nuclear freeze—because if those weapons go off, no one will be left standing at all.

This election is about our values.

Today, millions of American children are born in poverty. Many go to school hungry. Many don't learn to read, and don't learn to hope.

And nearly everything we've done as a nation to help those children has been cut back by this administration.

Today, there are Americans roaming the streets and sleeping on grates, bag women and broken men—and thousands of them plunged into that tragedy because this Administration threw them off the disability rolls.

Today, our country is peddling guns around the world. The African drought has brought massive starvation—but this Administration is shipping them less food, and more weapons.

The Republicans say they're for family values. But families don't disown their weaker children. What would we think of parents who taught their kids to think only of themselves, and not to care for their brothers and sisters? What would we say about parents who lived in high style—and left their children in debt as a result?

In this campaign, I will do everything I can to focus our nation on these questions—whatever the political consequences. It must never be said that in 1984, we did not know what we were doing.

I won't permit this crowd to steal the future from our children without a fight. I won't let them put ice in our soul without a struggle. They have a right to ask for your vote. But I'll be damned if I'll let them take away our conscience.

The other week, Mr. Reagan and I both spoke at the Italian-American Foundation dinner here in Washington.

He told a moving story about an Italian immigrant who came to America with nothing. One of his children was a milkman. One of his children, in turn, became a surgeon. And one day, the surgeon saved the life of a President of the United States who had been shot.

It was a fitting tribute to Dr. Joseph Giordano—head of the trauma team here at George Washington University Hospital.

The other day, Dr. Giordano wrote an article you may have seen. In it, he said: Mr. President, you only told us part of the story.

Yes, my parents sacrificed for me. But I was also helped through college by low-interest federal student loans.

Yes, I saved your life, and I was proud to do it. But the medical technology I used wouldn't have existed without years of federally-funded research.

And yes, my parents worked hard all their lives. But now they rely on Social Security, and more than once my father has benefitted from Medicare.

Mr. President, there are millions of Americans making it on their own. But there are millions of others who need some help once in a while—just as you needed some help the day Dr. Giordano saved your life.

That's the kind of people we are. That's the fight I'm waging. That's what's more important than the polls. That's what this election must be about. And that's why I ask for your help.

Thank you very much.

☆